FRANZ LISZT

The Man and his Music

BY ALAN WALKER

A Study in Musical Analysis
An Anatomy of Musical Criticism

EDITED BY ALAN WALKER

Frédéric Chopin:
profiles of the man and the musician

FRANZ LISZT (in 1881)
Oil Portrait by Lenbach

FRANZ LISZT

THE MAN AND HIS MUSIC

EDITED BY
ALAN WALKER

SACHEVERELL SITWELL
DAVID WILDE JOHN OGDON
HUMPHREY SEARLE ROBERT COLLET
LOUIS KENTNER ARTHUR HEDLEY
CHRISTOPHER HEADINGTON
ALAN WALKER

TAPLINGER PUBLISHING COMPANY
NEW YORK

First published in the United States in 1970 by
TAPLINGER PUBLISHING CO., INC.
New York, 10003

SBN 8008 2990 5

Library of Congress Catalog Number 72-108274

Printed in Great Britain

Contents

Illustrations

Music examples drawn by
Paul Courtenay

Acknowledgments

I should like to express my thanks

to Mr David Sharp, music adviser to Barrie and Jenkins, who helped prepare the typescript for the printers;
to Dr István Kecskeméti of the National Széchényi Library, Budapest, and Mr Edward Waters of the Library of Congress, Washington, who provided photostats;
to Mr and Mrs Christian B. Peper, who gave permission to reproduce Edward Lear's painting of the Villa d'Este;
to Mr Robin Harrison and Mr Thomas Rajna, who checked the final proofs;
to Miss Veronica Heighway, who typed the script, and Miss Carol Williams, who helped me with correspondence;
to the staffs of the BBC Music Library and the BBC Gramophone Library for the loan of essential materials.

A. W.

Editorial Note

Titles

The titles of Liszt's works feature at least three languages—French, German, Italian—a fact which reflects his cosmopolitan background. Unfortunately, this makes a consistent editorial policy, even on so seemingly simple a matter as what to call a given piece, curiously difficult to formulate; some of Liszt's titles exist quite happily in three languages simultaneously. My practice throughout this volume, therefore, has been to retain the original titles, *whatever their language*, in the belief that this is less confusing than the consistent use of English translations—to say nothing of foreign ones.

Thus, '*Waldesrauschen*' is preferred to '*Forest Murmers*'; '*Feux-follets*' is preferred to '*Will-o-the-Wisp*'; '*Totentanz*' is preferred to '*Dance of Death*'. This practice would also appear to reflect common usage among musicians in England. The only exceptions to this rule are where common usage itself has established an acceptable precedent for using English. Thus, '*Transcendental Studies*' is preferred to '*Etudes d'exécution transendante*'; '*St. Francis walking on the waters*' is preferred to '*St. François marchant sur les flots*'.

Throughout, the titles of most of Liszt's works take italics (e.g. *Gnomenreigen*, *Nuages Gris*, etc.). There are two chief exceptions to this rule:

(a) Nicknamed works (e.g. 'Malédiction' Concerto, 'Dante' Sonata, etc.) which take quotation marks instead; and
(b) Works with 'formal' titles (e.g. Concerto no. 2 in A major; Sonata in B minor, etc.).

Italics

Apart from their normal function of stress, italics are used throughout this volume

(a) for all foreign words which have not yet been assimilated into the English language, as opposed to those which have (e.g. compare *Zeitgeist* with Conservatoire);
(b) for certain types of musical titles (see above).

They are not used for Italian musical terms.

Capitals

Their obvious use in titles apart, they are employed

(a) to lead off on all Italian musical terms (e.g. Allegro con spirito); and
(b) to indicate technical terms (e.g. Introduction, Exposition, Coda, etc.).
(c) to indicate *particular* cases (e.g. the Second Rhapsody still retains its popularity) as opposed to *general* cases (e.g. the rhapsodies as a whole are neglected).

Punctuation

I take this to be a stylistic rather than an editorial matter; conformity is neither possible nor desirable in a book of this kind. Therefore, contributors will be seen to have exercised considerable freedom here, to say nothing of ingenuity in avoiding the more obvious abuses of the English language.

A. W.

Notes on Contributors

(1) ROBERT COLLET, pianist and writer on music, has been a professor of piano at the Guildhall School of Music, London, since 1952. He studied at Cambridge under C. B. Rootham and Edward Dent. His piano teacher was Frida Kindler (Mrs Van Dieren). Special interests include sixteenth century music, Bach, Rameau and Berlioz. He wrote the essay on the Studies and Preludes in the Chopin Symposium edited by Alan Walker.

(2) CHRISTOPHER HEADINGTON, composer, pianist and writer on music. Studied at the Royal Academy of Music, London. Author of *The Orchestra and its Instruments* (1965). Formerly in the Music Division of the BBC. In 1965 appointed Staff Tutor in music to the Extra-Mural Delegacy in the University of Oxford.

(3) ARTHUR HEDLEY, a leading authority on Chopin. Author of *Chopin* in the Master Musician Series and Editor of *Selected Correspondence of Chopin*. From 1949–65 Vice-Chairman of the Jury of the International Chopin Competitions in Warsaw. Created a Commander of the Order of Polonia Restituta on 17 October, 1949. In 1965 made Hon. member of Chopin Institute, Warsaw—an honour he shares only with Artur Rubinstein, Malcuzynski and the Late Queen of the Belgians.

(4) LOUIS KENTNER, Hungarian-born pianist and composer. President of the Liszt Society, London. Gave premiére of Bartók's second piano concerto under Klemperer in Budapest in 1933. Frequently serves on international juries. Resident in London since 1935 and now a British subject.

(5) JOHN OGDON, pianist and composer, was born in Mansfield and educated at Manchester Grammar School and the Royal Manchester College of Music, where he studied the piano with Claud Biggs. Later he studied with Denis Matthews, Ilona Kabos, Gordon Green and Egon Petri. He is very interested in contemporary music.

(6) HUMPHREY SEARLE, composer and writer on music, was a pupil of Anton Webern. He has translated Rufer's *Composition with Twelve Notes* into English. A leading authority on Liszt, he is the author of *The Music of Liszt* (1954), a standard work on the composer. From 1964–65 he was a visiting professor at Stanford University, California. Guest composer at the Aspen Music Festival, Colorado, in 1967.

(7) SIR SACHEVERELL SITWELL, writer and poet. Member of a famous artistic family which included Sir Osbert and Dame Edith Sitwell. Distinguished author of more than seventy books, including *Liszt* (1934), a standard biography of the composer.

(8) ALAN WALKER, author of *A Study in Musical Analysis* (1962) and *An Anatomy of Musical Criticism* (1967); Editor of a Symposium on Chopin (1966). Radio producer in the Music Division of the BBC. Doctor of Music in the University of Durham. Also composes and plays the piano.

(9) DAVID WILDE, pianist. Artist in Residence, Lancaster University. Elected Fellow, Royal Manchester College of Music, 1966. Winner of four major awards, including First Prize in the Liszt-Bartók competition, Budapest 1961. Soloist Proms, Edinburgh Festival, and in Europe and America.

Preface

Of all the great nineteenth-century composers, Liszt alone still remains to be fully explored. His contemporaries—Chopin, Schumann, Wagner—have long since come into their own. But Liszt's true posterity still lies in the future. Why?

In the first place, there is his vast output. Nobody knew better than Liszt himself the tremendous struggle it cost him, while still in his thirties, to shake off his brilliantly successful career as a pianist in order to devote himself to composing. The outcome of that struggle was a body of music—1,300 or more works—which, in sheer quantity, is unequalled by any other major composer, with the possible exception of Bach. Not even the experts know it all. Liszt, in fact, is a standing indictment against musicians and musicology alike, and it is nothing short of scandalous that almost a century after his death there are works by him still awaiting their publication—let alone their first performance.

Then there are the critics. In some quarters, the very name of Liszt has always provoked hostility, and it probably always will. He has been variously accused of vulgarity, showmanship, charlatanry even. In puritan England, especially, Liszt has had a rough time, and it is still considered to show 'lack of taste' to admire his more extrovert pieces such as the Hungarian rhapsodies and the operatic paraphrases. I have a theory which may reveal my own attitude towards such criticism, and that is that there is no emotional attribute in music, of any kind, which we ourselves do not put there. If we take music to be 'vulgar', that can only be because it reminds us of a side of our own artistic personalities which we do not like, and which we would sooner forget about. Music not only tells us something about the composer; it tells us something about ourselves, too. A great deal of the criticism projected on to Liszt is of this patently autobiographical type. But perhaps it is not up to me to try and explain why Liszt's detractors do not like him. Perhaps it is up to those detractors to explain why his admirers do, and to draw the conclusion. It has always seemed to me to be infinitely more rewarding to give up one's dislikes rather than one's likes, and I take it to be musically more fruitful as well.

As if it were not enough to have to survive one's critics, one has to survive one's interpreters too. It is difficult to think of another nineteenth-century composer who has been so brutally manhandled by his performers as Liszt has. This is especially true of the piano music which, for two generations or more, has taken a beating at the hands of large numbers of punch-drunk virtuosos, many of whom regard Liszt's music simply as a physical challenge—a sort of high-powered obstacle course over which to tone up their muscles in public. It is not often that a great composer suffers this double fate: that most of his music is never heard, and that when it is, it is wrongly heard. But it has been suffered by Liszt, and it seems to me high time matters were put right by a more intelligent interest in this wonderful and original musician.

The present volume is intended as a companion to my earlier symposium on Chopin. The choice of Liszt as its subject seemed inevitable. Liszt was an almost exact contemporary of Chopin; like Chopin, he became a leading figure in the Romantic era; and like Chopin, too, there is now a better chance that professional musicians (to whom the book is primarily addressed), having recently emerged from a dreary period of anti-Romanticism, will take a fresh look at him and view him more favourably than before. Like that earlier volume, this one concentrates on the music while not necessarily excluding the man. And I have allowed the same policy to govern the selection of contributors. That is to say, as far as possible each essay has been written by a musician—pianist, composer, or teacher—who carries Liszt's music in his ears and fingers, and who has lived on terms of intimacy with it for a long time—in some cases, for a lifetime.

ALAN WALKER

*Hampstead, N.W.*3
6 May 1968

FRANZ LISZT

The Man and his Music

SACHEVERELL SITWELL

Liszt: A Character Study

IN writing of this most famous of virtuosi in the whole history of music, other facets of his career and of his character have to be considered beside his mere virtuosity. Many, if not all of these, are contingent to or rising out of that, and by their sum of contradictions they paint the continuing importance and colour the mysteries of his fame. For Liszt is still a problem, and one which is little nearer to solution although he has been dead for over eighty years. From what we know of him, however, it is not unlikely that this wonderful, yet ambiguous being would prefer that the legend of his achievement should remain more of a question than an answer. There are artists in all the arts who stay, in life and death, on one side or the other of this barrier. Is there not a finality in Beethoven, or in Wagner; and are we to conceive of an alternative Verdi, or a second Rubens? They are of the race that fulfil themselves and leave no more to be said. But there is the other sort whose fascination is in what they have left unfinished and unanswered; who have put suggestions and not always made decisive statements. They have left discoveries and made experiments; and their failures are often more interesting than their successes. Unknown and neglected in their own lifetimes, they may be destined, as it were, for posthumous awards, and decorations.

But Liszt is not to be numbered among this group either, for while alive he was a great deal more than famous. He achieved a notoriety at once, encouraged by his personal bearing and feats of virtuosity, things inherent in him and in the very nature of his gifts and talents; and then, as resolutely, he renounced them—a renunciation which did not lead him from temptation either in affairs of music or of the heart; but then, there were exceptional temptations for him both as a man and a musician.

To have been in part neglected, alive and dead, just because nature has been so prodigal to you and you were so famous in your lifetime, is a rare predicament which puts its victims in a category to themselves. They are not locked up in limbo, two or three to a cell. It is solitary confinement in their purgatory, where they stay till the verdict is given, which in this instance has been long delayed. There can be too many talents in one person. The recipient of so many natural gifts is at once distrusted, particularly if he has gone out of his way to exploit them, an undeniable truth in Liszt's case. But, then, as the first of world-famous pianists, was it really to be expected of him that he should belittle his powers and pretend to ordinary talents? It is in respect of this side of his nature that he has been called 'a mixture of priest and circus rider', an inelegant phrase which does him less than justice and only harms its author.

There are personalities that are great, not because they are the same all through, but because of the very nature of their contradictions. It is the unannounced and unexpected which make the interest: that the great pianist should be the inventor of the symphonic poem; that the amorist musician should enter holy orders; that the lover of Lola Montez should be the Abbé Liszt; that the virtuoso in the black soutane with the long white hair should be, as well, the firework-specialist of the Waltz from Gounod's *Faust*. Today, the *zeitgeist*, or spirit of our time, is still hostile to the personality cult; in the Age of Everyman it is not expedient to excel in more than one thing at a time. But our epoch of Mies van der Rohe and Stravinsky, with its hatred of ornament and expression, is itself now ageing and going into deliquescence, and 'the less, the more' may no longer be the motto of the age that follows. 'Star quality', now restored to opera and ballet, if indeed they ever lacked it or could survive without it, and which is present again in the one person of Picasso, has long been established on the conductor's rostrum and is now returning to the concert platform. The interval since the age of the virtuosi which ended some thirty years ago is but a short one in musical history.

In considering the long life of Liszt as a whole, I think it may be true to say that the wisest move he ever made was in retiring from the concert platform when he was thirty-five years old in 1847; and in parenthesis let us remember that this was a hundred and twenty years ago, at the very beginning of the railway age. The more obvious countries apart, he had toured in Ireland, Spain and Portugal, and of course Russia, at a time when it was necessary to travel by post-chaise, but which took weeks instead of days. By retiring when he did, and only performing at charity concerts and giving lessons, he gave himself the time to compose and kept unimpaired the legend of his playing. He may have been influenced in this by the example of Rossini who had left off composing operas in 1830 at about the same age. But the one was devoting himself to the music of the future, while the other was taking his curtain and saying farewell to the music of the past, the old Italian music of which he had been the last great master. Both musicians preserved their legend in this fashion; the one by the drastic cessation of his energies, and the other by so prodigal an outpouring of music in nearly every imaginable form that the heaped masses of it at his feet obscure his stature. But, his music apart, the life story of Liszt is one of interest and fascination, of which, in default of the whole-length canvas, I now attempt to fill in the outline and paint him at least in the full colours of his generous nature, his genius, and, if they are to count as such, his failings, both as a man and as a musician.

*

Franz or Ferencz Liszt was born on 22 October 1811, in the year of the comet, when talk was of nothing but war. The star of Napoleon was waning, and the disastrous Moscow campaign threw its shadows before it. Yet Liszt's birthplace was quiet and peaceful enough. It was at Raiding, in the Austrian Burgenland, only some thirty miles from Vienna, and, before the Peace Treaty of 1920, equivocally in Austria or in Hungary. His father, Adam Liszt, was land steward on a small portion of the vast Esterházy estates. Their two country seats or palaces, Eisenstadt (where Haydn lived and worked) and Esterháza, are now respectively in Austria and in Hungary; but at Raiding, under the auspices of the Esterházy, the atmosphere was more Hungarian than German. Liszt's mother, Anna Lager, came from Lower Austria. It is perhaps only natural that Hungarian blood should be attributed to Liszt. In fact his descent was purely German and Austrian. The family name was List, a not uncommon name in Austria (Liszt himself was once heard to say that his father had added the 'z' to the name, to prevent it being pronounced 'Lischt' in the Magyar fashion). His name was even entered as 'List' in the baptismal registry at Raiding. Certainly there would have been native music at Raiding supplied by wandering bands of Gypsies, something never forgotten by Liszt though he left Hungary in 1821 and did not return there until 1839; but it was an influence he always felt in him, and to paraphrase the quotation in an earlier paragraph, you do not have to be born in a circus tent to love the circus.

At the age of nine Liszt gave his first concert, and a month later played at another of the Esterháza palaces where a number of Hungarian nobles in the audience raised a sum of money towards his musical education. This took him with his parents to Vienna, where he studied with Salieri and with Czerny; and this was the time also, so the story goes, of his being embraced by Beethoven and his meeting Schubert. Two years later the Liszt family moved to Paris; and by 1824 he was launched there as a child pianist. The same year, too, he played in London and to George IV at Windsor Castle. In 1827 Adam Liszt, his father, died at Boulogne, his last words to Franz being: 'Je crains pour toi les femmes', or, in Liszt's words, 'he feared that women would trouble my life and bring me under their sway'—a curiously prophetic utterance.

A year later, in the midst of religious doubts and longings to become a priest, he fell in love with one of his pupils, the sixteen-year-old Carolyne de Saint-Cricq. Their attachment became too ardent. They were discovered prolonging a music lesson till long after midnight, and Franz was ordered to leave the house and never return. As a result he had a nervous breakdown and suffered renewed worries of conscience over the next two years. But it is typical of Liszt that he never forgot his first love-affair. Meeting her again many years later at Pau, in the Pyrenees, when she had become Madame d'Artigaux, he dedicated some music to her; and he left her a ring in his will made at Rome in 1860, at the turning-point and most solemn moment in his life.

A year or two after this adolescent illness[1]—a disturbance of the psyche, as we may take it to have been—Liszt was still in Paris, had heard Paganini, and met Chopin and Berlioz; all three of which happenings had a profound effect upon his life and set him on the course he was to follow. From German being his spoken tongue—he never mastered Hungarian, either as a child or as an older man—he had now become French-speaking, as was only natural to a youth arriving in Paris at the age of thirteen and living mainly in the French capital for the next twelve years. His health had recovered, his nerves and his physical strength were strong enough to sustain him in his career as composer and virtuoso, and he had become the good-looking and romantic young man of Ingres's and Dévéria's drawings. These were the years of ferocious practice, with Paganini as his model whose effects, together with some tinge of his *diablerie*, it was Liszt's ambition to transfer to the keyboard;[2] an astonishing instance of this new obsession, written by the twenty-one-year-old pianist within a few months of first hearing Paganini play, being his 'Clochette' Fantasy of 1832, on *La Campanella*, in which the alternating and diabolical pianissimi and violent runs and bell-ringings are of almost poltergeist insistency and strangeness. It is to be discerned in this work that a new and tenacious force, limitless in scope, had arrived in music. The 'Paganini' studies, proper, were to follow some years later, but they lack that fiendish and painstaking rapture.

It was not likely that a young man of Liszt's looks and genius would be left

[1] Liszt was actually reported dead, and an obituary notice was published in Paris.
[2] There is a full discussion of Paganini's influence on Liszt on pp. 43–55.—*Ed.*

to himself for long in the French capital; and soon after he had been a witness at the wedding of Berlioz to Harriet Smithson (one of those weddings at which one could wish a photographer had been present) he had the fateful meeting with Comtesse d'Agoult, the introduction both to her and to George Sand being arranged, most typically, by the affected and over-amorous Alfred de Musset. Madame d'Agoult was twenty-eight years old and Liszt was twenty-two. Her parents were a French aristocrat and the daughter of a German–Jewish banker of Frankfurt, and her husband was a Frenchman who was twenty years her senior. She was handsome and serious-minded, with little sense of humour; romantically and sentimentally inclined, and mentally and physically less French than German. Where the planning of their lives was concerned she took the initiative with her lover, and before long they had eloped to Geneva. She was not especially musical, she already had two children,[1] and she was a rich woman; but from now onwards, whatever her virtues, Liszt's life was a subject of scandal. Their first daughter, Blandine, was born in the winter of 1835, and for some time they were cut off from Paris. But Madame d'Agoult at least encouraged Liszt to work during these months, mainly at collecting and arranging Swiss melodies, later to take different form in the first or 'Swiss' volume of the *Années de Pèlerinage*, and in transcribing Berlioz for the piano which can have been only less difficult and exciting a task than translating Paganini for the same medium.

The lovers returned to Paris during 1837 where they made in turn the fateful introduction of George Sand to Chopin and spent the three summer months with her at Nohant. During part of this time Liszt and George Sand were alone together without Madame d'Agoult; it would be a slur on George Sand's reputation to say that no flirtation took place between them; but whatever happened was soon interrupted by Madame d'Agoult who returned with the declared purpose of taking Liszt to Italy where they read Dante together—at a later stage it was to be, on alternate days, Dante, Shakespeare, Goethe and Tasso—and visited the picture galleries, a serious programme lulled by a sojourn of some weeks among the camellias and oleanders of Bellagio on Lake Como. And here, on Christmas Day 1837, their second daughter Cosima was born, named after her birthplace, the daughter who was to leave her husband and become the wife of Richard Wagner. But nothing could stop Liszt composing in this first flow of his genius, and during these months he completed the first version of the Twelve Transcendental Studies, the six 'Paganini' studies, and also the first sketch for his frightening *Totentanz* after seeing the fresco of the *Triumph of Death* at Pisa in the inevitable company of Madame d'Agoult. These

[1] One of whom had died just before her elopement with Liszt.

are his first mature compositions. He visited Florence, Rome and Venice, composed such pieces as *Sposalizio* (after Raphael's painting of that name in the Brera at Milan) one of the most beautiful works of the second or 'Italian' volume of his *Années de Pèlerinage* with, for companions, the three most exquisite and moving Petrach Sonnets, originally songs, now made into piano solos, as well as the 'Dante' Sonata (subtitled *Après une lecture du Dante*), a quasi-master-piece for which his Egeria can almost be forgiven her seriousness and lack of humour.

But the break in their relationship was coming, and in November 1839 the Countess returned to Paris with their by now three children,[1] while Liszt went back to Hungary where it would not have been possible for her to accompany him. Here he was welcomed with near delirium as a national celebrity, hobnobbed with the magnates who had helped him when he was a child, and was given a jewelled sabre which clanked from his waist on occasions when playing to Hungarian audiences during those weeks of frenzy. He revisited Raiding which he had not seen since he was ten years old, and heard the Tzigane cimbalom and violin in the Gypsy encampment on the outskirts of the little town. He described this and similar experiences in his book on Hungarian Gypsy music.

> They had built their fire under a colonnade of ash trees and were sitting round it, violin in hand, on the piled sheepskins that were their only furniture. The women were crashing their tambourines, and uttering little cries of mimicry while they danced. The men, who resembled each other like the sons of one mother, got up from the ground to look at some horses they had been given in exchange that day. This pleased them . . . and they started imitating castenets by cracking the joints of their fingers, which are always long and charged with electricity. Still uncertain, they began throwing their caps into the air, and followed this by strutting about like peacocks. Then, they looked at the horses again, and as if suddenly given the power to express their pleasure in the bargain, they flew to their violins and cymbals, and began playing in a fury of excitement.

And he describes the Gypsies moving off next morning in the rain, those who rode on horseback wearing their sheepskin pellisses with the wool outside because of the damp, which made them look like as many bears mounted on wild horses. Such scenes will have inspired some of his Hungarian Rhapsodies, which, in their day, were without precedent and in excess of anything hitherto written for the piano.

The career of Liszt was rising to a pitch of excitement, and before the year

[1] Daniel, the youngest child, had been born a few months earlier.

1840 was out he had met Wagner, an encounter that was to affect him for the rest of his days.[1] This was the year, too, in which he went back to London, was joined by the Countess, and, in mundane detail, played to Queen Victoria at Buckingham Palace, made friends with Lady Blessington and Count d'Orsay, and moved generally in circles into which it was again embarrassing for him to introduce the Countess, whom he left in an hotel at Richmond.

The situation between them could not last for much longer, and it was aggravated by his journeys further afield as far as St. Petersburg where he gave his first concert in 1842. He had an enthusiastic following in Russia which lay, then, under the hermetic tyranny of Nicholas I, a terrifying autocrat with much Prussian blood in him, and as Herzen describes him, with 'eyes of pewter'. It was a time when Russia was, to all intents and purposes, a closed kingdom. The influence of Liszt on the native school of composers was to extend far into the future.

In the next year or two his concert tours took him still further afield to Constantinople and to Spain and to Portugal, but up to nearly this point Liszt and the Countess and their three children still spent the summers together in the quasi-seclusion of Nonnenworth, an islet in the Rhine between Cologne and Coblenz, with a half-ruined convent, a chapel and a few fishermen's huts. It was the last home they had together. The slant of his life which was leading to his break with Madame d'Agoult was now taking him away from Paris and drawing him back to Central and Eastern Europe; and it was perhaps an unconscious symbol of this that he was holidaying on an island in the river between France and Germany and occupied in the main with making piano versions of Schubert's songs, many of which are indeed little masterpieces of perception and understanding.

Already, he had played in Weimar and conducted there, the latter activity being a new experience in his musical life and the opening of a fresh career for him, made possible by the Grand Duke Karl Alexander of Weimar appointing him musical director. The Grand Duke's wife Marie Pavlovna, the music-loving sister of Tsar Nicholas I, may have brought this about. But a year or two of recitals in most countries of Europe followed before Liszt was able to give all of his energies to his post at Weimar. And in the course of his travels, he started a new friendship which was to tie him in some sense for the rest of his life. It was while giving a series of concerts at Kiev, in the Ukraine, that he met Princess Carolyne of Sayn-Wittgenstein, eight years younger than himself and daughter of a great Polish landowner, who had been married at seventeen to a

[1] Liszt's musical relationship with Wagner is discussed by Alan Walker on pp. 67–76. See also John Ogdon, pp. 136–37.—*Ed.*

member of the Russian branch of this Westphalian family. The marriage was not a success, husband and wife had agreed on a separation, and the Princess had retired with her daughter to her Ukrainian estates. She attended Liszt's concerts; and within a few days had asked him to stay with her at Woronince, the chief of her properties, where she had inherited no fewer than thirty thousand serfs at her father's death. Life there was just as a reader of Turgeniev would expect it to be. Servants slept along the passages and outside the doors of bedrooms; and on snowy days and long winter nights they sang together in unison like a choir, or played the balalaika. But Liszt had not come to the Polish countryside to escape the reading he was accustomed to with Madame d'Agoult. Dante and Goethe, here as at Nonnenworth, or anywhere else the pair of them had lived together, were open on the table. And so was the cigar-box, for the Princess was an inveterate cigar-smoker. When Liszt left Woronince after a few weeks' stay it was only to perform at his last public concert. This final appearance as a professional pianist was at Elizabetgrad in the far south of Russia, now rechristened Stalingrad, after which he returned for four months' holiday to stay with Princess Wittgenstein, preparatory to taking up his post with all seriousness at Weimar. He eventually returned to Weimar in February 1848 through the winter snows. The Princess would join him there; she hoped to get the Tsar to grant her a divorce through the kind offices of his sister the Grand Duchess. He never played again in public for money for himself. The expenses of his post as musical director were paid by the Grand Duke; for the rest, he depended upon the small sums earned from the sale of his own music.

The new career of Liszt had begun.

*

Before continuing, let us look at him in retrospect during his years as a wandering virtuoso. Never before had a pianist received this degree of public adulation. It had been accorded to great singers a century before when the Italian *castrati*, Farinelli, Senesino and others, sang in Handel's operas at the Opera House in the Haymarket. And among composers, Handel himself was admired and made welcome in London, as elsewhere. But the performing virtuoso was another matter. We know the degree of social recognition that the church organist in a North German town used to receive; and Gabrieli, Marcello, and other choir-masters of St. Mark's in Venice, from whom Schütz and other North German musicians came to learn, had the status of a minor lawyer or a practitioner in medicine. John Dowland the lutenist, who was invited to Denmark by Christian IV, the uncle of our King Charles I, and given a salary equal to that of the prime minister, is about the only exception. Domenico Scarlatti, probably the greatest keyboard virtuoso before the coming of Liszt, who never gave what we would call a public concert in his life, spent the last thirty years of his life as music-master and personal musician to the Queen of Spain. She came of a musical family and was herself a fine performer, but apart from the favour and kindness shown him by the Queen, he may have been little more esteemed in the Royal Palace than the apothecary, or the man who came round to wind the clocks. The predecessors of Liszt in the generation just before him, pianist-composers like Hummel or John Field, are not to be envied in their careers. Field, it may be recalled, after an early phase as underpaid and half-starved salesman in Clementi's London warehouse, went to Russia where he was overwhelmed by the weight of music-lessons he was forced to give, became an alcoholic, was stranded in misery in Naples whence he was rescued by a Russian family, and died after anything but a happy or successful life, in Vienna.[1]

It was Paganini who showed to Liszt how technical prowess could be made to dazzle and excite an audience. But it is not to be denied that his gaunt and skeletal person, as revealed in the caricature-statuette of him by Dantan, was part and parcel of the effect he made. There were elements of the 'horror-comic' in Paganini, as we might agree were we enabled by some alchemy of time to have heard and seen him in his *Fandango Spagnuolo* with barnyard imitations, known under the title of *The Vagaries of the Farmyard*. But this is not to belittle a composer and virtuoso with more than the usual attributes of genius, an extraordinary appearance included, even if this histrionic side of him was to some small degree due to his physique rather than to the result of deliberate study. He was in all things unique. There could never be another Paganini.

The fascination exerted by Liszt, both in public and in private, was of another nature which it is difficult to define. Not all accounts agree, even as to his handsome appearance; one person at least described him as 'a very ugly man'. Certainly, as with Lord Byron, he was one of those males who are irresistible to women. But, first of all, it must be taken as proved that whatever the terrors of execution, and indeed the more of those the better, he could play the piano as no one had played the instrument before him.[2] The grand piano of the thirties and forties of the last century was a comparatively new invention; and the public, in so many of the towns where he performed on his concert tours, was

[1] John Field seems to have had a certain fascination for Liszt who published an edition of his Nocturnes in 1859, together with a perceptive essay about him.—*Ed.*

[2] In his later life, from 1847 onward, Liszt scarcely ever practised (neither, incidentally, did Paganini). Hence, no doubt, as with Paganini, the tendency to indulge in 'pranks' and the 'fiddle-faddle' of which Joachim complains in pious horror (see footnote p. 10).

unused to music. Amateurs, who were not so few in number, may well have been of far wider musical knowledge and sophistication than we would anticipate; but the audience in general would be astonished and dazzled by a Fantasia on 'William Tell' or 'Lucia de Lammermoor', not to mention Liszt's own, and favourite warhorse, his *Galop Chromatique*. They may have been used to 'arrangements' of overtures or airs from operas, but not to Liszt's operatic *Réminiscences* or Paraphrases, the best of which are works of art in their own right transcending and improving upon their originals.

With the authentic 'centaur-pianist', a phrase applied to Liszt whether in praise or disparagement, when the instrument and the virtuoso would appear to be one and the same, each is equally dependent upon the other. The mood of its interpreter conveys itself to the instrument; and the personality, more notably the physical attributes and mannerisms of the musician have their effect upon the audience. There is more than the merely mechanical about the transcendental in performance. Not that Liszt, in the accounts that are left to us of his playing, was the protagonist of noise and thunder. Quite the contrary. 'Liszt *hardly ever* used his muscular prowess . . . the great charm of his playing lay in the delicate and subtle, and *not* in the muscular and powerful . . . I was surprised to notice that as he left the piano, not a trace of perspiration or fatigue was noticeable on his face or hands.' Thus, Strelezki, who was a pupil; and there are many other concurrent accounts of his playing, with perhaps only the violinist Joachim for dissident.[1] But perhaps the last word can be left to Schumann who wrote to Clara Wieck to say that it was the greatest artistic experience of his lifetime to have heard Liszt, and he was astonished and spellbound by his own music as if he had never heard it before.

It is not to be denied that during these years of musical notoriety Liszt may have developed tricks and mannerisms of an annoying or aggravating kind. Facial expressions of disdain, of lofty sentiment, of selfless aspiration, and so on, may have irritated one part of his audience as much as they elevated the other. It is to be remembered that an unsophisticated public, altogether new to music, is nowhere to be found in our time except perhaps among the demonstrably music-loving penguins of Antarctica. Never again can there be such opportunity, even facility, to dazzle and hypnotize an audience; a golden age for the two or three lions of the arena, to culminate in the series of historical recitals

[1] Joachim repeatedly said what a wonderful experience it was to play sonatas or other chamber works with Liszt *for the first time*. At the second or third performance, however, he could not refrain from playing quite simple passages in octaves or thirds, converting ordinary trills into sixths, and indulging in 'fiddle-faddle' of this kind.

of Anton Rubinstein in 1886, at which cyclopaean events the members of the public actually hung from window-ledges and clung to the chandeliers. Paderewski was the last performer to be acclaimed with such transports, now only accorded to pop-singers.

But Liszt's career as a touring virtuoso was now over. By the year 1849, two years after his final concert at Elizabetgrad, we find him settled at Weimar. First of all he lived at the Erbprinz Hotel; but after a few months, when the Tsar had refused the Princess's petition for divorce, he moved into the Villa Altenburg with her, occupying a separate wing. This was to be their home for the next twelve years; a home untainted by aestheticism which after all was an English invention or affectation, and of an ugliness endemic to all nineteenth-century authors and musicians whether it be Flaubert at Croisset, Wagner in the Villa Wahnfried at Bayreuth, Victor Hugo in his villa in Jersey, or Tchaikowsky in his home at Klin. Musicians and authors perhaps work better in an unaesthetic setting. In any case during his years at Weimar the pre-occupation of Liszt was with the music of the future.

It was, it could be said, incidental to this ambition that at nearly forty years of age he took instruction in orchestration, largely under the tutelage of Raff, and began the composition of his Symphonic Poems, works of historical importance where later composers are concerned. It was a form, bound to come, that was of Liszt's invention; and in its progeny are to be included *Thamar*, *Schéhérazade*, *Till Eulenspiegel* and a host of works by Smetana, Dvořák, and others. But, as well, during these years of extraordinary productivity, Liszt was composing his 'Faust' Symphony and his Sonata in B minor—two of the key works of the whole Romantic movement—the 'Dante' Symphony, the two piano concertos, and the tremendous Fantasy and Fugue for organ on the chorale *Ad nos, ad salutarem undem*. All this was incidental to his work as conductor and producer. Wagner's *Lohengrin*, *Tannhäuser*, and the *Flying Dutchman*, Berlioz's *Benvenuto Cellini*, and indeed a week-long festival of Berlioz in 1852 and again in 1855, are but a few of the more outstanding examples of Liszt's energy, as an appendix to all of which it is to be noted that in the company of Berlioz he was one of the first orchestral conductors in the modern meaning of the term.[1] To represent, as has been done by writers

[1] Other operas produced at Weimar were: *Orpheus*, *Iphigenia*, *Armida*, and *Alceste* of Gluck; *Don Giovanni* and *The Magic Flute* of Mozart; *Euryanthe* of Weber; *La Gazza Ladra*, *L'Italiana in Algeri*, *Le Comte Ory* of Rossini; *Ernani* of Verdi; and operas by Cherubini, Spontini, and Meyerbeer. There were innumerable orchestral concerts as well.*

* Liszt's enterprise at this time was remarkable. See Humphrey Searle (p. 281) for an account of the orchestral forces Liszt had at his disposal.—*Ed.*

including Ernest Newman, that all this was in self-aggrandizement while involved in a whirl of idle flattery, is to shut your eyes and ears and ignore all else in favour of your idol Richard Wagner.

It is, also, easy enough to make fun of Princess Wittgenstein. True, she was not beautiful; but the oval face that looks out at one in later life in photographs is kind, if determined, and it is not difficult to imagine her 'clear blue eyes and blonde hair'. Her love for Liszt apart, which was the interest of her life, it is not to be forgotten that she urged Berlioz to compose *Les Troyens*, and kept up his courage when he was failing, and that he dedicated the opera to her. It is doubtful whether the work would have been undertaken at all, let alone completed, but for her encouragement. Of course, where length and indigestibility were concerned the Princess was a martyr for punishment, as witness her own masterwork, the twenty-four volumes of the *Causes intérieures de la faiblesse extérieure de l'Église*. Liszt later wrote to her from his clerical retreat at Grottammare that he had read in the *Moniteur* of a rival to her, the Japanese novelist Bakin, who had just completed his novel in one hundred and six volumes, having been working on it for thirty years. But Bakin's volumes were small by comparison. On one occasion, in Budapest, Liszt had to go specially to the Customs to rescue her third volume of 1149 pages by which the officials were intrigued; and he writes in answer to her that her next instalment, a thousand pages on the Episcopate, would indeed be a serious and grave task. Certainly the *Causes intérieures* is a mammoth publication, and the present writer may be one of the only dozen persons living who have had the curiosity to ask for it in a library.

It is also customary to denigrate Liszt for his literary works while blaming them, at the same time, on the Princess. It is true that the four hundred and fifty pages of his book on Hungarian Gypsy Music suggest her helping hand, but the best passages in it are certainly by him. When he describes his personal experiences in Gypsy encampments, listening to their music, he is not inferior to the finer pages of Borrow in *Lavengro* and *The Romany Rye*. And it is to be noted that although nearly every writer on the subject derides his work on Chopin there is hardly a book on the composer that does not quote from him. Probably it is the case that she wrote the more lengthy and uninteresting parts of the book on Gypsy Music and shaped and finished his articles and essays. But by this time—the book on *Chopin* came out in 1852 and *The Gypsies and their Music in Hungary* in 1859—he had reached a stage, experienced at times by most great individuals in their own lives, when everything he did was wrong. He was attacked for his love affairs, and in the same breath blamed because the Princess was eccentric, ill-favoured, and chain-smoked strong cigars. He had no men friends . . . 'is not a man of great intelligence . . . it is a settled system with him never to express an opinion upon anything, however unimportant it may be, so as not to compromise himself or offend anyone . . . and he smelt horribly of bad tobacco' . . . all this from the military historian von Bernhardi who was certainly no music lover, and whose observations about Liszt were based in the main on scraps of gossip picked up from the Liszt circle in Weimar, and one or two casual encounters with Liszt himself. Ernest Newman, in his book *The Man Liszt*[1] as might be expected from someone setting out with the express purpose of debunking the composer, regards Bernhardi's evidence as having a crucial bearing on Liszt's character. At one point, Bernhardi was busily pumping Liszt's own bodyguard for information about him, and Newman solemnly tells us, *à la* Bernhardi, that these worthies 'had at that time no great belief in him as a composer'![2] I shall have more to say about Newman's book shortly. The Bernhardi type is, alas, more common among human beings than men of the stature and genius of Liszt, whatever his faults, and it is wiser to take him and his achievements as against the mere opinion of a politician and Prussian military historian.

Naturally, there was a lot of mischief and gossip at Weimar; and the music of the future, as was inherent in its very name, from being music of the present, was over without excessive applause, and had quickly become music of the past. In the meantime, the Tsar had refused the Princess her divorce, confiscated her fortune, and even deprived her of her nationality, although no saint himself and in a hurry to marry morganatically as soon as the opportunity arrived. Bernhardi, however, writing some time before this financial loss, of course, knew better. The Princess, 'A small, dark, ugly, sickly, very clever and adroit Polish woman, with a slightly Jewish *nuance*'—how kindly Bernhardi writes!—'I happen to know has brought two million roubles away with her and put them in a safe place' . . . 'and at last Liszt himself came in—a very ugly man, *manières décousues*, who made on the whole a disagreeable impression.' But Bernhardi does at least end this passage in his *Memoirs* with the remark: 'I came away with a somewhat uncanny impression.' Strange to say, this had happened to other observers, too; perhaps it was the only effect his magnetic mind had on their stupid persons. But in reading Newman's *The Man Liszt* it is noticeable that almost every entry under Liszt's name in the index is used as a stick with which to hit him: 'Dual nature of; plays pranks with music; lack of discrimination; indulgence in stimulants [nine entries]; extravagance of; grand manner of; hectic life of; social inferiority of; defective education of; uncontrollable temper of; vanity of; arrogance of; his love for aristocracy; has difficulty in expressing

[1] London, 1934.

[2] *Op. cit.*, p. 187.

himself; indolence of; poses of; has no male friends; wastes time in answering letters; cruelty of; advantages of "publicity"'; etc., etc., etc. As against which, there is hardly an entry in the index of the book to his credit; and there only to his having recognized at once 'the superlative genius of Wagner, to his [Liszt's] eternal glory'.[1]

The Vie Trifurquée

In December 1858, after the failure of his production of Cornelius's *Barber of Bagdad*, Liszt resigned and his ten years' work at Weimar was at an end. There now follows the so-called Roman period of his life. After some further delay at Weimar, Liszt arrived in Rome in October 1861, preceded by the Princess, hoping to marry her a day or two later, on his fiftieth birthday. The church of San Carlo at Corso was already hung with flowers. But late that night, on the eve of their wedding, a messenger came from the Vatican to say that the Pope (Pius IX) had revoked his sanction for their wedding. They could not be married. Henceforth, Liszt continued to occupy his rooms at 113 Via Felice, and went every evening to see the Princess. There are accounts of him at this time in Gregorovius's *Roman Journal*; Gregorovius was an observer with a great deal more intelligence than Bernhardi. Here are some extracts: 'Have

[1] This is the place, I think, to comment briefly on Newman's book which enjoys a reputation in the Liszt literature out of all proportion to its true worth. Newman's aim was an 'objective' study of Liszt's personality, an attempt to get at the real man wrapped in the cocoon of legends woven around him by the 'romantic' biographers of the nineteenth century. This 'forensic' approach was an inevitable reaction to the idealized, hero-worshipping attitude of a previous generation which had tended to sweep under the carpet the less palatable facts about the great composers. Newman's declared purpose was to see Liszt as he really was, 'warts and all', however much his ruthless exposure might pain Liszt's admirers. It needs to be said here and now that as an 'objective' study Newman's book is a dismal failure. It is written with the kind of dogged persistence associated with the policeman lurking behind corners hoping to catch a petty thief with his hand in the till. Time and again, Newman gives the impression of being 'on to something' only to have his case collapse about him by the supreme unimportance of the evidence. Thus, Liszt liked cognac—so Newman writes like a man who has just signed the pledge; Liszt enjoyed female company—so Newman writes like a Trappist monk; Liszt occasionally misled people in his correspondence—so Newman becomes a high court judge. The interesting thing about Newman's book is that it starts out as an indictment against the nineteenth-century approach to biography, and it ends up as an indictment against Liszt himself. Somewhere along the line, the object of Newman's aggression was deflected on to the very thing he strove so hard to see in a 'factual' light. The result is a piece of malevolent mischief-making, not an 'objective' biography at all (I question whether an 'objective' biography, in Newman's sense, is possible or even desirable). *The Man Liszt* is, with respect, fascinating mainly for the light it throws on the man Newman.—*Ed.*

made Liszt's acquaintance, a striking, uncanny figure—tall, thin, and with long grey hair. Frau von S. maintains that he is burnt out and that only the outer walls remain, from whence a little ghost-like flame hisses forth' . . . 'I am glad that I heard him play again; he and the instrument seemed to be one, as it were a *piano-centaur*' . . . 'Yesterday I saw Liszt clad as an Abbé. He was getting out of a hackney carriage, his black silk cassock fluttering ironically behind him. Mephistopheles disguised as an Abbé. Such is the end of Lovelace.' It was surely such accounts of Liszt in his Roman period that inspired Busoni, possibly his only peer among pianists, though perhaps a genius *manqué* as a composer, to want Leonhardt, a character in his Hoffmannesque opera *Die Brautwahl* who had apparently lived for several centuries and was possessed of magical powers, 'to look like Liszt at the age of fifty', in fact during the very years he took minor orders. Liszt had indeed received four of the seven degrees of priesthood. He could not celebrate Mass, or hear confession. He could leave the priesthood when he wished, and it even left him at liberty to marry, did he so desire. But he was door-keeper, reader, acolyte, and exorcist. And an honorary canon as well.[1]

The magician in Liszt, and this was no small part of his physique and his metabolism, was now probably at the height of its powers, but those were diverted and absorbed in a new direction. That is why he was so strange and interesting a spectacle at this time. After a year or two during which he wrote little and was evidently under strong emotional stress—not merely play-acting as his detractors would have it—he was now composing again. How curious it is to think of him taking up his new apartment in the Vatican, opposite the *Loggie* of Raphael, on the very day of his reception into the Church! He remained there for some months, until he moved into the Villa d'Este at Tivoli, which his friend and patron Cardinal Hohenlohe, who was in charge of the Austrian interests at the Vatican, placed at his disposal. He seems to have thought his new vocation was to transform and renew church music,[2] in pursuance of which aim he completed his two oratorios *Christus* and *The Legend of St. Elizabeth*, and the *Hungarian Coronation Mass* of 1867. But, also, the musical experimentalist was starting to work in him again while indeed a new pattern in his life was forming. Already, as we have seen, he was established at the Villa d'Este, outside Rome; and now in 1869 he was invited back to Weimar, but, tactfully, without the Princess who remained in Rome working on her *Causes*

[1] Probably, therefore, the Rev. K. Chignell of the Charterhouse, Hull, who corrected in green ink the proofs of the life of Liszt that I wrote more than thirty years ago, was correct in striking out the word 'Abbé' wherever it came in my text and putting in its place the word 'curate', though I thought at the time that it diminished and threw a cold draught upon my narrative.

[2] See Collet, p. 319.—*Ed.*

intérieures. The Hofgärtnerei, a four-roomed house where the head gardener had lived, was furnished and placed at his disposal. Here he spent at least a part of each year for the next seventeen years, receiving his pupils and being visited by the leading musicians of the world. The months of April, May, and June were spent at Weimar and he gave lessons free of charge, as ever, to the most brilliant young pianists of all nations. At the Villa d'Este he stayed from July till Christmas, doing most of his composing. The first three months of every year from 1871 onwards he now spent at Budapest, teaching at the new Academy of Music which he helped to establish. Such was his *Vie trifurquée*, his threefold life, as he called it, and this was to continue until he died. The journeys must have sapped his strength—he travelled second-class on the long railway journeys—and from now onwards his works were on a smaller scale. He was starting on his ultimate, and in many ways most interesting phase, but I think it would be true to say that he had prematurely aged; this, on the evidence of his letters and from contemporary accounts, and from photographs.

And it was a time not without its ardours for him. Of these, one of the principal may have been the affair of Olga Janina, the 'Cossack Countess'. Like perhaps a few other of his fateful attachments it left no memorial behind it in the form of musical dedications, and so on. It was too serious for that. The years were 1869–71 when Liszt was approaching sixty years of age. Olga Janina, 'a Cossack girl of aristocratic birth' (as she is often described, though I have never seen the evidence for this assertion, nor indeed any details whatever of her origins or history) had married at fifteen, and on the morrow of her wedding horsewhipped her husband, and left him. She then went to Kiev, and, obsessed by the music of Chopin, took piano lessons at the Conservatoire. But violence always followed in her wake, and in her own words 'L'infortuné directeur du Conservatoire . . . mourut du gangrène, mordu par un tigre que notre Casaque [her bodyguard] promenait toujours à son côté.'[1] But before he died he had time to introduce the music of 'L' to her. All this from her novel *Souvenirs d'une Cosaque* published under the pseudonym Robert Franz in 1874.

The director dead, she wrote to 'L' at Rome begging him to take her as a pupil. He replied that he would do so if her talent seemed to him worth encouraging, thinking she was a young man. Within a fortnight he knew differently. For her first meeting with Liszt, in her own words: 'j'étais vêtue en crêpe de chine blanc, lamé d'argent. C'était une de ces toilettes comme Worth seul

[1] 'The ill-fated director of the Conservatoire . . . died of gangrene, bitten by a tiger that our Cossack bodyguard always had walking by his side.'

possède le secret.'[1] She accepted the offer of a cigar, and they both smoked walking up and down the room till late at night. She tells of the complicated sentiments which were inspired in his heart by 'cette petite sauvage de 18 à 19 ans'. As could be anticipated, other of Liszt's women friends, 'fans' we would call them, did not share her own views about herself. Janka Wohl describes her as 'still fairly young, but painfully thin. She had a pale, intelligent face, large black eyes, and pleasing manners,' and Janka Wohl adds, helpfully, that 'she reads Kant and Schopenhauer, and to amuse herself had studied the microscope and vivisection, and now she wanted at any price to become a pianist'.[2] But this was when Olga Janina had followed Liszt from Rome to Budapest. In the meantime, he had seen her intermittently during a year in Rome, at his clerical retreat in the cloister of Santa Francesca Romana and at the Villa d'Este, where she broke in dressed as a garden boy and then, or sooner or later, it is of little moment, they fell into each other's arms.

Worse was to come. She pursued Liszt to Hungary, or went at his invitation, it comes to the same thing; and at this point, hearing dramatically that she was ruined, and having gambled away all that was left at Baden-Baden, she sailed for New York to make her living as a pianist; only to return a few months later, burst into his room at Budapest, and after a fearful all-night scene took poison, but woke up alive in his apartment. By now the scandal had exploded and the Princess in Rome had heard about it. Liszt writes to her: 'I had a terrible disturbance last Saturday. . . . Forgive me the recital of her violences and furies—and have the kindness not to mention her to anyone at all. My guardian angel upheld me in this danger.' And he ends, tactfully, 'Your beautiful views on the development of music and the pre-eminence of religious music especially have deeply interested me.' After which, and doubtless with more scenes, the Cossack Countess disappears from history, leaving only her two novels *Souvenirs d'une Cosaque* and its sequel *Mémoires d'un pianiste* which purported to be Liszt's reply to her tirade. What happened to her subsequently I have been unable to discover; and even her true identity is uncertain.

Liszt was, let us remember, sixty years old at the time. Olga Janina's description of her first impression of him was of 'a man of high stature, distinguished carriage, and grand manner; ugly', as Newman of course loves to repeat, 'with

[1] 'I was dressed in white *crêpe de chine* lamèd with silver. It was one of those dresses of which Worth alone knew the secret.'

[2] Olga Janina's pen was more vitriolic. Writing of another woman friend of Liszt, Countess Moukhanoff-Kalergis, a former pupil of Chopin, whom she saw at Weimar with the master, she refers to her as 'the belle of the Berlin balconies', and continues, 'there was nothing genuine about her but an issue in her leg, and her breath. Leaning on his arm, this ruin wandered along the shady paths in the park, cooing her whole repertory of recitatives, nocturnes, and cantilenas.'

an abundance of beautiful hair, now almost white, which he wore long and thrown back from his forehead'. If he was 'ugly', the Cossack Countess certainly found this no impediment. Liszt was one of these males who are irresistible to women. How often has Baron Meyendorff—the son of his last and platonic love, who died only a year or two ago aged well over ninety—told me he must be the last person alive who knew and loved him, who had supper with his mother and Liszt many scores of times all the years they were at Weimar; and how often did old Baron Meyendorff ask me if Newman could not understand this, or had never heard of a man, especially a genius of this description! Now that we know the 'angelic' Mozart had a scatological side to him which emerges from his letters to his sister; and have been told over and over again of Beethoven's quirks and quarrels and his troubles with his publishers, it does not make either of them lose artistic stature—nor does it in the case of Liszt when we know of his love-affairs, and we can accept that a facet of his genius was that of the actor and the showman.

The more pleasant, indeed delightful description of those years at Weimar with his pupils must now be left till last, while the details of the music he was writing in his late years and of his final and last journeys are filled in. The 'Christmas Tree' Suite, twelve short pieces appeared in 1874–76; and later still come the Second Mephisto Waltz, originally written for orchestra, afterwards transferred to the piano; the Third Mephisto Waltz for piano, one of his masterpieces; the four *Valses Oubliées*; the four last Rhapsodies; the Csárdás Macabre and Csárdás Obstiné of 1881–82; the *Jeux d'Eaux à la Villa D'Este*; and transcriptions of Verdi's *Simone Boccanegra* and of the Polonaise from Tchaikowsky's *Eugène Onegin*. There are, as well, the short and controversial piano pieces of strange character; the two versions of *La Lugubre Gondola* written, curiously, some months *before* Wagner died in Venice; the nocturne *En Rêve*; *Schlaflos* (sleepless), *Frage und Antwort*; *Nuages Gris*; and the three pieces, *Unstern*, *Sinistre*, *Disastro*. One or two religious pieces should be mentioned, as well, like his motet *Ossa arida*—'O ye dry bones, hear ye the word of the Lord'; of truly terrifying effect, *pace* Humphrey Searle, in the vein, one surmises, of Liszt's *Totentanz*. For the rest, he left the unfinished oratorio of *St. Stanislaus*, the Polish counterpart to his St. Elizabeth (of Hungary) of which *Salve Polonia* and a polonaise or two survive, but are never played.

And so we arrive at his seventy-fifth year when he said farewell, we may think, knowingly, to the Princess and left Rome for the last time in January 1886. He arrived in London via Budapest and Paris, early in April. His pupil Sir Alexander Mackenzie, who knew him in Rome even before he became a priest, has told me of meeting him at the station, and of how he appeared out of the railway carriage in his top hat and soutane. He stayed a fortnight in London and was fêted at a number of concerts and private parties, at several of which he was persuaded to play, in most cases a Chopin *étude* or a nocturne.

On leaving London he went to Antwerp where he spent Holy Week; then he returned to Paris where his jubilee was celebrated as in London. After which he enjoyed a short rest at Weimar from where he wrote to a pupil: 'For a month past I have been quite unable to read and almost unable to write, with much labour, a couple of lines. Two secretaries kindly help me by reading to me and writing letters at my dictation.' He was tired out after his journeys to London and to Paris. Dropsy had been diagnosed, and he was to be operated on for cataract in September. In spite of this he managed to struggle as far as Luxembourg, where he stayed with the painter Munkacsy, and the Cardinal Primate of Hungary was another guest. He then proceeded, apparently alone, from Luxembourg to Bayreuth which must have entailed a night in the train. It is said that on the last stage of the journey the door of his second floor compartment was flung open and a honeymoon couple entered who sat before the open window, clasped in each other's arms. The cold air coming in struck a chill into him, but he would not ask for the window to be drawn up and had to take to his bed immediately he reached Bayreuth with a feverish cold. The next day he spent in bed, but in the evening he played a little whist. On the Sunday he insisted upon attending a performance of *Tristan*, sitting at the back of the theatre in the Wagner family box. After the death of Isolde, he asked to be carried back to the Villa Wahnfried. Next morning, pneumonia declared itself, and he lay dying all week. On Saturday, 31 July, at ten o'clock in the evening, his lips moved and he was heard to utter the word 'Tristan'. It was the greatest work of art he had been concerned with during his life. A couple of hours later he was dead.[1] As for Princess Wittgenstein, she lingered until the beginning of March 1887, having finished the last and twenty-fourth volume of her *Causes intérieures* a mere two weeks before she died.

*

There remains the picture of Liszt in his old age at Weimar holding court among his pupils, among whom at one time or another were numbered von Bulöw, Tausig, Emil Sauer, Eugène d'Albert (d. 1932), Frederick Lamond (d. 1948), and Moriz Rosenthal (d. 1946) who was generally reputed of the younger generation after Tausig to be the most talented pianist of them all. But, as could be expected, the best accounts of Liszt come from his female pupils, notably from Amy Fay, a young American girl from Chicago who writes of

[1] See pp. 76–78 for a further account of Liszt's death.—*Ed.*

Weimar in 1873–74. Her book *Music Study in Germany*, published in 1886, the year of Liszt's death, used to be a favourite prize for music students, but is nearly forgotten now. Amy Fay went to the theatre the night after she arrived in Weimar, and the first person she saw, in the box opposite, was Liszt. 'He was making himself agreeable to three ladies, one of whom was very pretty. . . . His mouth turns up at the corners, which gives him a most crafty and Mephistophelian expression when he smiles, and his whole appearance and manner have a sort of Jesuitical elegance and ease. . . . I cannot imagine how he must look when he is playing. He is all spirit, but half the time, at least a mocking spirit, I should say.' She meets him a day or two later. 'He is rather tall and narrow, and wears a long Abbé's coat reaching down nearly to his feet. He made me think of an old-time magician more than anything, and I felt that with a touch of his wand he could transform us all.'

Later, she goes to him three times a week for lessons.

> At home Liszt doesn't wear his long Abbé's coat, but a short one in which he looks much more artistic . . . I think he hates the trouble of speaking German for he mutters his words, and does not half finish his sentences. Yesterday when I was there he spoke to me in French all the time. . . . It is *so* delicious in that room of his. It was all furnished and put in order for him by the Grand Duchess herself. The walls are pale grey, with a gilded border running round the room, or rather two rooms, which are divided, but not separated, by crimson curtains. The furniture is crimson, and everything is *so* comfortable. . . . There is always a lighted candle standing on the writing table by which he and the gentlemen can light their cigars. . . . The more I see and hear Liszt, the more I am lost in amazement! I can neither eat nor sleep on the days that I go to him. . . . He goes far beyond all that I expected. Anything so perfectly beautiful as he looks when he sits at the piano I never saw, and yet he is almost an old man now. His personal magnetism is immense, and I can scarcely bear it when he plays. He can make me cry all he chooses. . . . Liszt knows well the influence he has on people, for he always fixes his eye on some one of us when he plays, and I believe he tries to wring our hearts. . . . I do not think he is the same when he is with aristocrats. He must be among artists to unsheathe his sword. When he is with 'swells' he is all grace and polish. He seems only to toy with his genius for their amusement, and is never serious. . . . Liszt is a complete actor who intends to carry away the public, who never forgets that he is before it, and who behaves accordingly. He subdues the people to him by the very way he walks on to the stage. He gives his proud head a toss,

throws an electric look out of his eagle eye, and seats himself at the piano with an air.

In the meantime Amy Fay had been made aware of Princess Gortschakow, *alias* Baroness Meyendorff. 'She is such a type of woman as I suppose only exists in Europe. She is a widow . . . always attired in black . . . yet nothing can conceal her innate elegance of figure. . . . I shall never forget the supercilious manner in which she took out her eyeglass and looked over me as I passed her one day in the park.' After which there is no space, alas! to tell of the summer excursions, she and the other pupils and the master undertook to nearby places like Tiefurt, and further afield to Sondershausen when the Baroness came in the train with them, too. And on another day they went to Jena with all the young musicians, and after dinner walked along the river to a place that Liszt called 'Paradise', and later had a picnic supper underneath the trees. Everyone except the master —and he had met Beethoven and Schubert and been the friend of Chopin!— was young, and the world was full of promise.

ARTHUR HEDLEY

Liszt the Pianist and Teacher

The Pianist

WHATEVER may have been the fluctuations and vicissitudes of Liszt's reputation as a composer, as a pianist he saw only once, and for a very brief moment, a shadow cast on his supremacy. From the age of twenty-six his fame was universal and unchallenged; and so it remained, and this in spite of the fact that for forty years he lived in what could be technically called 'retirement from the concert-stage'. It was inevitable that his name should be linked with that of Paganini, and Liszt welcomed the comparison. After the first shock of hearing the Italian he determined to show that he could in every respect achieve the same astounding and almost paralysing effect on his hearers. The assault was too much for some of his contemporaries, especially those of a severe academic outlook, and the observations of A. Marmontel (a typical professor of the Paris Conservatoire) illustrate the opposition that Liszt quickly ran into:

> Paganini and Liszt, both idols of the public, have more than once been tempted by this adoration and have defiled their prodigious talent in order to maintain their incomparable renown. They have themselves used artificial means to enhance the brilliance of the light by which they shine: time will soften it down.
>
> Far be it from me to run down such a forceful talent. I merely wish to convey something of the complex nervous impression produced by Liszt on sincere artists [including, of course, M. Marmontel himself]. I can still hear him at a soirée at Halévy's where he carried off his usual triumph. His mesmerising gaze directed at his audience, his rather long-drawn preludings, did not prevent me from being charmed by phrases adorably sung or passages of exquisite delicacy—I only regretted the more being aroused from my ecstasy by violent sounds, by effects which good style forbids.

> I trembled, not for the pianist but for the piano, expecting to see the strings break at any moment and the hammers fly into splinters.

On occasions a more serious charge was made: the accusation of charlatanry. The charlatan is essentially a bluffer, one who does not genuinely do what he claims to be doing, and this Liszt never was.[1] He had no need of bluffing, and for the good reason that his technique, the basic qualities of which were scarcely dimmed by advancing age and long periods without practice, was founded on the most solid training that a pianist has ever had.

The boy was a so-called 'wonder-child' and took to the piano as to a native element. His father, Adam Liszt, was enough of a pianist to place the child's fingers correctly on the keys and to teach him his notes, but it is doubtful whether he put him through any definite course of piano-playing. Little Franz played by the light of nature, and his first public appearances, which created a sensation, probably owed more to the novelty of a child doing things beyond the skill of an ordinary adult than to the actual quality of the playing. His first press-notice of November 1820, when he was nine, shows where the attraction lay.

'This artist's extraordinary agility together with his quick grasp of the most difficult music, playing at sight anything placed before him, excited general admiration and gives ground for the highest hopes.'

It was fortunate that Liszt's father realized that his son still had almost everything to learn, and did not allow his talent to run to seed in empty, small-town successes. The boy was taken to see Hummel in Weimar, a severe formalist under whom he would probably have done well. (On the other hand Hummel might have had a stultifying effect on a pupil of Liszt's impatient temperament. His family later held Liszt responsible for the 'deplorable decline of true piano-playing' after their father's death.) But Hummel's fees were too high, and so it was to Carl Czerny in Vienna that the boy was finally taken. Master and pupil were wonderfully adapted to each other for the production of a pianistic marvel. On Liszt's side incredible talent; on Czerny's equally remarkable industry, patience, and strictness, combined with a full appreciation of the problems of technique and a resolve to vanquish them, by hard work if by nothing else. It

[1] It was left to pianists like Dreyschock, who made a speciality of octaves, to pretend, by clever faking, to play things like Chopin's Revolutionary Study in octaves—a trick which should deceive no one. Once, in Russia during the 1840s, Dreyschock produced his stunt before the Imperial court. Being challenged to equal this, Liszt sat down and played Chopin's F minor Étude, Op. 25 No. 2, in a magical whisper. On reaching the last Cs in the right hand he held the note with his thumb, calmly opened his hand to take the octave, and then played the whole study at lightning speed and in genuine octaves. There was nothing more to be said.

was once fashionable to laugh at Czerny and his endless output of teaching material, his constant question 'Have you been working hard?' and his tiresome thoroughness. But his firm control was just what Liszt needed. For about eighteen months, at a critical time in his development, he had to submit to systematic training, a training which did not supress his natural tendencies but regulated them. Czerny taught Liszt to *think* about his playing. At a later stage, in Paris, when still greater demands were to be made on him, Liszt was able to sit down and ask himself: 'What do I need, and what must I do?'; and he could deliberately plan his progress as 'the pianist of the future'. Anyone who has observed young pianistic talents in action knows that it is not the length of time spent in technical slogging that counts in these early years but the quality of the practice and the rate at which new mental and muscular controls are established. A relatively short period with Czerny was sufficient for Liszt to develop his hand and brain along the right lines, and what he acquired in those months remained with him for the rest of his life. His fingers became and stayed obedient to his slightest volition, and his sight-reading powers were extended until they reached a miraculous comprehensiveness.

His hands were long, thin and 'nervous' (in the original sense of that word). In his early manhood they must have been beautiful to watch. They had none of that soft roundness and chubbiness so often associated with 'a lovely tone', but they were capable of producing electrifying effects of power alternating with delicacy, together with a veritable *orchestration* of the music he was performing, several strands of tone-colour being evoked simultaneously. As late as 1886, when he played privately in London, an otherwise hostile critic was forced to admit: 'Assuredly nothing like his playing has been heard here before. His touch is exquisite. Liszt, unlike his pupils, is no piano-smasher. He strokes the keys and seems to "coax" the tone out of them.'

One should not however disguise the fact that during the height of his virtuoso career Liszt did smash many of the flimsy wood-and-wire boxes that found themselves in his path, leaving a trail of wreckage behind as he moved from Madrid to St. Petersburg and Constantinople.[1] But that was in the 1840s, before the iron-frame instrument had been evolved to meet the challenge of the new school of piano-playing with its solo 'piano-recital'—a term originating in Liszt's own international tours. It was never part of Liszt's system to knock pianos to pieces in order to overwhelm his audiences, and he would have considered it disgraceful that anyone should break a string on a modern Stein-

[1] One wonders what sort of pianos he found in the English country-towns, Exeter, Plymouth, Mansfield, and so forth, in 1840–41. Many a local music-lover must have regretted lending his square piano for the itinerant virtuoso's rendering of the *William Tell* overture!

way. No one guilty of such an outrage has the right to shelter behind the claim that 'Liszt used to do the same'.

For sixty years he was the undisputed monarch of the piano, and volumes could be filled with accounts of his playing. Much of this material is however mere journalism, particularly the outpourings of French and German newspapermen as ignorant as their readers, and little is to be gained by working through their rhapsodical descriptions. Henry Chorley, a cold-blooded Englishman in Paris in 1837, is a safer guide. His instincts repelled him from all that Liszt represented. He despised what he called 'Bellini's broad and sickly melodies' and Berlioz's 'heated fancies'. He hated the whole atmosphere of Paris at the time when Liszt was winning his greatest triumphs. Yet he can speak of Liszt as being 'the real diamond among much that is paste—the *real* instrumentalist among many charlatans'. And he goes on to admit that 'the most limited among purists must confess his prodigious mastery over his instrument and must be willing to regard him not merely as the successor of Clementi, Hummel and Moscheles, but as one in whom the piano, so far from being the end, is but the *means* of expressing certain emotions'.

Chorley does not confine himself to generalities: he specifies the details of Liszt's superiority.

> In uniform richness and sweetness of tone he may have been surpassed. His manner of treating the piano—his total indifference to wood and wire in his search for effect, could hardly fail to preclude uniform care and finish. But his varieties of tone are remarkable; and as far as I have gone, unsurpassed. He can make the strings whisper with an aerial delicacy or utter voices as clear and as tiny as the very finest harp notes. Sometimes the thing becomes a trumpet and a sound is extracted from the unwilling strings as piercing and nasal as the tone of a clarion.
>
> With regard to the amount of difficulties vanquished, those who have the least comprehended Liszt's mind have been the most wonder-stricken by his attributes. Rapidity and evenness of finger consistent with the most self-controlling power of stopping or retarding a passage to introduce some freak of ornament, to improvise some *shade* of expression—grasp of intervals the most harassing and difficult (the bass-chords of many of his arrangements extending over two octaves and yet struck so certainly as almost to lose the effect of *arpeggio* necessary to their production)—the power of interweaving the richest and most fantastic accompaniments with a steadily moving melody—the maintenance of question and answer among several parts—add to these velocity, fire, poignancy in flights of octaves

> and in chromatic successions of chords. All these gifts, singly or in combination, are sternly or gamely under command of the moment's poetical imagining.

Chorley sincerely regrets that Liszt has been misled by the Romantic school which thinks that 'Passion must be allowed free sway, a momentary distortion being better than a chilling restraint', but he insists that

> the amount of his exuberances has been foolishly magnified. Many who have heard M. Liszt once only have been misled through the eye by the singularity of his appearance. Because he brings a superabundance of fire and passion to the reading of works fiery and passionate they have forgotten the delicious calmness which the artist could throw over music of a more tranquil character. What next? Will M. Liszt found a school of poetical pianism, in which its professors shall each—not only *impersonate*, but *be*—a Napoleon, a Hamlet, a Faust, still not forgetting the Fathers of the art without whose precepts and sound knowledge as a basis, such personifications would become mere ravings?

Monsieur Liszt was not just then 'founding a school of poetical pianism', but by quiet and persistent work during the decade 1830–40 he was creating for himself (with Chopin in the background) a new keyboard technique which put in the shade almost everything that had gone before. Academic critics like Fétis appeared to be quite blind to this fact. Fétis could actually see in Thalberg's sterile though flowery fantasias—*Home, Sweet Home* and the like—the Music of the Future! Liszt, he declared, was already a 'back-number'.

Liszt had what Chopin lacked: electric energy and unlimited physical resources. He could bring to their highest point aspects of pianism for which the ground had already been prepared by his predecessors but which awaited his master-hand. It was he, for example, who extended the use of octaves to its furthest limit, especially in episodes of 'pathetic' declamation, in which he achieved overpowering effects. When the octaves were shared between the hands (as in the third Paganini Étude) speed and power were carried to the *n*th degree. Liszt invented this effect and could claim: 'Chromatic passages divided between the hands are my property.'[1] He also treated in the boldest and most original manner the technique of 'wide skips'. It became a speciality of his and he seems to have been practically infallible. And so with his chromatic passage-work—those dazzling cadenzas which seemed to run out of his finger-tips—

[1] See p. 111, Ex. 45 for an illustration of the device.—*Ed.*

or the incisive, bafflingly rapid repeated notes to which only the best instruments could do justice. The whole keyboard from top to bottom was swallowed up with such confidence that it is not surprising that the caricaturists of the day usually represented him as possessing four hands and twenty fingers.

All this was not achieved without hard work. He writes:

> My mind and my fingers are working like two convicts. Homer, the Bible . . . Beethoven, Bach, Hummel, Mozart and Weber are all around me. I study them, meditate on them, devour them avidly. And I do four to five hours practice as well—thirds, sixths, octaves, tremolos, repeated notes, cadenzas etc. If I don't go mad you will find in me an ARTIST, yes, an artist such as is needed today.

And later:

> You see my piano is for me what his frigate is to a sailor, or his horse to an Arab—more indeed: it is my very self, my mother tongue, my life. Within its seven octaves it encloses the whole range of an orchestra, and a man's ten fingers have the power to reproduce the harmonies which are created by hundreds of performers.

Among the first fruits of this development was his astounding performance of Berlioz's 'Fantastic' Symphony.[1] (His first transcription of 1833 was not published.) Here indeed the pianist could give the illusion of taking the place of 'hundreds of performers'. And to show how great were his powers of assimilation he could, as a mere trifle, publicly perform from memory two of Chopin's most difficult Études half an hour after the composer had finished writing them down. Later the strain became terrific, and during his triumphal days in Berlin he gave 21 concerts between the end of December 1841 and the beginning of March 1842, taking a vast range of new material in his stride.

It was inevitable that, leading the life he did in 1838–47, constantly on the move, playing to all and sundry and often in quite degrading circumstances, Liszt should not have maintained the high standards he had set himself in the first flush of enthusiasm. He has been reproached with playing showy rubbish and performing tricks like a circus animal, when he might have done more to 'uplift' his audiences from Italy to Ireland. This is not really fair, and shows a failure of historical imagination. Could he be expected to play Beethoven's

[1] Sir Charles Hallé gave an eye-witness account of this performance. It is quoted on p. 43.—*Ed.*

Op. 111, or even the 'Moonlight' Sonata, to an audience at the Scala, Milan—chattering, having supper, conducting love-affairs and paying social calls throughout the performance? All the same, the memories of some of the 'highlights' of his tours must have later brought a guilty blush to the cheek of the Master at Weimar and Bayreuth. His critics were not slow to seize on these shortcomings and backslidings, and Liszt had only himself to blame for the reproaches (more in sorrow than anger!) of the virtuous Schumanns (Robert and Clara) or Mendelssohn and his circle. Mendelssohn writes (during the Berlin triumphs of 1842):

> Liszt has not given me half so much pleasure here as in other places: He has forfeited a good part of my esteem thanks to the idiotic pranks he played, not only with the public—which matters little—but with the music itself. He performed works by Beethoven, Bach, Handel, Mozart, and Weber in such a lamentably imperfect style, so uncleanly, so ignorantly that I could have listened to many an average pianist with more pleasure. Here six bars were added, there seven left out: now he played wrong harmonies which were subsequently cancelled out by others equally false. Then we had a horrible fortissimo employed in passages marked pianissimo—and so on, all kinds of deplorable misdeeds.

Against this should be set the opinion of Wagner on Liszt's Beethoven playing in later years. Wagner was the last person on earth to compromise in matters of musical standards: he could never unbend to spare someone's feelings. And therefore he must be taken seriously when he declared that in Liszt's interpretation of Beethoven (as revealed to him from about 1853) he found not a mere *reproduction* of the composer's thought but a *re-creation*, actually taking place in the listener's presence.

Unfortunately for Liszt these early indiscretions of his could not be easily lived down, and for a long time his very name was synonymous in academic quarters with 'flashy facility' and 'vulgar display'. This attitude towards him lasted until the end of his life, and the sarcastic tone comes out clearly in some press-notices of his last visit to London in 1886:

> Dr. Franz Liszt has agreeably disappointed those who prophesied that while in England he would not touch the piano. . . . Liszt himself declared he was too old to play, and that he now left his music safe in more youthful hands. . . . But all this it seems was mere modesty. It was 'only pretty Fanny's way'. Liszt, like the bashful young lady in the drawing-room, only

> needed pressing, and it is possible that, had he not been pressed, he would have been exceedingly dissatisfied.
>
> He has given his friends and the musical critics abundant opportunities to hear him, but always in a certain class of music. In the case of anybody else but Liszt, no experienced critic would care to offer a definite opinion of a pianist until he had heard him in a higher grade of pianoforte music... The most trenchant criticisms of Liszt have always been levelled at his playing of Beethoven. If he would perform the Op. 106 [Hammerklavier] or even the *Appassionata*, latter-day musicians would be better able to form their own opinion upon Liszt's claim to be the greatest of all pianists. Whether the great executant is, in the modern sense of the term, gifted with the higher mental qualifications of pianoforte playing cannot be determined. The music he performed gave no opportunity for the demonstration of such qualities.[1]

Liszt, alas, had only himself to blame: the memories of 1838–47 had not faded, and the wider European public knew nothing of his development after he abandoned his virtuoso life. There can be little doubt that the hostility (not unmixed with jealousy) which the *pianist* aroused in influential 'professional' quarters had a most damaging effect on his endeavours to establish himself as a *composer*. Whatever the merits or demerits of his works, they were rarely judged in a calm, unprejudiced or generous frame of mind: Liszt had left himself wide open to attack and denigration.

Today, 125 years after the epoch of his greatest impact on the general musical public, it is difficult to assess the exact 'quantity' of his virtuosity. Now that a formidable command of every possibility of the keyboard, including developments undreamt of by Liszt himself—Rachmaninov, Ravel, Debussy, Bartók, Prokofiev, etc.—is a commonplace familiar to the experience of vast audiences, and is open to close scrutiny thanks to recordings, one might be tempted to suppose that the 'innocent ears' of the 1840s were easily bewitched by anything noticeably outside the range of the domestic pianist, and that Liszt might find himself painfully 'cut down to size' in the presence of a Richter or Horowitz.[2] The idea might be entertained for a moment if we had no point of reference save the writings of contemporary journalists, the hysterical behaviour of ignorant audiences and the untrustworthy memories of 'favourite pupils'.

[1] *Illustrated London News*, April, 1886.

[2] Rumours have long circulated concerning a cylinder recording—only to be mentioned in whispers!—which Liszt is supposed to have made in 1885. There seems to be nothing in the story, and it is better so. What could such a pathetic relic tell us of the King of Pianists?

But friend and foe alike, among them the most serious musicians of an age rich in solid culture, did not hesitate to acknowledge Liszt's supremacy, his universality both in technique and interpretation. When Tausig and Anton Rubinstein admitted 'We are all children compared with Liszt' they were expressing the sentiments of all those who heard Liszt at the summit of his powers and were able to measure the extent of his achievement. The absolute mastery of every difficulty, the electric excitement, the caressing lyricism, the suggestion of 'things beyond tears' and the sensation of being in the presence of heaven-sent genius—these were things that he alone could offer. A duller and machine-dominated 'civilization' (if that is the right word) can only look back with regret and envy.

The Teacher

On entering upon even a brief discussion of Liszt as a teacher one must move with caution over a difficult stretch of ground. From the end of the last century up to the present day the value of any connection however remote or tenuous with the great man has not been overlooked by those who might claim to be in the direct line of succession and to be the heirs to his 'methods' and 'traditions'. To have received consecration from a pupil of a pupil of Liszt can still inspire, or if necessary console, the aspiring pianist who seeks to stand out among the host of his competitors. Nevertheless, a cool examination of this topic is both illuminating and instructive.

Liszt, of course, taught from his earliest years in Paris until his dying day, when a group of pupils waited in the moonlit garden at Bayreuth to learn that their revered Master would give no more lessons. Some accounts from his earliest pupils survive in the form of notes, but they convey practically nothing of real interest—nothing that would show Liszt to be very different from the ordinary run of lesser teachers. It does not help much to be told that he gave some young lady 'an admirable, admirable lesson' during which he 'shook his long silky hair and his eyes flashed lightening'. The fact is that he was not cut out for the life of a regular pedagogue, such as Chopin or Henselt made it their business to become. The lessons he gave before he began his profitable concert tours were either to make money or to relieve the boredom of confinement in a place like Geneva where, in 1835, he undertook the piano-classes in the recently founded Conservatoire and actually promised to write a piano-method for that institution. Nothing came of it, and all that remains of this brief period of teaching are the end-of-term reports on some fair pupils: 'Little hands—brilliant execution', or 'Pretty fingers—lovely eyes—might make a teacher'.

A pupil of 1828, Wilhelm von Lenz, shows Liszt using for practice an extremely heavy piano, specially prepared, we are told, 'so that to play one scale on it is as good as playing ten on another piano'.[1] There is no mention of any specific technical instruction: Liszt took it for granted that his pupils would arrive at results by steady practice; that they would observe him and try to produce the same effects. The piano world would have to wait until the arrival of teachers like Deppe, followed by others like Matthay, for an analytical approach to the problems of keyboard manipulation. If one *observed* how Liszt was doing certain things—the lie of his hand at an angle to the keyboard in scale-playing, for instance—one might learn. Liszt himself did not expect to give an exact account of his own mental-muscular adjustments. No one thought of piano-teaching in that light, although every teacher naturally had his own 'system' and empirical methods. (In his last years Chopin made a sketchy attempt to put something down on paper.) There was no lack of instruction-books and patent equipment, such as Kalkbrenner's notorious 'hand-guide', expressly designed to *restrict* freedom! What Liszt did give attention to was interpretation, and Lenz shows him taking a composition to pieces, bar by bar, to get to the heart of the composer's intentions. 'In the Andante of a Weber sonata I learnt more from Liszt in the first four bars than from all my previous teachers.'

In this matter of interpretation Liszt was quite exceptional, and it is here that his true function as a teacher appeared, especially during the years when he had abandoned his virtuoso career and had settled down in his 'triangle': Weimar, Rome, Budapest. Having reached a kind of pianistic Everest from which he could look down on the world below, Liszt could not be expected to take much interest in the mere mechanics of playing. His rôle was to create the atmosphere in which young talents could blossom by absorbing the radiations of his personal magnetism and by basking in the glow of his supreme achievement. As the man who had received the kiss of Beethoven and had been the intimate and co-equal of all the great figures of the recent past he enjoyed immense prestige. One may smile at the exaggerated enthusiasm of some of the 'fans' who sought him out, followed him on his journeys or exploited his benevolence, but one must recognize that they were in pursuit of something unique. To have one's ambition fired by such an example, and to be caught up in the magical atmosphere of romance and unsurpassable pianistic perfection was felt to be

[1] Liszt used a dumb keyboard throughout his career and even had one fixed in the coach he used for his tours.

an ample reward for the sacrifices to which some of these pupils had to consent.

There should be no illusions regarding the vast body—well over 400 are recorded—of those who gave themselves the proud title of 'Pupil of Liszt'. Many of them played to him once only, and even then they sometimes did not get beyond a page or two before they were unceremoniously bundled off the piano-stool, never to be seen or heard of again.

The relatively few exceptions were found among those in whom Liszt recognized outstanding talent and who were allowed to associate with him for long and worthwhile periods. Among such were Karl Tausig, his true heir, whose death at the age of twenty-nine in 1871 was a bitter blow; Hans von Bülow, his son-in-law; the Russians Siloti and Vera Timanoff, Reisenauer, the Englishman Walter Bache, and some others. On occasions there were as many as fifty young people in Weimar clamouring for acceptance as pupils. He could not possibly give his attention to all of them, although they came with testimonials and letters of recommendation from kings, princesses and musical celebrities—indispensable introductions, for after all Liszt had to impose some kind of 'passport system'. Most were sent away happy if they played once and had a word of commendation bestowed on them. For the rest of their lives they would draw inspiration (and reputation!) from their week or fortnight in Weimar.

The routine of these master-classes only became fully established after Liszt settled at the Court-gardener's House (Hofgärtnerei) in Weimar in January 1869. He had a large drawing-room on the first floor, provided with a splendid piano—a new one every year.[1] The pupils would present their letters of introduction privately beforehand and be invited to attend the next lesson. Three times a week while Liszt was 'in residence' the classes were held in the afternoon from 4 till 6. Liszt, having been up since 4 a.m., needed a siesta, after which he was ready to receive. The class being assembled (unpunctuality was a crime of *lèse-majesté*) and all the music being laid out on a table near the door, Liszt would appear, announced by the tense whisper: 'The Master comes!' All stood, and were greeted with royal courtesy. Then the business of the class began. Liszt picked up pieces of music, glanced at them, laid them aside. At last his eye would fall on something he chose to hear: 'Who plays this?'—and the lucky but fearful pupil stepped forward and took his seat, while the Master placed himself beside the pupil and gave a running commentary on the performance. Apart from Liszt's comments and suggestions it was the nerve-testing experience of

[1] A photo of the 1880s shows a group of thirty pupils waiting in the garden below while Liszt looks down from an open window.

LISZT'S MUSIC
ROOM IN THE
OFGÄRTNEREI

LISZT AND SOME OF HIS PUPILS (WEIMAR, SUMMER 1884)

From left to right: 1. Georg Liebling. 2. Alexander Siloti. 3. Moriz Rosenthal. 4. Miss Drawing. 5. Arthur Friedheim. 6. Mademoiselle Paramnoff. 7. Franz Liszt. 8. Emil Sauer. 9. Madame Friedheim. 10. Alfred Reisenauer. 11. Mannsfeldt. 12. A. W. Gottschalg

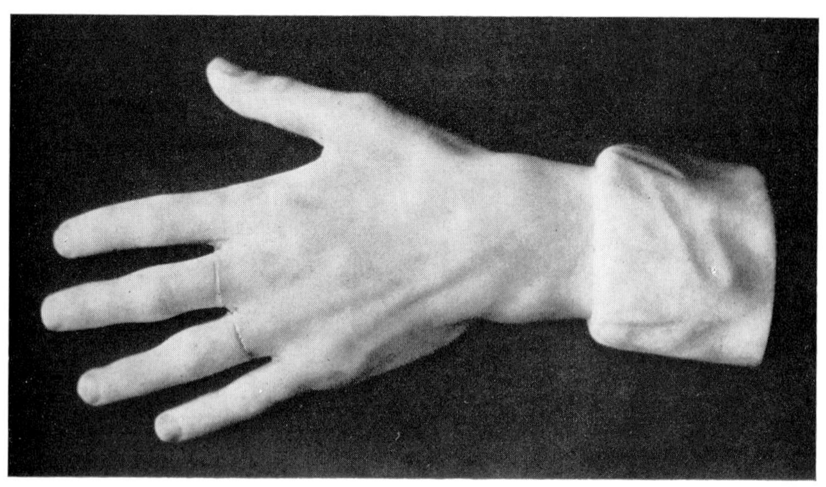

Above PLASTER CAST OF LISZT'S LEFT HAND

FRANZ LISZT (in 1838)
Lithograph by Kriehuber

playing before such a knowing and critical audience that was of value to the aspirants to fame. It either made them or broke them as candidates for public careers; anyone who could face up to *that* need not be afraid of a concert-audience.

The most trustworthy account of the classes comes from the clear-sighted young American, Miss Amy Fay,[1] who looked on the scene before her with a steady eye. She felt all the 'prestige' and quasi-mystical atmosphere, but she did not sink under it.

> July 15th, 1873
>
> Liszt is such an immense, inspiring force that one has to try and stride forward with him at double rate. To-day I'm more dead than alive as we had a lesson from him yesterday that lasted four hours. There were twenty artists present, all of whom were anxious to play, and as he was in high good-humour, he played ever so much himself in between. It was perfectly magnificent, but exhausting and exciting to the last degree. It is a fearful day's work every time I go to him. First, four hours practice in the morning. Then a nervous feeling that takes away my appetite and prevents me from eating my dinner. And then several hours at Liszt's where all sorts of tremendous things are played. You never know before whom you must play there, for it is the musical headquarters of the world.

Again:

> You feel so *free* with him, and he develops the very spirit of music in you. He doesn't keep nagging at you but leaves you your own conception. Now and then he will make a criticism, or play a passage, and with a few words give you enough to think of all the rest of your life. He doesn't tell you anything about the technique. *That* you must work out for yourself.

And here comes a notable point:

> We bring the same piece to him but once, and but once play it through. Our class has swelled to about a dozen persons now [it was early in the season] and a good many others come and play to him once or twice and then go . . . Fraulein Kahrer was one, but she only stayed three days.

It is easy to see how Liszt's generosity in accepting people into his classes was exploited, and how his own reputation suffered from the exaggerated piano-smashing and the eccentricities of those calling themselves his pupils. On one

[1] *Music Study in Germany*, Chicago, 1880.

memorable occasion the irascible Hans von Bülow attempted to clean out the Augean stables—the comparison is not inappropriate, since, as with Hercules, the dirt flew in through the window as fast as it was thrown out at the door—but as soon as his back was turned the crowd of hangers-on reappeared.

Liszt himself played relatively little during these lessons. He rarely allowed slovenly playing to pass, and many an incautious pupil was obliged to repeat a passage a dozen times, and might think himself lucky if Liszt did not snatch the music from the piano and dismiss the culprit with stern words: 'We don't wash dirty linen here—go back to your conservatoire!' The great occasions were those on which he would play a big work himself—Chopin's B minor Sonata, for example, which 'showed off all his powers . . . the Scherzo with its wonderful lightness and swiftness, the Adagio with its depth and pathos, and the last movement where the whole keyboard seemed to "thunder and lighten".' Beethoven he treated in his lessons with the greatest respect—a contrast with the cavalier approach of his early concert career, when he would play fast and loose with the text of concertos and sonatas. 'He always teaches Beethoven with notes, which shows how scrupulous he is about him, for he knows all the sonatas by heart. One day [when a Mr. Orth was playing Op. 110] he insisted on having it done in a particular way and made him go back and repeat it over and over again. One line is particularly hard. Liszt made everyone in the class sit down and try it. Most of them failed. "Ah yes," said he, laughing, "when once I begin to play the pedagogue I am not to be outdone."' His reactions when a mediocre student embarked on the *Appassionata* illustrate the atmosphere of tension and mental excitement that could exist at the Hofgärtnerei:

> It was a hot afternoon and the clouds had been gathering for a storm . . . a low growl of thunder was heard muttering in the distance. 'Ah', said Liszt who was standing at the window, 'a fitting accompaniment'. If only Liszt had played it himself the whole thing would have been like a poem. But he walked up and down and forced himself to listen, though he could scarcely bear it. A few times he pushed the student aside and played a few bars himself, and we saw the passion leap into his face like a glare of sheet lightening. Anything so magnificent as it was, the little that he *did* play, and the startling individuality of his conception, I never heard or imagined.

*

This, then, was Liszt's great contribution to the art of piano-playing. He occupied a unique position: no one could hope to impress him by mere technical brilliance, for there was nothing that anyone could do that he could not do better. He had behind him an unparalleled pianistic career and vast experience. His repertoire was enormous; in his time he had played everything and had known all the great composers for his instrument personally. And yet he was accessible and generous—not for him the exclusiveness of a Chopin or the petty clannishness of many of his successors. A regular student at his classes had the chance of hearing, in very fine performances accompanied by trenchant criticism and wise advice, the whole repertoire of the piano. Liszt concentrated indeed on the intellectual and spiritual content of the music, but as a late pupil, Stavenhagen, noted: 'If one is attentive one can learn enormously from him in technical matters. One must be swift to seize on the Master's technical secrets.'

Although the glory of the best Weimar days was later tarnished by the exaggerations and often spurious 'recollections' of certain pupils, for those who shared in the musical feasts that Liszt offered those golden afternoons at the Hofgärtnerei remained a blissful memory. We may leave Liszt the teacher as he appears in a tiny sketch from the memoirs of a genuine disciple:

> He played with me his Concerto Pathétique, then his Rákóczy March. This latter recalled to him his *Hexameron*. But I was frightened and ran away. They caught me and brought me back to him. 'Come on,' he said, 'I will take charge.' And so he did, playing all the difficult passages himself, even when they really fell to me. And then he improvised so poetically on Schubert . . . marvellously, unforgettably.

What other teacher could have led his pupils into such an enchanted world?

ALAN WALKER

Liszt's Musical Background

FOUR men dominated Liszt's musical background. All were outstanding musicians in their own right. All left an indelible stamp on his creative personality. Between them, they spanned his entire life—and it was a long one, lasting nearly 75 years, and stretching right across the nineteenth century. They hold the key to his music. They helped to make him what he was.

It is Liszt and his musical relationship to these four men—Czerny, Paganini, Chopin, and Wagner—that I want to consider.

Czerny (1791–1857)

When Liszt arrived in Vienna in 1821, accompanied by his father, it was to Carl Czerny that he turned for lessons. The choice was obvious. Czerny himself had been a pupil of Beethoven; his fame, both as a pianist and as a teacher, was spreading rapidly. A series of brilliant pupils had already passed through his hands, including the astonishing child prodigy Ninette von Belleville who made her master's name known in every capital in Europe. Czerny, at this time, was just thirty years old. He was a bachelor and lived in the house of his parents where he taught, sometimes for ten hours a day. His industry was staggering; apart from his heavy teaching programme, and his being constantly besieged by would-be pupils from every country, he still found time to compose no fewer than 1000 opuses, many of which consist of fifty numbers or more. Czerny the man was as disciplined as Czerny the artist. He was rarely observed to show emotion; he kept what was basically a warm, impulsive nature in tight check. To the outside world he was the supreme pedagogue. And the qualities which made him such a brilliant teacher—precision, fanatical thoroughness, a love of order—were carried over from his personal life which was meticulously organized down to the last detail. Nowadays, Czerny might well be classed as an obsessional neurotic.

Adam Liszt chose a bad time to approach Czerny who was grossly overworked and not disposed to take any more pupils. It was only with the greatest reluctance that Czerny agreed to hear young Liszt play at all, and he granted the audition only on the strict understanding that there was to be no question of regular lessons. The boy began to play, with Czerny looking on. After he had finished, Czerny, according to Lina Ramann, 'was now of another mind'. There is no doubt that the lad made a great impression on Czerny who taught him free of charge. Years afterwards, when writing his autobiography, Czerny recalled the event: 'It was evident at once that nature had intended him as a pianist.'

What Liszt learned from Czerny was discipline. Although Liszt was only with him for eighteen months, the experience proved enormously beneficial to him. Czerny drilled him in every branch of piano technique. Up to this time, his playing had the impulsive, improvisatory character of natural genius. Contemporary observers speak of the lad's fondness for wild rubatos and departures from the text during which he would rhapsodize over the thematic material quite freely. Some of the music he played he had not looked at, literally, for years. Czerny was a tyrant. He gave the boy massive doses of endurance exercises—including Clementi's *Gradus ad Parnassum*—and he forced him to play with meticulous regard to the text. An adherent of the 'finger equalization' school, Czerny spared no pains to give him a rigorous technical foundation. Even Liszt, used as he was to sitting long hours at the keyboard, found it tough going. Years later he got his own back by dedicating his fearsomely difficult 'Transcendental' Studies to his old master.

Liszt's first known composition dates from this period. It is of some interest because it shows something of Czerny's influence. In 1822, Diabelli the publisher sent a theme of his own composing to fifty musicians then living in Austria and invited them each to contribute a variation on it. Liszt, who was then eleven and the youngest contributor, was invited; so, too, was Czerny.[1] Liszt's contribution is not particularly outstanding; it might almost pass for a Czerny study (Ex. 1, p. 38).

Of far greater interest is Liszt's official Op. 1, the set of Twelve Grand Studies. Although these pieces were not written until he was fifteen, and no longer a pupil of Czerny, they are brilliant examples of their kind and strongly

[1] So, too, was Beethoven, who refused! Some months later, however, he relented and returned to Diabelli's theme—a 'cobbler's patch' he called it—eventually composing his *33 Variations on a theme by Diabelli*, arguably the finest set of variations in existence.

EX. 1

reflect the influence of his teacher. What makes them of crucial importance, as we shall see, is that Liszt returned to them many years later and used them as the basis of his epoch-making 'Transcendental' Studies.[1] Here is the beginning of the second of them. It is basically an exercise in broken octaves—in the best Czerny manner.

EX. 2

Young Liszt has never been given the credit he deserves for these brilliant pieces. They are worth anyone's while to perform. Not only are they skilfully laid

[1] See pp. 51–54.

out for the keyboard; nearly all of them are musically interesting, too. Perhaps the best of them is the one in D flat major—a little gem which exploits melody and accompaniment in the same hand.

EX. 3

One of the most dazzling studies in the set is the tenth in F minor. The fifteen-year-old boy here reveals an astonishing flair for making the keyboard sparkle from one end to the other.

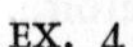
EX. 4

Liszt left Vienna—and Czerny—in 1823. He had been with the great pedagogue a mere year and a half. Yet the benefits were to remain with him all his life. Czerny's bone-breaking exercises, and his own unremitting labours, had given him an enviable technique. He might have stayed with Czerny longer. But his father was increasingly anxious for him to study composition and had high hopes of getting him into the Paris Conservatoire. With this end in view, the family packed their belongings and set out for the French capital.

Arrived in Paris, and armed with various letters of introduction, Adam Liszt set about securing a place for his son in the Paris Conservatoire. Had they known what a frosty reception that august establishment was to extend to them, they might well never have left Vienna. The principal of the Conservatoire at that time was Cherubini. Cherubini enjoyed a world-wide reputation as a composer; but as an administrator he appears to have been unadventurous, blinkered by the rules of his office. And the rules were quite clear concerning the admission of foreigners; only Frenchmen were allowed to study at the Conservatoire. Despite all his protestations, Adam Liszt found Cherubini quite unbending on that point. It was a bitter blow. Adam had pinned all his hopes on getting his son into the Conservatoire, which was one of the finest institutions in the world for grounding its students in the elements of composition. After a good deal of deliberation, it was decided to place Franz under the care of Reicha and Paer. Reicha, who had been a pupil of Michael Haydn, was one of the best theorists in Europe; while Paer, who came from Parma, was an established opera composer and enjoyed a wide popular following. The arrangement worked very well. Franz undoubtedly enjoyed far greater creative freedom under these two musicians than would have been allowed him had he been a Conservatoire student. Moreover, he quickly gained entrée into the fashionable *salons* of the French artistocracy and played before many of the best-known families in the land. Everywhere he went the 'little Litz' was lionized (the French always had trouble pronouncing his name) and it became obvious that he must set the seal on these private successes by having some public ones as well. Two concerts were arranged. These took place on 8 and 9 March 1824, at the Italian Opera. They can only be described as sensational. The press went wild.

> I cannot help it: since yesterday evening I am a believer in reincarnation. I am convinced that the soul and spirit of Mozart have passed into the body of young Liszt . . .
>
> His little arms can scarcely stretch to both ends of the keyboard, his little

> feet scarce reach the pedals, and yet this child is beyond compare; he is the first pianist in Europe. Moscheles himself would not feel offended by this affirmation.[1]

'Little Litz' became the darling of the French capital. His father, mightily pleased at the furore, immediately set about organizing more concerts. Within weeks they were in London. Liszt played at the Argyll Rooms, and then at Drury Lane, where he 'consented to display his inimitable powers on the New Grand Piano Forte, invented by Sebastian Erard'. Everywhere, his playing provoked the liveliest interest. The crowning touch came when he was received by George IV. Altogether, Liszt in his youth paid three visits to London. At the last of them, in 1827, he played for the Royal Philharmonic Society.

On his return to France, with three years of intensive concert-giving behind him, he fell ill. So much activity had overtaxed his strength. The doctors advised Adam to take the boy to Boulogne for sea baths. While they were there, tragedy struck. Adam succumbed to typhoid fever, and within days he was dead. Liszt, who was only fifteen, behaved with remarkable composure. Alone, in a strange city, he supervised the funeral arrangements, settled his father's debts, gently broke the news of the tragedy to his mother in a letter, and instructed her to meet him in Paris, where he now returned. A new chapter was about to begin.

The Piano-playing World of Paris

Paris was the centre of the pianistic world in those days. Everybody who was anybody revolved around it. Dozens of steel-fingered, chromium-plated virtuosi played there, locked in deadly combat, including Kalkbrenner, Herz, Hiller, Henselt, Pixis, Thalberg, Moscheles—the list is endless. And 'deadly combat' is not too strong a phrase to describe the open rivalry which existed among these men—gladiators of the piano, fighting it out in the open arena of the concert hall. These pianists spent their lives bringing their fingers to an unbelievable state of perfection. Some of them even specialized in a particular branch of technique. There was Dreyschock with his octaves, Kalkbrenner with his crystal-clear passage-work, Thalberg with his trick of making two hands sound like three. Nowadays, it is fashionable to sneer at such antics.

[1] A. Martainville, 'Le Drapeau Blanc', 9 March 1824.

But that generation of pianists solved some of the most intractable problems of piano playing. They pushed back the physical boundaries of the piano to such a degree that the instrument became the most comprehensive musical tool of the Romantic era. They founded modern pianism. There never was such a time in the history of the piano as this, and there never will be again. Paris was a riot of pianists, and the noise they made was heard across the world.

I mentioned Dreyschock's octaves. He would practise them solidly for many hours a day. In his prime, he reached the point where he could play them as quickly and as smoothly as single-note passages. He became famous for his rendering of Chopin's 'Revolutionary' Study and used to stagger his audiences by playing the difficult left-hand part entirely in octaves. He got the idea from his teacher Tomaschek. At one of their lessons Tomaschek happened to open Chopin's newly-published 'Revolutionary' Study and casually remarked that at the rate things were going a pianist might well emerge who was capable of playing the continuous left-hand semiquavers in octaves. Dreyschock took the hint. He went away and practised solidly for several weeks. When he came back he had completely mastered the problem. (Old Tomaschek's reaction has not been printed.) Of all his stunts, this was probably the most spectacular. Cramer and Moscheles, both trained observers, agreed that he probably had the greatest left hand in the business. As for Kalkbrenner, he was one of the best piano technicians of his generation. He used to sit motionless at the keyboard while accomplishing astonishing feats of finger dexterity. Ernest Pauer once described his playing as 'polished as a billiard ball' and said that Kalkbrenner 'controlled his obedient fingers like a captain directing a company of well-drilled soldiers'. Chopin seriously considered taking lessons from him. True, nothing came of the idea; but Chopin always retained a healthy respect for Kalkbrenner: 'He is a giant, walking over Herz and Czerny and all.' Thalberg falls into quite a different category. When he was on form he was a wonderfully refined artist who used the piano as a genuine means of musical expression. His personal magnetism was tremendous, and he held great sway over his audiences. Seated at the piano, Thalberg's attitude was one of absolute calm. His technique was impeccable; it never obtruded, yet it could meet the most difficult physical emergency. Chopin, it is true, was not all that impressed. His character-sketch of Thalberg has been widely quoted.

> As for Thalberg, he plays excellently, but he is not my man. Younger than I, pleases the ladies, makes potpourris from [Auber's] *La Muette*, gets his soft passages by the pedal, not the hand, takes tenths as easily as I take octaves—has diamond shirt-studs—does not admire Moscheles.

We should remember, however, that when Chopin wrote this from Vienna in 1830, Thalberg (who was not born until 1812) was a mere lad of eighteen. He matured considerably over the next ten years. I shall have more to say about Thalberg later, for in his hey-day he was an outstanding pianist, and he was the young Liszt's only serious rival.

The one truly great musical personality Liszt met at this time (1830), and who stands head and shoulders above the rest, was Hector Berlioz. The friendship was to be of inestimable artistic consequences to both men. It is necessary to mention it here because it led the young Liszt to produce one of his pianistic masterworks—his transcription of Berlioz's *Symphonie Fantastique*. This remarkable pianistic *tour de force* reveals clearly how far Liszt had advanced since his adolescent studies with Czerny. See the quotation from the *Marche au Supplice* Ex. 5 based on the plainchant for the dead, *Dies Irae*, probably Liszt's first artistic encounter with a melody which was to obsess him for many years.

As a young man, Sir Charles Hallé lived in Paris. He was in the audience on one occasion when Liszt played this work.

> At an orchestral concert given by [Liszt] and conducted by Berlioz, the *Marche au Supplice* from the latter's *Symphonie Fantastique*, that most gorgeously instrumented piece, was performed, at the conclusion of which Liszt sat down and played his own arrangement, for the piano alone, of the same movement, with an effect even surpassing that of the full orchestra, and creating an indescribable *furore*. The feat had been duly announced in the programme beforehand, a proof of his indomitable courage.

Liszt plunged into the pianistic turmoil that was Paris and became its undisputed leader. And here, having reached the top of his profession, he might have stopped. He was nineteen years old.

In the lives of most great men there comes a moment, often in a blinding flash of revelation, when they see their future destiny clearly mapped out before them. This happened to Liszt. And the 'blinding flash' occurred on the evening of 9 March 1831.

Paganini (1782–1840)

The foremost virtuoso at this time was not Liszt; it was Paganini. Already, during his lifetime, Paganini had become a legend. His virtuosity was such that

EX. 5

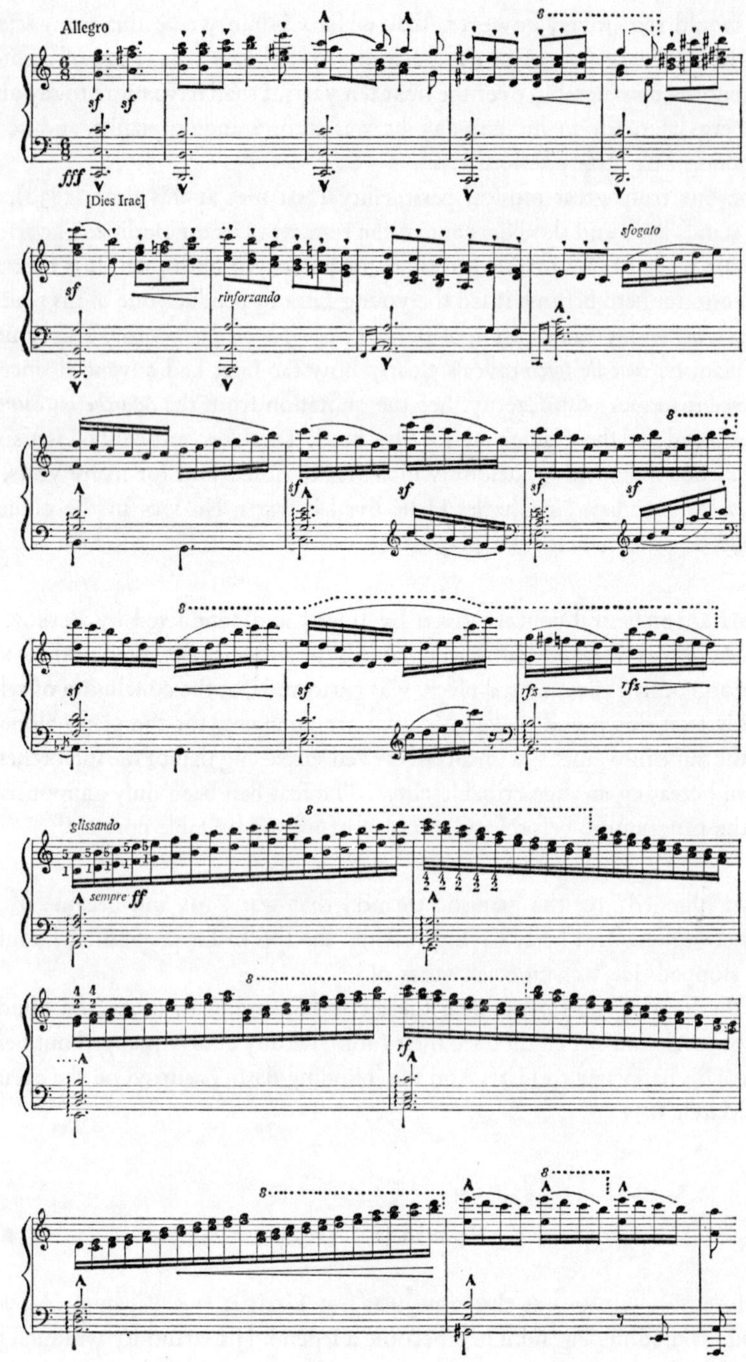

Allegro
[Dies Irae]
rinforzando
sfogato
glissando
sempre ff

in order to account for it at all musicians supposed him to be in league with the devil. Typical among the rumours which swept Europe was the one concerning his fourth string—from which he could draw ravishing sounds—which, superstition said, was the intestine of his wife whom he had killed by his own hand. It is easy to understand why such stories should circulate when we consider Paganini's appearance. When Liszt first saw him, in 1831, Paganini was forty-eight and was already wasting away from syphilis,[1] although he still had another ten slow years in which to die. His skeleton body, racked with pain, glided rather than walked on to the stage. He dressed in black. His dark, piercing eyes had receded deep into their sockets and this, together with his waxen complexion, gave him a spectral appearance which was enhanced by the dark blue glasses he sometimes wore—two black caverns set in a death-white face. The macabre impression was that of a bleached skull with a violin locked under its chin. Some hearers suspected he was Mephistopheles personified; and when he began to play they became convinced of it. Such sounds had never before been drawn from a violin. He could make the instrument do anything. He created and solved his own problems. The most rapid scales and arpeggios, triple and quadruple stopping, harmonics, every conceivable variety of bowing and tone-colour—these things were child's play to him, the most fantastic technical feats being thrown off without the slightest effort. When a string broke, he played equally well on three; if another broke, he played equally well on two; indeed, one of his specialities was to perform the most difficult pieces on one string only with which he would 'bring the house down'. He was, in short, the supreme virtuoso. Years of toil at his instrument made it unnecessary to practise and his reputation rested solely on his phenomenal performances in public—each of which kept him 'warmed up' for the next. He rarely touched the instrument in private, except to tune it, and when questioned about this he replied: 'I have laboured enough to acquire my talent; it is time that I rest.'

On 9 March 1831, Paganini glided on to the stage of the Paris Opera House and played to a packed audience. Liszt, who was there, was electrified. He was nineteen years old, and it is not too much to say that the experience changed the course of his life. He locked himself away and practised for ten, twelve, sometimes fourteen hours a day. His aim was very simple. He wanted to do for the piano what Paganini had done for the violin; he drove himself mercilessly to conquer the keyboard's last remaining secrets. And he succeeded. When he re-emerged, the term 'virtuoso' was no longer adequate to describe what he had become. Clara Schumann, not the most generous of critics, was bowled over.

[1] The immediate cause of his death was tuberculosis of the larynx.

> We have heard Liszt. He can be compared to no other virtuoso. He is the only one of his kind. He arouses fright and astonishment. His attitude at the piano cannot be described—he is original—he grows sombre at the piano.

It is probably true to say that during the years immediately following his encounter with Paganini, Liszt worked harder than at any time in his life. His transcendental technique was something he acquired by the sweat of his brow. Moreover, he identified himself so completely with Paganini that he also took over some of the Italian's platform mannerisms with startling success. From the moment Liszt walked on the stage he held the audience, quite literally, in the palms of his hands. He was more than a supreme pianist; like Paganini, he had become a supreme showman.

It is not easy to explain the extraordinary hold Paganini had over the young Liszt's imagination. Liszt was ill when he first encountered Paganini. For a year or more he had been in a state of severe psychological depression, occasioned by his thwarted love-affair with his former pupil Caroline St. Cricq. Rarely to be seen in public, he now spent most of his time indoors, in complete apathy, living in a small apartment in the Rue Montholon looked after by his mother. At one point he was actually reported dead, and an obituary notice appeared in the Paris *Étoile*. Liszt's state of mind at this time bordered on religious mania and he seriously contemplated entering the priesthood. Among his few friends was Chrétien Urhan, a bizarre character with a strong leaning towards mysticism, who led the violin section of the Paris Opera Orchestra.[1] Another friend in whose company Liszt sought consolation was the Abbé Lamennais, a French philosopher who filled Liszt's mind with religious aspirations. Both men were considerably older than Liszt and had a somewhat morbid influence over him. It seems essential to sketch in this much of Liszt's background because it helps to explain why he was so receptive to Paganini at this time.

T. S. Eliot tells us that all influence 'introduces one to oneself',[2] and on the deepest psychological level he is perfectly right. 'Influence' is what you need to be influenced by in order to develop; there is no clearer case in musical history than Liszt. Aged nineteen, he already had a dazzling concert career behind him. Young as he was, he had no rival as a pianist. Yet somewhere deep within him he knew that he was born to do more than simply play the piano better than other pianists: he must conquer the keyboard itself—a very different proposition.

[1] His moral principles were so strict, it is said, that whenever a woman dancer appeared on the stage he played with his gaze averted!

[2] *To Criticize the Critic:* London, 1964.

Liszt realized that there were technical resources at the piano still waiting to be explored, but in his apathetic frame of mind he had no real incentive to pursue them. Then Paganini appeared. Paganini brought Liszt, quite literally, back to music. In Mr. Eliot's phrase, he introduced him to himself. With startling clarity, Liszt saw himself mirrored in Paganini and he perceived where his future lay; henceforth, his mission was to unlock every secret of the keyboard—as Paganini had unlocked those of the violin—however intractable they were. He must become the Paganini of the piano. I now want to consider how he accomplished this.

The works with which Paganini used to enjoy his biggest success were his Twenty-four Caprices for unaccompanied Violin (op. 1). Everywhere they were regarded as unplayable; Paganini then used to turn up and play them. Liszt knew them well. He knew Paganini's performances of them too. During the years 1831–38 he literally lived with these pieces. He analysed their technical problems in the greatest detail, pondering how they might be re-expressed in terms of the piano keyboard. In 1838 he produced the results of his labours: the six *Études d'exécution transcendante d'après Paganini.* Five of these pieces are transcriptions from the Twenty-four Caprices; the remaining one—*La Campanella*—is a set of variations on the well-known tune of that name which Paganini had used in the Rondo of his B minor Violin Concerto. All six pieces are fearsomely difficult. It is true to say that only a tiny handful of pianists have ever been able to cope properly with their extraordinary difficulties. Some years later (1851) Liszt felt impelled to simplify them and make them generally more accessible. He ironed out their more intractable problems and re-published them under the less imposing title *Grandes Études de Paganini.* It is a pity that this last version, regularly played as it is, has had the effect of diverting attention away from the earlier one. The 1838 version is never heard, yet it sums up the young Liszt's unique brand of keyboard *diablerie* better than anything else he ever did. Consider the second piece in the set. In Paganini's original version, it runs like this.

EX. 6

It is obviously a study in scales and double stops. Now, merely to reproduce these notes on a keyboard would render childishly simple a work which happens to be very difficult indeed on the violin. With infinite cunning, the young Liszt set himself to re-express the intrinsic, violinistic problems of the piece in terms of the piano. He did this by deliberately handicapping himself, placing obstacles across the keyboard, as it were, so that in the act of overcoming them he encounters the same kind of physical resistance from the instrument as does the violinist from his. And all this while retaining the essence of Paganini's music.

EX. 7

Another of Liszt's effective 'translations' is to be found in the fourth piece of the set. It is an arpeggio study. Here is Paganini's original.

EX. 8

At his first attempt at re-composing it for the piano, Liszt hit upon the ingenious idea of having both hands unfolding arpeggios simultaneously.

EX. 9

[1838 1st Version]

But this was not difficult enough for the young lion. He immediately produced an alternative version, frightening to play, in which four streams of arpeggios flow up and down the keyboard in this diabolical fashion.

FRANZ LISZT (in 1847)
Oil Portrait by Barabás

FRANZ LISZT
(in 1839)
Oil Portrait by Lehmann

Below AUTOGRAPH PAGE OF POLONAISE IN C MINOR (1851)

EX. 10

And at the point at which Paganini's version moves into the tonic minor,

EX. 11

Liszt creates a master-stroke by composing against it an audacious counter melody in the bass.

EX. 12

This piece, more than any of the others in the set, testifies to the great leap forward Liszt took while still in his mid-twenties, a leap which placed him for a generation beyond the reach of all other pianists. Later in his life, when Liszt began to simplify his approach to the piano, he returned to Paganini's original and reproduced it intact, printing it on a single stave.

EX. 13

By far the best-known piece in the collection is *La Campanella*—a set of variations based on the popular Italian tune of that name.

EX. 14

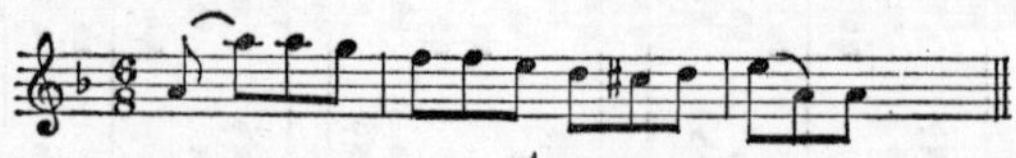

Liszt was obsessed by this melody. He must have known it long before he heard it turn up in the finale of Paganini's B minor Violin Concerto. The first results appeared in his *Grande Fantasie de bravoure sur la Clochette* which dates from 1831, and which presents the tune in every conceivable light. It was while he was revising this piece that Liszt hit upon the happy idea of re-writing it as a set of variations. Basically *La Campanella* is a study in rapid note-repetition. In many respects, it is an epoch-making work. It wins for the piano, once and for all time, a device which had hitherto been regarded as the sole preserve of the violin. Even in the hands of a bad violinist, rapid note-repetition is simplicity itself. But until Liszt came along, most musicians would have claimed that passages such as the following were simply not effective on the piano.

EX. 15

And they may have had a point. Until Sébastien Érard invented his 'double-escapement' action, pianists were compelled to let each key rise to the surface before sounding a repetition. This slowed them down considerably. But the double-escapement did away with all that by making it possible to repeat the same note endlessly from a point midway between key-surface and key-bed. Liszt exploited this new possibility to the full. When he came to revise *La Campanella* he was able to achieve some remarkably delicate effects which would have been unthinkable without Érard. Exx. 15 and 16, alternative versions of the same passage, are worth comparing.

EX 16.

Transcendental Studies

At the same time as Liszt was working on his 'Paganini' Studies, he was simultaneously bringing to fruition the first version of his 'Transcendental' Studies (1838). These pieces are so intimately connected with his encounter with Paganini, and they are so closely related in spirit to the 'Paganini' Studies, that it is convenient to consider them here.

It is not generally known that the 'Transcendental' Studies are based on the set of Twelve Studies, op. 1, which Liszt wrote as a boy of fifteen.[1] To say exactly why Liszt chose to work up those youthful pieces into a set of studies which are, technically, so complex that for a time he was the only pianist capable of playing them, is not easy. Rossini once said: 'The best way to compose a new piece is to use up an old one.' But this explanation is too facile to cover Liszt's motives. In the 'Transcendentals', Liszt unfolds a part of his musical

[1] See pp. 37–39. The only 'Transcendental' Study not to have its origins in op. 1 is the seventh of the set, called *Eroica*.

autobiography in public, so to speak; Liszt, the supreme virtuoso, openly reminisces about Liszt, the infant prodigy. I do not claim that it is essential to know Liszt's op. 1 before you can fully understand his 'Transcendentals'. But it will certainly colour your attitude towards them, in a positive sense, and it is bound to bring you more closely into line with Liszt's own attitude towards them, if you hear the 'Transcendentals' over that same musical background against which Liszt himself composed them.

Here is the Study in D minor, op. 1, no. 4.

EX. 17

It is a conventional study in double thirds, in the approved Czerny manner. But the astonishing thing about it is that it contains the kernel of the mighty *Mazeppa* study. The one can be heard shimmering behind the glittering façade of the other.

EX. 18

The child is father to the man.

When Schumann first reviewed the 'Transcendentals' he, like everybody else, was taken by their intractable physical problems. He knew little of their 'autobiographical' content. He rightly described them as 'studies in storm and dread for, at the most, ten or twelve players in the world'. Yet, studied side by side with op. 1, a certain amount of creative new light is thrown on them. Compare *Feux-follets*, for instance, with its early model.

EX. 19

Again, the one version shimmers behind the other. And the moment the player knows it, his performance of *Feux-follets* will be profoundly affected.[1]

[1] The crucial problem of *Feux-follets* is tempo. Liszt writes the piece in 2/4 time, Allegretto, and it is virtually impossible to play it at this speed. Unfortunately, this does not prevent today's steel-fingered virtuosi from wrecking the piece by trying to play it as rapidly as they think Liszt himself must have played it. But as soon as you hear *Feux-follets* for what it is, as a variation on the early B flat major study, op. 1, the rhythmic connection with that study (composed in 4/4 time) automatically clicks into place, and you naturally play *Feux-follets*

The Six 'Paganini' Studies, and the Twelve 'Transcendental' Studies between them provided Liszt with an unrivalled set of eighteen pieces covering every aspect of piano technique. They guaranteed his absolute supremacy as a virtuoso, and set the seal upon his long endeavours to transform himself into the Paganini of the piano.

Paganini Postscript

When Paganini died in 1840 Liszt suffered a genuine sense of loss—as his commemorative essay on Paganini shows—and he must have been one of the few musicians to grieve over the passing of that macabre personality. Even in death Paganini's tortured frame found no repose. The rumours about his 'black art' pursued him to the grave—and beyond. The church refused to allow his remains to be buried on consecrated ground. A bitter quarrel flared up between Paganini's friends and the church. For a month the body remained at Nice, where Paganini had died, unburied. The most shameful scenes occurred as the town's sensation seekers queued up to get a glimpse of the ghastly corpse. Its glassy eyes, which nobody had bothered to shut, stared sightless at the onlookers. On its head was perched a cotton nightcap at a bizarre angle. Its sagging jaws were held together by a bandage. People crossed themselves and rushed back into town to spread more lies about the great violinist. Meantime, the squalid wrangling over the burial arrangements continued. The stench given off by the decaying corpse made it imperative that a temporary abode should be found and at last a tomb, of sorts, was erected at Cap Saint-Hospice, on the property of Count de Pierlas, one of Paganini's admirers. It was to be thirty-six years before Paganini found a permanent resting place at Parma, and in the meantime the coffin was dug up several times, the gruesome corpse viewed, and placed in yet another grave. Paganini's posthumous to-ings and fro-ings scandalized Europe. The one sane voice to be raised in Paganini's defence, and which contrasts magnificently with the hysterical outbursts Paganini's name provoked elsewhere, was Liszt's. In a noble and generous tribute printed in the *Gazette Musicale* on 23 August 1840 Liszt wrote:

> The flame of Paganini's life is extinguished; with him vanished one of those wonders which Nature seems to bestow upon us only to reclaim it

in 4/8 time—that is, four, not two, beats to the bar. For those who argue that when Liszt writes 2/4 he does not mean 4/8, the simple answer is that until recently 4/8 time did not exist, and 2/4 time conventionally did duty for both.

> as hastily as possible—a miracle which the kingdom of art has seen but once.
>
> The unattainable, unsurpassable greatness of his genius frightens even those who try to follow in his footsteps. None will succeed him, none may be called his equal in fame. His name will never be mentioned in connection with another. For what artist's fame has enjoyed such unclouded sunlight; who is his equal in the enthusiastic and undivided opinion of the world, as ruler in the kingdom of art?

Liszt admired Paganini's art as he admired no one else's. It left an ineradicable impression upon him. And when Paganini died, Liszt felt as if he had lost a kindred spirit.

Liszt's Duel with Thalberg

It was in 1836 while Liszt was in Switzerland, in blissful seclusion with the Countess d'Agoult, that rumours began to reach him which bothered him. A young, unknown pianist called Sigismond Thalberg had appeared in Paris and was sweeping all before him. People were openly comparing him with Liszt. Thalberg, a year younger than Liszt, had two important advantages. The first was that he was born into the aristocracy;[1] he had no social or financial barriers standing in his way. The second was that he had discovered a new keyboard trick with which to fascinate his audiences. He used to bring out the melody with both thumbs in the middle of the piano, and surround it with arpeggios, thus creating the illusion of three hands. It was the kind of thing which the Parisiens loved, and they used to crane forward in their seats to see how it was done. The 'Thalberg sound' was, as it happens, an important contribution to the development of piano playing. (See Ex. 20, p. 56.)

Liszt grew nervous. He left his countess in Switzerland and hurried back to Paris. Once there, he discovered that things were even worse than he feared. Thalberg was being hailed as a greater pianist than Liszt himself. Liszt had been out of circulation for eighteen months and his public had been seduced away from him. To them, Liszt was now just a memory; Thalberg, on the other

[1] I suppose it would be truer to say that he was born out of it. He was the illegitimate son of Count Moritz von Dietrichstein and Baroness von Wetzler. It was his mother who gave him his name. After he was born she delivered herself of the following utterance: 'May this child be a peaceful valley (*Thal*), but may he someday become a mountain (*Berg*).' It remains only to add that Thalberg survived his mother's questionable talent for colourful imagery and went on to make a success of himself.

EX. 20

hand, was a reality, and he had wasted no time in firmly establishing himself in Liszt's absence. When Liszt heard Thalberg he was in no doubt that he was dealing with a second-rate pianist. After listening to the famous 'three-handed effect', he cuttingly remarked: 'Thalberg is the only man who plays the violin on the piano.' Privately, however, Liszt realized that unless he did something about it, Thalberg might well become a permanent threat.

Liszt fired his opening shot. On 8 January 1837 he wrote a scathing review of Thalberg's music for the *Gazette Musicale*. In a word, Liszt said, it was rubbish. Thalberg, not unnaturally, was cross. When asked if he would like to make a joint appearance with Liszt at a concert he retaliated: 'No. I do not like to be accompanied.' The remark is said to have swept Paris like wildfire and to have ruffled Liszt's feelings. In a letter to George Sand, Liszt observed sarcastically that he had decided he really must get to know the complete works of Thalberg, and that he had 'shut myself in for a whole afternoon to study them conscientiously'.[1] A public 'showdown' between the two pianists became imminent.

[1] Ernest Newman, in his *The Man Liszt*, quotes this letter and fails completely to see the joke by taking it to be a serious piece of evidence that Liszt could not possibly have known Thalberg's music very well because, on his own admission, Liszt only spent one afternoon studying it!

On 12 March 1837 Thalberg appeared at the Paris Conservatoire playing his 'Fantasia on God Save the King' and his 'Moses' Fantasia. There was no doubt in anyone's mind, least of all Thalberg's, that this was an open challenge to Liszt. The concert was highly successful; Liszt's followers were humiliated. Liszt met the challenge by announcing a concert of his own, for the following Sunday, at which he would play his 'Niobe' Fantasia and Weber's *Concertstück*—and for which purpose (a final insult to Thalberg) he proposed to rent the Opera House which held a far larger audience than the Conservatoire. That concert, too, was a great success; Thalberg's followers were dejected. The final crunch came on 31 March. Princess Belgiojoso invited both pianists to play at her *salon* in a charity concert in aid of the Italian refugees. All Paris was agog and the Princess charged 40 francs a ticket. The *Gazette Musicale*, announcing the forthcoming event, informed the public that Liszt and Thalberg would 'take turns' at the piano, and went on to liken the present uncertain state of play to the 'indecisive balance between Rome and Carthage'. Other musicians took part in the programme, but as far as the audience was concerned, they might just as well have stayed at home. All eyes were on 'Rome' and 'Carthage'. According to Lina Ramann, Thalberg played first and delivered himself of a glittering performance of 'Moses'. Liszt appeared later in the programme, and thus enjoyed a psychological advantage over his rival. By the time he walked on to the stage the audience was beside itself. Liszt sat down and attacked his *Niobe* Fantasy. Immediately, all doubts about Liszt's supremacy were dispelled; his hearers were riveted. When he had finished playing, the audience, doubtless

EX. 21

non legato egualmente

p dolce

feeling they had had more than their 40 francs worth, gave Liszt a hero's reception.

Having dragged his rival through the dust, Liszt went on to complete his victory by taking possession of the very device which had first rocketed Thalberg to fame. The 'three-handed effect' constantly turns up in Liszt's music after this date—part of the victor's spoils, so to speak—and it reaches one of its highest peaks of expressiveness in his D flat major Concert Study, Ex. 21.

Chopin (1810–49)

Liszt first met Chopin in 1831 while he was still reeling under the impact of Paganini. There is no doubt that Chopin's influence on Liszt was extensive and complex, and it lasted for many years. Chopin was a year older than Liszt, and at twenty-one, when he first encountered him, he was already fully matured as a composer. As Sacheverell Sitwell has said, he was, even at this early age, the full-grown Chopin we all know, and, if he improved, he never changed. Liszt, on the other hand, had composed nothing of consequence and he was only too ready to be inspired by Chopin's example—although, as we shall see, it took a somewhat unusual form. The two men were first introduced to one another by George Sand, and they immediately recognized each other's genius. Yet, from the very outset, there was something uneasy about the relationship. Superficially, it was marked by great cordiality, and in its early stages the friendship might even be described as a warm one. Yet Liszt was always more kindly disposed towards Chopin than Chopin was towards him. There was something in Liszt's make-up which repelled Chopin's refined manners—something of the showman, the trickster, the vulgar charlatan as he thought—and in his letters Chopin makes some cutting remarks about Liszt which should completely dispel the popular illusion of a romantic friendship between them.[1] Indeed, later on, owing to an unpardonable indiscretion on Liszt's part,[2] Chopin's growing coolness towards him turned into active dislike. Yet, even after the final break, Liszt remained a fervent admirer of Chopin's music, while Chopin, for his part, always acknowledged Liszt's superior stature as a per-

[1] Chopin especially disliked Liszt's hob-nobbing with the aristocracy. In a letter to Julian Fontana (1841) he says scornfully of Liszt: 'One of these days he'll be a member of Parliament or perhaps even the King of Abyssinia or the Congo.'

[2] While Chopin was out of Paris on one occasion Liszt took Mme. Pleyel, with whom he was having an affair, to Chopin's comfortable apartments in the Rue de la Chaussée d'Antin in order to enjoy her favours undisturbed. When Chopin got to hear about it he was furious as the husband M. Pleyel was a close friend of his.

former. The high point in their relationship came when Chopin dedicated to Liszt his set of Twelve Studies, op. 10. Liszt must have played these difficult pieces superbly. He was a past master at overcoming the kind of technical problems they contain. In a letter to Ferdinand Hiller (1833) Chopin said:

> I am writing [to you] without knowing what my pen is scribbling, because at this moment Liszt is playing my studies and putting honest thoughts out of my head: I should like to steal from him the way to play my own studies.

From op. 10 onwards, in fact, Liszt seems to have kept a very close watch indeed on what Chopin got up to. It was an interesting situation. Liszt had harboured all his life but one ambition: to conquer the keyboard. But having conquered it, it was Chopin who gave him clear notice that his achievement would crumble and turn to dust unless he put the fruits of his conquest into a more permanent form. For here was Chopin, creating in front of Liszt's ears, so to speak, a whole new world of piano music the like of which had never been seen before, and which Liszt in his undeveloped state as a composer could not yet hope to match. To Liszt, it probably seemed that Chopin had stolen his, Liszt's, prerogative. For Chopin's op. 10 Studies are a compendium of what was then modern piano technique—and everybody knew who was the master of modern piano technique! And Liszt hardly had time to recover before Chopin published his second set of twelve studies, op. 25 (1837) dedicated to—of all people!—Liszt's mistress, the Countess d'Agoult. It is uncertain when Liszt first conceived the idea of publishing his own 'Transcendental' Studies. But the fact remains that within a year of Chopin's op. 25 appearing, Liszt took the hint and brought out the first version of the 'Transcendentals' (1838) which rank among the most fearsomely difficult works he ever produced. When Schumann first heard them he expressed awe. What Chopin expressed has not been recorded.

As we have seen, several composers had a hand in the unique synthesis that was Liszt; but after 1849 and, for a period of about six years, none of them made such great inroads into his creative personality as did Chopin. Why 1849? This was the year in which Chopin died. And it is now that we must consider what I earlier described as the 'somewhat unusual form' in which Liszt succumbed to Chopin's influence. Practically all those works which show this influence at its strongest were written *after* Chopin died. Liszt composed virtually nothing which owes anything to Chopin while Chopin lived.[1] This fact,

[1] I have not forgotten the recently-discovered 'Duo' Sonata for violin and piano, an

which can easily be substantiated, surely calls for an explanation. It is as if there was a deep-rooted unconscious hostility towards Chopin, (which contrasts sharply with his conscious attitude of warm friendliness) which forced him to resist Chopin while Chopin lived, and to embrace him after he died—after he was, so to speak, no longer a rival. Indeed, Chopin's posthumous impact began to operate immediately.

EX. 22

Liszt wrote this piece—*Funérailles*—in memory of three of his Hungarian friends who died in the 1848 revolution. But it is significant that he actually composed

---

extended work based on Chopin's Mazurka in C sharp minor, op. 6, which only came to light in 1963. But there are strong grounds for believing that the date 1832–35, originally attached to this piece by its editor Tibor Serly, is wrong. Serly assumed that Liszt wrote the Sonata in Paris as a direct result of his youthful encounter with Chopin. This is doubtful on two counts. First, the advanced use of the 'metamorphosis of themes' technique contained in the Sonata points to the Weimar period of some twenty years later. Secondly, the Polish folk-song quoted by Liszt in the last movement was unknown to him until 1847 when he heard it for the first time at Woronince, one of the Polish estates of Princess Sayn-Wittgenstein. Liszt used this Polish folk-song in the second of the *Glanes de Woronince* pieces of 1847; the 'Duo' Sonata quotes the *Woronince* piece and must therefore post-date it.

My guess is that the Sonata belongs to the year 1851 and that Liszt started to compose it for the one violinist with whom he played chamber music consistently over a period of many months—Joachim. Joachim arrived at Weimar in October 1850 to lead the orchestra there, but left in a huff after a couple of years or so. The unfinished work was then shelved—permanently, as it happened.

As for the choice of Chopin's C sharp minor Mazurka as the basis of the work, I submit that this was prompted by the 'Chopin mania' to which Liszt succumbed in the 1850s and the Sonata was only one among many works from this period to be haunted by Chopin's memory.

it in October 1849—the very month in which Chopin died, and within days of hearing about his death. More than one musician has expressed the view that the piece is a threnody for Chopin, and my quotation from it 'brings back to life' the central episode of Chopin's A flat major Polonaise (op. 53). Here is Chopin's famous left-hand passage, based on alternating clockwise and anti-clockwise arm motion—an effect dutifully observed by Liszt (compare Ex. 22 with Ex. 23).

EX. 23

*I print this modulation in E flat major—Chopin uses the much more daring enharmonic notation of D sharp major—in order to facilitate comparison with the Liszt example above.

If you examine Liszt's output during the years immediately following Chopin's death, you will discover that he composed a number of pieces in forms which, up to that time, were quite foreign to him (some of them actually having been invented by Chopin) but which afterwards seemed to become second nature to him—as, indeed, in a mysterious way, they now were. Liszt's two Polonaises, the two Ballades, the two Mazurkas, the Berceuse and the Tarantella all date from this period. These are all forms which Chopin made famous, and while Chopin was alive Liszt never touched them. But after Chopin died he attempted to make them his own; I regard this as an unconscious symptom of his posthumous identification with Chopin. Liszt's *Berceuse*, for instance, is so closely modelled on Chopin's as almost to constitute a deliberate parody of it.

EX. 24

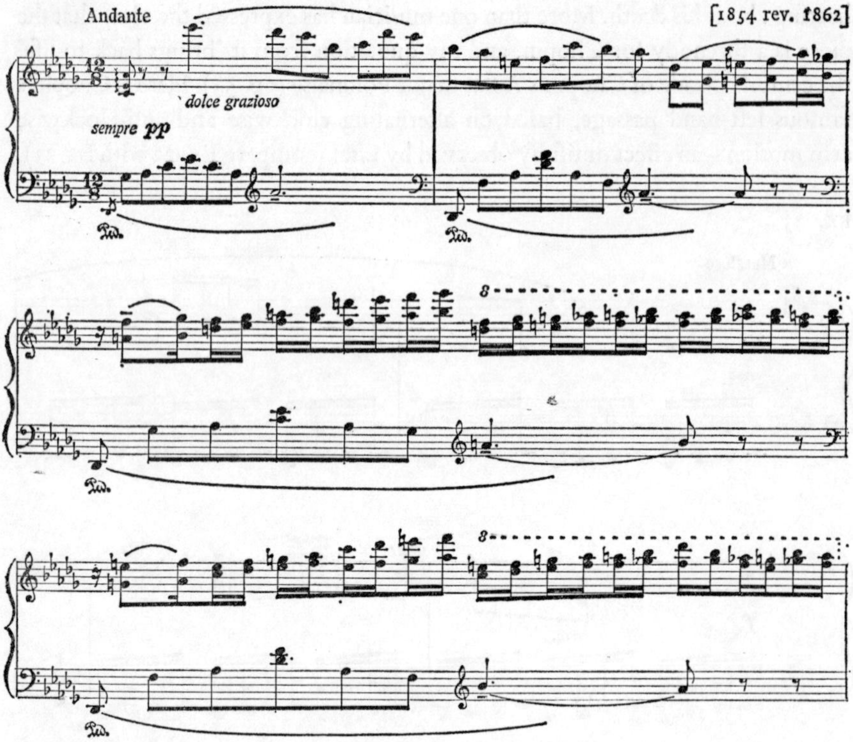
Andante
[1854 rev. 1862]
dolce grazioso
sempre pp
8
8

The connections are obvious. To begin with, it is in the same key—D flat major. Moreover, it, too, consists of elaborately varied figurations around a simple theme, not unlike Chopin's, and (a final touch, this!) there is even a tonic pedal sustained throughout the entire piece. Compare Exx. 24 and 25.

EX. 25

Andante
p
3
3
6

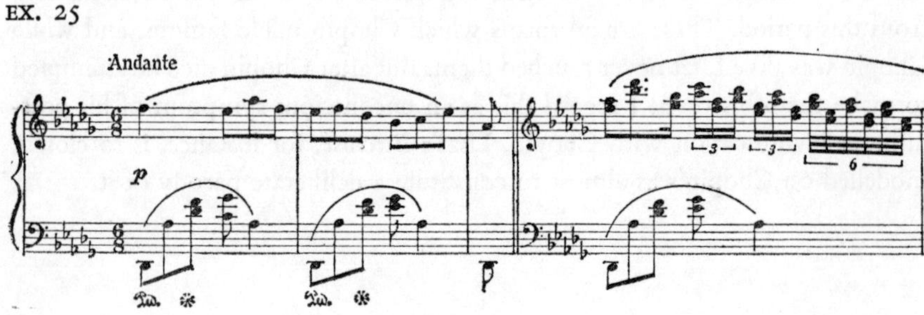

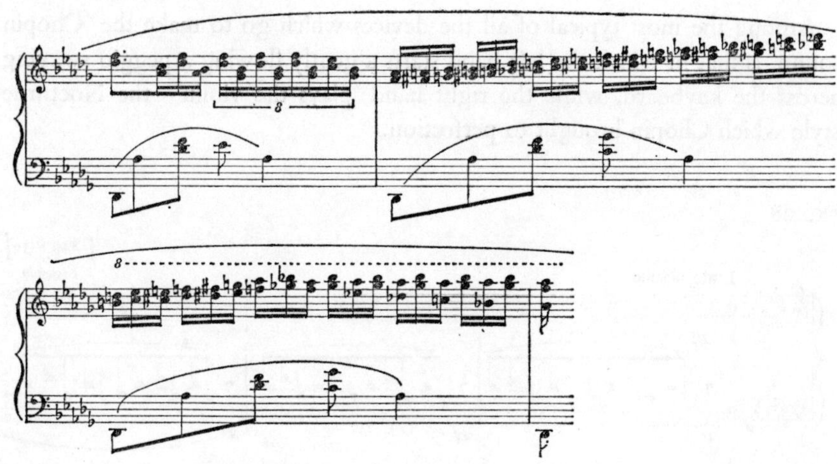

As for the other pieces which Chopin posthumously inspired Liszt to compose, the C minor Polonaise discloses turns of phrase which are practically indistinguishable from Chopin.

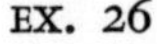
EX. 26

And they are elaborated with the same kind of filigree passage-work so typical of the Polish master.

EX. 27

Among the most typical of all the devices which go to make the 'Chopin sound' is that in which the left hand starts a gently flowing arpeggio swaying across the keyboard, while the right hand 'plays the violin'—the Nocturne style which Chopin brought to perfection.

EX. 28

Chopin's spirit broods heavily over this piece—Liszt's Consolation in D flat major—which could well have been inspired, and possibly was, by Chopin's Nocturne in D flat major, op. 27, no. 2.

EX. 29

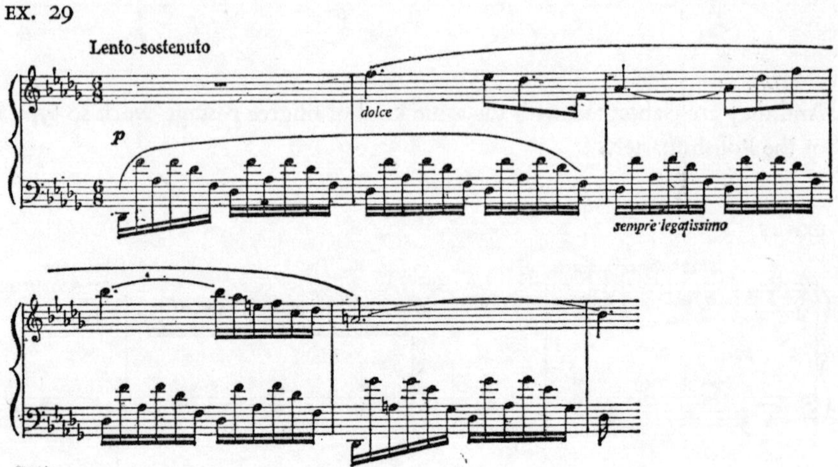

Liszt's crowning touch in paying posthumous homage to Chopin was to write a book about him (1852). There are very few examples in history of one composer taking time off to write a book about another.[1] The very opening sentence strikes a note of eulogy.

> However lamented he may be by all artists and persons who knew him, we doubt that the time has yet come for him (so deeply mourned and fully appreciated) to hold the high position of universal regard that the future likely reserves as his.

Again, we notice Liszt's magnanimity towards a fellow musician. His lifelong habit of repaying tenfold his artistic debts, and in public too, places him in a category of composers in which he is almost unique.

The Weimar Period

In 1847, Liszt took a momentous decision. He closed the piano and turned his back on the concert hall for good. The idea had long been germinating in his mind. He wanted leisure to compose. His career as a travelling virtuoso was becoming increasingly irksome to him. Yet what a career it had been! Not even Paganini's could rival it. In eight years of almost non-stop travel, he had visited practically every country in Europe—including Italy, Spain, Portugal, France, Rumania, Turkey, and Russia. Often he found himself playing in a different town each night—for nights on end. Tens of thousands of people heard him. His repertoire at this time was enormous. (On one occasion he gave twenty-one concerts in Berlin in ten weeks, performing eighty works—fifty of them from memory.[2] It must also be remembered that this was still the age of the stagecoach, and travelling was both time-consuming and exhausting. Nobody could keep up this pace for ever.

The last public recital Liszt ever gave for money was in Elisabetgrad. He was thirty-five years old.

Some time earlier (1842) he had been offered an appointment at the court of Weimar which he now decided to accept. The position seemed a desirable

[1] The quality of the book is, admittedly, debatable; it is indisputable that the Princess Sayn-Wittgenstein wrote at least a part of it. But the fact that Liszt desired to publish a book on Chopin at all, in the midst of all his other activities, points to an emotional commitment to Chopin's memory of an unusual order.

The book was republished in a new English translation by Edward N. Waters, in 1963.

[2] These figures are taken from Wallace, *op. cit.*, p. 38.

one. Weimar had an opera house and an orchestra. Moreover, his duties would be relatively light; he would have ample time for composing. The job also carried with it a free residence in the favour of the Duchy of Weimar, the Villa Altenburg, which Liszt was to make famous throughout the musical world (for this is where he held his first master-classes in piano playing). Liszt's brief was concise. He was to take charge of Weimar's musical life and turn it into a centre for all the arts.

While Liszt was laying his future plans, events took a new twist. Among the audience at his penultimate recital in Kiev was the Princess Carolyne Sayn-Wittgenstein. This was the woman who, for better and for worse, was to exercise a dominant influence on him for the rest of his life. The Princess was twenty-eight, extremely wealthy, and separated from her husband. Shortly after the recital they met privately, at the Princess's invitation, and Liszt's fate was sealed. Whatever Liszt's initial intentions (and there is some evidence to suggest that a passing flirtation is all he was interested in), the Princess soon made it clear that she would settle for nothing less than a total commitment on his part. A year later, they were both installed at the Altenburg.

The Altenburg still stands in Weimar today. It is an undistinguished house, even ugly, but its rooms are spacious and it made a comfortable home for Liszt, the first real one he had ever had. Liszt took over one small wing of the house as his own personal quarters—a bedroom with a linking door to his study—and it was here that he did all his composing. The rooms were modestly furnished, the largest item being a grand piano, a Bechstein, of which he seems to have been especially fond. There were only two pictures on the wall, an engraving of Dürer's 'Melancholia', and an artist's impression of 'St. Francis walking on the Waters'—which later inspired his piano composition of the same name. By contrast with these spartan surroundings, the rest of the house, which he shared with the Princess,[1] must have been a veritable treasure-trove of items which he had collected on his tours—medals, swords of honour, the valuable death-mask of Beethoven, Beethoven's piano, etc.—much of which had been provisionally stored with his mother in Paris until he could find a permanent place for it all. The Altenburg was not the kind of environment

[1] It is still possible to read that their relationship was a 'platonic' one. From all we know about Liszt, and his relations with women, it is incomprehensible how such a rumour could gain a secure grip on the literature. There were, it seems, three children of the union.* The Princess discreetly removed herself from Weimar on each occasion before the confinement, and the children were brought up by foster-parents in Brussels.

* Carl Maria Cornelius was quite emphatic about it. He was the son of Peter Cornelius, one of Liszt's colleagues at Weimar, and was in a position to observe events at first hand. (Ernest Newman, *op. cit.*, p. 182.)

one would have thought suitable for a man of Liszt's restless temperament. Yet it was to be his home for the next twelve years, and he was to produce some of his greatest compositions there, including the B minor Sonata and the 'Faust' Symphony.

It was also the time when one of the greatest musical influences he ever encountered was to enter his life—Richard Wagner.

Wagner (1813–83)

The friendship between Liszt and Wagner is one of the deepest and most complex in the history of music. It is no part of my present task to examine it. It has been very well examined elsewhere.[1] I simply, and briefly, want to say that the relationship was of the utmost value to both men, not only artistically but psychologically. Wagner the selfish egotist, demanded everything and gave nothing; Liszt, the selfless idealist, gave everything and demanded nothing. Liszt, in fact, came to realize that Wagner was a superior being, greater than Liszt himself even. He loved Wagner as a brother and conceived it to be his duty to put Wagner's cause before his own. He helped him financially, often at great cost to himself;[2] he gave preference to the performance of Wagner's music over his own at Weimar at a time when it was politically unwise to do so —he came close to compromising his own position there; and he harboured him from the law when Wagner, on the run from Dresden for his part in the 1849 Revolution, sought sanctuary with him. In fact, the more one studies the evidence, the more one is driven to the conclusion that there can hardly be a parallel to such magnanimity from one artist to another anywhere—inside music, or out. Without Liszt, it is difficult to imagine what might have become of Wagner. His genius would, of course, have still shone through; genius always does. But there is no doubt that Liszt smoothed over many a difficult problem

[1] *Wagner as Man and Artist*: Ernest Newman, London, 1924. *Liszt, Wagner and the Princess*: William Wallace, London, 1927.

[2] Liszt was not well off. After 1847 he never gave a recital for money. His annual stipend from Weimar was a paltry £200 a year. Moreover, although he had a great many pupils, he never charged for lessons. His chief source of income was from his published compositions which, as time went on, sold less and less. The fortune he had made in his younger days as a travelling virtuoso had been spent—thousands of pounds of it, it might be added, on others. And throughout all this time he was shouldering the financial responsibility of looking after his three children and his ageing mother in Paris.

On his death, Liszt left 82,000 kroner. Ernest Newman assumed this to be a large sum and, true to form, suggested that Liszt was not sincere when he confessed to being hard up. In fact, this sum was worth about £5,000 (the figure was provided by the National Institute of Bankers, London). The income it provided was hardly adequate to meet Liszt's liabilities.

for Wagner which might otherwise have deflected this wayward and tempestuous spirit, however temporarily, from achieving his objectives.

Liszt's first encounter with Wagner, in 1840, was an unpromising one; it gave no hint of the way their friendship was to ripen over the following years. Wagner, then a young man in his late twenties, had turned up in Paris, bearing a letter of introduction from the publisher Schlesinger. He was completely unknown, penniless and starving. Ushered into Liszt's presence, and observing the luxurious style in which the celebrated pianist was living (a style to which Wagner himself would dearly have liked to become accustomed, and later was), he became nervous and agitated. Liszt at that time could speak no German; Wagner could speak no French. The interview collapsed, and Wagner fled.

Two years later, they met again. Wagner's *Rienzi* was being staged in Dresden and Liszt went round to the artist's room to offer his congratulations. Again, the encounter was a frosty one. Accompanying Liszt was the notorious Lola Montez with whom he was living at that time. The affair was a sordid one, and the scandal of it rocked Europe; the adverse publicity Liszt received from it was to do him untold harm for many years to come.[1] And here they were, Liszt and his strumpet, at one of the important social events of the season, brazenly mingling with the various other dignitaries come to offer Wagner their congratulations! It was too much, even for Wagner. The atmosphere was chill. This time, it was Liszt who fled.

It was not until 1848 that the two men came to terms with each other. By that time, *Rienzi* and *The Flying Dutchman* had made Wagner's name resound throughout Europe. In the meanwhile, he had also completed *Tannhäuser* and *Lohengrin*. Wagner was becoming a force to be reckoned with. Liszt, who was fascinated by his music, packed his bags and made a special journey to Dresden to see him. Later that same year, Wagner, in turn, visited Liszt in Weimar and set the seal on their friendship.

It was one of the best things Wagner ever did for himself—it is difficult to put it less cynically—for almost at once the material and artistic benefits of Liszt's admiration began to flow his way. By February 1849, Liszt had already given a performance of *Tannhäuser* at Weimar. And the following year he also put on *Lohengrin* for the first time. These two operas cost Liszt

[1] Lola Montez (1818–61) was a dancer who exploited her undoubted physical assets to the full. She achieved notoriety by once baring her breasts on stage before Ludwig I of Bavaria. Liszt met her in 1841 and quickly became enamoured of her. As quickly, he tired of the affair, but found her difficult to shake off. She had the temper of a tigress. Eventually he bribed the hall-porter of their hotel to smuggle him and his luggage out of the building and to lock the lady in her room until he had made his getaway. She was imprisoned there for twelve hours, and not unnaturally she was cross. She broke every stick of furniture in sight, and when the trembling hotel staff finally let her out the room was in a complete shambles.

dearly in terms of the goodwill of the Weimar authorities, who were nervous about Wagner's undesirable political connections; but Liszt pushed them through because he passionately believed in them. As to the purely material benefits of Liszt's support, these were hardly less crucial. Wagner had foolishly become involved in the Dresden uprisings and was a fugitive from the law. He ran straight to Liszt. There is something comical about Liszt concealing Wagner in the Altenburg from the police; the mind boggles at how this almost operatic situation might have further developed had not the Princess Sayn-Wittgenstein, who did not like revolutionaries living under her roof, put her foot down. She told Wagner a few home truths and sent him packing—but not, it should be added, before he had managed to pump Liszt for a handsome loan.

Four years elapsed before they met again. Liszt, in the meantime, defiantly re-affirmed his faith in Wagner and treated the good citizens of Weimar to a performance of *The Flying Dutchman.* (Although Liszt did not know it, he was gradually committing artistic suicide for Wagner at this time. His persistent and unyielding championship of Wagner was a factor which forced his resignation from Weimar in 1858.[1]) When the two men eventually came together again, in Zürich in 1853,[2] Wagner was virtually established as the leading opera-composer of his time. Well might he write to Liszt: 'I regard you as the creator of my present position.' And he added this astonishing rider: 'When I compose and orchestrate I always think only of you.' The implications of this remark are so significant that I now want to take a closer look at it.

*

'When I compose and orchestrate, I always think only of you.' What did Wagner mean?

He had been listening to some of Liszt's music, and it had penetrated deeply. Had he not confessed it, his works would have confessed it for him. The sequence of events is revealing. During Liszt's visit to Zürich, the great pianist had played through some of his recent pieces to Wagner. Wagner at

[1] The immediate cause was his production of Cornelius's *Barber of Bagdad* (1858) which got a hostile reception, and which Liszt took to be directed against himself. But this was merely the last of a long series of artistic clashes he had at Weimar which all go back to the Wagner connection.

[2] There is a wonderful description of Wagner written by Liszt during this visit in which he tells of Wagner's delight at seeing him again. Wagner was 'screaming like young eagle laughing, weeping, dancing for at least a quarter of an hour . . . He loves me heart and soul, and never stops saying, "Look what you have made of me". When it is a question of matters relating to his reputation and popularity he has leapt to my neck twenty times in the day.' Wagner, as we have seen, had good reason to be grateful.

that time had composed nothing since *Lohengrin*—a gap of five years. Liszt's playing seemed to act as a catalyst on him.[1] Almost at once, he started work on *The Ring*; more than one observer has commented on the marked change of style. While *The Ring* was still in progress, Wagner had a second, and more serious brush with Liszt's music. It was the summer of 1856. Wagner was 'taking the cure' at Morneux. He spent his time studying Liszt's Symphonic Poems, seven of which had been published simultaneously that same year—*Tasso*, *Les Préludes*, *Orpheus*, *Prometheus*, *Mazeppa*, *Festklänge* and the *Bergsymphonie*. They were Liszt's testament of modern music, the fruits of his enormous labours at Weimar over the past five years and were intended to put modern music on the map. Wagner got to know them very well indeed. A short time later, he abandoned work on *The Ring* in order to compose *Tristan* at white heat. And here it might be worth considering some music examples.

Ten years before Wagner had even begun *Tristan* (1857–59) Liszt had already anticipated its famous opening in this phrase.[2]

EX. 30

It comes from one of Liszt's love-songs *Ich möchte hingehn* (*c.* 1845). Clearly, it later became *Tristan's* love-motif. Here is Wagner's version of the idea.

[1] Not for the only time. Wagner was highly susceptible to Liszt's piano playing. There is a delightful story, told by Count Apponyi, of Wagner's powerful reactions to a performance of Beethoven's 'Hammerklavier' Sonata at Wahnfried.

> When the last bars of that mysterious work had died away, we stood silent and motionless. Suddenly, from the gallery on the first floor, there came a tremendous uproar, and Richard Wagner in his nightshirt came thundering, rather than running, down the stairs. He flung his arms round Liszt's neck and, sobbing with emotion, thanked him in broken phrases for the wonderful gift he had received. His bedroom led on to the inner gallery, and he had apparently crept out in silence on hearing the first notes and remained there without giving a sign of his presence. Once more, I witnessed the meeting of those three—Beethoven, the great deceased master, and the two best qualified of all living men to guard his tradition. This experience still lives within me, and has confirmed and deepened my innermost conviction that *those three great men belonged to one another.* (My italics.)

[2] There is another remarkable resemblance between the opening of *Tristan* and Liszt's song *Die Lorlei* (1856). See Christopher Headington, Ex. 5, p. 231. The mutual influence between Wagner and Liszt is a complex topic which has been ably summarised by Humphrey Searle, *The Music of Liszt*, London 1954, p. 52.

EX. 31

It is impossible to say that Wagner knew Liszt's song; it is equally impossible to say that he didn't. Liszt, as he himself might have sardonically observed in later life, had a flair for robbing the future of some of its better ideas.

There was an interesting sequel to the 'Tristan' connection. In 1877, some years after *Tristan* itself had been written, Liszt composed his *Aux Cyprès de la Villa d'Este* (Threnodie II) which clearly develops the 'Tristan' idea a stage further.

EX. 32

It shows that Liszt occasionally looked back to Wagner as well as forward to him.

There is an obvious link between the main theme of Liszt's 'Faust' Symphony

EX. 33

and the second act of Wagner's *Walküre*.

EX. 34

Both compositions date from 1854, although Liszt had started work on the 'Faust' Symphony much earlier and had actually played parts of it to Wagner on the piano before the latter started serious work on *Walküre*.

A much more significant connection, commented on by both Wagner and Liszt, can be found between the 'Last Supper' motif which opens Wagner's *Parsifal* (1882) and the beginning of Liszt's *Excelsior!* (1874). Here are the two themes side by side.

EX. 35

The connection between these two passages has a long and complex history.[1] The final outcome was when Liszt used the 'Parsifal', or 'Excelsior' motif, call it what you will, in memory of Wagner in his astonishing *Am Grabe Richard Wagners* (1883). Here, the motif sounds broken and tortured—a piece of deliberate musical symbolism on Liszt's part. It has become an anguished moan, torn from Liszt by the shade of Wagner who, even beyond the grave, obsessed him.

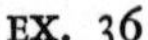

EX. 36

[1] It has been discussed at length by Arthur Marget in 'Liszt and Parsifal', *Music Review*, May 1953.

Liszt wrote on the manuscript: 'Wagner once reminded me of the likeness between his *Parsifal* motif and my previously written *Excelsior!* May this remembrance remain here. He has fulfilled the great and sublime in the art of the present day. F. Liszt, 22 May '83, Weimar.' The date, of course, was Wagner's birthday. Had he lived, he would have been seventy.

The belief, then, that Liszt was simply a slavish imitator of Wagner, with no ideas of his own, will hardly bear scrutiny. Yet it was widespread from the start. Here is Heinrich Esser, the influential conductor of the Vienna Court Opera, and an ardent Wagnerian.

> What will happen when [Wagner] is dead and can give us no more new works? Then will his imitators, the long-haired Lisztians, descend upon us *en masse*, and ruin, by their exaggerations, everything that the master has built up by a lifetime of work.[1]

The letter would hardly be worth quoting were it not to be unthinkingly echoed today, for this, it must be admitted, is the way that musical history has viewed the situation ever since. Wagner himself is partly to blame. There was something in his make-up which made it extraordinarily difficult for him to acknowledge his indebtedness to others. He studied Liszt's works in private, yet he lost no opportunity of keeping quiet about the fact in public. He was quite put out when Pohl (a Liszt disciple) published an analysis of *Tristan* and mentioned the influence of Liszt. Wagner wrote to von Bülow (1859):

> There are many matters on which we are quite frank among ourselves (for instance, that since my acquaintance with Liszt's compositions my treatment of harmony has become very different from what it was formerly), but it is indiscreet, to say the least, of friend Pohl to babble this secret to the whole world.

There is a basic lack of magnanimity here which contrasts oddly with Liszt's open-hearted friendliness towards Wagner.[2] It later prompted Busoni into remarking acidly that Wagner revealed about as much morality as a fraudulent bank.

The friendship between the two men deteriorated sharply about 1861. The immediate cause was the Princess Sayn-Wittgenstein who actively disliked

[1] Letter to Schott, 1872.

[2] See John Ogdon (p. 136) for an interesting discussion on the Wagner–Liszt relationship.

Wagner and all his works and attempted to set Liszt against him. And Liszt was ripe for it. Wagner's letters to him at this time reveal an increasing selfishness. In turn he begs, demands, beseeches, and commands Liszt to lend him money, to secure performances of this or that work, to drop everything and visit him forthwith, etc. Wagner, in short, had become a Wagnerian. Liszt's patience wore thin. His replies are curt and pointed. But far worse was to come. Unknown to Liszt, Wagner had formed an attachment for his younger daughter Cosima, already married to his favourite pupil Hans von Bülow. The affair burst into the open in 1865 (it was to drag on for several years, von Bülow not divorcing his wife until 1870). For Liszt, it was the last straw; and when, in 1867, Cosima gave birth to Wagner's child, he could contain himself no longer and travelled to Triebeschen to thrash the matter out with him. The interview was a stormy one. Afterwards, all Liszt would say about it was: 'It was as if I had seen Napoleon at St. Helena.'[1] They were not to meet again for five years. Yet, during all that time, there is nothing to suggest that they did not continue to hold each other's music in the highest regard. Artistically, at any rate, their relationship was incorruptible. Finally, it was Wagner who made the first move. The occasion was the laying of the foundation stone at Bayreuth in 1872. He wrote a letter to his old friend which, while it must have broken his pride to write it, surely ranks among the most human and moving documents one composer ever addressed to another.

> MY GREAT AND DEAR FRIEND, Cosima maintains that you would not come even if I were to invite you. We should have to endure that, as we have had to endure so many things! But I cannot forbear to invite you. And what is it I cry to you when I say 'Come'? You came into my life as the greatest man whom I could ever address as an intimate friend; you gradually went apart from me, perhaps because I had become less close to you than you were to me. In place of you there came to me your deepest new-born being, and completed my longing to know you very close to me. So you live in full beauty before me and in me, and we are one beyond the grave itself. You were the first to ennoble me by his love; to a second, higher life am I now wedded in *her*, and can accomplish what I should never have been able to accomplish alone. Thus you could become every-

[1] In 1865 Liszt had taken minor orders in the Roman Catholic Church, becoming an Abbé. The scandal of Cosima's elopement with Wagner was a severe psychological setback for him. Having lived down his own past life, he now saw himself having to live down his daughter's present one, a nightmare prospect for him. Liszt was extremely sensitive to his standing with the Church just now, and when he heard that Cosima had turned Protestant in order to marry Wagner he felt betrayed. This factor must always be borne in mind when considering the rift between himself and Wagner.

thing to me, while I could remain so little to you: how immeasurably greater is my gain!

If now I say to you 'Come', I thereby say to you 'Come to yourself!' For it is yourself that you will find. Blessings and love to you, whatever decision you may come to!

Your old friend,
Richard.

Liszt was too generous and magnanimous a being not to respond to Wagner on the same level. His reply of 20 May 1872 runs:

> DEAR AND NOBLE FRIEND, I am too deeply moved by your letter to be able to thank you in words. But from the depths of my heart I hope that every shadow of a circumstance that could hold me fettered may disappear, and that soon we may see each other again. Then shall you see in perfect clearness how inseparable is my soul from *you both*, and how intimately I live again in that 'second' and higher life of yours in which you are able to accomplish what you could never have accomplished alone. Herein is heaven's pardon for me: God's blessing on you both, and all my love.

These are extraordinarily moving letters. They deserve the closest study. For eleven years, the two men had not corresponded. For five years they had not even seen each other. Yet the old fire of their friendship proved impossible to quench, and burned as brightly as ever at the moment of Wagner's greatest triumph.

Wagner's Death

Two months before Wagner's death, Liszt had a premonition of it. It was December 1882. He was in Venice. The Wagners had invited him to spend the winter there with them. The funeral processions by gondola along the canals came to fascinate him. The thought that Wagner himself might soon die,[1] and his corpse float down the lagoons, began to exercise his imagination to a point where he wrote two extraordinary piano pieces: *La lugubre Gondola I and II.* Two months later, in fact, Wagner was dead, and his funeral procession glided down those same Venice canals. News of his death was brought to Liszt in Budapest, to where he had meanwhile travelled. He is said to have been

[1] The reference comes from Liszt himself.

composing at his desk at the time, and he did not even look up and register surprise. But he was overheard to whisper brokenly: 'He today, I tomorrow.'

Two works written under the immediate shadow of Wagner's death are *R.W.—Venezia* (1883) and *Am Grabe Richard Wagners* (1883). The latter piece, and its psychological significance for Liszt, I have already discussed on p. 72. The former, *R.W.—Venezia*, rises from the black depths of the keyboard, thus.

EX. 37

The tonal ambiguity of this passage leads, with simple pictorial symbolism, to a typical Wagnerian 'fanfare', which collapses after only a few bars, and the piece falls away again into the depths.

EX. 38

The Death of Liszt

Liszt's final years were not happy ones. Most of his closest friends were now dead, and he missed them sorely. His health, until now perfect, was showing signs of strain; his vision had deteriorated, a cataract having developed in one eye, and he was easily fatigued. He was also concerned about money problems.[1] Worst of all, he came to regard himself as an artistic failure. He looked back over a long life and saw that musical history had not gone his way.[2] Yet his

[1] Eduard Liszt, his cousin and financial adviser, had died and this increased his difficulties.
[2] It was later to do so, however. See my essay *Liszt and the Twentieth Century*, p. 350.

industry was staggering. He continued his usual practice of rising before dawn in order to compose; his list of works during the final years is a long one. And he continued to teach. His chief comfort was his pupils. They flocked to him from the four quarters, and followed him round his 'vie trifurquée'—the endless circle of his trips to Rome, Budapest, and Weimar.

If the circumstantial account of Liszt's death given by Julius Kapp[1] is true, then it is nothing short of a standing indictment against those in a position to ease his last moments.

In 1886, in mid July, the seventy-four-year-old Liszt set out for Bayreuth especially to hear the performances of *Parsifal*. The journey upset him. He arrived on 21 July, exhausted and with a racking cough. He took to his bed in his regular lodgings, a guest-house at 1 Siegfriedstrasse not far from Wahnfried. There was no one to nurse him. Cosima, his daughter, had her hands full with the Bayreuth Festival which, since Wagner's death, she now administered. A steady stream of distinguished visitors to the festival was starting to arrive and Liszt was left to cope with his illness as best he could. On 25 July he dragged himself to the theatre to hear *Tristan* because he had promised Cosima that he would. He sat in the Wagners' box, slumped in the shadows, a handkerchief to his mouth. He felt ill during the performance and went back to his bed, never to leave it. The following day Cosima summoned a doctor who made the foolish mistake of prohibiting all alcohol—Liszt had consumed large quantities of brandy for years as a matter of course. To make matters worse, the food at his lodgings was unsuitable and as no one came near him (Cosima had banned all visitors) he had nothing whatsoever to eat. His pupils—among them Siloti, Stavenhagen and Sophie Menter—gathered outside, confused by the situation, not knowing whether to break Cosima's ban or to leave their master in peace. By Friday, the 30th, he was delirious. Great spasms rent his body and he cried aloud. Cosima became alarmed. She called a second doctor, but it was already too late. Pneumonia was diagnosed. On Saturday, 31 July, Liszt sank rapidly and entered a coma. At 10.30 p.m. he was heard to say 'Tristan'. Fifteen minutes later he died.

His friends and pupils were outraged at the lack of respect shown to him. The other guests in the lodging house where Liszt was staying had objected to the presence of the body which was discreetly removed down the road to Wahnfried where it was placed in a side room in a hastily made coffin.

On 3 August the funeral took place. Despite the fact that Liszt was an Abbé in the Roman Catholic Church, there seems to have been no Requiem Mass for him, nor had he been given extreme unction. His pupils carried torches in the

[1] Julius Kapp: *Franz Liszt* (1924 rev.).

procession. One of them, Walter Bache, an English disciple who had travelled from London especially for the funeral, was stunned by the frivolity of some of the 'mourners', visitors to the Wagner festival who had come simply out of curiosity.

So all Bayreuth celebrated Wagner while Liszt was lowered into the ground. And perhaps this is how Liszt himself would have wished it.

List of Sources

Day, Lillian, *Paganini of Genoa*, New York, 1929.
Newman, Ernest, *The Man Liszt*, London, 1934.
Ramann, Lina, *F. Liszt als Künstler und Mensch*, 1880.
Schönberg, Harold, *The Great Pianists*, New York, 1967.
Searle, Humphrey, *The Music of Liszt*, London, 1954.
Sitwell, Sacheverell, *Liszt*, London, 1934.
Szabolcsi, Bence, *The Twilight of Liszt*, Budapest, 1959.
Wallace, William, *Liszt, Wagner and the Princess*, London, 1927.

LOUIS KENTNER

Solo Piano Music (1827–61)

It is tempting, when surveying Liszt's piano works until the end of the Weimar period, to try to impose upon them some sort of central tendency, a common denominator, something that is, to a greater or lesser degree, characteristic of them all. Tempting but, alas, almost impossible. It is, of course, true that they are all redolent of a strong personality, permeated by an unmistakable aroma of what can only be described as Lisztian culture, constructed wilfully but firmly within the framework of Lisztian pianism, of Lisztian harmony, in all of which the urge to innovate and reform is sometimes stronger than the primary creative urge. But when we have noted all this we have said nothing that could not be said of half-a-dozen other composers with equal truth. Nor is it the whole truth. For in at least one great work, the B minor Sonata, Liszt achieved his aim; here he succeeded in being both innovator and fulfiller, not only an inventor of novel sorts of brick but a great master builder.

What, then, if anything, is that elusive common factor, revealed only to the closest scrutiny, which makes the whole of his work, despite all its proliferation and diversity, seem of a piece? I think it is the gradual breaking away from the Romantic Movement which enslaved Liszt in his youth, from which he appears to have entirely freed himself in his old age. This battle, this wandering in deserts and oases, with a final glimpse of the Promised Land, the twentieth century, seems to me the whole story of his middle-period piano music.

Liszt and the Romantic Movement

Schumann, Chopin, Berlioz—these are the greatest names we associate with the Romantic Movement in music. Leaving Berlioz aside, who plays no part on our confined stage (though he influenced Liszt profoundly), we can see quite sharply the features of the Romantic age by looking at the two others. Liszt, in humbly accepting the part of disciple to two of the greatest masters of piano music, nevertheless preserved his different aims which demanded other means of expression. There was never an open rebellion on Liszt's part; he never ceased to admire what he once admired. We shall see presently that his admiration was not reciprocated.

But what was the Romantic Movement? Its roots were essentially literary (in the same way that Debussy borrowed the then novel philosophy of Impressionism from the visual arts); its aim was the revival of lofty ideals—beauty, originality, nobility—which seemed to be lost, after Beethoven's death, in a welter of worthless, pedantic, philistine stuff, or of frankly meretricious ministrations to a depraved public taste. The Romantics represented a rebellion. They were conscious of specific, well-defined objectives (unlike the Classics), and Schumann became the prime torch-bearer of the movement. He was a great composer of small-scale music.

Chopin's influence on Liszt was enormous. He never ceased to admire Chopin's aristocratic, poised, meticulous and reserved artistry, the perfect balance of form and content, a perfection comparable only with the classical mastery of a Mozart, and yet romantic by reason of its wholly sentiment-inspired lyricism and its self-imposed discipline of the small form as the best means of expression for that lyricism. Add to this an ardent nationalist feeling (with French culture overlaying it), the use of folk melodies, the extraordinarily sensitive and single-minded exploration of keyboard sonority—and you have some of the things Chopin had in common with Liszt, his friend who loved him but who got only ambivalent feelings from Chopin in return for his friendship. Then there was Schumann. In a somewhat cool appraisal of the 'Transcendental' Studies (1838 version) Schumann had compared them unfavourably with one of the fifteen-year-old Liszt's first attempts at composition (first version of the Studies), piously complaining that Liszt, the adolescent, had apparently not yet achieved perfect peace of mind. ('Schumann, the Davidsbündler', commented Busoni, 'recommending peace of mind!') Later biographers recorded how Schumann reacted to the great B minor Sonata, played to him by Liszt himself, with horrified and stony silence. Brahms, a late arrival to the circle around Schumann, behaved even worse: he fell asleep during Liszt's performance of the Sonata, totally unappreciative of the rare honour accorded to him. Chopin lavished praise on Liszt the pianist but withheld it from Liszt the composer: 'He (Liszt) may one day become Deputy or even King of Abyssinia or of the Congo. But his works will be buried for ever in souvenir albums, together with volumes and volumes of German poetry.'

What, then, was the reason for this coldness, this ill-concealed contempt, this total refusal to understand the aims of one who quite sincerely wished to be one of them, on the part of the Romantic masters? Discounting personal reasons, the flamboyance of a virtuoso career, the public life of the man—a certain easy-going politeness creating doubts in some minds as to his sincerity—discounting all this as insufficient grounds, one must conclude that deeper grounds existed.

★

The German Romantic revolution had, by about 1835, run its course. It had won the day, and its protagonists, safely ensconced in snug positions as critics, teachers, conductors, were settling down to a comfortable enjoyment of the fruits of their richly deserved success. Schumann, an undisputed arbiter of taste, by virtue of his critical sharp-sightedness, dispensed good and bad marks in the *Neue Zeitschrift für Musik* (where he had hailed Chopin as a genius). He was also trying to inflate himself into a 'big' composer from a merely 'great' one, a composer of symphonies, oratorios, operas, in which enterprise he was doomed to failure. Mendelssohn, near-genius but no fully committed Romantic, made perhaps a more valuable contribution than anyone by re-discovering and giving model performances of the then forgotten choral masterpieces of Bach. The affiliated members of the group (Chopin, Berlioz and later Brahms) were all successful, recognized, admired, each without a rival in his own field. Into this snug little world burst Liszt, an ardent young Prometheus, ready to draw fire down from Heaven; but everyone else was quite cosy sitting by their own firesides, using matches and plywood to keep them going (at a moderate heat). Who wanted a Prometheus? Who wanted fire from Heaven?

Soon there was evidence, too, that Liszt was going his own way, not content to compose 'nice' piano pieces of the 'Blumenstück', 'Nachtstück', 'Romanze' type, or simple effusions of a modestly emotional kind often called 'Intermezzo' or 'Capriccio'. Indeed, the brutal harshness of the B minor Sonata must have come as a stunning blow to its dedicatee Schumann—almost as a declaration of war to the whole tight little world of bourgeois romanticism.

Liszt involved himself deeply in what was going on in the world, politically and socially; in this and other things (one of which was the influence religion had on his thinking) he was the diametrical opposite of the romantic artist of his time. His sources of inspiration—nature, poetry, works of art—did not indeed replace romantic sentiment but went some way to making it seem less important.

The coolness of the Romantics towards Liszt was caused (if the foregoing argument is accepted) not by philistinism or a monstrous misunderstanding but by an unfailing instinct that made the correct diagnosis: that Liszt, though a genius, was not flesh of their flesh, not blood of their blood. Liszt's own reactions? His references to Mendelssohn and Brahms, though not unkind, show a marked lack of enthusiasm. These and some contemptuous remarks on what he called 'Leipzigerisch' in Schumann's work, are indications of some bitterness or hurt pride caused no doubt by the rejection of his work; a bitterness and pride (however skilfully disguised by courtly manners), which could have become a force compelling him to turn, first, to new gods (Wagner) and, in due course, to become an anti-Romantic, a 'modern' composer—one who put the stamp of his personality on our own century.

I want to examine in some detail the chief works of this middle period, this period of transformation, and see to what extent, if any, they are in line with the theory here propounded.

Liszt and Sonata Form

When Beethoven improvised, the result was a sonata. When Chopin or Schumann set out to construct a sonata form, it tended to sound like an improvisation.

I incline to take issue with some theorists of our day who argue that the Classics were not conscious of writing in sonata form but that this, the sonata form, was simply their most natural way of expressing themselves. There is, in fact, no contradiction between these two propositions. Bach certainly must have found fugue the easiest and most natural form in which to express himself, yet there can be no doubt that he was conscious of writing in this form. Likewise, it is difficult to see how Beethoven (and his predecessors) could have composed hundreds of works which, by some miraculous series of accidents, always formed themselves into what we have come to call sonata form, or rondo form, or a combination of both, without conscious intention taking a very decisive hand in the matter. Form must remain the composer's greatest problem; it is not the inventing of themes which makes a composer, nor the harmonic imagination, however daring or interesting, but the ability to build, to construct architectural designs in music, great or small, long or short, and with whatever kind of emotional appeal. Composers who set their faces against the concept of 'technique', who proclaim loudly that form is nothing, expression everything, are either master builders like Beethoven and *mutatis mutandis* Liszt, supreme technicians who can afford to despise technique and turn their whole attention to expression (perhaps not realizing that there is no very clear dividing line)—or else they are the amateurish kind of composer who sees the creation of a symphony in terms of inventing a few good tunes and stringing them together.

Liszt's temperament was certainly not analytical, but intuitive; yet he was conscious of the exigencies of craftsmanship. How could it have been otherwise, since he had spent years creating and perfecting a new kind of piano technique? He made no bones about the many hours daily spent in practising. There is much evidence of revising and rewriting compositions which did not satisfy him (which is the equivalent of the instrumentalist's practising, transferred to the creative sphere); and if it is true that he spoke contemptuously of 'form for its own sake', he was no less anxious to master classical form than any other composer, and did in fact master it.

It is fascinating to examine Liszt's ever-changing ways of approach to the sonata. Fascinating because here is one of the clues that show him to be a very different sort of artist from those Romantics who simply received the sonata form as handed down by Beethoven and Schubert, with whatever modifications and freedoms that implied, and tried to 'fill' it, like an old bottle, with some kind of new wine, with the ardent, glowing, sentimental, small-scale, deeply felt outpourings of their German souls. But this was a battle lost before it was begun. Form and content being indivisible in the ultimate work of art, a perfect fusion is not possible unless the one determines the other in a process of mutual fertilization in which the component elements become almost indistinguishable. Form, in short, must be an epidermis, not a garment.

Sonata in B minor (1853)

The B minor Sonata is without doubt Liszt's pianistic masterpiece. He completed it in 1853 while living in Weimar and the first performance was given in Berlin in 1857 by his pupil Hans von Bülow. The Sonata unfolds about half-an-hour's unbroken music and is, in fact, the first sonata to roll its contrasting movements into one. Along with the 'Faust' Symphony, the 'Christus' Oratorio, and the great organ Fantasy and Fugue on *Ad nos*, it bears witness not only to Liszt's extraordinary creative energy, not only to his ability to paint a great self-portrait but, also, it shows him concerned with things beyond the merely personal, things of metaphysical, or even cosmic, import. In this, as in other things, Liszt breaks away from that Romantic self-limitation which put the microcosmos of individual emotion and its precise expression above any other aim of the artist; indeed, he reaches out towards late Beethoven, and makes the boldest bid made by any nineteenth-century composer to continue where Beethoven had left off. The importance of the B minor Sonata has to be restated here because it has suffered adverse criticism even from Lisztians. Oddly enough, its towering greatness has been generally, if grudgingly, admitted by anti-Lisztians over the last century, though it is a pity that so many virtuoso performers have misinterpreted it into a kind of undistinguished piece of fireworks to demonstrate their muscular prowess, instead of the searing, searching, fiery self-revelation that it really is.

In the B minor Sonata Liszt uses the device of presenting, in a short Introduction, three seemingly incongruous elements, ideas slightly reminiscent of the Wagnerian *Leitmotiv* (Ex. 1 (*a*), (*b*) and (*c*)),

EX. 1

and then proceeds to demonstrate how these can be welded into a unity of such compactness, of such compelling power, that it convinces even the unregenerate. It is an interesting fact about the Lisztian 'metamorphosis' technique that it is the opposite of what Wagner did with his *Leitmotiv*. Wagner invents a short, characteristic, extremely meaningful and plastic motif, attaches it to a person, a feeling, a thought, a situation or even an inanimate object (like Siegfried's sword), almost like a tag, visible from a long way off, and whenever the dramatic situation requires it the *Leitmotiv* is sounded in a virtually unchanged form—an admirable though perhaps a little over-simplified device for driving a point home, in case the goings-on both on and off the stage should be a bit obscure in themselves. A *Leitmotiv* then, is broadly speaking, always the same and always means the same. Liszt handles his motifs differently; he twists and bends them, gives them different meanings (sometimes diametrically opposed ones); they appear in slow or fast tempi, rhythmically re-shaped to fit into the *musical* design—since there is, of course, no *dramatic* situation to illustrate. The identity of the motif is always recognizable, but may, on occasion, elude the uninitiated.[1] Liszt was not the first to use this technique (which Eduard Hanslick, the Viennese critic, called 'a monstrous, anti-musical procedure'); Schubert made use of it in one single work, the 'Wanderer' Fantasy. Liszt's obvious affinity with that work, his partiality to and deep sympathy with it, have often been noticed and mentioned. The B minor Sonata is Liszt's 'Wanderer' Fantasy, only it covers a wider range of emotional experience. It comes from greater depths and reaches greater heights. Above all, it makes better sound.

Before the curtain goes up there is the Prologue. It differs greatly from the Classical introduction. The Classics used the introduction to generate tension, rouse expectancy, generally set the stage for things to come. But they did not give away what the drama was going to be about. (Only Beethoven occasionally felt the need to strengthen the psychological motivation of his Introductions by re-introducing fragments of them at later stages of the work, as in the 'Pathétique' Sonata.) Generally, Classical introductions are thematically unconnected with the main body of the work, sometimes almost detachable. Schumann and Brahms follow the Classics in this respect, with few exceptions. Liszt, in this Prologue, passes three of the main *Dramatis Personæ* in review (see Ex. 1). He shows them in their *Urform* as if to say: 'These are the characters who will be acting upon the stage; they will cry, laugh, suffer, live and die, all according to the laws of their natures'—rather in the style of the *Commedia dell'Arte*. Every particle of the material used derives from the three basic ideas already quoted (all except the Andante sostenuto theme, Ex. 8); but these particles in the course of living out their predetermined lives nonetheless form themselves into a 'sonata' on the Classical pattern, albeit with wider arches than those built by the Classical masters. It is possible to disagree with the widespread assumption that the tonality of the opening (Ex. 1*a*) is G minor. I associate this Introduction with 'dominant' rather than 'tonic' ambience—and the beginning G naturals seem to me to be the dominant of C minor, rather than the tonic of G minor. This seems to be borne out by the A flat at the end of the third bar. The B minor Sonata starts in C minor, a semitone high—as if by mistake!

The first subject, when it is eventually fully disclosed, is found to be already familiar from the Prologue; but now there is nothing hesitant or tentative about it, and its two elements form easily and naturally a main subject—indeed, so

[1] For further discussion of Liszt's 'transformation of themes' technique see Humphrey Searle (pp. 281–83) and Robert Collet (pp. 249–50).—*Ed.*

naturally that one wonders how they could ever have been separated. The music sweeps along irresistibly, carried on waves of rushing semiquavers (played by alternating hands) and these semiquavers (bracket 'x'), when carefully examined, are found to derive from the main theme as well (Ex. 2).

EX. 2

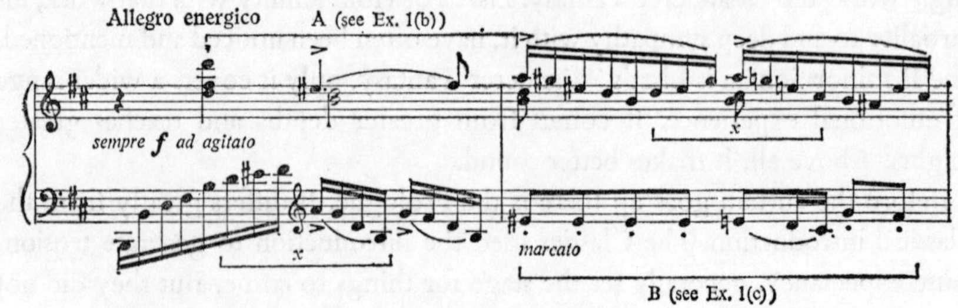

No 'tune and accompaniment' here, but real counterpoint (which ought not to be obscured by too fast a tempo or too heavy pedalling).

The torrent of the music rages through many modulations into a kind of 'bridge' which, starting in B flat and using the main subject in a curiously 'canonic' way, modulates on through the famous dreaded double-octave passages until it comes to rest on another dominant, that of D major, under which the ominous opening re-appears[1]

EX. 3

[1] This funeral march-like theme (see the opening of the Sonata, Ex. 1*a*), appears only at crucial points of the composition: the beginning, the lead into the optimistic Grandioso, the end of the slow movement (just before the Fugato), in the Recapitulation where it plays an important part in leading back to the Grandioso in B—and finally at the end of the work, just before the curtain comes down. In other words, it serves the purpose of separating the main acts of this great drama.

leading to the triumphant entry of the Grandioso second subject.

EX. 4

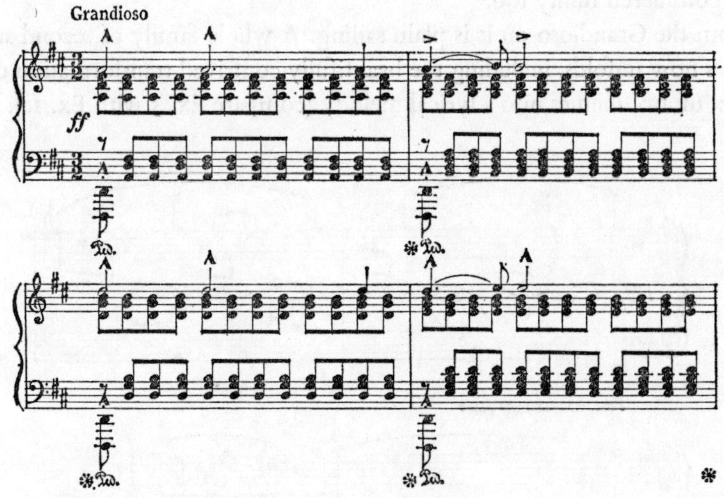

One often hears sneering references to the 'grand manner', and presumably what is meant by this is the nineteenth-century image of the long-haired etiolated-looking virtuoso who has many cheap tricks up his sleeve to make up for the absence of solid worth. In a strangely ambivalent book on Liszt, Walter Beckett makes half-mocking, half-serious allusion to the 'ardent virtuoso, head thrown back, his face responding to the ecstatic fullness of the music'.[1] This is reminiscent of some contemporary caricatures of Liszt, or Anton Rubinstein, and (later) of Paderewski and Emil Sauer. Oddly enough, Dr. Beckett associates his image with this truly great 'Grandioso' subject of the B minor Sonata, but complains, illogically, that the whole episode only lasts ten bars 'then he goes on to something else'. Leaving aside as irrelevant the atavistic British dislike of 'pose' or 'attitudes', there is nothing reprehensible, or comic, in the grand manner, if by this is meant that the artist, under the stress of great emotion, is not in complete control of his facial expression, or the movements of his body—as long as the performance is commensurate with the manner in grandeur and emotional impact. No sound judge will find

[1] Walter Beckett: *Franz Liszt* (*Master Musician Series*), London, 1956, pp. 84–5.

anything funny in such overspill of emotion, unless the line

The poet's eye in sacred frenzy rolling

were considered funny too.[1]

From the Grandioso on it is plain sailing. A whole family of second subject themes now unfolds, including the beautifully contrived transformation of one of the 'motto' themes into a lyrical melody (compare Ex. 5 with Ex. 1*c*).

EX. 5

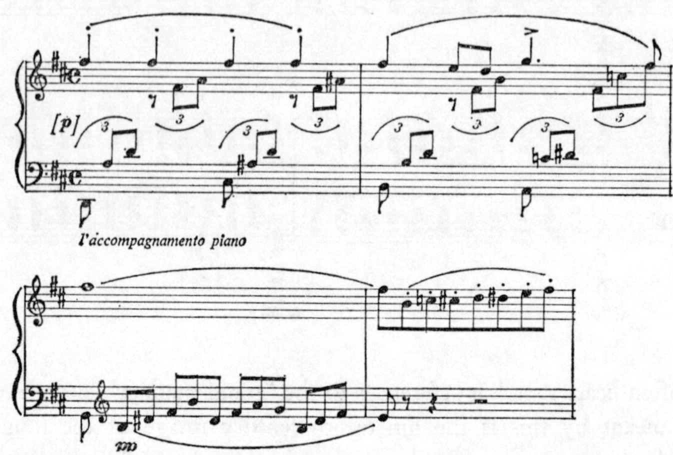

Beethoven's way of contrasting the so-called 'masculine' and 'feminine' elements in his sonata expositions (first and second subjects respectively) was not Liszt's way. The 'feminine' does not really make an appearance until the Andante sostenuto which is no less than a complete slow movement and one of Liszt's most beautiful inspirations. Before it begins, it is introduced, eased into the key of F sharp major, as it were.

EX. 6

[1] It is a remarkable fact that the English, so tolerant towards eccentricity of behaviour in every other walk of life or art, discourage any such tendencies in musicians; and this view is reflected in the way English musicians do in fact behave. Compare, for instance, the posturing flamboyance of a Lord Byron or Tennyson (great and wonderful poets both)

The modulation is, of course, the enharmonic kind, and Chopin might have carefully written it out like this.

EX. 7

Liszt's spelling, if less correct, is more practical, and easier on the eye.

It is difficult to give an adequate idea of the beauty, serenity and simplicity of this 'Gretchen' theme.

EX. 8

It is, of course, an entirely new idea, in total contrast with what has gone before. Nor is it ever subjected to the Mephistophelian dissecting, sarcastic, degrading tearing-to-pieces process which is applied to the 'Faust' heroics—since the Eternal Feminine could not be touched by the Devil, in Liszt's (and Goethe's) religion. The procedure is the same in the 'Faust' Symphony.[1] On the other hand, some of the previous themes, the grandiose, the threatening, are passed in review in the course of this heavenly intermezzo, but transformed, touched

---

with the sober, gentlemanly ways of Sir Edward Elgar, who all but disclaimed being a musician at all. It is not difficult to see a connection between this trait of the English national character, and Liszt's marked lack of success in England.

[1] There is a long tradition behind the view, here suggested by Louis Kentner, that Liszt had Goethe's 'Faust' in mind when composing the B minor Sonata, and that it is possible to regard the contrasting themes of the work as representing the personalities of 'Faust', 'Gretchen' and 'Mephistopheles' respectively. This interpretation, which is doubtless helpful to pianists, has had some distinguished support in the past, some of it from Liszt's own pupils. But I have never heard of any evidence to show that Liszt himself ever even mentioned it.—*Ed.*

with sweetness and gentleness, and a nascent and virginal passion. The Andante theme returns in a blaze of glory which is quickly extinguished again.

Bartók, in his edition of Bach's 'Forty-Eight', expresses the opinion that Bach's display of contrapuntal ingenuity, of sheer technical skill, always grew in proportion as he aimed at more intense expression of feeling—thus, the deepest of his fugues are also invariably the richest in fugal devices of every kind. Be that as it may, it is certainly true of the fugues—not great in number—with which Liszt enriches the canvasses of some of his bigger works, including the one in the B minor Sonata.

EX. 9

The fugue here stands in place of the customary Development (Beethoven did the same thing in op. 101 and elsewhere) and it must be regarded as the Mephistophelian part of Liszt's self-portrait: the spirit of mockery, of negation and savage distorting caricature. This is done with so much elegance and skill that one suspects the Abbé of being perhaps a little more in sympathy with the Devil than with God. The fugue's exposition (which takes the theme through three voices) is followed by a modulating Development, using scraps of the theme in contrapuntal juxtaposition; then follows the theme in inversion—but without its second half—while the rest of the voices juggle about the rhythmically changed form of the original theme, as if playfully tearing it to shreds.

EX. 10

The fugue also acts as a lead-back to the Recapitulation which begins with a reappearance of Ex. 2, and then Liszt proceeds to review all the main ideas of the Exposition, although with a good deal of compression. The piano writing unfolds more and more richly, reaching a climax in the jubilant coda

EX. 11

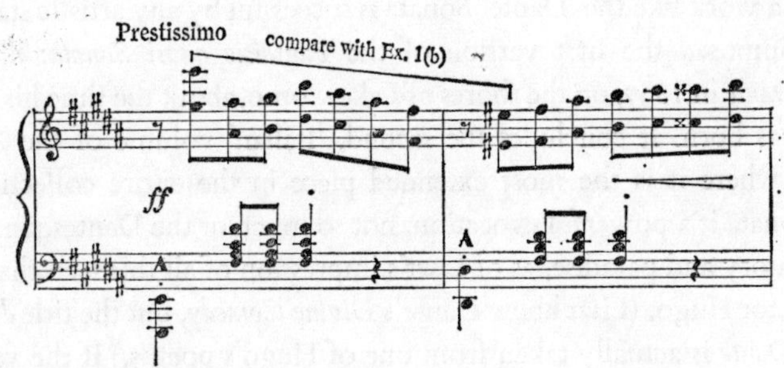

which is all too often treated as an octave exercise by Giants of the Keyboard, whereas in actual fact it is yet another 'transformation' of the main subject (compare with Exx. 1*b* and 2). It leads to the biggest of all climaxes, perhaps, in piano literature. The Grandioso reappears like a burning Valhalla in the skies.

EX. 12

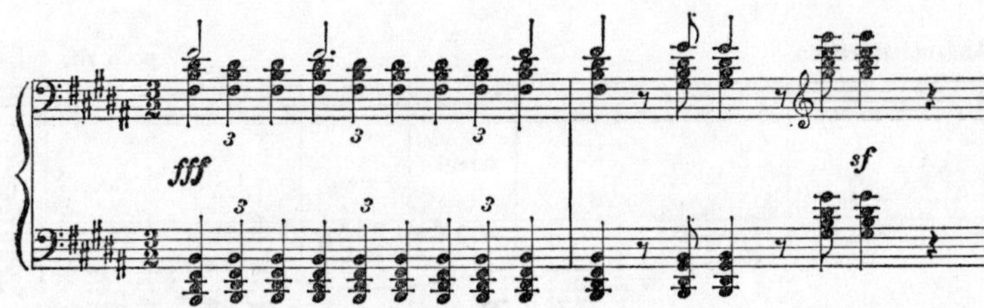

A sudden silence falls (this must be very long!) and the still small voice of the Andante sostenuto is heard singing a heart-rendingly beautiful epilogue. Certainly some of the greatest music Liszt ever wrote is on these two pages to which no analysis can do justice, and only very few performances.

Perhaps analysis should not attempt to break the seals of the mystery that is artistic creation anyway, but should say with humility: 'We are in the presence of genius.' The alchemy of genius will, thank God, for ever remain a secret.

'Dante' Sonata (1849)

'Liszt', says C. M. Breithaupt, speaking of the B minor Sonata, 'never reached such heights again.' But, one wonders, is not the distinguished author of *Die natürliche Klaviertechnik* making a judgment in which the magnitude of the task the artist has set himself is considered paramount and not the degree of success with which he tackled it? For it must be maintained that within its more limited intentions a work like the 'Dante' Sonata is successful by any artistic standard.

Liszt composed the first version of the *Fantaisie quasi Sonata: d'après une lecture du Dante* in 1837, on the shores of Lake Como, about the time his daughter Cosima was born. It concludes the second, 'Italian' volume of the *Années de Pèlerinage* where it is the most extended piece in the entire collection.[1] The 'Dante' Sonata is a powerful evocation, not so much of the Dantesque world of hell, purgatory and paradise, as of Liszt's impression of all this seen through the eyes of Victor Hugo. (Liszt knew Dante's *Divine Comedy*, but the title *d'après une lecture du Dante* is actually taken from one of Hugo's poems.) If the vastness of Dante's conception is cut down to size—the size of a single piano!—the sonorous Hugo rhetoric is nonetheless perfectly matched by Liszt's austere grandeur.

The Introduction abounds in far-reaching modulations, and the tritone with which the work opens ('Abandon hope all ye who enter here') lends itself admirably to the Lisztian technique of keeping us in suspense over the tonic key.

EX. 13

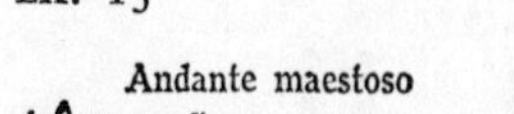

[1] The other pieces in the set are discussed on pp. 120–25.—*Ed.*

As soon as the Presto agitato section starts, however, there is no doubt that here is the first subject in D minor.[1]

EX. 14

The chromatic wailing of these flitting shadows, gradually thickening to a deafening roar (marked 'disperato'), is one of Liszt's most exciting experiments —an experiment in the sense that few other composers would have treated this material the way Liszt did, as the main subject of a sonata. But it is entirely successful. The raging hellfire is eventually quenched by a chorale-like second theme, undoubtedly a close relation to the Grandioso theme of the B minor Sonata. The piano writing is very florid at first with thundering double octaves rushing down the keyboard to decorate the chorale.

EX. 15

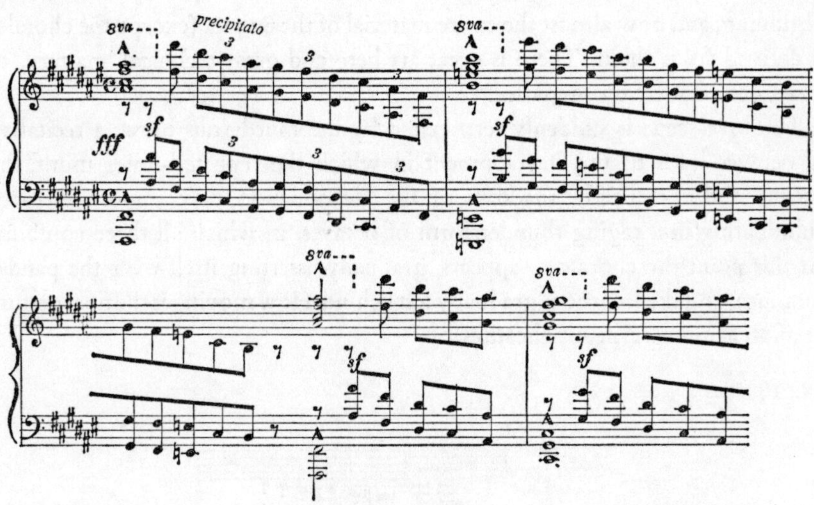

[1] See Louis Kentner's remarks on the pedalling of this passage, p. 216.—*Ed.*

The tritone of the opening is sounded once again, and the chorale is transformed into this love duet,

EX. 16

which leads into the beautiful 'Francesca da Rimini' episode.

EX. 17

Observe how this lyrical island grows out of the two repeated notes of the beginning, and how almost the entire material of the Sonata (except the chorale) is derived from them. There is great art here and great technical mastery, to those not blinded by prejudice.

The love-scene is suddenly terminated by the murderous blow, a recitative in octaves leads to the Development in which the repeated-notes motif, the tritone and the flitting shadows of the Introduction play important parts, culminating in a raging thunderstorm of octaves, in which all three combine. At this point the chorale re-appears, gradually asserting itself over the pandemonium, and the Inferno is gradually left behind. How moving is the final gesture as of an arm raised in supplication,

EX. 18

then dropped in despair as the heavy gate closes on the lost souls wailing behind it!

EX. 19

If the last section falls below the rest in musical interest, the reason is obvious. In the 'Dante' Symphony, Liszt desisted, possibly on Wagner's advice, from giving a musical counterpart to *Il Paradiso*, on the grounds that no music could adequately express the beauty of Paradise. The glimpse into Paradise, attempted in the Sonata is—not surprisingly—disappointing.

EX. 20

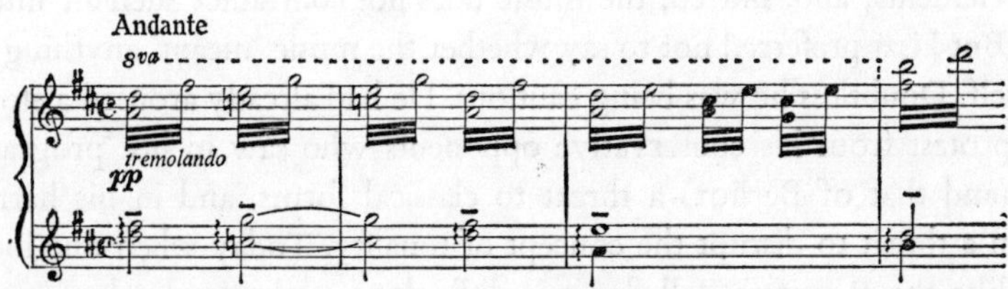

By comparison, Hell is much more interesting! But a superb Coda, a summing-up of all the thematic material of the work, rounds it off with stunning effect. In the final bars Liszt has some unusual 'modal' harmonies

EX. 21

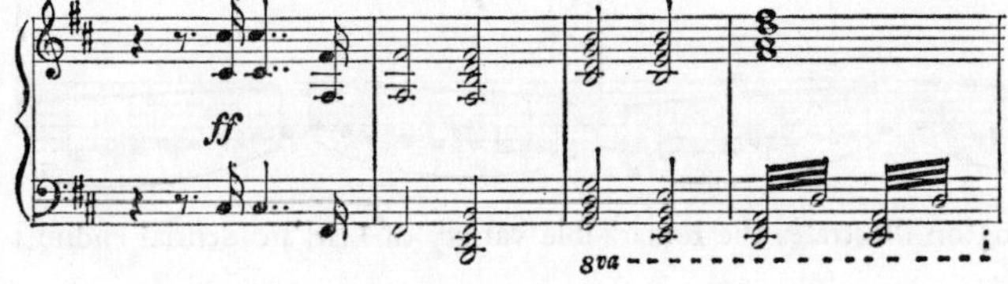

which create a completely satisfactory tonal cadence without once using the dominant-tonic progression—a symptom, perhaps, of Liszt's growing desire to avoid the obvious, the formula, the 'device'.[1] From here, the cross-roads leading to the harmonic experiments of his late period are not very far away.

Ballade in B minor (1853)

The Ballade in B minor, despite its title, belongs to the category of 'absolute' music (as opposed to what used to be called descriptive or 'programme' music) with special leanings towards sonata form, which is one of the reasons I want to discuss it here. True, there is in the case of the Ballade a vague tradition of some Hero and Leander type of story about constant love triumphing over the raging elements; and, indeed, the music does not contradict such an interpretation. But Liszt preferred not to say whether the music 'meant' anything other than itself. Doubtless he was being cautious. He had already aroused a storm of angry protest from his conservative opponents who saw in his 'programme' music (and that of Berlioz) a threat to classical forms, and in his harmonic freedom a threat to disrupt the concept of tonality. Today when one looks at works like the B minor Ballade, it is difficult to understand what upset the diehards so much; certainly, sonata form is freely dealt with, extended (but not much more than in the case of Schubert), given new psychological twists, especially in the recapitulation section where Liszt tries to avoid the routine of bringing back everything unchanged, as if nothing had happened, which he must have thought a trifle dull.

The thematic material of the B minor Ballade is essentially sonata material—broad, big, plastic, with a long 'breath', firmly rooted in the tonality. Its main subject strides mightily over chromatic waves in the bass,

EX. 22

[1] Christopher Headington illustrates the remarkable variety of Liszt's cadential endings on p. 243, Ex. 14.—*Ed.*

until a second part of the same theme takes over, gentle, contrasted in character to the first part, yet poetically somehow consistent with it,

EX. 23

making an unusually long first subject in which the germs of the coming conflict are presented as in a prologue. How different from the short-lived, nervous four-bar phrases in Schumann! They cry out for symphonic treatment (and receive it) instead of having to be blown up by repetition to look bigger than they sound.

The Recapitulation starts, unusually, with the second subject,

EX. 24

while Liszt reserves his biggest surprise until the end when he re-introduces the main subject as a Coda, but in this transformed version.

EX. 25

Compare with Ex. 21. This gradually grows in a volume towards a grandiose and triumphant climax, but—and this is a more typical Lisztian touch than is generally admitted—the Ballade instead of continuing the grandiloquent apotheosis of the first subject ends quickly, dying away as the second half of the first subject (Ex. 22) is quoted once more.

Scherzo and March (1851)

The Scherzo and March, a relatively unknown work, must be given a place of distinction for its brilliance and sustained energy and for its originality of form. The first section (Scherzo) is in itself a complete full-length sonata form preceded by an Introduction in which ghostly, leaping shadows play a mocking game,

EX. 26

and the chattering main subject

EX. 27

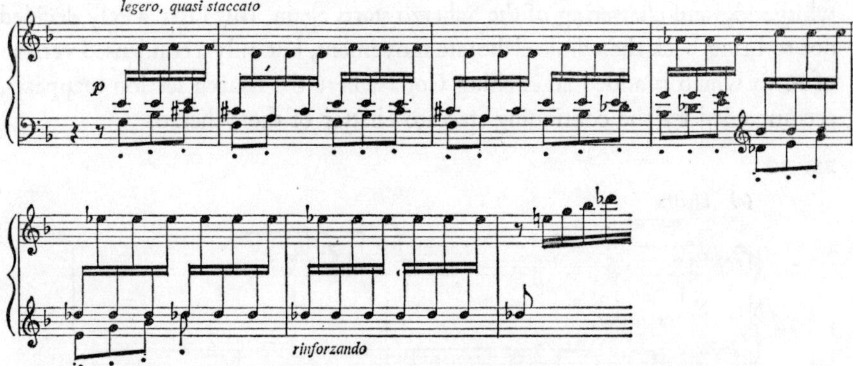

maintains a mood of macabre, nocturnal hellishness, unrelieved by any contrast, even when the second subject makes its appearance.

EX. 28

With this material Liszt constructs a superb piece of *diablerie*. It comes to a full stop in D minor, the main key, rather like the Scherzo of Beethoven's Ninth Symphony (also a full-length sonata form). The March which Liszt uses as a middle section, or trio, has a slightly ecclesiastic character, oddly contrasting with the devilish Scherzo.

EX. 29

It is as if a Witches' Sabbath were interrupted by a procession of monks, carrying torches and chanting. From the muted beginning the March rises gradually to a tremendous climax and, just as quickly as it came, fades out; then the ghostly whispering and chattering of the Scherzo starts again. But Liszt wisely decided not to bring back the whole elaborate movement, but only a condensed version of it, to which is added an exciting Coda where the March section reappears, accompanied by the continuing staccato chatter of the Scherzo.

EX. 30

It is as if religion were doing battle with the Devil. In the end there is victory for religion, but not as unqualified as is usual in Liszt. Altogether a significant composition, unjustly neglected.

Mephisto Waltz, No. 1 (1860)

Liszt was a devout Catholic: he feared God, but he loved the Devil. Of the many and diverse personalities that co-existed in him none was more fascinating than the 'Diaboliszt' (if the pun be allowed). The innumerable works in which Mephisto appears, openly or disguised, deserve a special monograph to themselves, for the psychological background of Liszt's pre-occupation with diabolism has never, to my knowledge, received attention from biographers who seem to ignore its value as a clue to Liszt the artist.

Germans tend to exaggerate the artistic greatness of Goethe's 'Faust'. But, if it is perhaps not all great poetry, there is no doubt that it had a profound influence on German thought, an influence from which Liszt was not immune, living as he did in Germany, surrounded by German culture which he absorbed as eagerly as he had absorbed French culture a few years earlier. But the Mephisto we are dealing with here does not come from Goethe's 'Faust'. He comes from another German poet, Lenau, with whom Liszt had special affinities; like Liszt, Lenau was a Hungarian expatriate, like Liszt, he was writing in a foreign tongue but with a note of nostalgic remembrance of the country in which they were both born. Unlike Liszt, however, Lenau was not a well-balanced man: he died young, in a mental home.

The first Mephisto Waltz (or 'The Dance in the Village Inn') is also an orchestral work, the second of 'Two Episodes from Lenau's Faust'.[1] To the eternal shame of orchestral societies everywhere the work is hardly ever heard in this version, although the piano transcription is popular enough with pianists. The half-epic, half-dramatic poem describes how Faust and Mephistopheles stray into a village inn where wedding festivities are in full swing; how Mephistopheles (a jovial enough character, hardly the embodiment of Evil) seizes a violin from one of the band and, by the demoniacal fire of his playing whips the dancers into a frenzy. Faster and faster gets the dance, more and more unbridled the dancers; Faust finds himself a beautiful wench with whom he dances out into the open, followed by the sound of Mephisto's violin, into the wood where only the sound of the nightingale's song is heard and where the couple are 'swallowed by the roaring sea of lust'.

Liszt's music follows the story closely enough to be described as 'programme music'. But the purely musical excitement of the work is enough to fascinate the listener, whether or not he is familiar with the poem. If the Mephisto of the poem does not quite convince the reader of his evil nature, the Mephisto of Liszt's music will, for it does in fact express Evil (if such a thing is possible); the marvellous opening, with its piling-up of perfect fifths on top of one another—the Devil tuning up his fiddle—is surely one of the most daring things created by any pre-Bartók composer.

EX. 31

[1] There is some doubt as to which version came first. See Humphrey Searle, p. 314.—*Ed.*

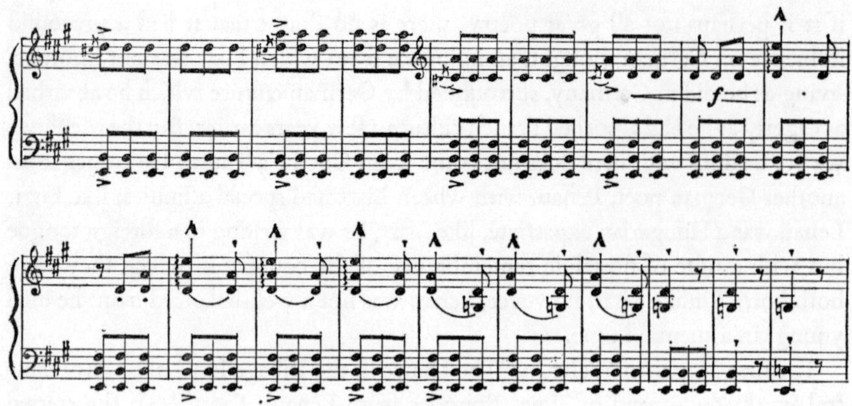

From the 'tuning up' section emerges eventually the main subject.

EX. 32

This gives way to the waltz proper, Faust's theme, with its swaying, clinging eroticism.

EX. 33

It is in the purple key of D flat and dominates the rest of the work. As it falls under Mephisto's spell, however, it undergoes a series of brilliant, demoniacal transformations. It re-appears, first, in this 2/8 *cum* 3/8 form;

EX. 34

on a later occasion in 6/8 time, in the form of crazy leaps;

EX. 35

and, at the close of the orgiastic love-scene, as a slow yearning melody leading to the 'nightingale' solo.

EX. 36

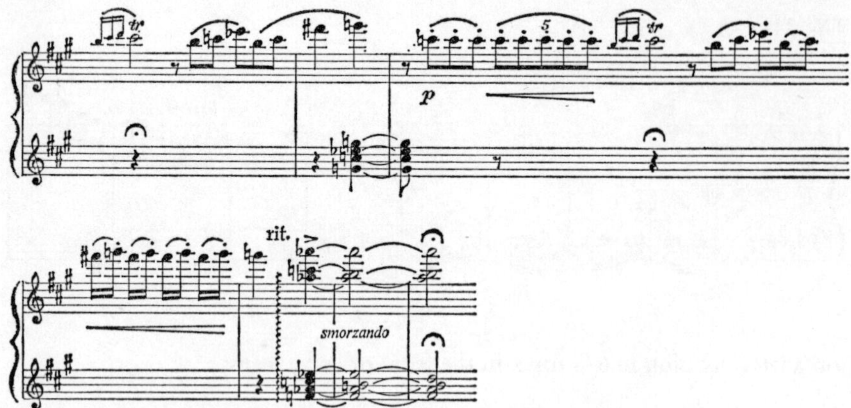

There is a rich range of thematic material used in this 'symphonic poem'—symphonic because in it Liszt not only uses the technique of thematic transformation, but uses it within the framework of what is not far removed from the classical sonata form to which he reverted so often in his life.

*

From all this diversity a pattern finally emerges: it is in this case, an un-Romantic, anti-Romantic pattern even. Liszt behaves as if he felt at ease in big forms—a reversal of the popular view about him. He has no particular wish to revolutionize the Classical sonata form. He uses it in the traditional way (as we have seen in the 'Scherzo and March' and the 'Dante' Sonata, for instance), or he extends it by adding new material to its bulk, and yet at the same time reverts to the one-movement sonata of the pre-Haydn age, thus creating that seemingly contradictory amalgam of condensation and proliferation, the huge B minor Sonata.

Liszt, then, was a large-scale composer—a point relevant to the main argument of this essay—and it is only in the light of this truth that we can hope to understand even his small-scale works (many of which group themselves into larger hierarchies anyway) which I now want to examine.[1]

[1] It must be stated, however, that the morbid giantism that affected German late-nineteenth-century music so disastrously was a Wagnerian by-product, not a Lisztian one.

Twelve 'Transcendental' Studies (1851)

Liszt, in his later years, treated with royal contempt all tendencies on the part of his pupils to put showmanship and manual dexterity above truth of expression. 'Do you think I care how fast you can play octaves?' he once thundered at an unfortunate pupil who displayed this special aptitude a trifle too flamboyantly. Was there, perhaps, an element of self-castigation in this outburst of Liszt's, a guilty recollection of his own early days as a travelling virtuoso? Perhaps.

The important thing about the Twelve 'Transcendental' Studies is not that they are concerned with technical problems. It is that they constitute *one* work, rather than a set of twelve separate pieces. They are a cycle in the same sense that Chopin's Twenty-four Preludes are also a cycle, and each depends on the cumulative effect of its constituent parts. This does not mean that some of these parts (not all, however) cannot be taken out of context and performed separately; they can be, and frequently are. But if Chopin wished to prove anything by offering the world a prelude in every existing key, and in a special key-sequence too, that purpose is obviously sacrificed when only one or two preludes are performed. Admittedly, the sheer beauty of the single pieces sometimes justifies the sacrifice. But the Preludes as a whole create a special unity by describing a complete circle of ascending fifths, one in each major and minor key; the first is in C major, the second is in its relative minor, then on to G major, and E minor, D major and B minor, and so on through all the keys. The 'Transcendentals' reverse this process; Liszt orders his Studies in a *descending* circle of fifths, leaving the cycle half finished.[1] (See list of keys on p. 106.)

If the original purpose of these 'exercises' was technical—and it might well have been when the fifteen-year-old Liszt composed the first, naïvely primitive version—this was lost sight of, undoubtedly because his own technique had reached such proportions that its further development ceased to interest him. What did not cease to interest him, however, was the vitality of the subject-matter, and he realized its potentialities in a frighteningly difficult second version (1838) verging on the unplayable. This was later simplified, and the result was the final version (1851) as we know and use it today. In this last version Liszt added a descriptive or poetic title to most of the Studies—and what else are

[1] It seems to have been Liszt's intention to complete it, but he never did so. Liapanoff, an enthusiastic Russian Lisztian, actually wrote twelve more Transcendental Studies to finish the Liszt cycle (beginning at F sharp major, the next key in Liszt's circle of fifths) and he dedicated his admirable effort to the memory of Franz Liszt.

these titles but another simplification, an aid offered by the composer for easier access to the character of the music?

1. *Prelude—C major*
2. *Molto vivace—A minor*
3. *Paysage—F major*
4. *Mazeppa—D minor*
5. *Feux-follets—B flat major*
6. *Vision—G minor*
7. *Eroica—E flat major*
8. *Wilde Jagd—C minor*
9. *Ricordanza—A flat major*
10. *Allegro agitato—F minor*
11. *Harmonies du soir—D flat major*
12. *Chasse-neige—B flat minor*

Only two Studies have no titles, perhaps because Liszt thought they needed no such aid to the imagination: no. 2 in A minor, which could be called 'Diablerie', and no. 10 in F minor which Busoni christened 'Appassionata', possibly stimulated by the key of F minor.

With the exception of the first, *Prelude*, a slightish piece of appropriately improvisatory character (which I would not recommend for performance on its own: it is so much a 'prelude' that one involuntarily expects something to follow it), all the Studies can be performed separately. They vary in length and interest, a 'genre-piece' like *Paysage* being followed by the great *Mazeppa*. This last piece has the stature of a symphonic poem; and it did, in fact, later become one, Liszt transcribing it for orchestra and welding the Mazeppa legend onto the result. Mazeppa was a Cossack chieftain whose enemies, according to myth, tied him to a wild horse which galloped across plains, rivers and mountains until it finally collapsed from exhaustion—not only horses collapse under the strain of Mazeppa!—and he is eventually released by the Cossacks and leads them in a great uprising. But the interesting thing about *Mazeppa* is not so much its story (this, as I said, came later anyway) as its piano textures, some of which—this 'three-handed' effect, for example—

EX. 37

help to give the word 'transcendental' its real meaning.

Equally hair-raising in its dramatic impact and technical difficulty, is the shimmering *Feux-follets.*

EX. 38

This piece retains more of the bearing of a 'concert study' than any of the others. It lies uneasily next to the somewhat pretentious *Vision*—which can at least be made to sound technically interesting if one follows Liszt's injunction to play the first three pages with the left hand alone. Few pianists do, for obvious reasons.

EX. 39

Eroica is neatly constructed and can be made to sound like an orchestra (but one must know how to orchestrate it).

Wilde Jagd, the next Study, is in no way to be regarded as 'programme music', nor is King Arthur's ghostly chase what this piece is 'about', except as an aid to those, listeners and performers alike, whose imagination is not immediately fired by the music alone. It should be remembered again that the 'Transcendental' Studies, in their first and second versions, were composed and published years before the poetic titles were superimposed. For the musician, a point of interest in this fine work is that Liszt makes no use of the transformation technique but presents contrasting themes in what appears to be a remarkably well-constructed sonata form on Schubertian lines (omitting the recapitulation of the first subject). *Wilde Jagd* is a mixture of savagery and subtlety, and requires an interpreter whose temperament has both these elements to a marked degree.

Ricordanza, although a bit too long, has nevertheless great charm of a Chopinesque, nostalgic kind, which led Busoni to liken it to a bundle of faded love-letters.

EX. 40

The F minor, number 10, is a perfect masterpiece. It maintains a tension, and creates a fever heat of excitement, not often equalled in Liszt's piano music.

EX. 41

It is incomprehensible that this noble piece is still neglected by the virtuosi.

Harmonies du Soir is like an impressionist canvas, so vividly painted that it is as if one hears not only the sounds but also smells the perfumes drifting across the warm evening air. There is an impression of bells softly ringing from distant spires.

EX. 42

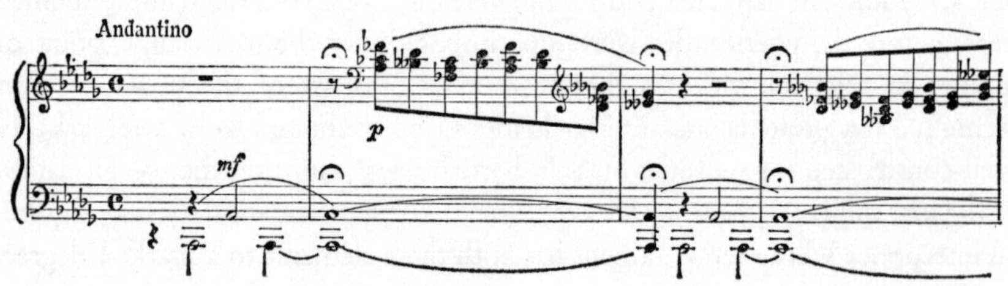

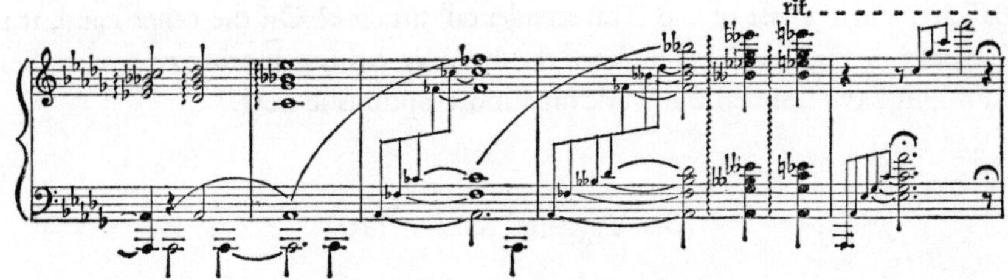

It is not difficult to see what technical purpose Liszt had in mind in this Study: the judicious and imaginative use of pedalling. There is here an unmistakable glimmer of Debussy's impressionism.

Many Lisztians look upon the concluding piece *Chasse-neige* as the greatest of the Studies. Indeed, it is unique in its mood of desolation. It is as if the softly falling snowflakes gradully covered the whole world, burying man and beast, while the wind moans.

EX. 43

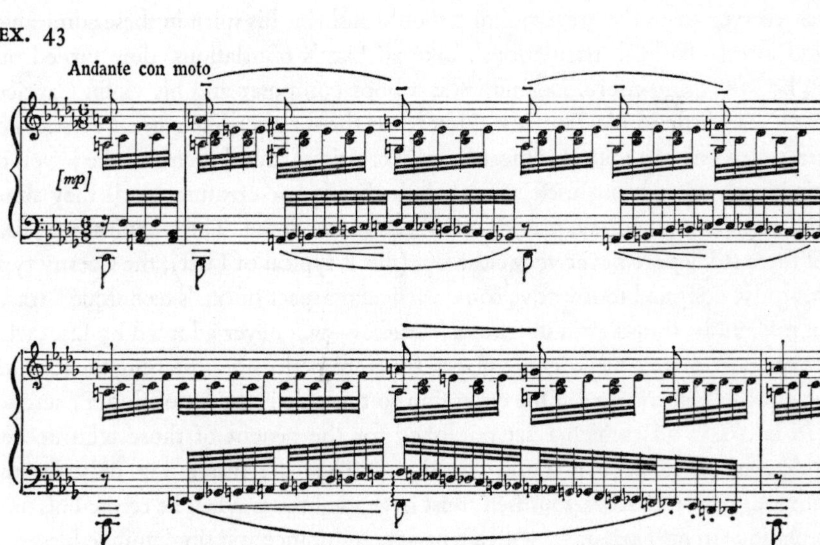

A study of nature at her most merciless. It is more typical of Liszt than is generally admitted to end a series in which virtuosity and brilliance are, after all, very much what the whole thing is 'about', with something far away from the expected final fireworks—a note of sadness verging on despair. To those who still look upon Liszt as a mountebank, as someone who writes 'for effect', I would recommend a glance at the end of the B minor Sonata, the B minor

Ballade, and the last of the 'Transcendental' Studies.[1] On the other hand, it is just possible that had he completed the cycle by writing another twelve studies, he might have finished the work on a more optimistic note.

Six 'Paganini' Studies (1851)

This note of optimism is certainly not absent from the 'Paganini' Studies. These are skilful piano transcriptions of five of Paganini's caprices for solo violin, together with one of 'La Campanella' from the finale of the B minor Violin Concerto. The collection is dedicated to Clara Schumann.

It is common knowledge that Paganini's phenomenal violin playing was the chief impetus behind Liszt's own researches into the technique of piano playing[2]—researches that led to the creation of the most unique, most shattering and all-powerful virtuosity the world has ever known. What could be more natural than that Liszt, perhaps moved by gratitude for the tremendous stimulation he received from the great violinist, should enshrine his spirit in these admirable, and utterly faithful 'translations'. Like all Liszt's translations, they turned out to be something more. Paganini was a poor composer and his violin Caprices have very little musical interest. Liszt treats them rather like a great dressmaker treats dummies; he puts his most fanciful creations round them, all the jewels of his imagination being used to embellish these poor creatures until they shine and sparkle with finery, leaving the skeleton unaltered. The technical purposes of these studies are never very clear-cut (this is typical of Liszt); the Czerny type of study, designed to improve some particular aspect of one's technique—traces of this can be found even in Chopin's studies—was never adopted by Liszt who wrote poetic descriptive 'genre pieces' for pianists already possessing the formidable technique required. One exception to this rule is the set of finger exercises (12 books in all) which Liszt published for the benefit of those who needed guidance on how to practise 'technique'. They are interesting only for the obvious reason that Liszt himself must have used them when he created his new technique in his Paris days, with a tenacity, endurance and singlemindedness one can only marvel at.

The first Study, in G minor, features a tremolo, mainly for the left hand, which takes the melody and the tremolo accompaniment simultaneously.

[1] The 'Transcendentals' receive further discussion on pp. 51–53.—*Ed.*

[2] See pp. 43–51 for a full account of Paganini's influence on Liszt.—*Ed.*

EX. 44

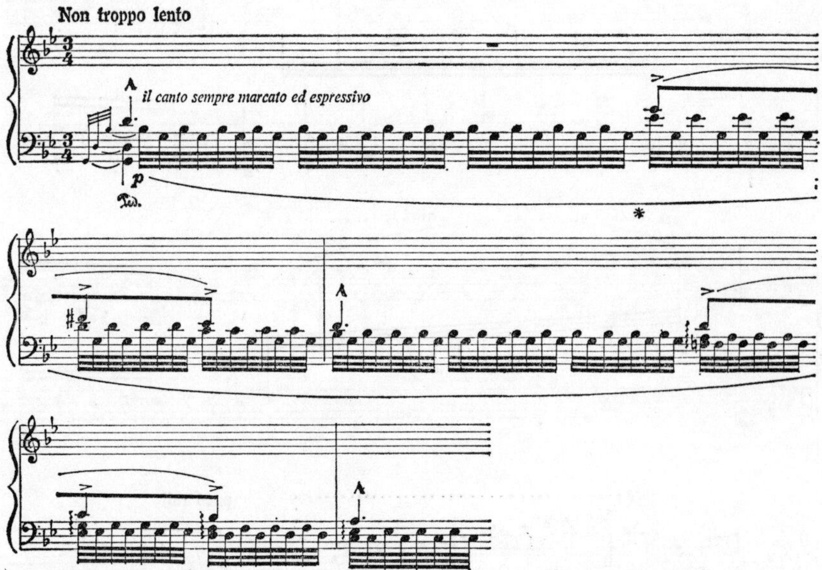

When Liszt first published this Study he printed above it, bar for bar in its entirety, Schumann's transcription of the same piece which had appeared a short time earlier. Was this an act of deference to Clara's husband? Or was it, as Busoni asks, a mephistophelian whim on Liszt's part? A comparison of the two transcriptions leaves one in no doubt as to whose is the more brilliant.

The next Study, in E flat major, is basically for scales and double octaves. It makes copious use of what have come to be known as 'Liszt octaves', double octaves played by alternating hands,[1] both in diatonic and chromatic scales. Such octaves should be executed with the two thumbs prominent, for evenness of sound.

EX. 45

ff

con strepito

[1] Liszt appears to have invented this effect. See p. 144 for further comment.—*Ed.*

The third of the 'Paganini' Studies is the well-known *La Campanella.* It starts as a study in wide leaps,

EX. 46

but this is soon lost sight of in a welter of trills, repeated notes, chromatic and diatonic runs and repeated octaves—altogether a marvellous exploration of the piano's possibilities and dynamic range, both taxing and rewarding from the virtuoso's point of view.

EX. 47

It speaks well of the vitality of this hackneyed old battle horse that no amount of denigration has so far done any damage to its popularity which is as great today as it ever was. Both Paganini and Liszt used the tune repeatedly.

Study No. 4, in E major, is an outstanding example of self-limitation on Liszt's part. Instead of a florid transcription, he does no more than virtually transfer the piece, as Paganini left it, to the keyboard, using only one stave, leaving it to the player to produce a convincing imitation of the violin's spiccato up-and-down arpeggios.

EX. 48

Two previous solutions to the problem of 'translating' this violin caprice to the keyboard were discarded by Liszt[1]—as were the first versions of the other studies—the re-writing being done, needless to say, in the spirit of simplification.

The fifth Study of the set is known as *La Chasse*, a title given to it by Paganini, not by Liszt. It is a charming 'hunting piece', in which the piano imitates flutes and horns. The piece was a great favourite with Paganini who used it to show off his mastery of harmonics in double-stops, an effect beautifully captured by Liszt in this passage.

[1] See pp. 48–49 for a fuller discussion.—*Ed.*

EX 49

Musically, this Study is not far removed from Scarlatti, to whom so much Italian eighteenth-century music seems indebted. I have never understood why Liszt's catholicity of taste did not extend to that great master whose virtuosity failed to arouse his interest.

The last of the 'Paganini' Studies, a set of variations on the theme that served Brahms and Rachmaninov so well,

EX. 50

is no more than a skilful and effective piano transcription of Paganini's original Caprice—itself a set of variations. The subsequent efforts of the other two composers did indeed prove that there was more to the perky little tune than Paganini himself realized. Liszt, however, did not attempt to go any further than Paganini and contented himself with transcribing his variations as faithfully as he could. Perhaps it should be emphasized here that Liszt, when writing transcriptions, as opposed to paraphrases or fantasias could, and did, proceed with the most scrupulous respect for the original text. His transcriptions of some of Bach's organ works are models in this respect.[1]

Three Concert Studies (1848)

No one, not even the most superficial student of musical history, can fail to notice how musical terms change their meanings in the course of time. The

[1] See David Wilde, pp. 178–79. The 'Paganini' Studies receive further discussion on pp. 47–51.—*Ed.*

word 'sonata', for example, once designated any piece which was played, as opposed to one which was sung. Nowadays, the term can mean either a certain way of grouping thematic material (sonata form) or it can mean a cyclic work in several movements, at least one of which is in sonata form. But already, with some modern composers, even this concept is crumbling away.

The term 'Étude', or 'Study', which once meant simply a technical exercise designed to develop the fingers, wrists and arms, has passed through a similar kind of transformation since the times of Czerny and Clementi. Both men were serious composers who stifled their talent for composition when designing these exercises, which were not meant to be enjoyed by the public, but to be profited by (and suffered from) by music students. Chopin, genius that he was, refused to be so limited in his aims; he made musical history by writing studies which were poetic genre-pieces while still bearing the stamp of the technical purposes inspiring their creation. In this, as in many other respects, Chopin's Studies are unique, masterly, and epoch-making.

Liszt carried this process a step further. He created the 'Concert Study' (surely a contradiction in terms) from which virtually all vestiges of the exercise idea seem to have vanished. The Three Concert Studies, like the 'Transcendentals', are not for music students, but for artists who already possess the technique needed for them. The element of 'display', obviously, cannot be absent from any concert study; but Liszt's demands in this respect are not too exacting. There is, however, a poetic quality about them, an elusive, fragile charm, which places them beyond the reach of some of the soul-less 'manualists' of our time. The poetic titles which were bestowed on the Three Concert Studies, presumably by publishers, are quite useful in aiding the less imaginative to grasp what was meant by Liszt, though the naturally musical can dispense with them.

No. 1 in A flat (called *Il Lamento*) is a romantic improvisation on a melody that at times sounds almost like Schumann.

EX. 51

It is perhaps more passionate than one would expect a lament to be and rises to great heights of pianistic ingenuity. Something between a 'Liebestraum' and a concert paraphrase, this piece deserves better performances from pianists than it usually receives.

No. 2 in F minor (*La Leggierezza*) is the finest of the set, and possibly one of the best concert studies Liszt ever wrote; it shows also how near was Chopin's nostalgic tone to Liszt's heart.

EX. 52

Only, unlike Chopin, Liszt does not stay in this mood of nostalgia for long. Cascades of leggiero passages (which give the piece its name) consisting mainly of variations on the main idea

EX. 53

lead to a big climax eventually subsiding and finishing in a melancholy, autumnal mood.

If No. 3 in D flat (*Un sospiro*) is more popular than the two others, the reason is its easy melodic appeal. This is not to say that it is either vulgar or meretricious; on the contrary, the principal melody, embedded in arpeggio-like up-and-down figuration is not without distinction.

EX. 54

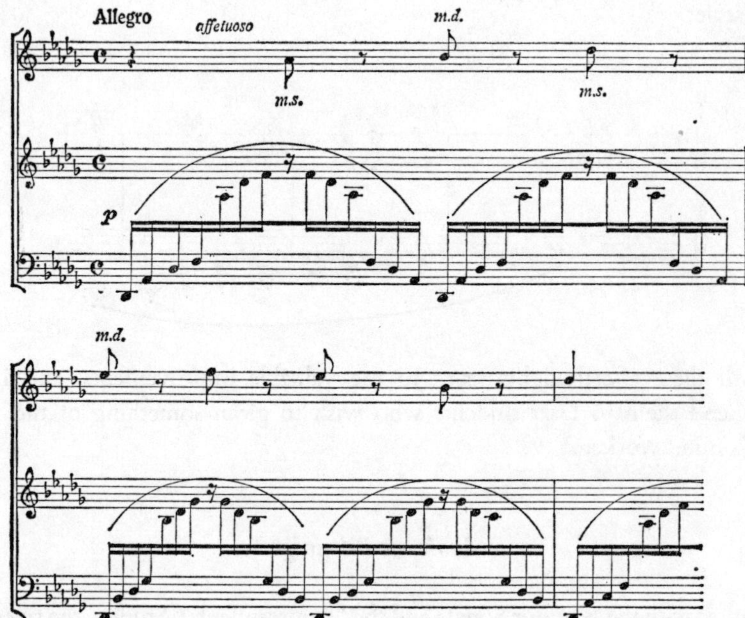

This Study has a more easily recognizable technical purpose (the crossing of hands) than the other two. Liszt made two revisions of this work: he inserted a slow 'Cadenza' before the recapitulation

EX. 55

and he also experimented with an alternative ending making use of the whole-tone scale:

EX. 56

Both these afterthoughts seem to me valuable improvements, and I recommend them to Liszt students who wish to glean something of the way Liszt's mind worked.[1]

Années de Pèlerinage

Together with the B minor Sonata and the 'Transcendental' Studies, the twenty-six pieces which comprise the three volumes of the *Années de Pèlerinage* form a series of self-portraits more searching and more complete than was given to the world by any other nineteenth-century musician. In the Sonata we see Liszt in his Faustian world of doubting, questioning, at odds with metaphysical issues; in the 'Transcendental' Studies he is the supreme virtuoso; but in the *Années de Pèlerinage* he is the vigorous, full-blooded enjoyer of the world he lives in—the world of nature, art, and poetry. The *Années* are mostly descriptive pieces, and some of them foreshadow in quite a remarkable way the music of the French Impressionists. The 'Swiss' book is concerned with nature and scenery, the 'Italian' book with great works of painting and literature. Needless to say, despite his boundless adoration of Michelangelo, Raphael, Petrarch, and Victor Hugo, Liszt was primarily a musician and anyone ignorant of the literary and extra-musical aspects of these pieces can still enjoy them as pure music.

[1] Two of the remaining three Concert Studies, *Waldesrauschen* and *Gnomenreigen*, are discussed by John Ogdon on pp. 140–42. The other one, *Ab Irato* (the title means literally 'In a rage'), appeared in 1852. Liszt composed it for a piano method published by Fétis. It is a brilliant show-piece, unaccountably neglected by pianists.—*Ed.*

Première Année: 'Suisse' (1848–53)

Most of these pieces date from Liszt's mid-twenties, first appearing in the early collection *Album d'un Voyageur*. But Liszt subsequently revised them, during his Weimar years, and he published them in their present form as late as 1855. They are musical reminiscences of the sights and sounds of Switzerland, and they bear these descriptive titles:

Chapelle de Guillaume Tell
Au Lac de Wallenstadt
Pastorale
Au bord d'une source
Orage
Vallée d'Obermann
Eglogue
Le mal du pays
Les cloches de Genève

The most important piece in the 'Swiss' volume is *Vallée d'Obermann*—a miniature symphonic poem—in which the 'thematic transformation' technique is used with great mastery and assurance to underline the many expressive changes in the music. ('Obermann' was the title of a novel Liszt admired, and the piece is dedicated to its author de Senancourt. There is a long quotation from the book at the head of the score.) There is an unmistakable resemblance between the opening theme of the piece

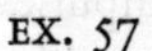

and Tchaikovsky's 'Letter Song' from *Eugene Onegin*, but I have no evidence to suppose that this was anything more than an odd coincidence. Tchaikovsky was no Lisztian.

The *Vallée d'Obermann* is a profoundly romantic piece of nature music, but of nature seen through the eyes of literature. The other Swiss pieces are pure nature sounds—lakes, springs, cow-bells, church-bells, Alpine horn—all these effects appear, drawn with astonishing precision by the hand of a master. Typical is *Au bord d'une source*, one of the most perfect 'water-pieces' ever written.

EX. 58

The piece is headed by some lines from Schiller: 'In murmuring coolness the play of young Nature begins.'

Most of the 'Swiss' volume of the *Années* has a purity and simplicity, not expected in the urbane, worldly young Liszt. They may not possess the vividness and epigrammatic conciseness, the deeper creative impulse which lies behind some of Chopin's miniatures; but, then, Liszt was not really a miniaturist, he needed space to expand in, leaving nothing unsaid.

Deuxième Année: 'Italie' (1846–49)

The 'Italian' book of the *Années de Pèlerinage*, better known than the 'Swiss' one, is based not on nature impressions, but on experiences in the realm of great art. Instead of sunshine and thunderstorm, lakes and mountain-tops, the impulses to write these pieces came from pictures, sculpture, poetry. Most of them, like those in the 'Swiss' book, were written when Liszt was a young man in his twenties and date from his travels through Italy with the Countess d'Agoult. They were revised during the Weimar period and published in 1858. Since the centrepiece of the collection, the 'Dante' Sonata (already discussed, pp. 92–93), is a great work of shattering impact, the purely musical value of the set is both favourably and unfavourably affected; favourably, because the specific weight of noble metal there offered is, in the aggregate, much higher; unfavourably, because the 'Dante' Sonata through its dimensions and its grandeur, dwarfs the other pieces in the set, beautiful though they are. Thus an impression of disproportion would be inevitable should anyone attempt to perform the 'Italian' part of the *Années* as a whole. The 'Swiss' part is a far better proposition from this point of view.

The titles are:

Sposalizio
Il Penseroso
Canzonetta del Salvator Rosa
Sonetto 47 del Petrarca
Sonetto 104 del Petrarca
Sonetto 123 del Petrarca
Après une lecture du Dante, Fantasia quasi Sonata

It is a pity that a beautiful, noble piece of restrained lyricism such as *Sposalizio* (inspired by the painting of that name by Raphael) is so rarely heard on our concert platforms. It is simple and recondite, like Raphael was, and like Raphael very Italian. Its lovely ending

EX. 59

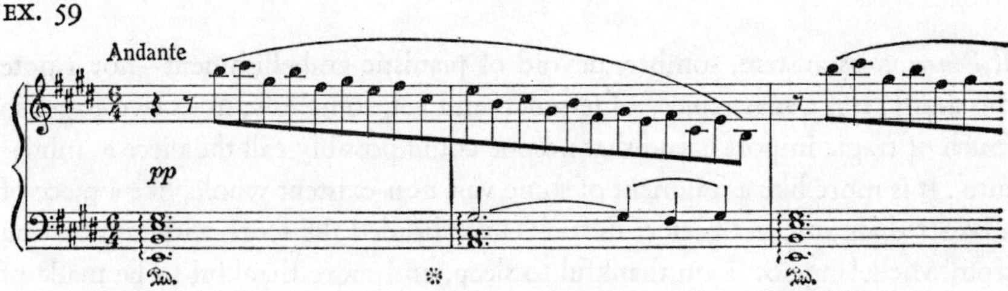

looks forward to Debussy's E major Arabesque.

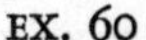
EX. 60

Liszt's textures are here actually more impressionistic than Debussy's, though writing nearly a century earlier.

In the short, but by no means slight, *Il Penseroso* (after the celebrated sculpture, 'The Thinker' by Michelangelo) Liszt shows himself so much ahead of his time as a harmonist that Wagner's admission of Liszt's decisive influence on his own harmonic thinking seems a grudging tribute—though Wagner no doubt meant it to be generous.

EX. 61

Il Penseroso is austere, sombre, devoid of pianistic embellishment—not a note too many. It is a masterpiece of terseness and yet, somehow, in its two pages so much of tragic import is said that no one could possibly call the piece a 'miniature'. It is more like a fragment of some vast non-existent whole, like a piece of a larger diamond, yet perfect in itself. Liszt headed the score with a quotation from Michelangelo: 'I am thankful to sleep, and more thankful to be made of stone. So long as injustice and shame remain on earth, I count it a blessing not to see or feel; so do not wake me—speak softly!'[1]

The jaunty little *Canzonetta del Salvator Rosa* (painter, bandit and—according to the evidence of this attractive tune—musician) is simply but effectively harmonized, not too difficult to play, and makes a rewarding concert piece or an encore off the beaten track. I have rarely heard this charming number played in public.

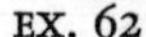
EX. 62

[1] According to Humphrey Searle (*The Music of Liszt*, p. 31) the piece had a great personal significance for Liszt. It turned up more than twenty years later as the basis of the second of the *Trois Odes Funèbre* which he intended to be his own requiem.—*Ed.*

Although the three Petrarch Sonnets are among Liszt's better known works, it is not generally realized that they are transcriptions and that in their original form they were songs. Liszt here shows himself to be a past master in the art of transcription, an art which, even when applied to his own music no less than to that of other composers, he clearly recognized as being an art of re-creation, not just a matter of re-arranging material to suit another medium. A remarkable freedom reigns in making subtle changes here and there, in selecting piano sonorities, in serving the purposes of expression and intensity rather than those of strict textual truth. I have no doubt that this is the right way, and in accordance with Liszt's detestation of pedantry.

The poems of which the Petrarch Sonnets are settings are quoted by way of preface in each case, not so much to help the player over any difficulties of prosody or phrasing, as to acquaint him with the underlying mood of each sonnet; but I find that the music by itself is so eloquent that it can hardly be misunderstood, even without Petrarch's words. *Sonnet No. 47* ('Benedetto sia il giorno') is a song of thanksgiving for the pleasures and sufferings of first love. Liszt bases it upon the idea of syncopation, giving it an agitated, unquiet character not to be found in the song.[1]

EX. 63

The words of *Sonnet No. 104* ('Pace non trovo') speak of restlessness, tears, self-hate, vain search for inner peace—all caused by the loved one. If the music falls short of expressing such depth of despair, it certainly expresses a passion which is entirely Liszt's own and which makes the piano soar like a bird. This is the best known of the Sonnets. It is understandable that pianists revel in its eloquence.

[1] See p. 236 for this passage in its original form. It is instructive to compare the two versions.—*Ed.*

EX. 64

molto appassionato

ff

8va

poco rall.

Sonnet No. 123 is full of the peace vainly searched for in the previous piece. The mood is mellow, dreamy, still and happy. ('I saw on earth the peace of angels' is the meaning of the first stanza.)

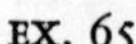
EX. 65

All brutal accents are avoided, even the climax, though passionate, is restrained like a nocturne by Chopin. At the blissful ending, sound so subtly melts into silence that it is hardly possible to say where the one leaves off and the other begins.

EX. 66

Venezia e Napoli (1859)
(Supplément aux Années de Pèlerinage: 'Italie')

Gondoliera–Canzone–Tarantella

If anyone should wonder why Liszt did not include these three pieces in the main body of the 'Years of Pilgrimage', but gave them a kind of less important status within the work by calling them collectively a 'supplement' (like encores after a piano recital), the reason is that they all belong to the Concert Paraphrase type of composition, a type otherwise absent in the set. All three are based on melodies by other composers, and therefore differ basically from the Petrarch Sonnets which are piano transcriptions of Liszt's own songs. Virtuosity must be the key-note of the *Venezia e Napoli* pieces, and we should not look for profundity in them.

The melody of the *Gondoliera* is a song by a Cavaliere Ponchini 'La Biondina in Gondoletta',

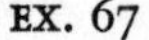
EX. 67

and Liszt is inexhaustible in inventing pianistic finery with which to deck this out. Beyond such limited aims there is also a very compelling feeling of Venice in the piece, particularly in the nocturnal dying-away chords of the ending.

Local colour is difficult to see in the *Canzone* (the melody comes from Rossini's *Otello*, the words are 'Nessun maggior dolore') which is altogether less successfully handled.

EX. 68

Berlioz, in one of his letters, complained that Wagner used too much tremolo in the *Flying Dutchman* and went on to attribute this to 'mental laziness' on the part of the composer who just did not bother to invent something more interesting. This may be unjust to Wagner. But, when applied to the little work in question, which rather painfully overworks the already boring device of tremolo, one wonders if there could be some truth in Berlioz's stricture. Liszt seems to have done the job like a portrait painter would an unsympathetic sitter—*senza amore.*[1]

In the *Tarantella* we are in a different world, a world of Neapolitan sunshine, vibrant, glowing, passionate; in this piece virtuosity runs riot, as it should. The central tune—about which Liszt only tells us that it is a 'Canzone Napolitana' attributed to one Guillaume Louis Cottrau—is anticipated in the first part of the work in this swaggering fashion.

EX. 69

[1] On the other hand, Liszt's tremolo technique, at its best, creates the illusion that the piano has been transformed into a sustaining instrument. See David Wilde (pp. 197–98).—*Ed.*

But when the song is stated in full it goes like this:

EX. 70

There is a wonderful transformation of this idea which evokes the sound of distant guitars.

EX. 71

Finally, the theme returns in Tarantella rhythm at the end of the work in a paroxysm of gaiety.

If these are fair examples of the Lisztian technique of thematic transformation they go a long way to prove that Liszt, in this one example at least, went further than merely producing a brilliant piece of pianistic bravura. If one might generalize: it is the musicianly thought, the formal mastery, the fertility of imagination, that in the end will enable such Lisztian 'bravura pieces' to survive in an anti-bravura age, while other productions of nineteenth-century pianism, equally brilliant but lacking in these qualities, will be consigned to oblivion.

Harmonies poétiques et religieuses (1845–52)

In the year 1834 Liszt published a short but significant piano piece called *Harmonies poétiques et religieuses*. The title and the dedication ('Ces vers ne s'adressent qu'à un petit nombre') are borrowed from Lamartine whose religious poetry had a profound influence on Liszt's own thinking—not, indeed, as is sometimes wrongly thought, by converting the pagan Liszt to Christianity, for he was a believing Christian all his life, but by helping him to resolve some of the tormenting doubts that co-existed with his fundamental devoutness. Liszt later repudiated, perhaps a little too harshly, this interesting piece, possibly not so much for artistic reasons but because it expressed doubt and torment more than faith and inner harmony, thus contradicting the serene *Weltanschauung* he fashioned for himself in later years. At all events, this early *Harmonies poétiques et religieuses* became the germ of the set of eight pieces collectively given the same title, the fourth piece in the set (now called *Pensée des Morts*) being a revised version of that early piece; it is technically an advance on the clumsier early version but many Lisztians still prefer the 1834 version, perhaps because it is experimental and has a gloomy ending.

The significance of *Harmonies poétiques et religieuses* (composed between 1845–52) is not only that it is the only piano work of this period of Liszt's life which is directly concerned with religion—such religious music as he composed he would normally entrust to the organ, orchestra or voices, until much later—but it consists in the fact that this collection of piano pieces, generally uneven in quality, includes two of the mightiest piano compositions Liszt ever created: they are *Bénédiction de Dieu dans la Solitude* and *Funérailles.*

Funérailles, Oct. 1849, is not, strictly speaking, a 'religious' work, nor does Lamartine have any part in it. It is a powerfully constructed funeral march of shattering impact, heroic in character, and with a slight Hungarian flavour. Because the middle section (a long crescendo built on an ostinato left-hand figure) reminds some people of Chopin's A flat major Polonaise, and because in one or two of the consolatory passages Chopin's ghost does seem to appear for a moment or two, it has been suggested that the date of October 1849 in the title of the work refers to Chopin's death. But Liszt researchers claim to have established that this is not so, and that the grief expressed in the work is a national rather than a personal one which relates to the victims of the heroic but vanquished Hungarian revolution of 1848–49.[1] Perhaps the most impressive part of *Funérailles* is the introduction: the clangour of bells builds up to a truly deafening roar.

EX. 72

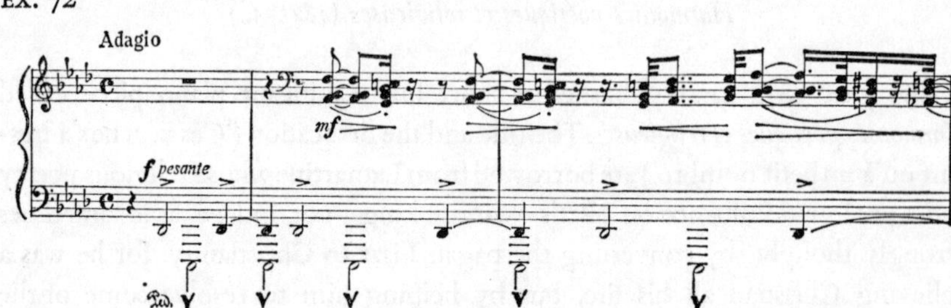

[1] See p. 60, however, for a discussion of the Chopin connection.—*Ed.*

FRANZ LISZT (in 1856)
Oil Portrait by Kaulbach

(c. 1854) by Dosnay

(in 1852) by Ernst Rietschel

(in 1857) by Christian Mohr

(in 1857) by L. von Schwanthaler

FOUR MEDALS STRUCK IN LISZT'S HOUNOUR

Here, as elsewhere, the carefully calculated pedal markings of Liszt ought to be respected to get the full grandeur of the sound which can be quite overwhelming.

After the bitter despair of *Funérailles*, the peace, mystical serenity and tranquillity (not without its ecstatic climaxes) of the *Bénédiction* is a very great contrast indeed. The piece is prefaced by a quotation from Lamartine: 'Whence comes, O God, this peace that overwhelms me? Whence comes this faith with which my heart overflows?' *Bénédiction* is painted on a large canvas, the form (ABA) being very clear-cut, and the piano writing showing the astonishing fertility of Liszt's pianistic imagination. He is inexhaustible in inventing new figuration, like the following for the right hand alone

EX. 73

which sounds like two voices and is very effective to play. José Vianna da Motta points out that the opening melody in the left hand could well have been (unconsciously) moulded to fit the words of Lamartine's poem, like a song or aria.

EX. 74

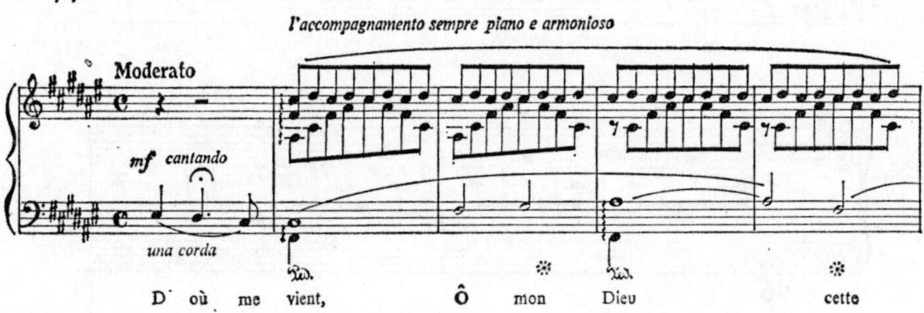

The middle section (which begins after a complete break, like a second movement, and which proves itself to be congruous and organically consistent with the rest of the piece, to one's surprise, at the end of the work) breathes heavenly calm, its fervour seeming to point straight to César Franck.

EX. 75

A parlando section in B flat major

EX. 76

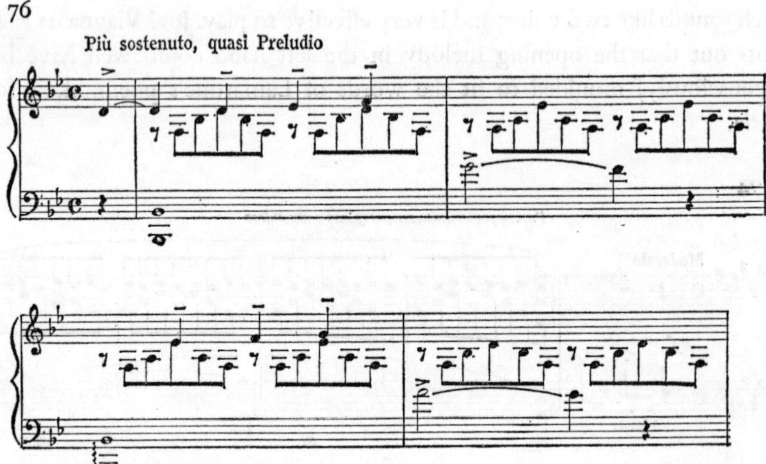

leads back to the first melody in a somewhat condensed form. A Coda in which all previous themes are reviewed, not unusual in Liszt, rounds off this beautiful and moving work.[1]

Fifteen Hungarian Rhapsodies (1846–52)

Other composers, such as Brahms, composed pieces which they called rhapsodies. And in the case of Brahms, they are very neatly and tidily composed, on strictly classical lines. But are they rhapsodies? Despite the beautiful music contained in these pieces, the answer must be no. For a rhapsody is not 'composed'; it is improvised, seemingly regardless of any rules of form, a free outpouring guided only by the instinct of the creative musician and the mood seeking expression. A rhapsody is basically the same as a fantasia with perhaps a little more stress on the untrammelled, the fortuitous, the unpremeditated in the composer's method of creation. Nevertheless, Liszt's rhapsodies are far from formless, for he had the instinct for form that protects the real creative artist from that danger. He saw to it, too, that the forms of the pieces varied from each other sufficiently to justify the claim that all the rhapsodies were one great work, a kind of national Hungarian epic in which there is unity in variety and variety in unity.[2]

Liszt's Rhapsodies have been attacked on three main grounds: first, that the composer uses in them thematic material not of his own invention; secondly, that this material is itself of doubtful value and authenticity; and, thirdly, that Liszt's treatment of the material is unsuitable because, instead of emphasizing its essential simplicity, he uses all the resources of brilliance and rich sonority available on the pianoforte. Let me take these points in turn.

The use by a composer of melodies not his own is not necessarily a crime, or a sign of failing powers, just as, conversely, the ready invention of tunes does not, in itself, make a composer. From time immemorial all composers, great and small, have made copious use, consciously or unconsciously, of the folk-tune material of their own countries; it is only because our ears are so conditioned, through centuries of listening to the German Classics and Romantics, to the sound

[1] The other pieces in the collection are of minor importance and can be left undiscussed. Only 'Hymne de l'enfant a son reveil' foreshadows something of the touching simplicity of the later sacred choral music; it is said to have been originally written for female voices, harmonium and harp. Two other pieces are vocal in origin, one of them being a piano arrangement of a *Miserere* by Palestrina.

[2] I would like to emphasize here that *all* the Rhapsodies except the last four, written about thirty years later, and therefore not part of the Weimar period, were contemplated by Liszt as *one* epic work, and should be so considered when critical standards are applied to them.

of their musical language, that we no longer realize how deeply rooted that language was in the German 'Volkslied'. But, even apart from folk-tunes, did not composers long before Liszt make use of each other's melodies without the slightest compunction? Did not Mozart (no mean melodist himself!) make use of the theme of a Clementi piano sonata for the Magic Flute Overture?[1] There are many more examples. In our own age, Strauss, Bartók, Stravinsky and countless others, used folk tunes and melodies written by known composers, without arousing the moral indignation of critics whose intolerance is directed only, it seems, against Liszt.

The second accusation against the rhapsodies concerns the value and authenticity of the material used, and here we are on more uncertain ground. There is very little information available on Liszt's sources of supply: a large collection of folk-tunes which he is said to have possessed is lost, according to his biographer Raabe. Liszt, in his admiration for the Gypsies, put forward a theory identifying them and their music with Hungarian folk music. In this, as we know now, he was mistaken, and the theory was exploded by later researches into the great reservoir of peasant music which gave such strong impetus to Bartók and other Hungarian composers of the post-Lisztian era. Nevertheless, though Liszt was undoubtedly wrong, it must be admitted that the Gypsies did to some extent further the cause of Hungarian folk-music. They did, in fact, perform genuine folk-tunes, as well as other songs, frequently written by amateurs, or even by the Gypsies themselves. (After all, the only difference between a folk-song and any other melody is that in the one case we do not know the name of the author, in the other we do.) It is, therefore, reasonable to assume that Liszt used for his rhapsodies some popular songs written by known composers, and some genuine, indubitable folk songs—and possibly even some melodies of his own.

As for the rightness or wrongness of his treatment of these melodies, let me quote Béla Bartók who in a lecture 'Liszt problems' (1936) said:

> To understand how Liszt was able to merge those diverse elements into a style of his own, it must be emphasized from the very start that that which the hands of Franz Liszt touched was first crushed to a pulp, then moulded together and so completely reconstructed that his individuality was indelibly stamped on it, as though it had been his original idea from the beginning. What he ultimately created through this seeming mixture of foreign elements became the music of Franz Liszt and none other.

[1] It is an established fact that Mozart had heard Clementi play the sonata in question.

There is, it seems to me, a strong case for Liszt's rhapsodies. But perhaps in the final analysis it would be merely silly to defend them against those music critics who complain about their loose construction, or 'disjointedness', which is like complaining about the long neck of a giraffe (or the long ears of some music critics!).[1]

Conclusion

It has not been my aim to provide an answer to the fundamental question: Was Liszt, the artist who aimed so high, blessed with the creative strength commensurate with his lofty ideals, and, if he fell short of those ideals, did he not share a common fate of all artists, even the greatest? Furthermore, in admitting such shortcomings as undoubtedly exist in him, should we not hasten to add that, human failings notwithstanding, there is more than enough left to admire? Let abler critical minds than mine decide whether Liszt, certainly no Classicist, and no Romantic either (if the foregoing arguments be accepted), deserves on the strength of his middle-period piano works alone, to be considered by us a founder of modern music. This is not suggested as yet another convenient pigeon-hole, that disastrous refuge of intellectual laziness, but rather as a stimulus to further thinking on the subject. We live in an age which has discarded many conventional beliefs. If some of the thoughts here expressed start yet another process of re-thinking in some readers of my essay, then it has fulfilled its purpose.

[1] Louis Kentner discusses the Hungarian Rhapsodies at greater length in his essay on Liszt interpretation (pp. 205–9).—*Ed.*

JOHN OGDON

Solo Piano Music (1861–86)

NOWADAYS it has become critically respectable to try to assess the unity lying behind a composer's creative diversity. Stravinsky's abrupt changes of style, the unexpected musical development of Messiaen and Prokofiev, the return to tonality in Schoenberg's later years—these are all an incentive to find an underlying *sequitur*. In literature, too, when William Golding follows the metaphysical *Spire* with his *Pyramid* of keen social observation, we are not surprised, although a hundred years ago such re-orientations of the creative process were almost unheard-of.

Thus, when Liszt's style of composition underwent a radical change in the last twenty years of his life, it is important to realize how unprecedented a change this was at that time. The tradition of music was one of unified progression, even to the extent of Brahms's First Symphony being known as 'Beethoven's Tenth'. As for Beethoven himself, his 'three periods' are, by comparison, a monolithic unity. That Liszt's change of style is far more radical than anything that had gone before is both visually and aurally obvious. Gone are those pages thick with hemidemisemiquavers.

EX. I

In their place are rests and notes possessing the ambiguous quality of a Delphic prophecy.

EX. 2

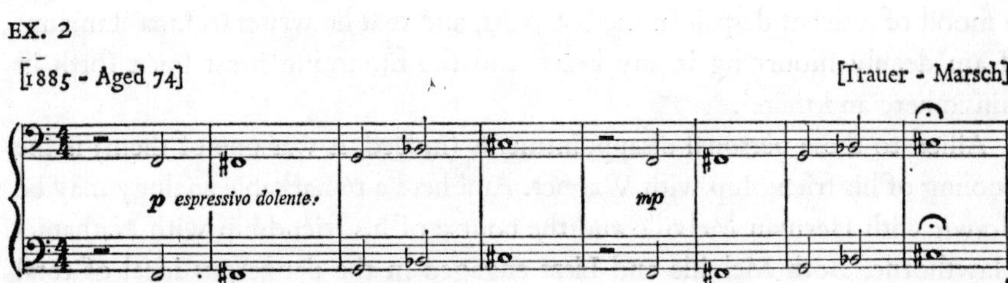

Transformed, too, is his 'unerring though unrecognized instinct for form',[1] and largely vanished is his desire of the Weimar period (1847–59) to graft the body of German classicism onto the spirit of cosmopolitan romanticism; indeed, in some of the late works one detects an almost anti-symphonic, anti-constructivist spirit. Why is this?

*

Three main reasons for Liszt's change of style in his last years are readily apparent. These are: tragedy in his personal life, the course of his friendship with Wagner, and his increasing interest in Hungarian and other national schools of composition—as opposed to the more cosmopolitan style prevailing in his youth.

The personal tragedies included, first, the breakdown of his endeavours to consummate legally his marriage to the Princess Carolyne Sayn-Wittgenstein who, as Szabolcsi says, was 'surely far from being such a ruinous demon as we find her described by certain biographers of Liszt'.[2] As Liszt himself once said: 'All my joys are hers, and my sufferings go to her to be appeased'. The Vatican's decision, at the last minute, not to grant his application to marry the Princess was a double blow, directed as it was against the person for whom he felt most affection, and coming as it did from the institution for which he felt most respect. Also he had lost children, a grievous blow; and his dream of Weimar as a city 'where Wagner and myself should have been the leading lights, as, in former times, Goethe and Schiller' had come to naught. When one adds to this the fact that, even at the cost of giving up his successful career as a virtuoso, he did not find an ordered domestic or professional life (since his teaching commitments still involved him in a 'vie trifurquée' divided between Rome, Budapest, and Weimar) and when one also remembers the enormous amount of energy which he poured out of his life for over twenty years in the service of others, one realizes that at this time (1860–61) Liszt must have become emotionally exhausted. It is hardly surprising, then, that his old enthusiasms alternate more with

[1] Constant Lambert: *Music Ho!*, London, 1934.
[2] Bence Szabolcsi: *The Twilight of Liszt*, Budapest, 1959.

a mood of reticent despair in the last years, and that he writes to Lina Ramann: 'I am deeply mourning in my heart, and the mourning must burst forth in music here and there'.

Allied to these personal disappointments (indeed, it was one of them) is the cooling of his friendship with Wagner. And here a remarkable analogy may be drawn with Herman Melville and the course of his friendship with Nathaniel Hawthorne. Both Melville and Liszt engaged in the dangerous ideal of total artistic friendship; in both cases these were at first fruitful, but later disappointing. Perhaps not at first, but eventually, Wagner and Hawthorne brought to these friendships less of soul-sharing and more of watchful calculation. Hawthorne drew back from Melville's growing antipathy to temporal society, while Wagner eventually disowned Liszt's prophetic vision to such an extent as to draw from Szabolcsi the cry: 'Was it in *this* light, that his closest and most intimate friend saw him? If so, what could he expect from his enemies?'[1]

Hawthorne's unilateral de-escalation of a once fervent friendship, drew from Melville his beautiful poem 'Monody'.

To have known him, to have loved him
After loneness long;
And then to be estranged in life,
And neither in the wrong;
And now for death to set his seal—
Ease me, a little ease, my song!

By wintry hills his hermit-mound
The sheeted snow-drift drape,
And houseless there the snow-bird flits
Beneath the fir-trees' crape;
Glazed now, with ice the cloistral vine
That hid the shyest grape.

And Liszt, from such an unnerving experience, also approached the 'monody' of his last years.

Other analogies between Liszt and Melville are possible. Both were successful in their early years, and highly extrovert. But in later life they exemplified, against the experience of humanity as a whole, a marked personality change, a withdrawal into complete introversion; and this kind of transformation is still not common. At the height of his career Melville wrote to Hawthorne: 'I have

[1] Szabolcsi, *op. cit.*, p. 24.

almost made up my mind to be annihilated', which closely parallels Liszt's: 'It seems to me, now, high time that I should be somewhat forgotten'.

But even as Melville followed his *cri de coeur* with a novel longer and more ambitious than *Moby-Dick*—his 'battle with the Kraken', *Pierre*—so Liszt for some time after his aside to von Herbeck did not cease to write large-scale works, continuing the traditions of the Weimar period. The 'early' late works of Liszt, which include the two *Franciscan Legends*, the two *Etudes de Concert*, the *Rhapsodie Espagnole*, the *Weinen, Klagen* variations and the *Fantasia and Fugue on B.A.C.H.* are, so to speak, annotations of the Weimar period, still displaying his interest of that time in the larger forms, in pianistic virtuosity and in romantic flamboyance. I shall now look at these pieces in more detail.

Two Franciscan Legends (1863)

The Franciscan Legends blend symphonic thought with the impressionism of *Les Jeux d'Eaux à la Villa d'Este*. There was no successor to the first of them, *St. Francis of Assisi preaching to the birds*, until Messiaen's recent interest in representing bird-song in pianistic terms. Compare, for instance, the opening of the Legend

EX. 3

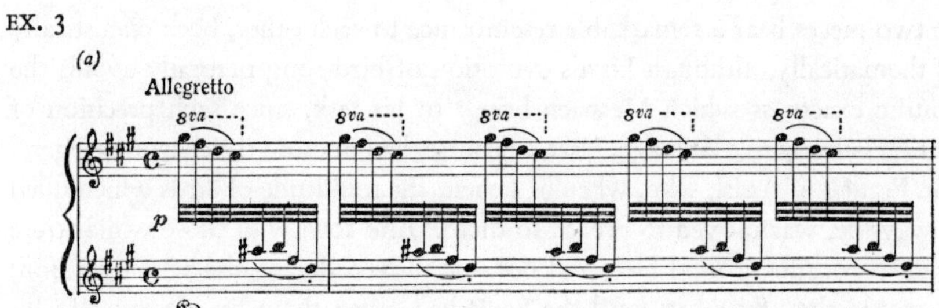

with Messiaen's *Régard des Hauteurs,*[1]

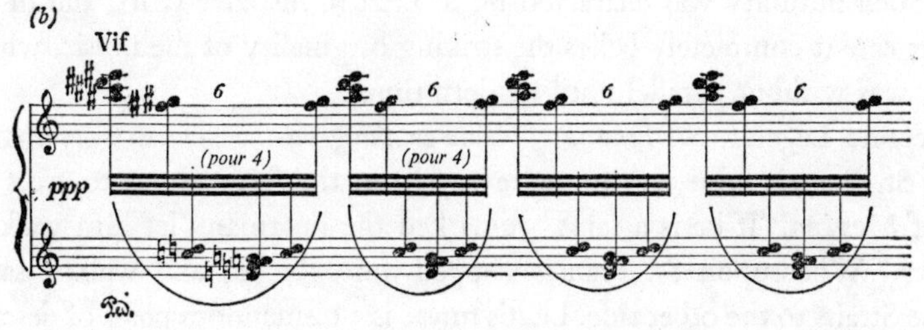

[1] From *Vingt Régards sur l'enfant-Jésus.*

also, the Legend's middle section

EX. 4

with Messiaen's 'Theme of Joy' from the same work.

The two pieces bear a remarkable resemblance to each other, both pianistically and thematically, although Liszt's evocation of bird-song naturally avoids the scientific exactness which Messiaen brings to his task, since such precision of notation belongs to a later age. Liszt, of course, had in mind the charming legend of St. Francis of Assisi, who, when he beheld the multitude of birds which filled the wayside, was moved to preach to them. 'And forthwith those which were in the trees came around him, and not one moved during the whole sermon; nor would they fly away until the Saint had given them his blessing.' In his preface, Liszt apologizes for his 'lack of ingenuity' and asks to be forgiven for 'impoverishing the wonderful profusion of the text of the "Sermon to the birds".' Such humility was characteristic of Liszt in his later years, and in this particular case it completely belies the striking originality of the music, which, as I said, was without parallel until modern times.

The second Legend, *St. Francis of Paola walking on the waves,* concerns the story of St. Francis who was turned away from the ferry about to cross the Straits of Messina. 'If he is a saint,' remarked the boatman, 'let him walk on the water.' Whereupon St. Francis stepped onto the sea and walked safely across the Straits to the other side. Liszt's music is a tremendous piece of descriptive writing, wonderfully executed, with St. Francis's theme heard against the menacing background of rolling waves.[1] This Legend demands Busoni's monumental performance, with the theme sculpted in relief, the accompaniment a wash of sound. The bare octaves, and the interval of a fourth at the beginning (Ex. 5*a*) have a pagan ring which only draws into itself the ethos of Christianity in its later effulgent harmonizations.

EX. 5

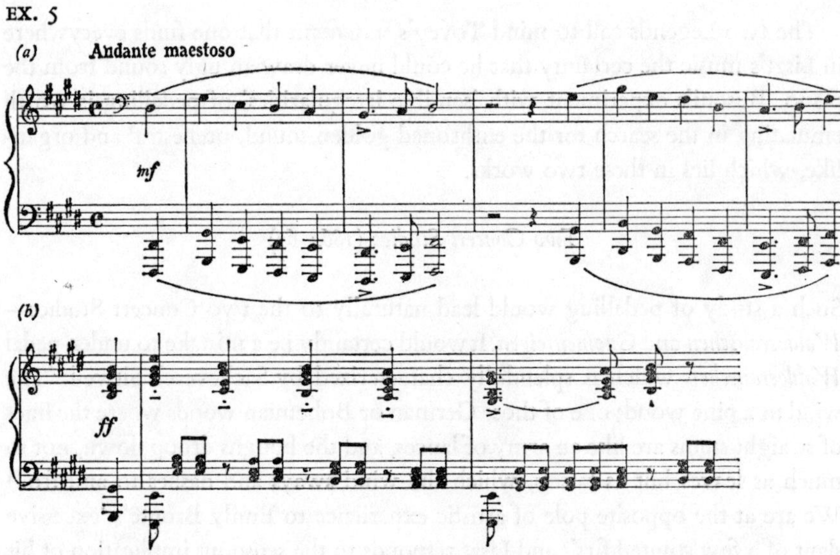

The use of the *caesura* towards the end is a dramatic gesture characteristic of the Weimar period (the B minor Sonata, for instance); this gesture, in which sincerity and theatricality combine, is one of the most imaginative uses of *silence* in the music of the nineteenth century, producing an almost physical impact; we literally hear the piano cease playing.

EX. 6

[1] For many years, Liszt had hanging in his study a painting of this scene. St. Francis of Paola was Liszt's patron saint.—*Ed.*

The two Legends call to mind Tovey's statement that one finds everywhere in Liszt's music the certainty that he could never draw an ugly sound from the piano. Busoni's experiment with 'sensible irregularities' of pedalling is worth emulating in the search for the enthroned golden sound, orchestral and organ-like, which lies in these two works.

Two Concert Studies (1862–63)

Such a study of pedalling would lead naturally to the two Concert Studies—*Waldesrauschen* and *Gnomenreigen*. It would certainly be a mistake to under-pedal *Waldesrauschen* which is splendidly characterized by Sacheverell Sitwell: 'The wind in a pine wood; one of those German or Bohemian woods where the lines of straight stems are like an army of lances, and the boughs droop down, not so much as leaves but as tassels, which the wind sways and dashes to and fro.'[1] We are at the opposite pole of artistic experience to Emily Brontë's 'excessive slant of a few stunted firs', and Liszt responds to the sensuous implication of his subject with one of his most shimmering themes.

EX. 7

[1] Sacheverell Sitwell: *Liszt*, London, 1955, p. 247.

This opening of *Waldesrauschen* is prophetic of Ravel's Ondine. It reminds one of Stephen Heller's observation that when Liszt played the piano it was as if the electricity flowed out of his arms.

In *Gnomenreigen* Liszt inhabits the world of Berlioz's 'Queen Mab' Scherzo and Mendelssohn's *Midsummer Night's Dream.* Music can be visually, as well as aurally mysterious. That the fantastic *legerdemain* of Ex. 8*a*

EX. 8

should give us this theme (Ex. 8*b*),

is almost as surprising as that the first and second violins in Tchaikovsky's 'Pathétique' Symphony (Ex. 8*c*)

should combine in this result (Ex. 8*d*).

The surprise in Liszt's case is achieved by subtly alternating hand position The second theme contains a magical, spine-shivering chord (Ex. 9, see *)

exciting in its implication of two dominants, *V* of B flat major and *V* of F

EX. 9

major, underpinned by an unsounded C. Mendelssohn might have written the passage thus (Ex. 10):

EX. 10

Spanish Rhapsody (1863)

More grandiose is the *Spanish Rhapsody*. Liszt composed this work in 1863. It consists of a set of free variations on two Spanish themes—*La Folia* (immortalized by Corelli) and the *Jota Aragonesa*. Years earlier, Liszt had included Spain in his European tours, and he probably first came to know these tunes at that time. *La Folia* dominates the first part of the *Spanish Rhapsody*.

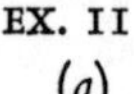
EX. 11

(*a*)

The second part features the *Jota Aragonesa*—a brilliant contrast.

EX. 12

The lyrical central section of the *Jota* (Ex. 13)

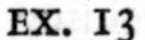

which is transformed to extraordinary effect in the final section (reminding us of Balakirev's debt to Liszt—*vide Islamey*),

EX. 14

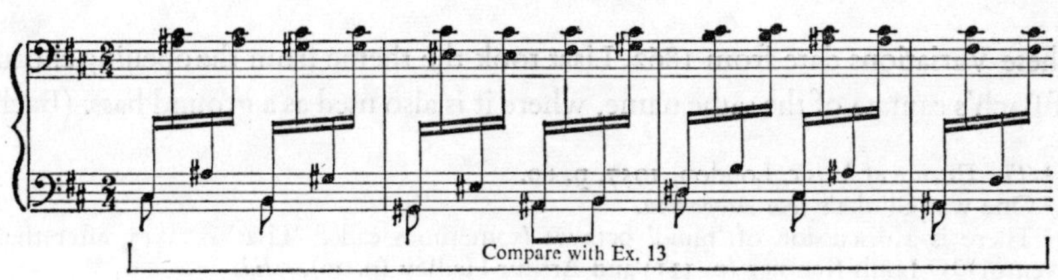

recurs years later in Mahler's Third Symphony, prompting Busoni's question: 'How does it get there?'[1]

As an evocation of Spain, the *Spanish Rhapsody* had few precedents;[2] the musical Hispanicism of Debussy, Ravel and Szymanowsky, and the nationalist compositions of Albeniz and Granados, were all to come later. The Rhapsody opens, incidentally, with one of the finest cadenzas in Liszt's output, one showing his sensitivity to glittering enharmonic relationships, a feature which recurs many times in the later works. Pianistically, the use of 'blind' octaves is unusually prevalent and exciting.[3]

EX. 15

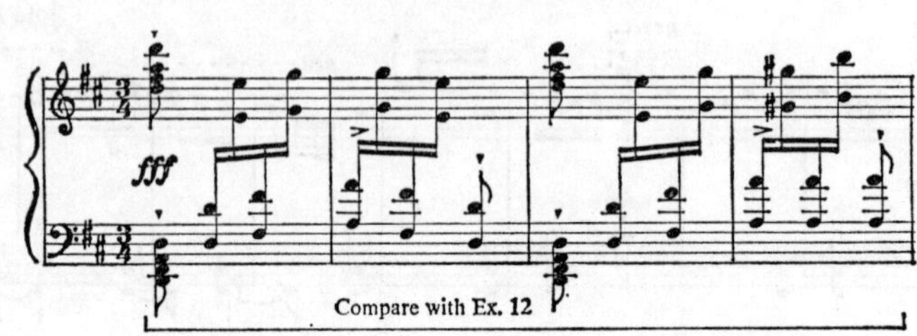

Busoni's transcription for piano and orchestra, which was first performed by Bartók in 1904 in Manchester, extends the final section of the work. I think this is justifiable, since Liszt sometimes experienced a curious difficulty in deciding on the best and most effective endings for some of his works.

The last of the 'early' late works which relate back spiritually to the Weimar period are two, inspired by Bach: the *Weinen, Klagen* Variations (1862), and the *Fantasy and Fugue on B.A.C.H.* (1871). Liszt was deeply interested in Bach, and his interest must have been further stimulated by the knowledge that Bach himself, a hundred years earlier, had lived and worked in Weimar.

Variations: 'Weinen, Klagen, Sorgen, Zagen' (1862)

These Variations date from 1862. Liszt took the theme from the opening chorus of Bach's cantata of the same name, where it is also used as a ground bass. (Bach,

[1] *The Essence of Music*, London, 1957, p. 89.
[2] One was Glinka's *Jota Aragonesa*.
[3] There is a discussion of 'blind' octaves (sometimes called 'Liszt' octaves, after their inventor) by Louis Kentner (p. 111) and Arthur Hedley (p. 26).—*Ed.*

AUTOGRAPH PAGE OF 'ST. FRANCIS WALKING ON THE WATERS'
(c. 1893)

FRANZ LISZT (in 1863)
Oil Portrait by Stein

incidentally, used the same theme again in the Crucifixus of the B minor Mass—also as a ground bass.) Here is Bach's version of the theme.

EX. 16

And here is how Liszt transforms it for the impressive opening of the Variations.

EX. 17

The piano writing throughout is superb. Appropriately, the work is dedicated to Anton Rubinstein.

Weinen, Klagen ranks as one of the most ambitious and masterly of Liszt's later compositions. Liszt, like Bach, was evidently taken by the theme's poignancy, and he made no attempt to diffuse its latent unity in the main body of the Variations, but conceives a structure analogous to that of Bach's own Chaconne, and likewise based on a triple metre and the regular recurrence of the tonic every four bars. The main variations begin gently and sadly, rising to climaxes of passionate fire.

EX. 18

Liszt's intuitively rhapsodic approach eventually slackens the rhythmic strictness of the variations, so that the music eventually finds itself barred in quadruple, sextuple, and, in the final recitative, irregular time-signatures. This metrical metamorphosis, as it were, enables Liszt to introduce, without any feeling of dislocation, the final chorale 'Was Gott thut, das ist wohlgethan', which also, incidentally, ends the Bach cantata.

EX. 19

The placing of the chorale after the variations works so well, partly because the metrical freedom of some of the later variations helps us to accept the change of mood and pace it represents. Also, the cadenza leading up to the chorale tentatively feels its way towards it with a melodic shape that adumbrates its leading phrase.

EX. 20

Slender, but enough. An effect of real serenity is obtained in this final section which, unlike the rest of the work, lies mainly outside the realm of chromaticism, and unfolds in the cooler world of diatonicism.

Pianistically, the Variations contain many master touches, and it is not surprising that they were frequently played by Rachmaninov.

Fantasy and Fugue on B.A.C.H. (1871)

This is a later work, completed in 1871; it was transcribed from the original composition for organ, the Prelude and Fugue on B.A.C.H. which Liszt had composed some years earlier.[1] The Fantasy presents Liszt in an unfamiliar,

[1] Liszt's organ music is dealt with on pp. 345–49.—*Ed.*

Cagliostro-like guise, as acrostician; mathematics and music usually co-exist rather uneasily in Liszt, yet we find here a tremendously interesting and inventive work, perhaps the first we have yet considered which truly gives out the emotional impact of the 'typical' late works. It opens with one of the darkest-sounding chords in piano literature, over the notes B.A.C.H.

EX. 21

The exposition of the Fugue verges at times on atonality, and almost even adumbrates a note-row.

EX. 22

But this should surprise nobody who knows the 'Faust' Symphony.[1] Later statements of the Fugue's subject presage Vaughan Williams and Messiaen in their alternations of gloom and bell-like brightness, while its middle section becomes a Mahlerian ride to the abyss, veering through F sharp minor and D flat major, to B minor. One later passage insists on quotation: it is a chord (achieved by a tremendous build-up across the entire range of the keyboard) which, like the tortoise of Hindu mythology, appears capable of carrying the heavens on its back (Ex. 23).

[1] See p. 362.—*Ed.*

EX. 23

The chord (Ex. 24) obtains its effect by simultaneously striking an acciaccatura

EX. 24

with its resolution—the most shattering moments in Liszt are often susceptible of a quite orthodox explanation. The passage's colossal effect also obtains from holding the sustaining pedal down. Liszt's music now, as Beethoven's formerly, is frequently under-pedalled or inaccurately pedalled, due in part to the still wide circulation of corrupt editions.[1] To have heard Liszt play this work must have been a revelation. It gives one a hint of what Rubinstein might have meant when he said: 'Compared to Liszt, all other pianists are children.'

The Final Period

Coming to the typical works of Liszt's old age, we see so marked a contrast to the style of the Weimar period, most obviously in texture, that we must ask: *how* did his style change after 1865?

Melody is shortened drastically, reduced sometimes to a handful of basic shapes, frequently four notes or fewer. To see this development in Liszt's art is astonishing, and, as I remarked earlier, it is without precedent in musical history. The change can be observed quite clearly if we compare a work from his early or middle years with one taken from his old age. The main theme of *Bénédiction de Dieu* (1845), for example, creates Classical four-bar and eight-bar phrase structures.

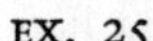

In this kind of theme, flowingly romantic though it is, one notices a structural balance between antecedent and consequent which stamps Liszt at this time as

[1] Louis Kentner writes about Liszt's pedalling on pp. 215–18.—*Ed.*

a composer with a Classical background. How different is the situation in the late works—the hesitant, Scriabinesque yearnings of the Third Mephisto Waltz, the virtual absence of melody in the *Trauervorspiel und Marsch*, the almost amorphous theme of the *La Lugubre Gondola—I* (1882).

EX. 26

The basic rhythmic unit ('x'), instead of becoming the foundation of an expansive Romantic melody, like the *Bénédiction*, is a stark end-product in itself. A thistle replacing a *fleur-de-Lys*, as it were. Throughout these last works, in fact, we see an ever freer, improvisatory form of melody, yet one derived from the very tightest structural cells Liszt could conceive.

While Liszt's melodic adventurousness is iconoclastic in these last years—only Berlioz and Mussorgsky fully parallel its fluidity and plasticity—his harmonic experiments in these late works are not without precedent, either in his own music or that of other composers. The augmented triads of *Unstern!* (*c.* 1885) had already appeared in the 'Faust' Symphony, and the bare fifths of the *Csárdás Macabre* (1882) had already helped the devil to tune up in the First Mephisto Waltz. Liszt does, however, make much more use of implied harmony. Chords hang in the air unresolved (see the close of *Nuages Gris*, Ex. 49), and melodies are unaccompanied (Ex. 27).

EX. 27

If revolution is merely a speeding up of the evolutionary process, and not something totally separate (a nice philosophical debating point, this) then we begin to understand Liszt's 'revolution' in old age—which is as traceable to his earlier works as to his later ones.

Liszt's interest in unusual scales and modes increased greatly in his last years.

His growing involvement in the political and musical destiny of Hungary, and indeed in nationalistic music generally, led him to explore anew, and in greater detail, the scalic constituents of Hungarian and east European music. Note, for instance, the opening of *Sunt Lachrymae Rerum* (Ex. 28) from the third volume of the *Années de Pèlerinage*, where both the rhythmic shape and the theme and its scalic organization shows its national origin.

EX. 28

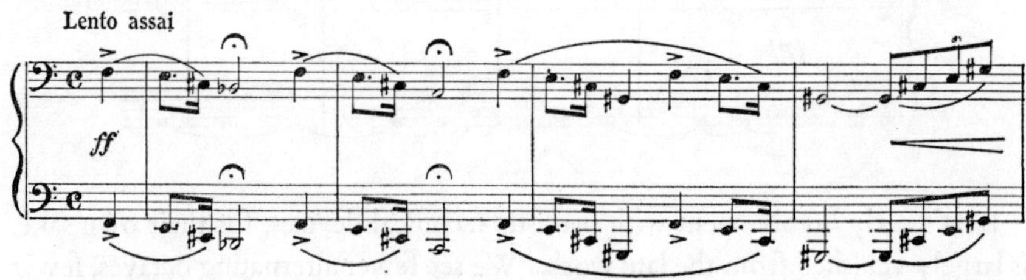

Liszt's exploration of a specifically Hungarian mode of expression was, of course, to have a profound influence on Bartók. Another scale which came to fascinate Liszt the more as he got older was the whole-tone scale. This scale, whose invention is attributed to Dargomijzsky, provides, in Liszt's usage, an interesting link between the nationalist Russian school of composers, and his later influence on Debussy and Ravel (see pp. 354–55).

In Liszt's late works rhythm, like melody, is fined down to its tightest cells. Moreover, he uses rhythm in a special way, to express the basic concept of a piece. The more elegaic works are pervaded by a trochaic rhythm which, over the centuries, has become irreversibly associated with grief. It is, of course, the rhythm pervading much funeral music (Chopin's Funeral March in the B flat minor Sonata is the most famous example) and the melancholy of much of Liszt's later music is directly attributable to its consistent use.[1] The sadness of some of these works leads Liszt occasionally to abandon all sense of rhythmic pulse; the lapping waves of sound in *La Lugubre Gondola* and *Nuages Gris* reflect the auto-hypnosis of a tired mind which approaches at these times Beethoven's direction 'ermattet'—exhausted.

Liszt's renewed interest in Hungarian music led him to apply, with a new authenticity, the rhythms of the *Csárdás* and the *Verbunkos*. There is a new

[1] Other examples of this 'grief-motif' can be found in the funeral marches of Mahler's First Symphony and Beethoven's 'Eroica' Symphony, and also the funeral march of the latter's piano Sonata in A flat major, op. 26. See also Ex. 40 of John Ogdon's essay, from the Elegy on the death of László Teleki.—*Ed.*

plasticity, and a lack of dogmatic construction; it is unlikely that the 5/4 sections of the *Elegy* in memory of Mosonyi, and the refined rhythmic augmentation in the last of the *Five Hungarian Folksongs* (Ex. 29) would have occurred to Liszt as points of rhythmic subtlety worth making in earlier years.

EX. 29

Liszt's early involvement with pianistic technical devices, for their own sake, is largely vanished from the late works. We see fewer alternating octaves, fewer effects 'a tre mani'; in general, Liszt turns away from the prodigious *legerdemain* which brought him such marked success in his early years, both as a composer and as a pianist. Significantly, some of the last pieces (notably *Am Grabe Richard Wagners*, the First Elegy, and the *Csárdás Macabre*) were conceived as pure music, existing independently of any instrumental colouring. Certainly, some of the earlier works had been executed in different media (e.g. *Mazeppa* and the First 'Mephisto' Waltz) thus indicating a certain absence of interest in the colour aspect of the music; but this direction of Liszt's thought, particularly in *Am Grabe Richard Wagners* represents an unexpected move towards Busoni's ideal that music exists in itself, irrespective of its instrumentation. Pianistic questions of colour, phrasing and pedalling pose a constant problem in Liszt's late music, as in his earlier works.

As for Liszt's approach to musical form at this time, his whole-hearted occupation with symphonic structure that produced the masterpieces of the Weimar years is largely sunk without trace. Instead, as Szabolcsi says, 'everything is visionary, everything is sweeping forth storm-like in a few seconds, everything is pervaded by a spirit of improvisation', and, 'the concepts of repeat, crescendo and variation are assuming a constantly widening and more and more special sense in Liszt's late compositions'.[1]

★

We come now to the last of the piano works. There are two groups of pieces which, as sets, stand somewhat apart—the third volume of the *Années de Pèleri-*

[1] *Op. cit.*, p. 47.

nage and the *Weihnachtsbaum* ('Christmas Tree') Suite. The bulk of the remainder are short, single pieces of a highly experimental character.

Années de Pèlerinage: Troisième Année (1867–77)

The stylistic contrast between volume three of the *Années* (which was not published until 1883) and the two earlier volumes is marked.[1] There are seven pieces in this last volume. Their titles are:

Angelus, Prière aux Anges Gardiens
Aux Cyprès de la Villa d'Este—Threnodie I
Aux Cyprès de la Villa d'Este—Threnodie II
Les Jeux d'eaux à la Villa d'Este
Sunt lacrymae rerum—en Mode hongroise
Marche funèbre (in memory of the Emperor Maximilian I of Mexico, 19 June 1867)
Sursam corda.

The opening *Angelus* underlines the piety and simplicity never far behind Liszt's flamboyance. Its simplicity is not false; one must believe in it. Tonally and atmospherically the little piece resembles the beautiful prelude to the oratorio *St. Elizabeth*, and is a miniature sonata first movement. Here is the opening.

EX. 30

There is a charming account of Liszt playing the *Angelus* to one of his visitors at the Villa d'Este. It is taken from the memoirs of the Rev. H. Haweis who saw Liszt there in 1880.

> 'You know,' said Liszt, turning to me, 'they ring the "Angelus" in Italy carelessly; the bells swing irregularly, and leave off, and the cadences are

[1] The two earlier volumes are dealt with by Louis Kentner on pp. 119–20 and 120–25 respectively.—*Ed.*

> often broken up thus': and he began a little swaying passage in the treble—like bells tossing high up in the evening air: it ceased, but so softly that the half-bar of silence made itself felt, and the listening ear still carried the broken rhythm through the pause. The Abbate himself seemed to fall into a dream; his fingers fell again lightly on the keys, and the bells went on, leaving off in the middle of a phrase. Then rose from the bass the ring of the Angelus, or rather, it seemed like the vague emotion of one who, as he passes, hears, in the ruins of some wayside cloister, the ghosts of old monks humming their drowsy melodies, as the sun goes down rapidly, and the purple shadows of Italy steal over the land, out of the orange west!
>
> We sat motionless . . . (Liszt's) fingers seemed quite independent, chance ministers of his soul. The dream was broken by a pause; then came back the little swaying passage, of bells, tossing high up in the evening air, the half-bar of silence, the broken rhythm—and the Angelus was rung.

The Villa d'Este, at Tivoli, where this scene took place, was the famous home of Cardinal Hohenlohe, a close personal friend of Liszt's, who had placed his magnificent residence at Liszt's disposal whenever he visited Rome. The Villa had, and still has, some of the most magnificent gardens in the world, renowned for their beautiful cypress trees and the ceaseless play of their hundreds of fountains.[1] Sacheverell Sitwell has described the source of the inspiration of the two Threnodies. 'For three whole days, in September 1877, he spent every hour of sunlight and as much of night as was made visible by the moon, in admiration of the cypresses. They obsessed his thoughts to the exclusion of all else, and two of the pieces in the third volume of the *Années de Pèlerinage* are the result of this.'

Harmonically, the Threnodies traverse the language of music from Beethoven to Wagner. In fact, the second Threnody owes much to Wagner, the opening sounding like a reminiscence of *Tristan*.

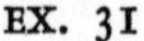

EX. 31

[1] Liszt once described the Villa d'Este as his 'El Dorado'. He spent some of his happiest days in old age there. See Edward Lear's painting (facing p. 352).—*Ed.*

This Threnody is more pictorially immediate than its companion. At one point there is an almost onomatopoeic representation of the wind soughing through the trees.

EX. 32

The coda is of particular beauty, a moonweft dream of silver glades.

EX. 33

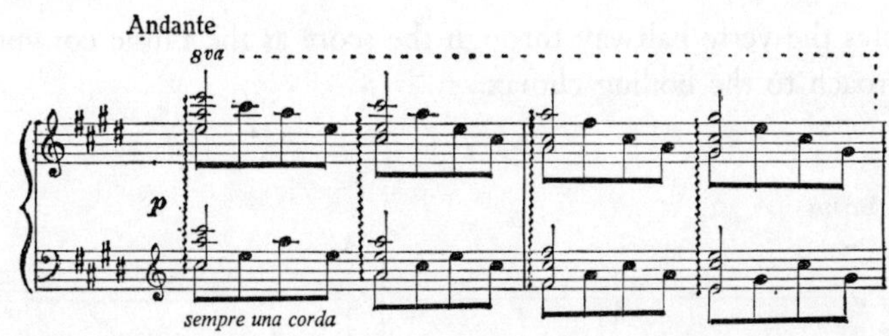

The masterpiece of the set is *Les Jeux d'Eaux à la Villa d'Este* which is superb in its impressionistic atmosphere, and important in being historically *avant-garde*. The cascading, upward-shooting, dominant ninths at the opening set the mood of the entire work.

EX. 34

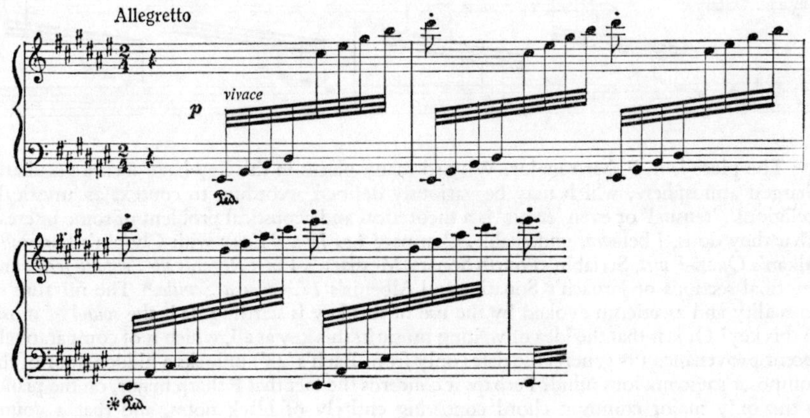

It is said that Liszt was spellbound by the wonderful spectacle of the fountains at the Villa d'Este. The experience affected him so deeply that it resulted in a masterwork of musical impressionism[1] which is so advanced for its time that it had no successor until Ravel composed his own *Jeux d'eau* some thirty years afterwards. The two pieces are worth comparing. But whereas Ravel's piece is 'water music' pure and simple,[2] Liszt has transcended the entire meaning of that kind of visual imagery by turning his cascading fountains into mystical symbols and associating them with the well-known verse from the Gospel according to St. John.

> But whosoever drinketh of the water that I shall give him, shall never thirst; but the water that I shall give him shall be in him a well of water springing up into everlasting life.

Liszt quotes the verse halfway through the score as the music commences its long approach to the boiling climax.

EX. 35

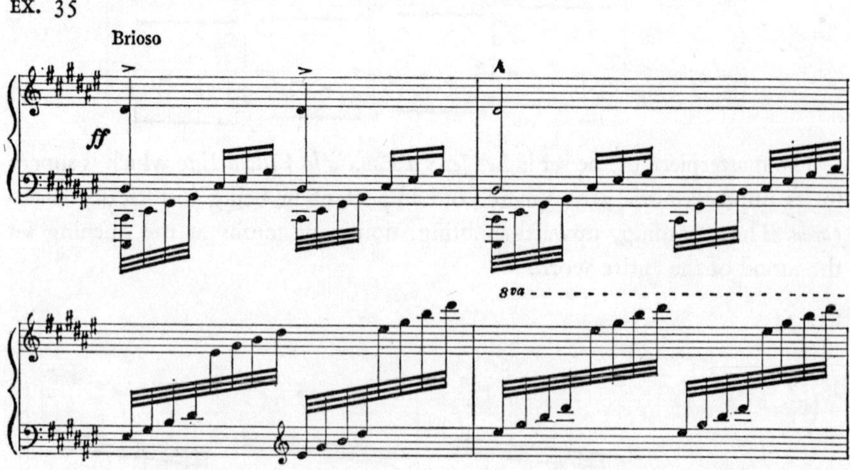

[1] The piece is in F sharp major. Why so many pieces in this key have such a peculiarly charged atmosphere, which may be variously defined according to context as 'mystical', 'religious', 'sensual' or even 'erotic' is a theoretical and acoustical problem of some interest. That they do is, I believe, undeniable. Compare *Les Jeux d'Eaux* with Chopin's *Barcarolle*, Alkan's *Quasi-Faust*, Scriabin's Fourth Sonata, Messiaen's *Vingt Regards sur l'enfant-Jesus*, and the final sections of Jarnach's Sonatina and Albeniz's *Fête-dieu à Seville.** The mixture of sensuality and asceticism evoked by the use of this key is startling. Is it the *sound* of music in this key? Or is it that the idea of writing music in this key at all, which is of comparatively recent provenance (its general use dates only from Bach's '48') unlocks a hidden door of the composer's unconscious mind? Perhaps it concerns the fact that F sharp major, on the piano, is the only major common chord consisting entirely of black notes, and that a young

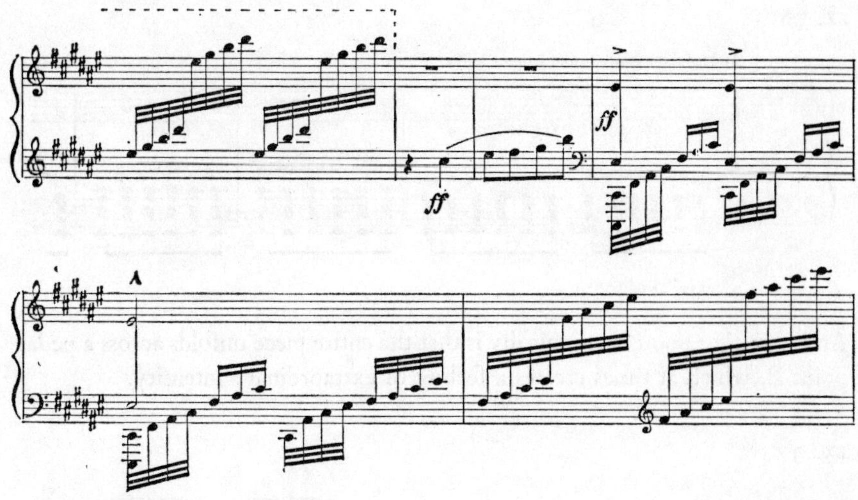

This wonderful work underlines how little justice he did himself when he said: 'How dry and unsatisfactory omnipotent Nature's sonorous laments and sighs sound on the piano.'

The next two pieces in the set, *Sunt Lachrymae Rerum* (which takes its title from the well-known lines of Virgil: 'The sense of tears in mortal things'),[1] and *Marche Funèbre* (composed in memory of the luckless Emperor Maximillian of Mexico, who was shot by insurgents on 19 June, 1867) reveal Liszt's increasing interest in national subjects. The rhythmic and scalic origins of both these works are strongly nationalistic. Both pieces show marked affinities with Bartók, although curiously enough it was the last piece of the set, *Sursam Corda* (with which one would have thought Bartók had less in common) that Bartók actually recorded. The grandiloquent title (which means 'The Heart Above') is one of the sentences intoned in the Latin mass before the singing of the 'Sanctus', and these words are symbolized by Liszt's use of the rising seventh.

---

composer's first explorations of tonality would intuitively place the black notes, in terms of emotional mystery and complexity, at the opposite pole to C major's open simplicity. Suffice it to say that in my view, Liszt, in *Les Jeux d'Eaux*, succumbed to this key as a direct result of the element of mysticism which, as we shall see (p. 156), he wished to express in it.

[2] Ravel inscribes his score with a quotation from Henri de Regnier: 'The river-god laughing at the waters as they caress him.'

* To which might be added Liszt's own *Bénédiction de Dieu dans la Solitude.—Ed.*

[1] *The Aeneid*—Book I.—*Ed.*

EX. 36

An interesting point harmonically is that the entire piece unfolds across a pedal-point E, which at times creates a feeling of extraordinary intensity.

EX. 37
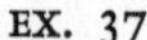

Such impassioned oratory is a fitting close to Liszt's years of pilgrimage, both musical and spiritual.

'Christmas Tree' Suite (1875–76)

The 'Christmas Tree' Suite is a slighter work which Liszt composed during the years 1875–76 for his grand-daughter Daniele von Bülow. There is much to interest both amateurs and professionals in these charming miniatures, some of which are arrangements of old Christmas carols, including 'Good Christian Men Rejoice!' (*In Dulci Jubilo*) and 'O come! all ye faithful!' (*Adeste Fideles!*). The homophony of 'Holy Night' (not to be confused with the other, more famous carol of the same name) reminds us of Liszt's very real interest in medieval music. The unresolved ending of 'Carillon' is entrancing;

EX. 38

while the Scherzo 'Lighting the candles on the Christmas Tree' exemplifies Liszt's resplendent modulations to mediant and submediant. The final pieces use, as Szabolcsi points out, Hungarian and Polish rhythms in homage to Liszt and the Princess Carolyne respectively. Altogether, the suite is a most beautiful, successful and, from Liszt, unexpected composition.

The 'Elegaic' Works

The elegaic compositions of Liszt's old age are numerous. They reflect his increasing obsession with thoughts of death.

Liszt's artistic 'death-fixation' was not a morbid one. He did not fear death. He was a devout Catholic and he derived great strength from his faith. Yet his constant return to 'death themes' takes some explaining. We know too little about the psychology of old age—modern research places the emphasis on the psychology of the young—to say with certainty why a man of Liszt's tremendous vitality and exuberance should undergo such a dramatic personality change in his fifties, and why it should come out in his art. There are dozens of the elegaic works scattered across the last twenty years of Liszt's life; we must assume, therefore, that it was a source of deep comfort and satisfaction to his complex personality to write them, and to keep on writing them. Moreover, some of them happen to be highly original pieces, pieces of extraordinary experiment, which forecast in a quite remarkable manner some of the main trends of twentieth-century music.

Among the many short elegaical sketches of Liszt's old age, the most important single group are the seven *Hungarian Historical Portraits*. Each of these pieces commemorates the death of a Hungarian artist or statesman of the nineteenth century for whom Liszt, in his dedication to the ideals of Hungarian unity, had the greatest admiration. The *Portraits*, in fact, are musical memorials, each one bearing the name of its particular subject. The seven men are:

Széchenyi Istvân
Eőtvős József
Vörősmarty Mihâly
Teleki Lászlő
Deák Ferenc
Petőfi Sándor
Mosonyi Mihláy

Although the *Portraits* were not published as a set until 1956, we know from Liszt's correspondence that he regarded them as a cycle, and the title *Hungarian Historical Portraits* was, in fact, his own. Apart from the mood link between these pieces, the internal unity of the set is further enhanced by the fact that three of them are thematically linked—Séchenyi, Eötvös, and Deák.

The most powerful and telling movement of the set is *Teleki Lászlő* whose tragic political career ended in his suicide in 1861.[1] This elegy, composed in march-style, is based on a four-note *ostinato* ('x') derived from a Gypsy scale.

EX. 39

The tonal ambiguity of the piece—do you hear it in G minor, or do you hear it as a sort of macabre *malagueña* in 4/4 time, on the dominant of B minor—is swept away by the colossal, frightening crescendo and the unstinting use of an orchestral-like tremolando which lend the piece a note of undisguised ferocity.

[1] By a curious coincidence his grandson Pál Teleki, who became Hungary's prime minister in 1920, also committed suicide. He shot himself while still in office in 1921.—*Ed.*

EX. 40

The most poetical of the *Portraits* is the last one, dedicated to Mosonyi who died in 1870. Mosonyi was a minor Hungarian composer and a friend of Liszt's. Liszt once promised to produce his opera 'Kaiser Max' at Weimar, but nothing ever came of the idea. Mosonyi, for his part, was a lifelong champion of Liszt, and Liszt felt deeply enough about him when he died to write this commemorative piece. Here is the beginning of the main idea:

EX. 41

which takes on towering proportions when it is eventually recapitulated.

EX. 42

The *Historical Portraits*, which remain almost totally unplayed, deserve to be better known, for they show Liszt's Hungarian nationalistic sympathies—a fundamental side of his character—as well as anything he ever did.

The two elegies *Lugubre Gondola I and II* (composed in 1882) are premonitive elegies for Wagner, whose body Liszt saw in his mind's eye being carried in funeral cortège in Venice, some months before this event was actually to happen. These 'two pieces' are, in fact, different versions of the same work, and it is fascinating to compare the way Liszt re-works the same musical ideas in two different ways. As far as I know, there is no evidence to suggest that the second version was intended as an alternative to the first one; rather, a consecutive performance of the two pieces is what Liszt probably intended. The latter way is certainly impressive, and it gives us an interesting glimpse into Liszt's creative process. Here is the opening of *Lugubre Gondola I.*

EX. 43

Here is the same passage as the one I have just quoted—in its recomposed version in *Lugubre Gondola II.*

EX. 44

Andante mesto, accentato il canto

mp

With *Unstern!* (Evil Star) we meet a stranger, deeper piece, to which Terence White Gervais's epithet (apropos of Busoni) 'Mefausto', is applicable. Witness Liszt's consistent use of the augmented fourth—*Diabolus in Musica.*

EX. 45

It sounds extraordinarily modern. The opening motif is based on the degrees *III IV VII I* of the C major scale, although the doubled tritone and the doubled leading-note produce an effect that is quite bizarre. At the point '*' an *implied* dominant, in the key of C major, is felt. The fact that it *fails* to materialize is significant; for in the piece's development the long passage over a pedal F *fails* to reach the appropriate resolution chord (an augmented triad on C sharp, two octaves above the chord it started with), and in the climactic re-statement of the opening theme the apotheotic dissonance (*)

EX. 46

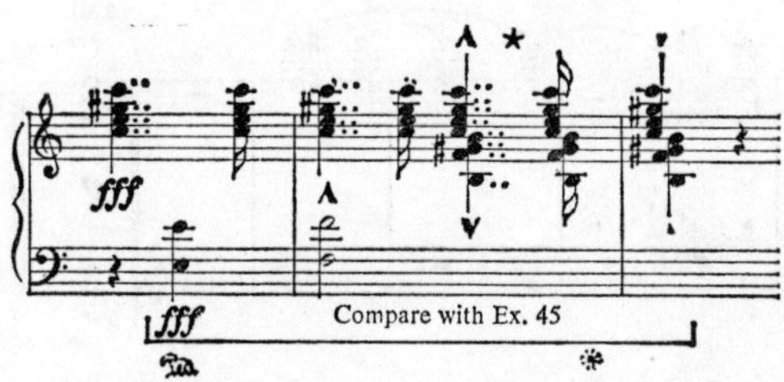

again *fails* to make the expected resolution to C major, and winds its way tortuously to B major instead (Ex. 47) in which key it ends. The whole piece

EX. 47

exemplifies, I believe, what psychologists term a 'frustrated conation'; to this, its uniquely disturbing impact is due. Its final section is a poetical recollection; the earlier pedal point on F now becomes an inverted pedal-point on F sharp and G. The final tonic cadence (in B) *fails* to materialize, as the dominant had *failed* earlier, and the piece literally dies out. A final non-statement of intent.

EX. 48

Some of the elegies take on the character of mood pictures, impressionistic tone-poems almost. This genre, containing the most intimate and touching of all Liszt's works, includes *En Rêve*, a delicate meditation of Mozartian simplicity on a dominant pedal-point, *Vier Kleine Klavierstück* and the *Five Hungarian Folksongs*. These last pieces are a blend of dance and fantasy, charmingly simple—except in notation (Liszt's notation in his Hungarian-inspired works generally maintains its early complexity); a charming *Toccata* slightly foreshadows Debussy's *Tierces Alternées* in its texture, and the wonderful *Nuages Gris* (Grey Clouds) was described as beautiful and perfect by both Debussy and Stravinsky; its wonderous close deserves quotation.

EX. 49

Perhaps the most beautiful and moving of all these short mood pictures is Liszt's 'Farewell' (1885). A combination of two Russian folk-songs, the piece has an incomparable serenity. It is available in England only as an appendix to Szabolcsi's book *The Twilight of Liszt.*

Dance forms

One broad category of works remains for consideration—Liszt's continued use of dance forms in his last years. His lifelong interest in the forms and spirit of dance never deserted him and, indeed, bore fruit in some of the finest of his late works, notably the two *Csàrdàs*, the first two *Valses Oubliées* and the *Third 'Mephisto' Waltz*.

The Csárdâs Macabre is traditional pianistically, but harmonically its opening bare fifths (which are supposed to have been written to irritate Hanslick) are typical of the experiments Liszt engaged upon in his last years.

EX. 50

Do you hear the fifth of the first bar as a flattened supertonic appoggiatura to the second bar, or do you hear it as a real tonic? Such tonal ambiguities are quite common in late Liszt. The structure is a miniature sonata form. Its second theme, appropriately, has a bizarre affinity with the *Dies Irae*; indeed, it was this affinity which prompted Liszt to give the piece its name.

EX. 51

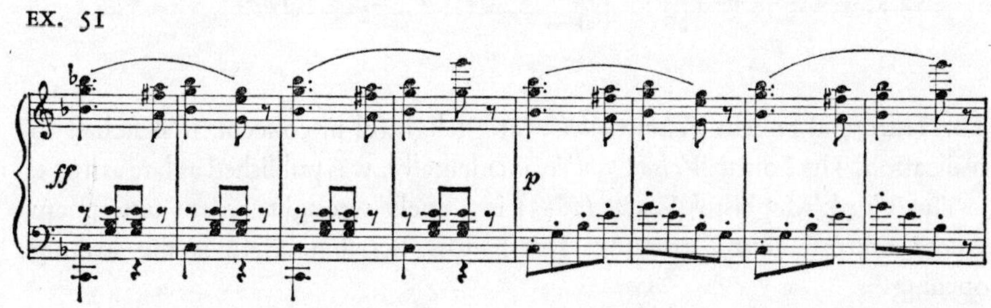

More interesting musically, I think, is the *Csárdâs Obstiné*. This piece is obsessed with a descending four-note notif (x). The splendour of Liszt's tonal excursions into the mediant and submediant, which procedurally lie somewhere between Schumann and Mahler, is memorable. We are reminded of what Liszt did to develop the fields of tonal relationship throughout his life, and of his influence in this respect on Franck, Wagner, Rimsky-Korsakov, Debussy and Ravel.

EX. 52

The four *Valses Oubliées* give the lie to the assertion that Liszt's last years were entirely gloomy. The first, immortalized by Horowitz, is almost Scriabinesque in its mystic watchfulness. An interesting development is the rhythmic refinement underlying the Second *Valse Oubliée*.

EX. 53

The Third and Fourth *Valses Oubliées* are delightful in concept, if sketchier in realization. The Fourth *Valse Oubliée*, incidentally, was published as late as 1955.

The Third 'Mephisto' Waltz (1883) is a finely wrought, ardent tone-poem whose unusual chord structures foreshadow Scriabin. Here is the striking opening.[1]

EX. 54

[1] See p. 360 for more comment on this remarkable passage.—*Ed.*

Again, the question arises: how do you hear it? It could be based on the dominant of F sharp major; but it could also be based on the tonic of A sharp (= B flat) minor. In fact, Liszt lends yet a further twist to it: after unfolding most of the Waltz in F sharp major, he quiets the passage in D sharp minor—in which key the Waltz unexpectedly ends.

EX. 55

Liszt's harmonic, scalic and melodic experiments are magnificently integrated in this work, while the piano writing has a sulphuric fitfulness which deservedly ranks the piece with its more famous predecessor.

*

What is the significance of Liszt's approach to composition in the last twenty-five years of his life? I should say that more than any other musician, Liszt was responsible for breaking the Germanic stranglehold on nineteenth-century composers, and scattering the seeds of modern music almost literally to the four winds. His music shows an *avant-garde* attitude to the problems of composing which was without parallel in the nineteenth century. But what I think I admire most about the aged Liszt is his continuing humility in the face of so splendid an achievement. He lived out his extraordinary life as if guided by the words that William Golding was to write eighty years later: 'There's a kinship among men who have sat by a dying fire and measured the worth of their life by it.'[1]

[1] *The Spire:* William Golding.

DAVID WILDE

Transcriptions for Piano

LISZT wrote one hundred and ninety-three transcriptions for the piano, of which forty-eight were re-arrangements of his own music; the rest were derived from a variety of different sources, from Bach to Wagner. They divide into two main types: *paraphrases*, in which the original work is transformed and freely recomposed; and *partitions*, in which Liszt faithfully transcribes a work from one medium to another, sometimes not deviating from the original by so much as a single note. The earliest example is of the first type, the *Fantasie sur la Tyroliènne de l'opera 'La Fiancée par Auber'* composed in 1829, when Liszt was eighteen. The last example is of the second type, a transcription of Cui's Tarantella which Liszt made in 1885, a year before his death. The fifty-six years between the two saw immense changes in music, in Liszt's own outlook, in the social conditions and attitudes of the period, and in the piano itself, which has changed little since Liszt died, but which was almost unrecognizably different when he was born.

Let us look now at some of the factors which led to Liszt's immense productivity in this field, and the inevitable differences between his criteria of relevant musical standards and ours.

Purely practical considerations have often initiated important artistic achievements. While Liszt's transcriptions, at their best, transcend the purely utilitarian role which has often been claimed for them, there can be little doubt that his burning desire to bring inaccessible music to the people was nevertheless an important motivating factor. In the preface to his sober and respectful transcriptions of the Beethoven Symphonies, Liszt makes this quite clear. He writes:

> The name of Beethoven is sacred in art. His Symphonies are now universally acknowledged to be masterpieces . . . For this reason every way or manner of making them accessible and popular has a certain merit . . .

If we consider the differences between music-making in Liszt's day and in ours, we see at once how urgent was the need that Liszt was anxious to meet. Today, there is no practical reason why everybody should not be acquainted with the whole world of music, from Monteverdi and Byrd, to Dallapiccola and Britten. Quite apart from broadcast and recorded music, which is available everywhere, many cities have symphony orchestras of excellent quality, and almost every town has its music club, visited regularly by professional musicians of high calibre. Travel is relatively easy and quick, enabling listeners and players to come together with a frequency which was unthinkable a hundred years ago. How different was the situation in Liszt's day! Then, every performance was heard once only, and only by the small number of people present at the time, and travel was too expensive and difficult for orchestras to journey about as they do now.

Together with Liszt's desire to bring acknowledged masterpieces to a wider public went a desire to put his glamorous reputation at the disposal of his less fortunate colleagues, by introducing his own versions of their music into his recital programmes. The charge against Liszt that 'he couldn't keep his hands off other people's music' is therefore unjust, and there is evidence to suggest that some, at least, of the composers whose music he is said to have molested were grateful for his trouble. Here, for instance, is part of a letter[1] from Meyerbeer, concerning No. 1 of Liszt's set of 'Illustrations' of Meyerbeer's *Le Prophète*, composed in 1849–50. The letter is dated 8 February 1852.

> Dear and illustrious colleague,
>
> Monsieur Schlesinger has spoken to me about a letter you wrote him in which you say that you have composed a large piano composition on the Anabaptists' hymn from 'Le Prophète', and that you intend to dedicate this work to me when it is published, but first you wish to write to me directly.
>
> I shall not wait for the arrival of that letter to tell you how happy I am that one of my songs impresses you as worthy to be used as a motif for one of your piano compositions, destined to be heard throughout Europe and intoxicate those who have the good fortune to hear them played by your wonderful, poetic fingers. However, I feel even more honoured at the mark of sympathy you offer me in dedicating your work to me, for if it is an honour to see my name linked with yours, it is even more agreeable to me that you make it known in this manner that we are friends.

[1] *Letters of Composers:* an Anthology by Miriam Shrifte and Gertrude Norman, New York, 1946, p. 107.

Given, then, the practical motivation behind them, it is understandable that the transcriptions fell into neglect and disrepute when improved conditions made them no longer necessary. However, there would now seem to be a case for re-considering them as musical creations in their own right.

As a starting-point, we could hardly do better than to quote Busoni's thoughts on the subject. They are very far-reaching. In answer to the charge that transcriptions take undue liberties with the original, Busoni points out that in Variation Form (generally considered 'legitimate') departure from the original is regarded as a virtue; whereas in Transcription (considered 'illegitimate') it is regarded as a vice. This is a revealing contradiction. Equally revealing is the following declaration:

> The human being can certainly not create, he can only employ what is in existence on the earth. And for the musician there are sounds and rhythms in existence.[1]

In other words, music exists independently of the composer, a thought which is in line with observations by composers of widely differing persuasions. Elgar is reported to have said that one must 'pluck music out of the air'; Rachmaninov, we are told, regarded himself as a medium of transmission rather than as a point of origin; and Stravinsky has said: 'I am the vessel through which "Le Sacre du Printemps" passed.' All these thoughts seem to suggest that the art of transcription does not differ radically from the art of composition. Originality is relative anyway, and composers who try to be absolutely original succeed only in becoming totally incomprehensible.

Clearly, these ideas relate more to the art of *paraphrase* than to the art of *partition*, and Liszt was evidently aware of the difference. I quote again from his Preface to the *partition* of the Beethoven symphonies.

> My aim has been attained if I stand on a level with the intelligent engraver, the conscientious translator, who comprehend the spirit of a work . . .

According to Sir Donald Tovey, Liszt's aim was indeed attained.

> The arrangements (of Beethoven's symphonies) . . . prove conclusively . . . that Liszt was by far the most wonderful interpreter of orchestral scores on the pianoforte the world is ever likely to see.[2]

[1] *The Essence of Music*, London, p. 89.
[2] Sir Donald Tovey: *Essays in Musical Analysis*, Vol. 1, p. 193.

The Beethoven Symphonies

Let us start with the Introduction to the First Symphony. Liszt wrote two versions of the first four bars. In the first version, the range of pitch is confined to close position, omitting the flutes and eliding some of the inner parts. In the alternative version, however, the range is as wide as in Beethoven's original, and the harmony is complete.

EX. I

The main problem in transcribing these bars is to imitate sustained woodwinds and pizzicato strings, simultaneously. Liszt suggests the pizzicato by a spread leap in the left hand—aptly, since orchestral plucking often gives the impression of being slightly spread and ahead of the wind instruments. But in the first version the left hand leaps to a single C, while in the 'Ossia' it leaps to a four-note chord, of which the two lowest notes also belong to the plucked strings, and are written as quavers. The second chord is also more complete in the 'Ossia' and is, like the first, preceded by a pizzicato bass leap. I believe it was probably this second chord which made Liszt think again, since in the first version he has been compelled to abandon the sustained horn C, so leaving the second chord without a fifth. This, and the inclusion of the flute parts which give such spaciousness to the original, make the 'Ossia' preferable, though more difficult. Throughout the Symphonies, there are places where, as here, Liszt has written two possible versions.

Another interesting passage in the First Symphony is the Trio to the third movement. Liszt writes the wind chords at the beginning exactly as in the original, on two staves, marked 'Una Corda'. At the sixth bar, he writes the violin parts, divided between the hands, on a third stave, while the wind chord

EX. 2

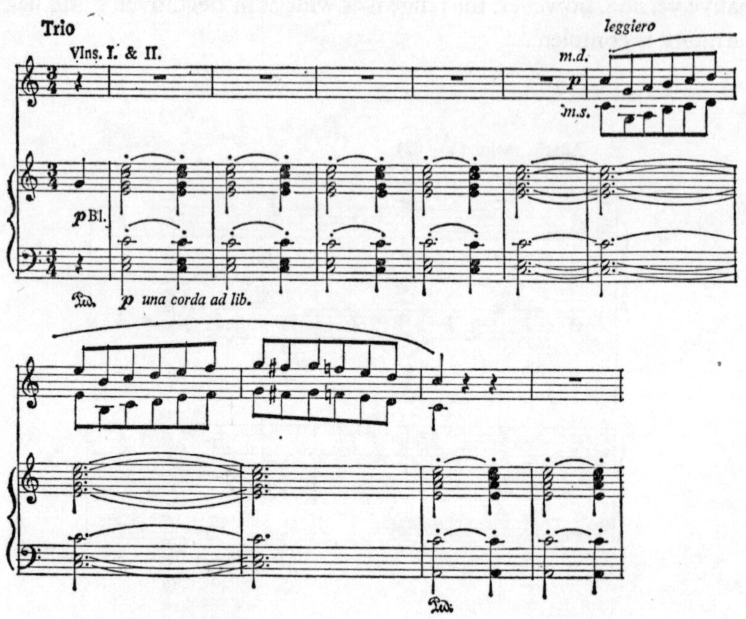

is still sustained. As it stands, this passage is virtually impossible without the modern 'sostenuto' pedal, which Liszt never knew. Typically, Liszt would not allow himself an easy compromise as, for instance, in this routine arrangement of the same passage.

EX. 3

TRIO

p

p.

Ped.

Instead, he wrote down his ideal, in the hope that one day it might be achieved —as indeed it has.

The 'Eroica' Symphony presents a challenge which must have delighted the romantic Liszt, who matches Beethoven's grand concept with piano writing in the grand manner. The 'hero' of this transcription of the Symphony might well be the pianist. Although, as we shall see, Liszt took great care over preserving the part-writing where it is vital to the sense, he was not pedantic about this. He was aware that the true sound was to be discovered not in the exact notes as written in the score, but in the complex of instrumental timbres, whose upper partials can combine to create aural illusions not evident on paper. The opening chords of the 'Eroica' are an example of this kind of 'sense for sense', rather than 'word for word', translation. Liszt transfers the spread chords for the violins to the bass,

EX. 4

and writes a pianistic 'tenth' chord which includes the fifth (B flat) two octaves lower than its counterpart, in Beethoven's original, on the first violins. Also Liszt puts G at the top, knowing that the ear selects this (played by the first oboe and first violins) as the 'melody' note, despite the B flat and E flat played above it by the flutes. In contrast, many routine arrangements merely have a chord of E flat, close root position, in each hand, with E flat at the top.

In the following passage, a single line is divided among sharply contrasted instruments. Liszt writes out the original melody as it stands, marks the instrumentation (as he often does) and separates the phrases by writing stems alternately up and down.

EX. 5

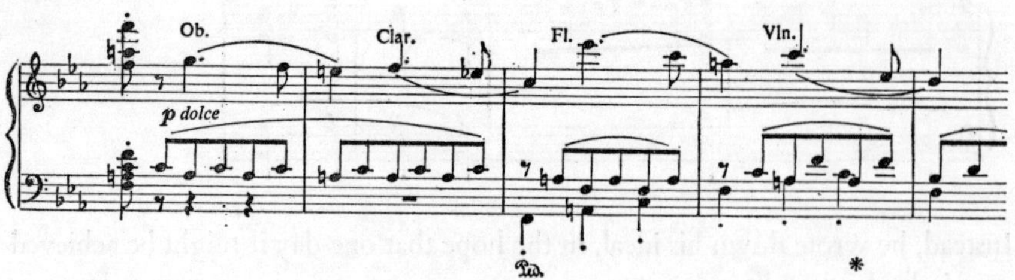

Similar procedures are to be found throughout the Symphonies. A glance through them reveals very few 'block' chords; instead, there is a great deal of careful placing of note-stems to clarify the part-writing. This can be complicated, but it is never confused. Here is an example from the 'Funeral March' of the 'Eroica'.

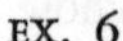
EX. 6

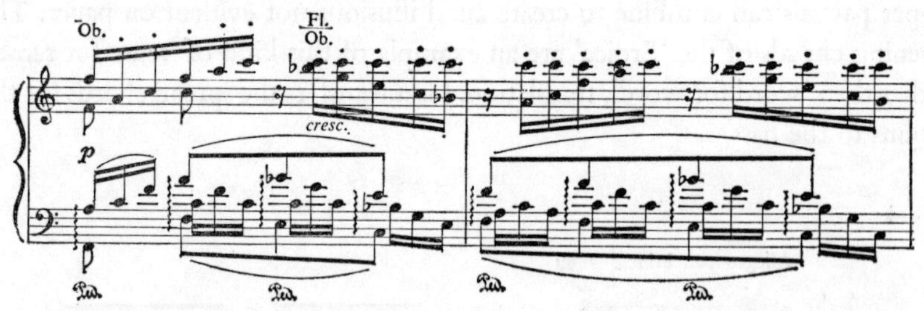

Occasionally, Liszt adds a third stave above the normal two, and writes on it either a part of the original he finds impossible to include in the arrangement, or (as in this instance from the finale of the 'Eroica') the original version of a passage he has been compelled to alter.

EX. 7

The slow movement of the Fourth Symphony is a marvellous example of imaginative re-thinking. Throughout the movement, Liszt has apparently absorbed every detail of the original and created it again in pianistic terms. To describe the results of this process in detail would merely be boring. Time and again, Liszt's part-writing approximates to the original so effectively as to deceive the listener into believing that nothing has been changed. In purely mechanical terms, a great deal has been changed, but nothing, or surprisingly little, has been lost.

EX. 8

This movement may be said to epitomize the whole problem of the 'Partition' as Liszt saw it.

> I confess that I should have to consider it a rather useless employment of my time, if I had but added one more to the numerous hitherto published piano-arrangements, following in their rut; but I consider my time well employed if I have succeeded in transferring to the piano not only the grand outlines of Beethoven's compositions but also all those numerous fine details, and smaller traits that so powerfully contribute to the completion of the ensemble.[1]

It is a question, then, not of fitting as much as possible into two staves and two hands, but of abstracting the sense and re-casting it in terms applicable to the new medium. This is a task which demands not only a complete knowledge of the works, and mastery of both the orchestra and the piano, but the ability to distinguish between that which is essential to the musical concept, and must be retained, and that which is special to the orchestra, and must be re-thought. This re-thinking, we must remember, was undertaken by the supreme master of the piano, and it often results in immense technical difficulties. Sometimes the

[1] From Liszt's Preface to his Partitions of the Beethoven symphonies.

element of difficulty already exists in the orchestral writing, as for instance in the notorious cello and double-bass octave passage from the Scherzo of the Fifth Symphony, presented in Liszt's version as an equally difficult octave passage for the left hand.

EX. 9

At other times, it occurs in the process of adaptation, as in this excerpt from the first movement of the 'Pastoral'.

EX. 10

Sometimes Liszt seems to introduce an element of difficulty deliberately, as if to prevent too facile an interpretation. In the middle section of the 'Peasants' Merry-Making' from the 'Pastoral', for instance, he doubles both violin and flute parts in octaves.

EX. 11

Of course, the greatest challenge of all is the 'Choral' Symphony; indeed, Liszt seriously doubted if the last movement could be transcribed at all. On 14 September 1864 he wrote to Brietkopf and Härtel as follows:

> After various endeavours one way and another, I became inevitably and distinctly convinced of the impossibility of making any pianoforte arrangement of the 4th movement for *two hands*, that could in any way be even approximately effective or satisfactory. I trust you will not bear me any ill-will for failing in this, and that you will consider my work with the Beethoven Symphonies as concluded with the 3rd movement of the 9th, for it was not a part of my task to provide a simple *pianoforte score* of this overwhelming 4th movement for the use of chorus directors. Arrangements of this kind have already been made, and I maintain that I am *not* able to furnish a better or a more satisfactory one for helpless pianofortes and pianists, and I believe that there is no one nowadays who could manage it.

The crux of the matter is in the words 'for two hands', for Liszt goes on to point out that in his version for two pianos, prepared for Schott, he gave the 'orchestra-polyphony' to one piano, and the chorus parts to the other: 'But to screw both parts, the instrumental and vocal, into two hands cannot be done either *à peu près* or *à beaucoup près*!'

Breitkopf and Härtel, however, were not so easily put off, and in response to their insistence, Liszt agreed, in a letter dated 1 October 1864, that he would 'again make an attempt to "adapt" the 4th movement of the 9th Symphony

EX. 12

to the piano'. He referred to the project, doubtfully, as 'the required *tentative*' and hoped that the proverb 'Tant y a la cruche à l'eau qu'a la fin . . . *elle s'emplit*'[1] might prove true.

In the version which he eventually submitted, Liszt wrote out the vocal parts throughout the finale on separate staves above the piano part, thus leaving the pianist in no doubt about the texture (Ex. 12).

It is impossible, in a single essay, to do justice to such an undertaking as this partition of the 'Choral' Symphony, or, indeed, to those of any of the Beethoven symphonies. It is worth noting, however, that numbers five, six, and seven were already finished by 1837, that is, when Liszt was twenty-six; the Funeral March of the 'Eroica' was completed by 1843, when he was thirty-two; the remainder were completed in 1863 and 1864, and the complete collection was published in Rome in 1865. These facts contradict the popular notion that Liszt's early years were spent entirely on frivolities, and that only in later life did he take his talents seriously enough. For the rest, I commend Liszt's 'Partitions' of the Beethoven symphonies to the reader. It is doubtful whether there is any point in playing them today in the concert hall in view of the marvellous orchestral performances so readily available, and the vastly increased repertoire of original music for the piano. But they repay study. They can give insight, both into the piano and into the symphonies themselves.

The Bach Transcriptions

The arrangements of Bach's organ works are as literal as could be. They are a special case, because Bach's originals are already conceived in terms of the keyboard. Liszt's problem was to substitute the piano's main advantage over the organ—the sustaining pedal—for the organ's main advantage over the piano—the pedal keyboard. He resolved the problem with no fuss, and without imposing his own personality. Curiously, he has not always been praised for doing so. Max Reger, for instance, in a letter to Busoni dated 11 May, 1895, writes: 'It's too bad that Franz Liszt did such a bad job on his transcriptions of Bach's organ pieces—they're nothing but hackwork'.[2] Paradoxically, 'hack-work' is not far off the mark, but not in Reger's sense of the term. The fact that Liszt was content to undertake this routine task, suppressing his own gigantic personality in the interests of Bach's music, was an act of humility with few parallels in the nineteenth century. Here is part of the Fugue in A minor.

[1] 'So often goes the pitcher to water that at last it is filled.'
[2] Schrifte and Norman, *op. cit.*, p. 336.

EX. 13

Liszt adheres scrupulously to Bach's original, not so much as adding a single phrase or dynamic marking.

The large number of partitions which remain range from the towering *Symphonie Fantastique* of Berlioz,[1] to the many relatively small-scale song transcriptions, some of which I will now discuss.

Song Arrangements

In his song arrangements, Liszt stands midway between the 'partition' and the 'paraphrase', and the degree of departure from the original differs among the songs. This 'half-way house' presented aesthetic problems which were not always solved; see, for instance, the quaint 'echo' effect in Schubert's Serenade, or the exaggerated grandeur of his Ave Maria. In addition to Schubert, these arrangements include songs by Beethoven (including the whole of the cycle *An die ferne Geliebte*), Chopin, Mendelssohn, Schumann, and Liszt himself.

Beethoven seemed to bring out the best in Liszt, and his version of *An die ferne Geliebte* shows the same respect and discretion which characterize the Symphonies. The arrangements of songs by Liszt's contemporaries, Chopin and Schumann, are amongst the most effective. Of Schubert's songs, those which are dramatic (e.g. *Die junge Nonne*), or fanciful (*Hark, Hark! the Lark*), and those in which the piano figuration is already florid and significant in the original (*Auf dem Wasser zu singen*) tend to be more successful; those of lyrical simplicity less so.

Die junge Nonne is a literal transcription.[2] The introduction is exactly as Schubert wrote it. When the voice enters, however, Liszt is faced with the problem of how to separate it from the piano part, without placing it too high

[1] See pp. 43–44.—*Ed.*

[2] The only change is in the final 'Alleluja!', where Liszt alters Schubert's inconclusive ending on the mediant to a more final (and, to my ear, more banal) ending on the tonic.

and thus anticipating the later dramatic tension. His solution is to continue the bass octaves of the introduction into the melodic line, so that at any point of the melody either the top or the bottom note of the octave is independent of the accompaniment. Compare Schubert's version with Liszt's (Exx. 14*a* and *b*).

Liszt often makes a virtue of this kind of necessity, as, for instance, at the words 'Und finster die Nacht'. Here, he has to bring the bass octave, the tremolo, and the voice part (which together span three-and-a-half octaves) within the scope of the two hands. He does so by altering the tremolo pattern from close to open position, divided between the overlapping hands, and holding the bass octave with the pedal. The result is a radical change of colour at just the moment the song requires it.

EX. 15

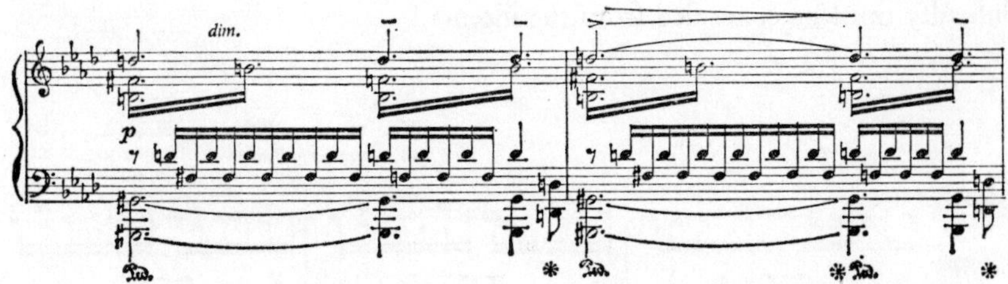

Not until the strong declaration of faith contained in the words 'Nun tobe du wilder gewalter Sturm' does Liszt expand the piano sonorities, doubling both the tremolo and the tune in octaves, and filling out the bass harmonies. To my mind, this is just acceptable—the song can take this degree of grandiosity, and no more. More questionable, perhaps, is the doubling of the melody in triads at 'Es lockt mich das süsse Getöh', but here, too, Liszt could find justification in the words.

With a strophic song like *Auf dem wasser zu singen* Liszt is freer to employ the variation techniques which lie at the heart of the operatic fantasies. Here, Liszt uses each of the three stanzas of the original song to explore a different way of solving the pianistic problem. He seems less concerned with the expression contained in the words, and more with the instrumental sonorities suggested by the figuration in the accompaniment. The tune is played an octave higher in each stanza, with accumulative effect, and then Liszt adds a fourth stanza of his own, expanding the sonorities far beyond the limits of the original, introducing great rolling bass figures, menacing broken octaves, and joyous leaps. This piece is not so much an arrangement as a piano study derived from the song.

EX. 16

Particularly fine is *Gretchen am Spinnrade*, a song which combines dramatic content with a florid accompaniment. Like much of Liszt's piano music, *Gretchen* can suffer from too much conscious 'virtuosity' on the part of the player. It is not a display piece, but a miniature tone-poem, whose technical difficulty must be concealed from the listener.[1]

EX. 17

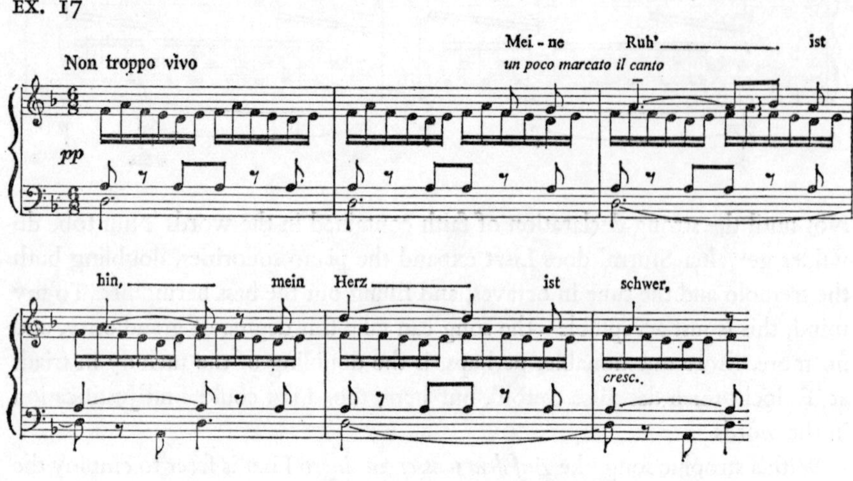

Operatic Transcriptions

The greatest variety of composers are represented in the operatic transcriptions, which treat a vast range of styles, from Mozart to Meyerbeer, in a number of different ways. Some are arrangements of passages from operas as they stand, as, for instance, the 'Liebestod' from *Tristan and Isolde*; some, like the *Tannhäuser* Overture, are, in effect, 'Partitions' of orchestral pieces; others, like the 'Tarantella' from Auber's *La Muette de Portici*, are short bravura studies, while the true paraphrases are in all sorts of styles and lengths. Sometimes Liszt merely juxtaposes two contrasting scenes, as in the Waltz from Gounod's *Faust*; sometimes he writes vast extravaganzas like the *Don Juan* and *Norma* Reminiscences; and then he surprises us with the slow and contemplative *Réminiscences de Boccanegra*.

In the operatic transcriptions, more than in any others, Liszt explores aspects of piano technique which were then new and are still challenging. Indeed, this part of his output provided him with a piano workshop as important to the growth of his ideas—and therefore to the history of pianism—as the 'Transcendental' Studies. Fixing his imagination on realms of sound which seemed irrelevant to the physical nature of the instrument before him, Liszt managed

[1] It would be difficult to imagine a better performance than that recorded by Egon Petri (Columbia LX 739).

to discover ways of overcoming the limitations of fingers, wood, felt, and steel, which perhaps even he could not have found by contemplating the piano alone.

Consider, for instance, his treatment of the descending string passages in the *Tannhäuser* Overture—already a startling innovation in Wagner's original. Liszt writes an octave followed by a single note in place of each pair of octaves; but the mental ear provides the missing note. The result is far more powerful and less strenuous than two complete octaves would be, and the natural gesture, of passing the hand over the thumb, ensures the appropriate phrasing.

EX. 18

This was written in 1848. Years later, we find Brahms developing this device still further, to produce a glittering cascade of sound, in his 'Paganini' Variations.

EX. 19

In *Tannhäuser*, Liszt was concerned with finding a direct pianistic equivalent to an orchestral effect. In the free fantasies, however, he set himself a much bigger task, that of re-creating in pianistic terms his own impressions of the opera concerned, as an imaginative concept. Liszt's colossal mastery of pianistic means enabled him to give full rein to his equally colossal imagination.

Let us now consider one of the finest and most elaborate of these works, the Reminiscences of Bellini's *Norma*. It was composed in 1841, during the active lifetime of Chopin, Schumann, and Mendelssohn. In it, Liszt employs techniques of piano writing not used by these composers, and prophesies many later developments. These techniques can be divided roughly into the following categories:

1. Effects dependent on the sustaining pedal
2. Effects dependent on the 'double escapement' and involving repeated notes
3. Rapid octave work and leaps
4. Rapidly changing chords and double notes.

All these are combined in various ways.[1]

It is difficult to be sure what Liszt meant by the title 'Reminiscences'. Was

[1] While it is clear that these new departures presented a physical challenge to the player, some of them also presented a challenge to the designers of instruments. In fact they may be further grouped into two types: those presenting a primarily acoustical and mechanical problem (numbers 1 and 2), in which the player has to master the mechanism and judge the sound, and those presenting a primarily physiological problem (numbers 3 and 4), in which he has to conquer the limitations of his own body. To put it another way, it is technically possible for a skilled pianist to play rapid octaves and some double note passages on a Cristofori piano of 1709. But rapid repetition, and effects in which notes must be free to sound after the hand has left them are not possible on instruments made before the invention of the double escapement and the sustaining pedal respectively.

The sustaining pedal was first introduced by Adam Beyer in 1777, and was adopted,

it the public who were invited to remember an opera which they were presumed to know? Or was it Liszt himself who was reminiscing? Perhaps he meant it both ways; but I like to think of him elated after a thrilling opera performance, returning to his piano and using his gigantic talents to express for his own pleasure the excitement he felt. This idea seems to be supported by some slight, and apparently pointless, deviations from the original, which suggest the sort of dreamy approximations which might have occurred to Liszt as he sat at his piano. It could account, too, for the fact that although Liszt's piece begins at the beginning of the opera, and ends (more or less) at the end, the sequence of events between the two is altered—rather as one might recall the moment of tension as the curtain rose, and the excitement of the finale, touching (but not necessarily in order) on the most memorable incidents between the two.

Norma begins with an introduction in G minor—a piece of sombre mood setting involving some characteristic diminished sevenths, a menacing bass 'tremolo', and a diabolical flourish which seems to prophesy the First 'Mephisto' Waltz (1860). It suggests, but does not literally quote, the opening of Bellini's Overture.

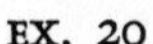

developed, and, in 1873, patented by Broadwood. Cristofori added a 'check' to his action in 1726, and this paved the way for Érard's 'double escapement' of 1821 (when Liszt was already ten years old). We have become so used to the standardization of pianos that it may come as a surprise to learn how many factors, now regarded as universal, were still in question in Liszt's day. For instance, as late as 1856 felt was only one of a range of possible hammer coverings, of which others included sponge, india-rubber, gutta-percha, and leather-covered cork!

The first all-metal frame was patented by Babcock of Boston, U.S.A., in 1825, but took many years to gain universal recognition. William Pole, describing pianos exhibited at the Great Exhibition of 1851, complained of the 'growing tendency to use too much metal in the construction of pianos'.

An interesting example of an early Bösendorfer is to be seen in the Goldmark museum at Kesthely in Hungary. Built in the 1840s, this piano has a hammer-stroke set back-to-front, and dampers operating from below. In contrast, the Chickering grand built for Liszt in 1886 and now kept in the Liszt Museum in Budapest is like a modern piano, except that the middle pedal (for single note 'sostenuto' effects nowadays) is a sustaining pedal for the lower half of the instrument. It seems, then, that in writing music such as the 'Norma Reminiscences' in 1841, Liszt was not only taking the maximum advantage of the piano as it was, but was pointing the way for later developments.

The main part of the work begins in G major. The whole of the succeeding passage is based on the two contrasting ideas in the opera's Introductory Chorus *Ite sul colle, e Druidi*. The first of these ideas rises expansively over a 'treading' bass;

EX. 21

while the second, after a meandering link passage and a cascade of octaves, is of a martial character, and is marked 'Allegro deciso'.

EX. 22

As in the opera, one of the motifs in the Allegro deciso occurs in a gentler form (marked 'nobilmente') in the first part of this section. Ex. 22 is followed by a series of bravura studies in free variation form.

Next, we hear again the Introduction, but this time, for heightened tension, stated a semitone higher, in G sharp minor. There follows a recitative, which leads to the next section in B minor, marked 'Andante con agitazione'.

EX. 23

Andante con agitazione
sempre legato

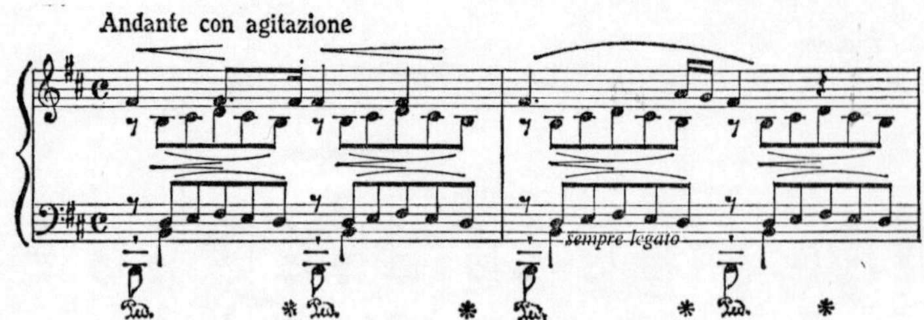

This is based on the first part of Norma's aria *Deh! non volerli vittime*. This, and the next theme, *Qual cor tradisti*, in B major, are taken from the finale of the opera where they occur in the reverse order. Surely the combined geniuses of Bellini and Liszt have produced, in this section, one of the most sublime passages in Romantic piano music.

EX. 24

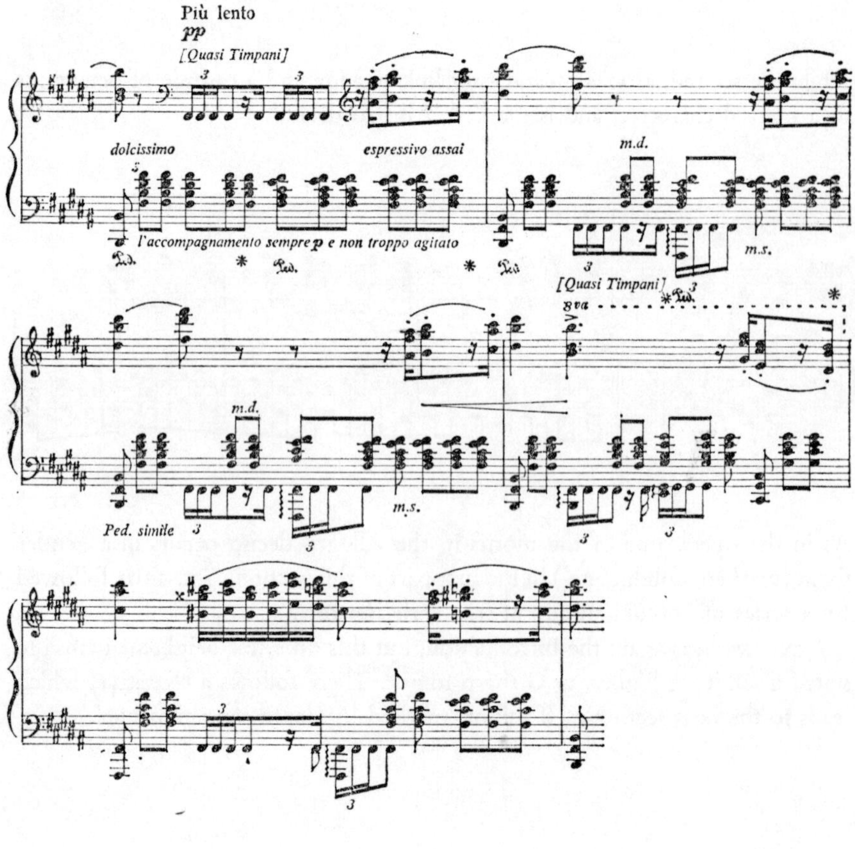

Più lento
pp
[Quasi Timpani]
dolcissimo
espressivo assai
l'accompagnamento sempre p e non troppo agitato
m.d.
m.s.
[Quasi Timpani]
8va
Ped. simile

Busoni remarked that 'anyone who has listened to or played . . . the middle section in B major in the 'Reminiscences' of Bellini's *Norma* without being moved has not yet arrived at Liszt'. Whether or not the reverse is true would not be for me to say, but when I first encountered the piece, it was this passage which transported and absorbed me for days. Quite apart from the beauty of the musical thought, for which Bellini must take much of the credit, this episode is a kaleidoscope of piano sonorities. Throughout the passage, Liszt makes the fullest use of the sustaining pedal. As elsewhere in this work, Liszt adopts the pedalling techniques originated by his rival Thalberg, who also composed operatic fantasies. The main difference between the Thalberg–Liszt approach to the sustaining pedal and that of their contemporaries and predecessors is that, whereas other composers used it to liberate the right hand, Thalberg and Liszt used it to liberate both. The result is either a clear three-handed effect, or, as in *Qual cor tradisti* (Ex. 24) a continuous sonority throughout the keyboard, in which the listener has little idea which hand is playing at any given moment. Thalbergian pedalling may be likened to juggling with three balls. They are kept constantly on the move, and at least one of them is in the air all the time.

EX. 25

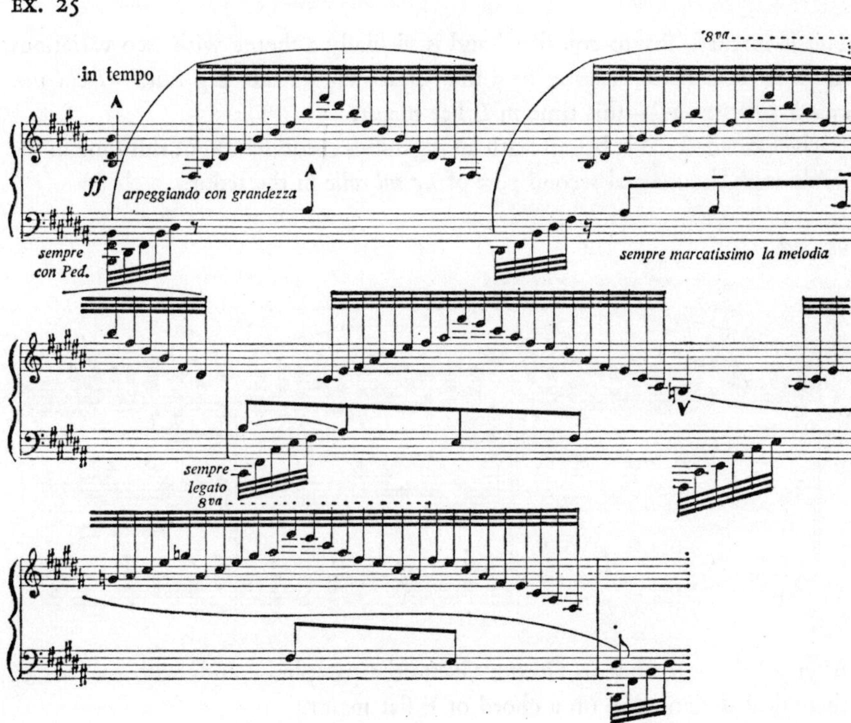

However, far from saying 'Look how clever I am', the performer must conceal his skill and leave the listener free to enjoy the continuous stream of shimmering sounds. Liszt now uses *Deh! non volerli vittime* as the basis of a grandioso melody in B major, surrounded by a swirling mass of sound covering virtually the whole range of the instrument (Ex. 25).

A transition passage follows in two sections. The first is based on part two of *Deh! non volerli*, and the second (marked 'Tempestuoso') on the chorus *Guerra, Guerra* (also from the finale), from which is derived the next section, in E flat minor.

EX. 26

This is marked 'Presto con furia' and is virtually a theme with two variations and a short codetta, leading to a final statement of the 'big tune'—*Deh! non volerli* (see Ex. 25)—this time in E flat major.

The extended Coda begins with an ingenious combination of this tune in the treble with the martial second part of *Ite sul colle* in the tenor.

EX. 27

After a brief reference to *Guerra, Guerra* the paraphrase ends with six bars of rhetorical declamation on a chord of E flat major.

Section by section, *Norma* gradually accumulates energy. A glance at the key-scheme helps to show why. The three tonalities involved outline the

EX. 28

G minor	G major	B minor	B major	E flat minor	E flat major
Intro.	'Ite sul colle' [bars 28 - 144]	'Deh ! Non Volerli' [bars 171 - 187]	'Qual cor tradisti' and 'Deh ! Non Volerli' [bars 190 - 238]	'Guerra, Guerra' [bars 249 - 331]	'Deh ! Non Volerli' and Coda [bars 332 - 372]

augmented triad of G, B and D sharp (= E flat), and each section begins in the dark minor mode and progresses to the brighter major mode. The total effect is one of gradually lightening mood until the work finishes in a blaze of glory. (This, by the way, is contrary to the opera's tragic ending, and suggests, again, that Liszt was recalling his own enthusiastic response to a specific performance, rather than the opera score itself.) The tonality of B is the halfway point in his scheme, and it is the point at which Liszt suspends the action with his incredibly beautiful version of *Qual cor tradisti*. In Italian song, as in Welsh, the major third is often given a wistful, far-away quality, and Liszt captures this mood by mounting Bellini's melody (whose opening phrases are themselves centred on the mediant), in a tonal frame of B, a major third away from the opening tonality of G.

Liszt's fascination with the Faust legend is well known,[1] and it is not surprising that, in 1861, he paraphrased part of Gounod's opera. Although he calls this paraphrase 'Waltz', it contains a contrasting middle section comprising two other scenes. The popular waltz-theme itself is treated very freely. In the original, the first idea exploits the various positions of a single, major triad, breaking them up into a striking rhythmic pattern, leaving Liszt free to apply this pattern to any chords he chooses without obscuring the tune.

EX. 29

[1] See Louis Kentner, p. 101, and Humphrey Searle, p. 314.—*Ed.*

So we find all kinds of harmonic sequences broken up rhythmically in the same way as Gounod's major triad. Compare Ex. 29 with Ex. 30.

EX. 30

To some extent, the same is true of the second idea. A vivid rhythmic pattern in the original is retained as the foundation on which to build more adventurous harmonic sequences later on. Compare Ex. 31*a* with Ex. 31*b*.

EX. 31

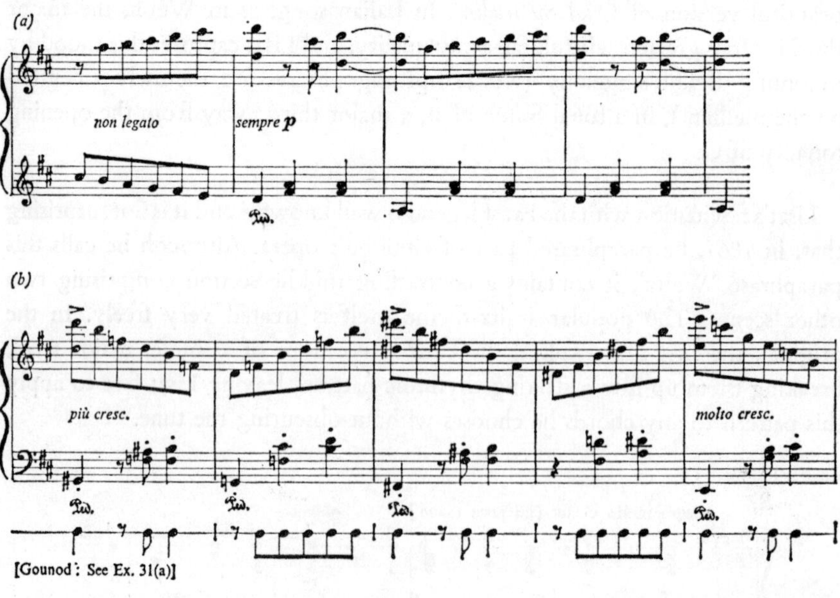

With his harmonic imagination thus released by the static nature of the original, Liszt revels in the colourful modulations like a child moulding clay or making sand-pies—the ultimate shape matters little, it's joy in the material that counts. The piece contains some delicious touches, as, for instance, at the

Gaëtano Donizetti (1797–1848)

Giacomo Meyerbeer (1791–1864)

Vincenzo Bellini (1801–35)

Gioaccino Rossini (1792–1868)

FANTAISIES AND RÉMINISCENCES
Four Composers who inspired Liszt's Operatic Paraphrases

ABBÉ LISZT (c. 1884)

following moment, where Liszt takes hold of the D sharp (see Ex. 32) and transforms it into the submediant of F sharp major, with magical results.

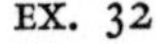

The middle section is preceded by a quotation from the libretto in which Marguerite refuses Faust's offer of his arm—to the music which follows.

Faust: Ne permettrez vous pas, ma belle demoiselle,
Qu'on vous offre le bras, pour faire le chemin?
Marguerite: Non, Monsieur, je ne suis demoiselle, ni belle,
Et je n'ai pas besoin qu'on me donne la main.

In contrast to the brilliant gaiety of the Waltz, this passage has a devotional quality, especially at the introduction to Faust's protestation of love, 'O nuit d'amour' from Act III. The contrast is accentuated by the solemn change to common time eight bars earlier.

EX. 33

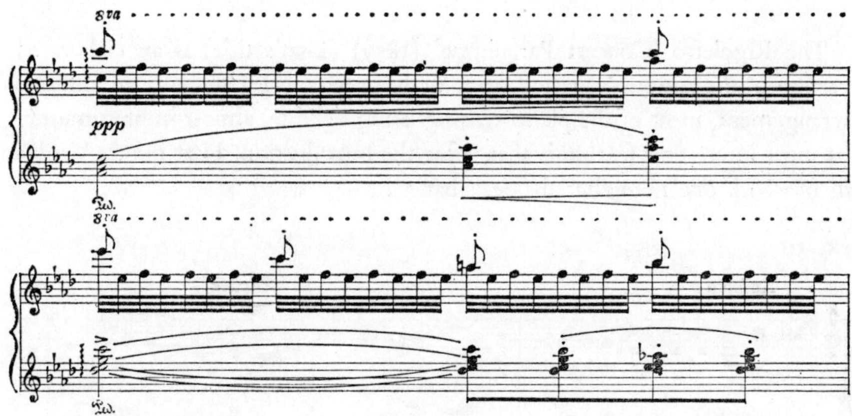

This section leads, by way of one of Liszt's inexhaustibly varied note cascades, to a reprise of the Waltz (Ex. 34), beginning quietly but brilliantly with a marvellously pianistic variation of Ex. 32.

EX. 34

This in turn leads to a fortissimo restatement of the first theme, during which Liszt audibly laughs with delight, leaping aside from D major to F major with an outrageous version of the second theme (Ex. 31*a*) containing an audacious glissando which recurs several times in succession (Ex. 35).

EX. 35

The final section is marked 'Stretta Presto', and is full of gay abandon.

The Rigoletto 'Concert Paraphrase' (1859) (Liszt's title) is an elaborated version of the famous 'Quartet' from Verdi's opera. It is essentially an intimate arrangement, most of the piano writing being delicate, almost impressionistic. Its most interesting feature is that, after the Introduction, Liszt quotes Verdi's theme with one note altered (see * bar 3).

EX. 36

In so doing he changes typical Verdi into typical Liszt in a single stroke. Later on, he juxtaposes the resultant tritone (E flat to B double flat) with Verdi's original perfect fifth in an ethereal dream sequence.

EX. 37

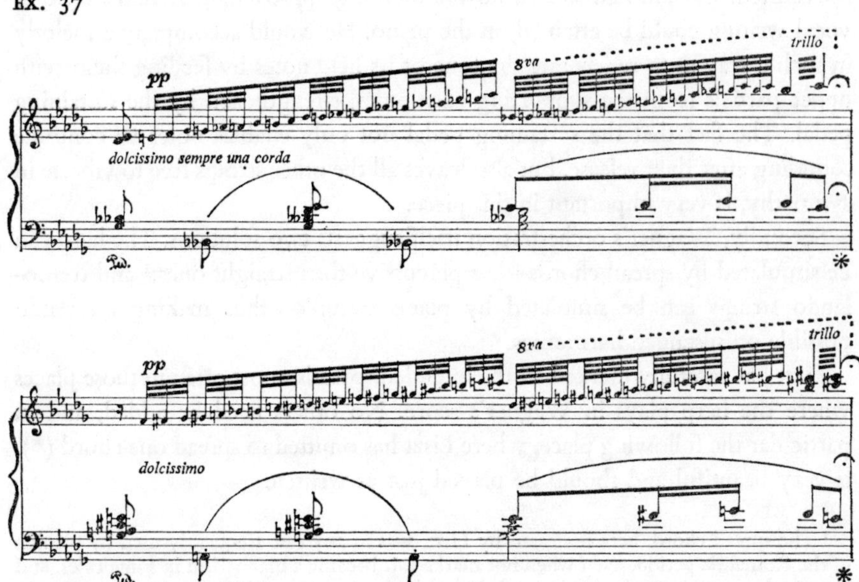

During the Coda, there is a passage in repeated octaves which should sound gentle and tremulous. This must have been more practicable on the lighter, shallower actions of 1860 than on most modern instruments, on which it can sometimes sound too brilliant.

The *Liebestod* from Wagner's *Tristan and Isolde* is a Partition, with a four-bar introduction added. It is dated 1867.

It is especially interesting because it seems technically such unpromising material for the piano. Despite its vast potential of timbres, the piano remains an essentially percussive instrument. The *Liebestod*, on the other hand, contains no percussive element at all, and is full of surging crescendos on sustained chords. So Liszt's problem here was no less than to free the instrument of its most basic limitation.

This idea was not new, of course. From the earliest years of the piano, musicians had tried to escape from its percussiveness, and the ideal of 'singing tone' lay at the heart of the approach of all the great Romantic piano composers. The

Liebestod is different only in degree; it seemed to present Liszt with the ultimate challenge to conjure from the instrument illusions of sustained sound.

How is it done? Firstly, by extending and developing the kind of writing explored by (in particular) Chopin, during the early years of the Romantic movement. Chopin had shown how something approaching Bellini's style of vocal writing could be attained on the piano. He would accompany a melody in such a way as to regenerate the tone of its held notes by feeding them with upper partials from the supporting harmonies, strengthened by the sustaining pedal. The fact that the sustaining pedal not only enables notes to continue sounding after their release, but also leaves all the other strings free to vibrate in sympathy, is very important in this piece.

Secondly, Wagner's orchestration itself suggests two solutions. The harp can be simulated by spread chords—less percussive than straight ones;[1] and tremolando strings can be simulated by piano tremolo—thus making crescendo possible on sustained harmonies.

Liszt has carefully marked all the intended spreads, most often in those places where the harp plays in Wagner's score. No others need be added, and in particular the following place, where Liszt has omitted to spread one chord (*), is very beautiful and should be played just as written.

[1] The spread chord, here indicated by Liszt, was in any case frequently used by pianists of the Romantic period, even when not marked. It became a mannerism in some cases, and is now almost universally condemned. But it is time to reconsider its use, where it seems applicable. It is the sort of subtle, personal device which cannot always be exactly notated. Its main value is that (as in the *Liebestod*) it prevents chords from sounding like hard blocks. Paderewski, whose 'left before right' mannerism did much to create the present climate of opinion, often used it to clarify the part-writing and colour the harmonies. He didn't always spread chords straight up from the bass, but would break them in a variety of different ways. Cortot would use a spread left-hand chord, sometimes with an added octave, as a preparatory rhythmic gesture—a rolled 'R' before the vowel, as it were. A similar device to these which I often adopt, is to sound the bass note, with pedal, slightly before the melody note in such a place as the beginning of Chopin's B major Nocturne.

The D sharp rings out with richer sonority when thus added to the column of sound emanating from the low B.

These ways of accommodating the piano's limitations and tapping its resources are logical developments of similar harpsichord techniques, and I see no reason why they should not be used, with care.

EX. 38

The tremolo has come to be regarded as a cheap trick, and I have heard the *Liebestod* transcription criticized because it contains too much of it. This is unjust. Liszt strictly confines its use to those places where Wagner has written tremolando string passages, and there is even one such place where he has managed without it. Furthermore, he has used the tremolo in many different

EX. 39

(a)

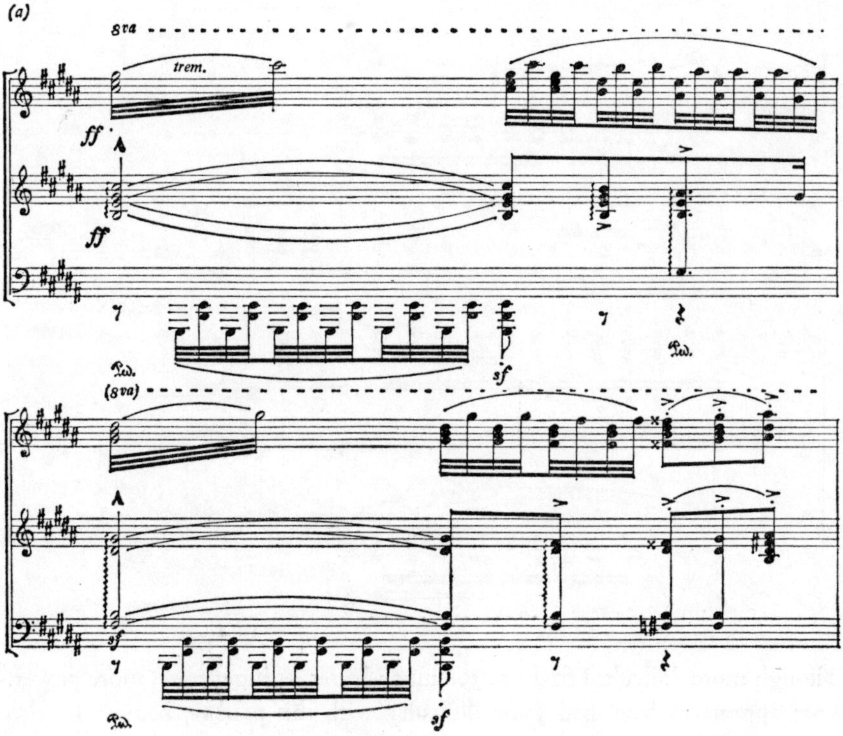

ways and with great subtlety; he presents in this manner not only octaves, but also sixths, fifths, fourths, third, three-note chords, and four-note chords. The tremolo appears in the bass, in the treble, and in the inner parts. It is never an added effect, but always an integral part of the musical texture.

There are two passages in the *Liebestod* where different versions have been published. The second is worth quoting here, since it occurs at the climax of the whole work (compare Exx. 39*a* and *b*).

EX. 39

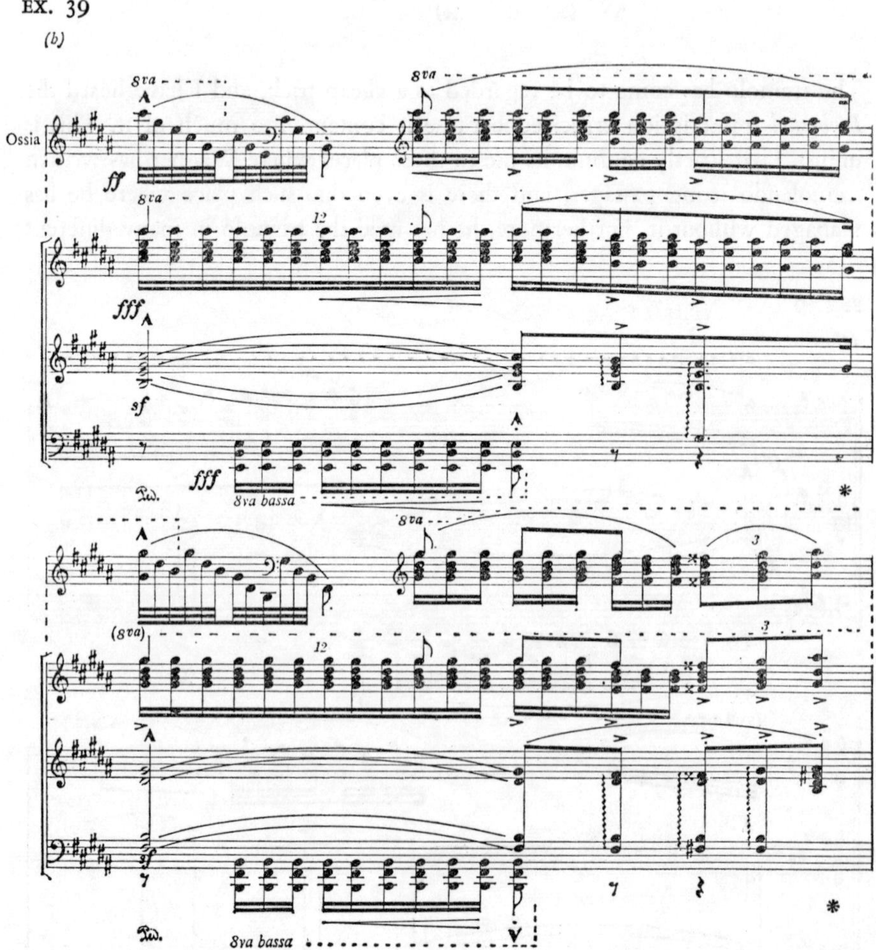

Though more difficult, I find Ex. 39*b* much better, as it generates more power. Liszt appears to have had some difficulty with this passage, because he also suggests as an 'Ossia' a third version of the right-hand part, substituting a descending arpeggio for the first few repeated chords.

If the *Liebestod* presented a challenge to its transcriber, it presents no less of a challenge to the performer. The ideal here is continuous reverberation—the soundboard must never be at rest. The fortissimos must seem not like hammer-blows, but like an overwhelming flood of sound. Since the act of depressing the keys constantly negates this ideal, the pianist must try to remain physically detached, yet sensuously alive—a difficult duality.

The *Réminiscences de Don Juan*, based on themes from Mozart's opera, has become so legendary that it must be mentioned even in a short essay like this.[1] The work has always aroused controversy, and I am one of those to whom it is unacceptable, not because of any inadequacy in Liszt's handling of it, but because I feel that Mozart's opera is not suited to this kind of treatment. Even Busoni, ardent Lisztian though he was, supports this view. Although he has glowing praise for Liszt's 'excellent instincts', his 'unerring perception of what is important', and his 'majestic mastery of all the possibilities of the pianoforte', he nevertheless writes: 'We willingly agree with the strict purists who maintain that the Don Juan Fantasy treats sacred themes in altogether too worldly a fashion.' Although a Paraphrase leads an independent life, the source work is nevertheless contained within it, and in this case the two seem incompatible. Something of this incompatibility can be felt in other of Liszt's free adaptations of music written before his time (as, for instance, in some of the Schubert songs), and I believe that we are confronted here not only with too great a disparity between the ethos of Mozart and Liszt, but with an altogether wider division which throws light on the spirit of Liszt's age—and of ours. Modern scholarship, recording, and the vast divergence of compositional styles and techniques since the First World War, have brought about a strong sense of musical history in our time. Even styles of performance can now be faithfully compared without reliance on fallible human memory. The problem of the extent to which works of previous ages should receive 'authentic' performances is being constantly aired. In addition, our whole outlook has been changed by the impact of such radical thinkers as Marx, Darwin, and Freud; all of whom laid great stress on the 'interpretation of history'—Marx, the history of society, Darwin of the race, and Freud of the individual. Consequently, we have become aware that human thought is accumulative. Specifically, this means that music of a former time was written for minds and ears differently conditioned[2] to ours, and

[1] Busoni has already made a superb analysis of it in *The Essence of Music*, pp. 89–95.

[2] Even the word has only come to be used with just this meaning in recent years.

therefore was in some respects actually heard differently. We know, for example, that ears which have learnt to accept 'Le Sacre' or even 'La Mer', must hear 'Norma' and 'Don Giovanni' differently to those which have not.

In contrast, even the most adventurous spirits of the nineteenth century were to some degree limited by a certain naïvety in their attitude to the past. Music did not escape the anomalies produced by this attitude, as can be seen in the Victorian 'editing' of Purcell's music—expurgated of 'false relations' and provided with 'good' harmonies. Styles of performance reflected this spirit, too, as can be heard in the recorded performances of Paderewski, who tended to play all music in the 'romantic' style.[1]

Liszt, with his interest in the 'music of the future', must often have asked himself, 'Where are we going?' and was to this extent above the historical self-containment of his contemporaries. But even he may not have asked quite so frequently, 'How have we arrived at this point?' or have been fully aware of the dangers presented by recasting in the idiom of one era ideas conceived in an earlier one. It is to his credit that the vast majority of his paraphrases are based on nineteenth-century sources, and that 'Don Giovanni' is the only one he completed on themes by Mozart. Apart from the unfinished 'Figaro' Fantasy, the only other occasions when this composer appears in the catalogue of Liszt's transcriptions are in a Partition of two movements from the 'Requiem' and in a religious tone-picture called 'A la chapelle Sixtine', based on Allegri's 'Miserere' and Mozart's 'Ave verum corpus'—a comparatively modest and discreet work. This fact suggests that Liszt's musical instincts served him well.

What is the overall impression left by the transcriptions, and how do they affect our image of Liszt? This must depend to some extent on our individual outlook; I can speak only for myself.

Firstly, I feel awed by the staggering range of Liszt's achievement, and by the colossal talents that made it possible. What a pianist, that could postulate problems beyond everyone else's wildest dreams, make them real, and, apparently, solve them in his own playing—all in one move! What a musician, that could enter into the mind of Beethoven, and re-create his Symphonies for another medium! What a man, indeed, who could achieve so much in one lifetime. Did he never sleep . . . ?

[1] But we have over-compensated, rejecting a nineteenth-century style of performance even where appropriate, and so have lost as much as we have gained. For instance, I know of no present-day pianist who could achieve anything comparable to Paderewski's incredibly beautiful performance of Schumann's 'Warum?'

On the debit side, in the transcriptions as elsewhere in Liszt's music, I sometimes miss that precious and indefinable quality to be found in, say, Mozart's 'Dove Sono' or Chopin's 'Barcarolle'. This could explain why, in his arrangements, Liszt often failed to capture the intimacy that lies at the heart of German song.

Sir Herbert Read has pointed out that each age throws up one artist who (though not necessarily the greatest) is the most characteristic of the period. He has named Stravinsky as the representative artist of the twentieth century. Perhaps Liszt might be regarded in a similar way as the representative artist of the Romantic movement. He was certainly very much a child of his time, a comprehensive figure, summing up the nineteenth century in all its strengths and weaknesses. But Liszt was big enough to absorb all these attributes into a character which, happily, possessed other, greater, qualities, and, at its best, his universal genius transcended the limitations of period. His courage was immense, for he was prepared to face any problem no matter how great, as can clearly be seen in the Partitions of the Beethoven Symphonies, which are an impressive testament of dedication, mastery, and strength of will. When he failed, it was because he attempted too much. In this he is surely more to be commended than those who always succeed because they dare not take risks.

Charles Lamb, writing to Wordsworth, once described S. T. Coleridge as 'an Archangel, a little damaged'.

He might well have been writing of Franz Liszt.

LOUIS KENTNER

The Interpretation of Liszt's Piano Music

'ARCHITECTURE is frozen music.'[1] Do not let us quarrel for the moment with this dictum, trite and banal though it may seem. Let us accept it, for the sake of the argument which follows. For I would like to postulate that the reverse is also true: music is melted architecture. To know where every note belongs, to create a structure exactly corresponding to what the composer put down on paper, is one thing; to make it communicate, speak eloquently, naturally and flowingly, even to move us to tears, to make this 'form', this 'architecture' lose all rigidity, all static existence in space, in other words to 'melt' into something that happens spontaneously in time—that is another. And it is, incidentally, what 'interpretation' means. And yet the two things must go hand in hand if we want it to be complete. An artist too exclusively concerned with architecture will tend to turn all performances into intellectual exercises, chilly and chilling, stiff and heartless. At the opposite extreme, while it must be admitted that animal warmth and spontaneity can compensate for many failings, it is equally certain that it will sooner or later make itself felt in many unpleasing ways: untidiness, false notes, insufficient attention to detail, slurred indistinct diction—these are not so much technical shortcomings as is generally assumed.

Liszt, who repudiated classical form in theory but could never quite break away from it in practice, did certainly put expression first, form second. In ranging ourselves firmly on his side, we come up against one of the linch-pins of academic conservatism. When one listens to the dreary, soulless, expressionless execution of the classics—and 'execution' is the *mot juste* in these cases—so often perpetrated in the name of 'classical style', one wonders if there ever was any composer, classical or romantic, who liked to hear his music murdered in the way so current in our age. 'Just play the notes, strictly in time, observe the dynamic markings, and no nonsense.' How often have I heard this admonition addressed by pedants of the older generation, who should have known better,

[1] Friedrich von Schelling (1775–1854). German Philosopher. *Philosophie der Kunst* (1797).

to young students guilty of liking their music with plenty of nonsense—a deplorable feature of modern music teaching when the unimaginative and untalented do their level best to strangle musicianly instinct and spontaneous feeling in the minds of the young. 'But', someone might object, 'this is all very well, but it does more or less apply to all music. In what way is the Liszt style different from the classical style? Is there such a thing as a Liszt style?'

It is obvious that an artist who has been variously called mountebank, wizard, Gypsy, priest, revolutionary, snob, Casanova, saint—and all these with some degree of justification at various times—must have expressed all these aspects of his personality in his artistic output. From this follows a bewildering diversity of styles. We need many keys to open many doors. (Indeed, the naïve urge for uninhibited self-expression which uncritically reveals the shoddier elements of this personality, as well as the lofty ones, refutes the accusation of insincerity. An insincere artist would not have shown himself to the world in all his nakedness.)

*

Thoughts on musical interpretation in general cannot be kept out when the special field of Liszt interpretation comes under scrutiny, and many such thoughts are obviously applicable also to the music of other composers, in varying degrees. Perhaps this is the moment to warn Liszt enthusiasts against becoming too exclusively Liszt *specialists*; or, at least, to make sure, by extensive ground work aiming at the greatest possible versatility, that Liszt really is what their musical metabolism mostly (or even exclusively) needs. This result must be the end of a long process of experiment and elimination which amounts, of course, to education. Thus, a good Liszt player must be a good Beethoven player, Mozart, Schubert and Bach player, he must see how far Liszt looked into the future and make Debussy and Bartók integral parts of his musical diet. A Liszt interpreter who interprets only Liszt cannot have a complete understanding of Liszt because such self-limitation creates ignorance of the wider issues, of the total picture, and ultimately produces a narrow-mindedness quite opposed to what Liszt stood for. In this, as in many other respects, Busoni is still a model worth following: his omnivorous catholicity of taste covered all music, from Bach to Schoenberg, with Liszt as some sort of musical lodestar.

The Composer–Interpreter Relationship

What is the composer–interpreter relationship? Should there be a clearly-defined line of demarcation where one ends and the other begins? I think not.

It is a popular simplification that the composer creates music and the instrumentalist carries out the composer's intentions. Actually, he does far more. First of all, a composer does not create music, he only writes a score. A score is not music; it becomes music only when it becomes sound. In certain ideal cases, like those of Chopin, Liszt, Beethoven, Mozart, and others, we have the natural unity of creator and interpreter, ready, provided by nature. In other cases this unity has to be achieved, sometimes by hard work and much bitter wrestling with God's angel.

Modern criticism tends to adopt a rather rigid view on the accurate observance of the printed text, perhaps as a natural and understandable reaction to the laxity shown by the older generation of artists in this respect. Certainly the classics (especially Beethoven) should be treated with the respect due to their often carefully-arrived-at text; but too much pedantry is to be deplored. Liszt himself was tolerant to the point of negligence—as long as the spirit of the music was there. After all, dynamic markings, put there by human beings, *can* be erroneous, original metronome figures *may* represent an early, already superseded view of the composer, and words like 'allegro' or 'andante' can have many meanings. Nor is the initial tempo, even if no change is indicated, necessarily valid for the whole piece—not in the classics, even less in Liszt (who has so far been left alone by purists, a fact thankfully to be recorded).

Perhaps the most important point in the philosophy of interpretation is that of the unity of composer and performer, because it implies total identification, whether by natural affinity or voluntary merging of personalities. Any 'critical' or 'objective' attitude would be fatal and is therefore inadmissible; cool detachment kills all possibility of communication with an audience, antagonistic or friendly. Even worthless music can and must be played with total conviction; indeed, the more worthless the music, the more conviction is needed. The late James Agate used to say that it was easy to act Shakespeare; but to put across, say, a French farce needed a *real* actor.

A Busoni, the intellectual-virtuoso type of artist, could do justice to works like the B minor Sonata, the 'Transcendental' Studies or the 'Norma' Fantasy and many others of the kind; but judging by a few surviving recordings, even he failed in the Hungarian Rhapsodies. Here eloquence, red-hot intensity, go hand in hand with a looseness, a making-it-up-as-you-go-along style that perhaps only Gypsies from Hungary (and probably Liszt himself) could so elegantly beguile our ears with, and which is within the powers of only very few living musicians. Fiery temperament, a deadly rhythmic urge, and above all, animal warmth—these things cannot be learned, one must be born with them.

The German language has a subtle distinction unknown to English: a 'Musiker' is simply a musician (he could be a composer, conductor, instrumentalist or singer); a 'Musikant', however, is one who is not, strictly speaking, a concert artist but more like an entertainer mainly concerned with the lighter kind of music, a player in a band, a Gypsy fiddler, a bar pianist—all these come under the heading 'Musikant'. Not using the term in any pejorative sense, it could mean a musician not spoilt by too much erudition (or too little knowledge), ardent, instinctive, earthy, untamed, a savage with savage rhythm still in his blood, and a natural-born aptitude for his instrument—the Hungarian Gypsy or the Negro jazz player for instance—the naturalistic yet sophisticated 'Musikant'. Now, if all Musiker had a little of the Musikant in their make-up, the world of music would be a better place to live in. Every serious musician should be able to turn himself into a Gypsy, if only for the short time it takes to play a Hungarian rhapsody by Liszt. For this is the territory of the Gypsy *par excellence*. Then he will know intuitively what Liszt meant by 'tempo rubato' or 'quasi recitativo'; he will know that bar lines are not important events in the life of a piece of music to be triumphantly demonstrated by vicious and unnecessary accents, but merely facilities for reading, accents being a means of expression, only to be used as such (and very often in opposition to the beat); that 'fast' and 'slow' are relative terms dependent on musical judgment, not on the sporting standard of what is physically possible—all this and a lot more. The younger generation of talented pianists might be reminded that speed itself does not constitute virtuosity, and that sometimes it is more difficult to play slower rather than faster, as well as less boring to hear.

If the subject-matter that forms the basis of Liszt's Hungarian rhapsodies had been recorded for posterity—quite a big part of the tunes can today be accepted as genuine folk-tunes only slightly distorted by the Gypsy interpretations—Liszt's own notation would no doubt have been more accurate. But in pre-Bartók times, even the most genuine folk-tunes came to be printed in clumsy, or mutilated versions, badly harmonized by amateurs; no wonder that Liszt himself, who spoke no Hungarian, sometimes accepted too unquestioningly those melodies which, at best, crudely follow the metre of the language, at worst having nothing at all in common with its prosody. For example, the F minor Rhapsody (and the Hungarian Fantasy for piano and orchestra) has as one major subject the following tune.

EX. I

Liszt's phrasing of this, ♩. ♪ ♪ ♩. if taken too seriously, would cut a word in two, and divide the two halves even more by a tenuto separation. Correctly phrased, the fourth note in the first bar should not be held too long, and the same applies to the first note. The 'choriambus' was too widely accepted as a typical Hungarian rhythm, and many melodies were forced into it by transcribers whether they fitted or not. The above melody, if sung with the traditional words, would sound more like this.

EX. 2

Liszt used the melody as it was presented to him and we must, of course, play it as 'Liszt' rather than 'Hungarian music', since he did, by some magical chemistry of his genius, transform everything he touched, if not into gold, then certainly into some Lisztian metal. It might in some cases be useful to know that the Hungarian language always stresses the first syllable (when the words are available to us), that the rhythm ♪♩. frequently veers towards ♬♩.. and that these things must be divined rather than deduced from the score which more often than not gives incomplete information; instinct, being at the bottom of creation, must be complemented by a kindred instinct in the *re*-creation (which is interpretation). Nothing, no amount of erudition or devotion to the cause, can compensate for the absence of instinct. In the much abused Second Rhapsody this phrase occurs:

EX. 3

I have heard a Gypsy play it as follows:

EX. 4

I myself adopted this style (not necessarily in all details) for this kind of music.

Taste, as an omnipresent censorship and protection against vulgar excess, cannot be discarded, any more than in the classical masters; but it must be the Lisztian taste, not that of his critics or detractors; too perfect, or too exquisite a taste can militate against genius which is not always possessed of these attributes. The Ninth Rhapsody ('Pesther Carneval') presents the player with some charming examples of characterization—not too nationally coloured—from the swaggering chevaleresque opening,

EX. 5

to the delightful 'scene' where a pretty masked female tries her powers of seduction (Ex. 6)

EX. 6

and receives a gruff refusal (Ex. 7) from the elderly gentleman, her intended victim.

EX. 7

This part of the music is so realistic that I had guessed its descriptive purport long before I heard that such a tradition actually existed. The whole piece requires, in my opinion, a sense of irony and an elegance of technique rarely to be found among modern pianists.[1]

To those who wish to do justice to the other Hungarian rhapsodies, I recommend for special attention the entirely novel and characteristically Lisztian effect of the 'quasi cimbalom', rapidly repeated notes or broken chords, often played by alternating right and left hands

EX. 8

and the quick 'vibrato' octaves which also stem from the cimbalom and require a very loose forearm and wrist technique. The cimbalom imitations are entirely Lisztian, but the player who has grappled successfully with the piano part of Schubert's *Erlking* or Schumann's *Toccata* will not be unduly distressed by the Sixth Rhapsody of Liszt.

EX. 9

The 'late' Rhapsodies (Nos. 16–19) present no great technical problems. We have here works which belong essentially to Liszt's last period; all florid piano writing is gone and is replaced by a stark simplicity and economy, going hand

[1] Rachmaninov, who made a superb recording of it, had both the irony and the surface polish. His Liszt interpretations were models in every respect. The same cannot be said of Paderewski who, his tremendous native fire and eloquence notwithstanding, sometimes fell short of manual perfection and faithful text reading; in both these respects, sins of omission and commission are only too noticeable (though I admire his passage-work in the *Leggierezza* recording).

AUTOGRAPH PAGE OF HUNGARIAN RHAPSODY NO. 1, IN C SHARP MINOR (1846)

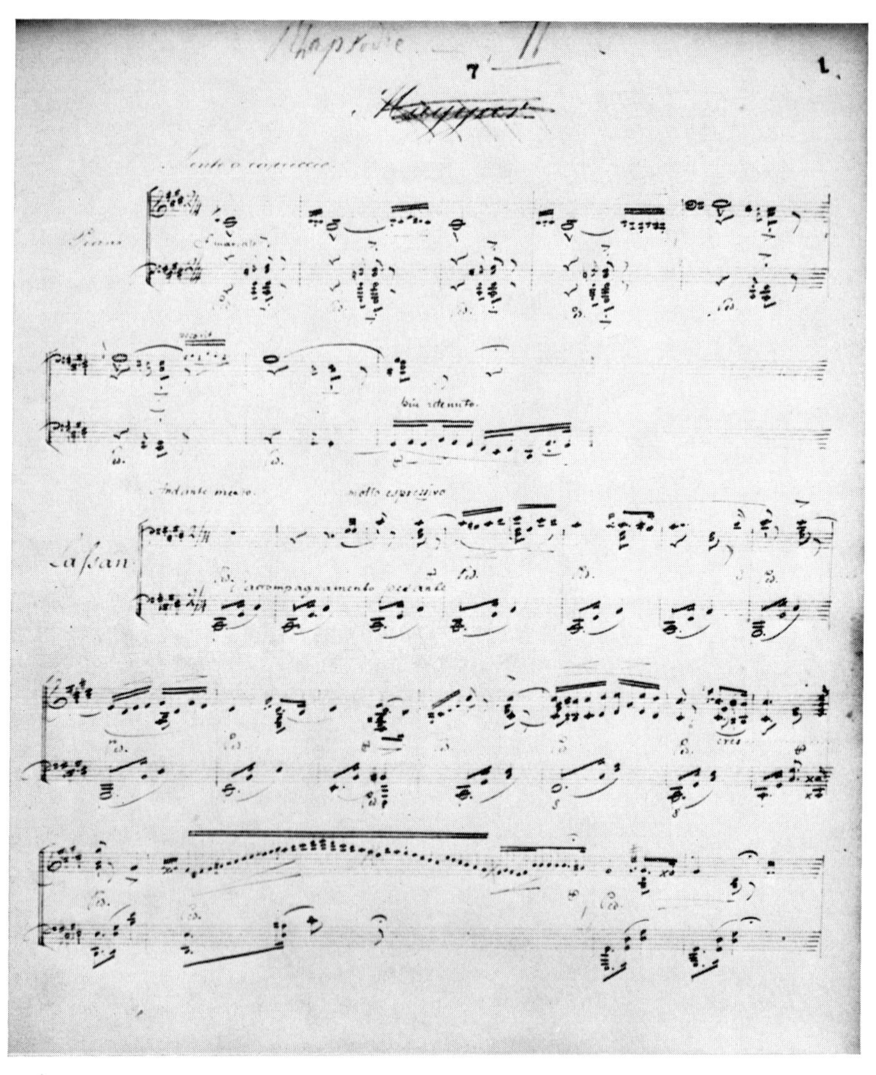

AUTOGRAPH PAGE OF HUNGARIAN RHAPSODY NO. 2, IN C SHARP MINOR (1847)

in hand with recondite harmony, requiring affectionate understanding of subtle shades on the part of the performer. The Gypsy 'Musikant' is less in evidence here than the intelligent musician who has the harmonic language of Liszt (so different from that of Wagner or Chopin or Berlioz) at his fingertips: a forward-looking language from which Bartók took his point of departure.[1] The same applies to the Rumanian Rhapsody where the Bartókian element can be detected even more strongly in the oriental-sounding main section. Very wide stretches limit this interesting work to performers with large (or very supple) hands.

EX. 10

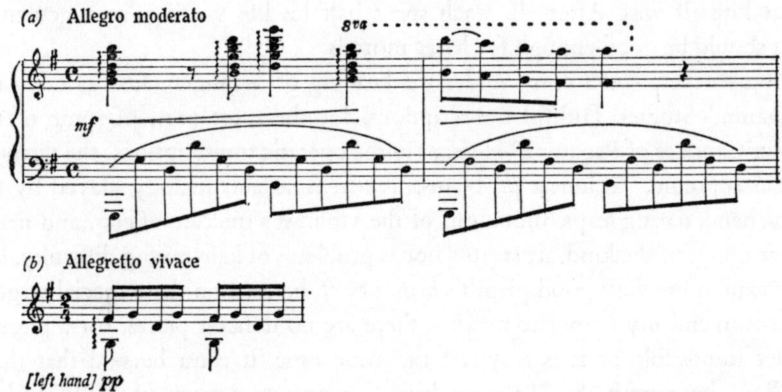

To the student of Liszt the Operatic Fantasies, or Paraphrases, or Reminiscences as they are sometimes called, all present a similar challenge: they must be played like original works of Liszt in which melodies from Mozart, Bellini, Verdi, and Donizetti are used with amazing and entirely Lisztian instrumental ingenuity. These melodies are not the principal thing in them, any more than are the themes on which earlier composers wrote variations. They are merely an excuse for the composer to show his ingenuity in transforming them into something else. Any performer of the terrific 'Don Giovanni' Fantasy will soon realize that he must forget all about Mozart if he wishes to play this work, must forget all about Gounod or Mendelssohn, although the 'climate' of these composers seems to come alive because of, rather than in spite of, Liszt's treatment of them, and he must only remember Liszt, his tremendous joy in his own

[1] Only No. 19 seems to return to the old-fashioned 'Csárdás' style, with its *Lassan* and *Friska* sections. Incidentally, as Bartók already pointed out, the term 'Friska' is a corrupted, Slavicized version of the Hungarian 'Friss' (meaning 'brisk' or 'lively'), while the word 'Lassan' ('slowly') is not used by Gypsies who prefer 'Lassu' ('slow') instead. As I said earlier, in matters of Hungarianisms Liszt is not the ultimate authority.

strength and his zeal as a propagandist for the composers whose works he transcribed. Liszt made these works his own while yet preserving what was best in them in that curiously Lisztian way, at once faithful and faithless, autocratic and subservient, always infectiously enthusiastic, as well as challenging to the pianist. This is not the place to put the case for the defence with regard to 'arrangements'—it has been done elsewhere in this book[1]—but it should be emphasized that nothing very good can come of a half-hearted adoption of that case, in view of the possible philistine objections to be encountered on the way, which have clogged the advance of all Liszt's music for a century. Anyone who plays Liszt's operatic transcriptions must be a fervent propagandist; he must be as Liszt himself was. After all, Bach spent half his life writing 'arrangements'; that should be good enough for lesser mortals.

Many other works come under the heading of 'arrangements', notably the 'Paganini' Studies, faithful transcriptions, for the most part, of some of the violin Caprices of Paganini.[2] Here, as in the operatic transcriptions, the virtuoso reigns supreme. Technical problems, like tremolo and melody played by the same hand, daring leaps, imitations of the violinist's spiccato effects, and many other things of the kind, are treated not as problems of hair-raising difficulty, but as weapons in every good pianist's armoury to be used on these special targets. I recommend my favourite maxim: there are no difficult pieces, for a piece is either impossible or it is easy. At the same time, it must be said that these studies, along with the 'Transcendentals' constitute a very good 'bridge' of technical exercises whereby the migration from the impossible to the easy class can be effected. In this context, the twelve paperback volumes of purely technical exercises—presumably as used by Liszt himself in his early days—should be mentioned.

Liszt and Technique

And this brings us to the question of technique. Liszt's own technique, according to the unanimous contemporary verdict, was omnipotent and omniscient. He had boundless confidence in what the piano could do, an incredible fertility in inventing new sound-effects and a pair of hands capable of reproducing without hesitation on the keyboard what flashed through his mind. The word 'transcendental' was so often used by him that there can be no doubt as to what technique, with its connotations of hard-working efficiency, of struggle with some recalcitrant matter, meant to him: nothing at all. He created what seemed

[1] See David Wilde, p. 170.—*Ed.* [2] See pp. 47–51 and 110–14.—*Ed.*

to all the world insurmountable difficulties; wrote, in everybody's opinion, unplayable piano music, and then proceeded to demonstrate calmly and negligently that the difficulties did not exist, that everything was not only playable but easy. We of a less naturally gifted generation must be content if we can do justice by hard work to what he created with such ease.

And yet it is a well-known fact that Liszt's early years were not unmarked by hard work, when he practised many hours every day—scales, thirds, sixths, octaves, repeated notes—in short, fashioned for himself a new technique (inspired by Paganini's example) capable of expressing new ideas. There is no contradiction between the years of hard work and those of easy mastery. Everybody has to learn to walk before he can run.

Piano technique had taken a great leap forward with Beethoven (in whose lifetime the instrument gained greatly in compass and sonority) who, himself a brilliant pianist, created new piano effects—as did Liszt, later—by introducing the pedal as a new factor to make the sonority richer, less percussive, and, when he wished, to blur even different harmonies into one blend; he also used the unusual effects of simultaneously sounding highest and lowest registers, passages in double thirds, octaves, glissandos, etc. Liszt, who was Czerny's pupil, and therefore Beethoven's 'grandchild', took up where Beethoven left off. Undoubtedly Weber, Mendelssohn and Chopin—all great piano composers—played important parts in the development of Liszt's style, and influenced him in various ways; but we are here concerned with the supreme master who, after years of apprenticeship, could make the piano do anything he wished it to do, like a lion-tamer does a lion. Only this lion and this tamer were tied together by bonds of mutual affection.

The most widespread of popular misconceptions is that all Liszt's music is 'difficult', and that you need big hands or long fingers to play it. Nothing could be further from the truth. Any pianist capable of tackling, say, Chopin's Ballades and Preludes will find such works as *Paysage*, *Sposalizio*, the Petrarch Sonnets and many other pieces well within his scope, speaking entirely from the manual point of view. Need one say that there are also a great number of 'easy' pieces, like the *Liebesträume*, the Consolations and the Five Hungarian Folk Tunes (almost Bartókian in their stark simplicity, although not meant for children). In addition, Liszt wrote the charming set of twelve pieces called 'The Christmas Tree' which are meant to be played by children and are limited, musically and technically, by that consideration. But I would go even further and say that the deeper one gets into the era of virtuoso piano writing (post-Beethoven era) the easier of execution the music is found to be because of the knowledge of the instrument that virtuoso composers like Chopin and Liszt (and Mendelssohn and Schumann before them) developed through their ability to feel the nature of the instrument. Their sound effects, however brilliant or miraculously iridiscent, were tested by ten gifted fingers. There is a basic difference here. Beethoven put down on paper what he heard in his mind with a sovereign disregard of the ten fingers ('Does the fellow think I have his miserable instrument in mind when I compose?'). Schubert composed for his own technique in which chords and repeated octaves play a great part, but in which passage-work is almost entirely absent. Schumann, by some odd quirk of his mind, deliberately chose to write some unplayable passages along with some wonderfully original and inspired piano writing. Only Chopin and Liszt were real piano composers *sui generi*; and of the two, Liszt was the more comprehensive. In many ways, Liszt's music is easier to perform than Chopin's because the latter, though he wisely limited himself almost entirely to the piano, nevertheless retained a certain abstract and idiosyncratic quality, a proud insistence that the music comes first and that difficulties simply had to be overcome (a demand Chopin himself was not always able to fulfil), whereas Liszt obviously never wrote anything down that he at least could not play immediately. This makes the solution of any problem in his writing a matter of instant mental adaptability; a thing that looks impossible on paper becomes easy once the mind takes the jump to the right conclusion—which is often using the hand in a certain way, or using a certain fingering.[1] In this sense, Chopin often requires more diligent practising than Liszt. All the same, we have it on record that Chopin confessed to envying the way Liszt played his (Chopin's) Studies. Liszt's tendency, both as composer and as 'manipulator' of his instrument, was to proceed from the complicated to the simple: all his life he revised his piano works to make them more easily playable, less overloaded with decorative by-play (some early versions of the Studies and of the *Années de Pèlerinage* are really hair-raising; they make us realize with a shudder of what this young man must have been capable, technically). His technical arsenal included practically everything: passage-work, trills, both long and short, octaves used with a sort of defiant negligence (as if they were single notes), tremolo, vibrato in chords, single notes and octaves, every kind of double notes, and—incredibly—the simplest kind of piano writing since Mozart, like this.

[1] Busoni's observations are worth quoting. He says: 'An eye-witness relates how Liszt—pondering over a cadenza—sat down at the piano and tried three or four dozen variations of it, playing each one right through until he had made his choice.' What was the secret of this choice? 'The secret of Liszt's ornamentation', Busoni concludes, 'is its symmetry.'—*Ed.*

EX. 11

EX. 12

The disadvantage of having small hands has been exaggerated. Several of the world's greatest players—Eugène d'Albert, Pachmann, Godowsky and Josef Hoffman among them—had extremely small hands. Greater agility evens out the advantage of long fingers. Liszt's own hands were remarkable not so much for their size or length of their fingers as for the low-lying mass of sinews and connective tissue which gave the fingers unusual freedom of movement.[1]

The Lisztian octave technique depends not so much on what you do with your wrist, arm, and shoulder—important though these things are—as on phrasing. Since it is obviously impracticable in rapid octaves to raise the whole arm separately for each octave, a grouping of several octaves becomes necessary; how they are grouped can only be decided by the player's instinct; a feeling for the topography of the keyboard combines here with a feeling of what musically belongs together. The arm, in these cases, is only raised from the shoulder once, the forearm (or wrist) articulates the individual octaves.

[1] See photograph facing p. 33.—*Ed.*

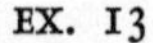

EX. 13

EX. 14

Phrasing, in a deeper sense, and pedalling, enter into the concept of what is often mis-called 'touch'. For, the piano being basically a harp, it requires more than an act of 'touch' to transform it into an organ. What we call 'touch' is a compound of loud and soft tone in single notes, the proportional or relative strength of notes within chords (the degree of preponderance given to the upper voice or to any of the subordinate voices), the shape of a melody, in terms of ever-so-slight crescendi and decrescendi, of continuous agogic fluctuation (= phrasing), and, finally, what Anton Rubinstein rightly called 'the soul of the piano', that mechanical device capable of making this percussion instrument sing—the pedal. A melody can be phrased more or less impetuously, or more or less pensively, the same theme can be given a passionate or lyrical or even sarcastic expression—Liszt frequently demands all possible variations—and all this, plus the thousand different ways the pedal can be used, translates itself into sound impressions in the mind of the listener who then says that 'X' has a different touch from 'Y', or that he makes the same piano, in the same piece of music, sound quite differently.

Liszt's phrasing is not essentially different from that of the classics. Less painstaking than Chopin, less negligent than Beethoven—that is how his markings can be characterized. Looseness and spontaneity are the keynotes. The music is so direct, so vivid and accessible, that only a very poor musician can miss the places where a *caesura* or break is needed, even if not marked in the score; in tempo rubato, less restraint than in Chopin is in order. Liszt's passion was more unbridled, his taste less aristocratic, without being vulgar.[1]

[1] Admittedly, lapses from fastidiousness do occur—and when they do we must go along unblushingly and all the way. And let those who never wept with emotion at certain

Perhaps this is a good opportunity for a word on rhythm. Liszt generally did not favour, either as interpreter or composer, a strictly mathematical, or metronomic, time-keeping. His tempo fluctuates, his rhythm is taut but not too taut to prevent it from being flexible. Tempo rubato, its merits and demerits, or its applicability to the classics, are not part of this discussion. It is at any rate certain that the metronomic type of musician has very little chance of getting Liszt's style into his inelastic grasp. Scholarly hair-splitting gets us nowhere near the true meaning of some of Liszt's somewhat negligent notation.

EX. 15

But to the musicianly instinct it will not only easily yield its secrets, it will also assume that compelling, quasi hypnotic plasticity which makes Liszt's scores perhaps the least difficult to sightread.

The use of the pedal in Liszt is so omnipresent, its shades so subtle and numerous that it would take a whole volume to deal exhaustively with this topic; it is not an exaggeration to say that pedal-less playing is an exception, a measure necessitated by certain special effects. The rule is: pedal, or the heart of the music ceases to beat.[1] Having said that, and having added that taste and judgment as to how much and how often, are as indispensable as a good ear and a knowledge of harmony (on which proper pedalling depends), I will limit myself to a few places where Liszt expressly indicates his wishes. These markings 'Ped. *' which are sometimes quite extended, always designate a deliberate blur, often comprising a whole series of harmonies, in the service of a definite poetic idea. Beethoven was the first composer to use this device (in the finale of the 'Waldstein' Sonata, for example) and many critics declared that his deafness, or the weaker sonority of the instrument of his time, must have been the

---

vulgarities in Tchaikovsky or Rachmaninov cast the first stone at the Second Hungarian Rhapsody or the Second *Liebesträum*. Liszt offers no apology, and neither should we, his interpreters.

[1] See also John Ogdon, p. 149.—*Ed.*

cause of his infraction of the all-important aim of clarity; but the advent of Debussy did something to bring home the fact that clarity is not always the only aim. Liszt often indicates the opposite intention.

EX. 16

"Dante" Sonata

Presto agitato assai

p *lamentoso*

I should hesitate to change this into something more 'clear-sounding' without careful examination of the case. At the end of *Harmonies du Soir* I pedal as follows.

EX. 17

The effect is magical, like dying sounds and smells all softly mingling in a bluish crespuscular haze, finally settling down in the clear D flat major of the end—all Nature at peace.

The rule on when to pedal is the time-honoured one: pedal *after* the sound (syncopated pedalling); but in arpeggios, when the hand is forced to relinquish a bass note immediately, the rule is suspended and the pedal is taken *simultaneously* so as to 'catch' the bass of the chord. In very rare cases, it is a good idea to press the pedal *before* the sound to get an 'ethereal' effect without attack. Some pianists advocate the use of 'harmonics' by silently depressing a chord, to relieve the possible emptiness of sound in single-note passages.

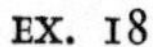
EX. 18

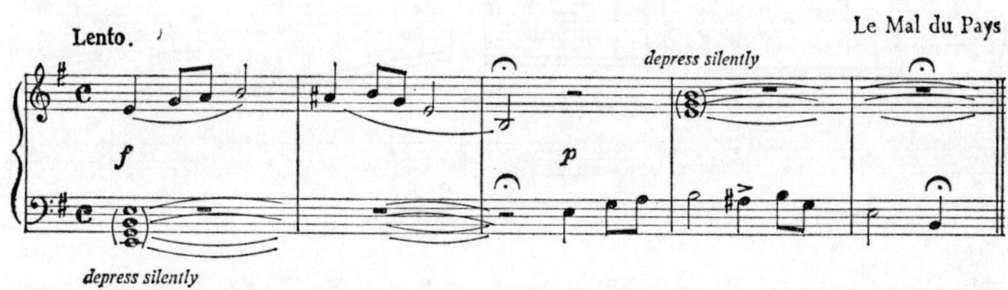

This is a good device when carefully managed, bearing in mind that some such monodistic passages need no 'accompaniment' and are meant to sound bleak. For instance, in the 'Dante' Sonata, the lachrymose 'clarinet solo', with the marvellously contrasting luscious episode following it, would lose all psychological motivation if it were made to sound rich and fruity.

EX. 19

An interesting, wholly Lisztian piano effect is the 'quasi arpa' or 'non legato' sound in rapid passage-work like the following. (Exx. 20*a* and *b*).

EX. 20

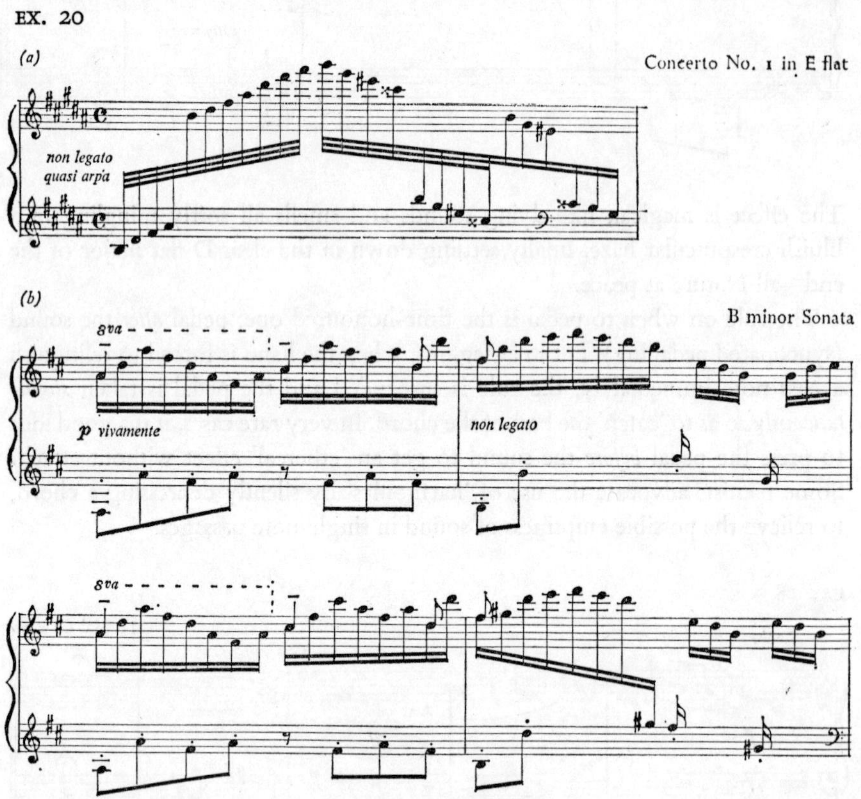

Closely related to the 'perlé' or 'leggiero' touch, known to Mozart and Scarlatti, this is produced by the fingers 'plucking' at the keys as if they were strings. The importance to any Liszt player of studying the sound of an orchestra in detail, of having an orchestrally orientated imagination, cannot be sufficiently stressed. Good piano sound is often the result of diligent score-reading.

Liszt's fingerings are worth attention.[1] When they seem odd at first sight, as in *Mazeppa*

[1] In addition to the examples given by Louis Kentner on the following page, Liszt's unorthodox fingerings can also be seen reproduced on p. 44, Ex. 5 ('Fantastic' Symphony); p. 129, Ex. 73 ('Bénédiction de Dieu'); p. 175, Ex. 8 (Beethoven's Fourth Symphony); p. 183, Ex. 18 (Wagner's 'Tannhäuser' Overture); and p. 239, Ex. 12 ('Go not, happy day'). —*Ed.*

EX. 21

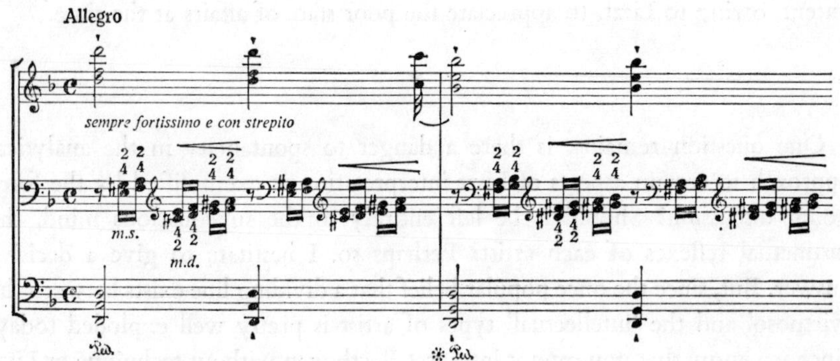

or the sixth 'Paganini' Study,

EX. 22

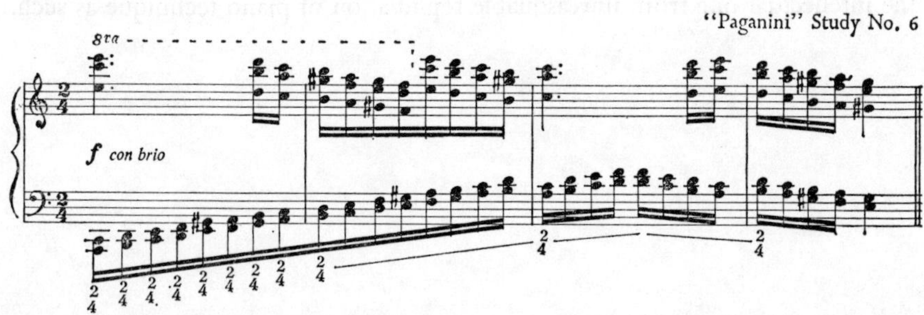

they often prove the only possible way, and sometimes they are surprisingly easy. Once or twice, his suggested fingerings, uncomfortable or even impossible for small hands, like this

EX. 23

are easily changed to eliminate the wide stretch. (I use in this piece the fingering 2312521 in the left hand.) Elsewhere, the fingerings indicated by Liszt are so easy and so natural that one wonders what sort of pianist Liszt had in mind who could not be trusted to find his own fingerings in those places. But one must bear in mind the strides pianism has made since Liszt, and, to a great extent, owing to Liszt, to appreciate the poor state of affairs at the time.

*

One question remains: is there a danger to spontaneity in the analytical approach to certain aspects of Liszt interpretation as exemplified by the foregoing discussion? Should it be left entirely to the subconscious mind, the instinctual reflexes of each artist? Perhaps so. I hestitate to give a decisive answer. But, since the once popular belief that a dividing line exists between the 'virtuoso' and the 'intellectual' types of artist is pretty well exploded today, since we know that you cannot interpret Beethoven without technique or Liszt without intellect, it may be found that instinct and analysis can co-exist, too. All my analysis is based on years of practical experience. I hope it may help to protect the instinctive student from much mechanical, soul-less practising, and the intellectual one from unreasonable repudiation of piano technique as such.

CHRISTOPHER HEADINGTON

The Songs

Introduction

LISZT'S songs, considered as a whole, could hardly be claimed to rank among his greatest achievements. His dream of an alliance between music and poetry was principally realized in terms of instrumental music, ranging from evocative piano pieces to the programmatic symphonic poems and symphonies. 'A poetic language more apt perhaps than poetry itself', was his way of describing the new, purely instrumental language which was his first love. Such a concept, shared by Berlioz among others, was perhaps French rather than German. Yet Liszt's *songs*, in Sitwell's words, show him 'moving away in spirit from France to Germany'.

1840 seems to have been the critical year in this period of change. It is the year of Liszt's first meetings with Wagner and Schumann. Wagner, who was on his beam-ends in Paris and loathed the artistic climate of the city, seems to have made little impression on him at that time, though later on his influence was to be considerable. But the meeting with Schumann may have been more significant. The two men spent a day together, and felt as if they had known each other for twenty years; they had, indeed, already had a very friendly correspondence. Both were highly articulate and given to philosophical speculation, and both were much concerned with the future of music and their vocation as artists. Yet they were not exactly kindred spirits. Schumann wrote to Clara that Liszt had magnificence but 'too much tinsel', and lacked the 'fine inwardness' which he and Clara so much valued; 'we are already quite rude to one another'.

No wonder if Liszt was rude and, as Schumann put it, 'moody'. Here was the greatest performer of the time giving himself freely in the cause of German music, including Schumann's own.[1] Yet he seems to have received something other than the starry-eyed admiration and praise for his selflessness which he might have expected. He had to endure the accusation that he was misusing his talents; of course, a certain natural bitterness may have come into this, in view of Schumann's own tragically frustrated virtuoso career. Had Schumann come to feel that certain forms of romanticism were *élite*-ist? Did he feel that the search for the infinite and the inaccessible[2] was as nothing beside the humanity of *Fidelio* or the finale of the Ninth Symphony? that these goals were unworthy of Liszt the humanitarian, the composer who claimed Beethoven as a guide? If he said so, Liszt was ready to respond to the challenge.

Liszt had already, in two separate letters of 1838 and 1839, encouraged Schumann to write chamber music. In 1839, Schumann had admitted that the piano was becoming 'too narrow' for his thoughts; and in 1841 and 1842 he did indeed turn for the first time, and in copious measure, to the orchestra and to chamber music. But in 1840, the year of the meeting with Liszt, he was passionately absorbed in the discovery of his powers *as a song writer*. No less than a hundred and thirty-eight songs date from that year, and he wrote to Clara of his joy in song composition: 'Too long have I been a stranger to it.'

If Schumann took Liszt's advice with regard to ensemble pieces, was there a *quid pro quo*—did Liszt agree to turn his hand to song? For it is now that the long series of settings of German poetry begins, Schumann's favourites—Heine and Goethe—featuring among Liszt's choices of poets. Meeting Schumann in that composer's great song year, he may have come to feel that songs were a medium of expression which he had too long neglected. In song, he might indeed come closer to the world at large than an exclusively instrumental language would permit; emotions explicit in words, he might have thought, are to be shared more readily. But he composed *Lieder* only as Handel had written Italian opera, adapting himself to an alien tradition—and he never learned to speak German perfectly.

Inevitably, we wonder whether an explicit text was in some way a handicap to Liszt's musical thought. Did this thought find a happier outlet in instrumental pieces, where extra-musical ideas emerge from creative fires, phoenix-like, as entirely *musical* poetry? It would be unwise to answer categorically one way or the other. Like most artists, Liszt was more versatile than theories, even his own, would suggest. He was, in any case, too intellectually curious to confine himself altogether to one line of artistic exploration: for example, moving to

[1] This was the time of Liszt's benefit concerts for the Beethoven memorial, 1839–41.

[2] Liszt had written of music's power to express, 'inaccessible depths . . . infinite presentiments'.

Rome after Weimar, he wrote that having solved the symphonic problem as far as he could, he now intended to tackle the oratorio problem! The appearance of a collected edition of the songs in his lifetime, with numerous revisions, gives adequate ground for feeling that Liszt would wish us to give them our full consideration. They deserve to be measured by the standards which we would confidently apply to the more familiar and well-proved music. If their quality proves uneven, facing the facts will still help our understanding of the composer. Whether or not we will go as far as Bartók and agree that 'there is no work in which we can doubt the greatness of his creative power', we still need not fear the truth.

Liszt wrote over seventy songs. It is difficult to give the number more precisely than this, for most of the early songs, those written before 1850, were revised, some very drastically. The revisions date from the period after 1855 (he had at that time written no songs for about five years); an older and perhaps wiser composer was reconsidering his work in the light of the preparation for publication of a collected edition of songs, the main part of which appeared in 1859. From the late 1850s and the year 1860, too, date sixteen new songs. Then comes another gap; the remaining songs, again sixteen in number, date from 1871–83. It is thus possible to divide the songs into three groups, in the approved but somewhat uninspired fashion with which we are all familiar. But in this case, we should not place too much emphasis on differences between one period and the next; or, at least, we should not allow convenience of approach to dull our observation. It is always fairly obvious that the same composer is at work, facing the same problems, and not necessarily finding brand-new solutions in the light of increasing experience. Nonetheless, he became more cautious, more modest and respectful in his treatment of words, as he grew older.

The Relationship between Words and Music

According to Raabe, the young Liszt showed greater independence than his contemporaries in that he 'did violence to words', rather than accept restrictions imposed by a text upon the flow of his musical creativity. Raabe goes so far as to speak of a 'Kampf der Musik mit dem Wort'—a conflict between music and words—in the early songs. It is true that Liszt was not a 'natural' song composer; and the numerous song transcriptions for piano which preceded the songs themselves must have encouraged him to think that words, so easily dispensable, needed to be little more than a springboard from which his thought might leap.

To do 'violence to words' is, however, not necessarily a crime. Stravinsky has remarked that he has in a sense 'violated' Pergolesi and Tchaikovsky, objects of his love if not his scholarly respect; but from such violation comes new artistic creation. Nobody who sets a poem to music can escape the charge of doing some 'violence' to the text, for he is imposing his thought upon it. The song composer, like a speaker, establishes a mode of declamation of the words; in this way he becomes an interpreter of the poem. If we allow that to *interpret* is not in fact to do violence, then we reserve our strictures for the composer who *mis*interprets. To set a gentle lyric in praise of spring flowers as a military march, to misplace certain natural stresses, to repeat words so much that they lose their force, to write accompaniments which obscure the text—such practices do justly earn our censure.

On the positive side, the situation seems to be more or less as follows: the song must be of poetic appropriateness as well as musical value; music, that is, must illuminate and enhance the words. Poetic appropriateness, however, may easily conflict with musical demands. In a line such as 'In rapture or grief, with swiftness or sloth', each noun can be musically 'painted', but the result will probably sound discontinuous and even rather silly. If a composer must set these words, he will either space them out at length or, as Schubert might have done, avoid detailed word-painting altogether. The latter course is obviously the one adopted in a strophic song—how can it be otherwise when the same music serves different verses? But if we dispense with strophic form, we find that the song composer has at his disposal a spectrum of styles, of approaches to the words: it ranges from vocalization through progressively less melismatic and repetitious aria, arioso, measured recitative, unmeasured recitative and speech-song to actual speech. In other words, the relative importance of text and music in a given passage will be somewhere in a range extending from maximum musical weight to maximum textual weight.[1] We have already noted that Liszt became more respectful to words as he grew older; the music becomes more discreet in almost every revision of a song which he made.

[1] This is perhaps the place for a very brief mention of Liszt's six recitations with accompaniment. We cannot here speak of a true alliance of text and music, of a real fusion; the music simply goes alongside the spoken words. Schumann, too, experimented with melodrama, as this form is called. Asked about his own use of it, Stravinsky has said: 'Do not ask. Sins cannot be undone, only forgiven!'

Language

Liszt wrote songs in five languages. In order of frequency they are German (most of them), then French, Italian, Hungarian and English—the single example of the latter being a setting of Tennyson's 'Go not, happy day' from 'Maud'. How far complete mastery of a language is necessary for the song composer is debatable; Britten, no polyglot, has successfully set as many languages as Liszt, whose command of German, as we have noted, was less than perfect.

EX. 1(*a*)

Mistakes in the setting of language—that is, those due to imperfect knowledge rather than any error of taste—are of two kinds. The more subtle of these is the result of misunderstanding words or poetic emphases; the more obvious is a simple fault in stress. In the first version of *Mignons Lied*, the sheer cliffs of Goethe's poem, with their waterfall, become a great rock falling, because a particular use of the verb 'stürzen' has been misunderstood; but in the second version the error seems to have been recognized, and the octave leap, previously downwards, now rises. The stresses on 'du' and 'die' in the first phrase are also unnatural and are duly put right in the second version. Compare Exx. 1*a* and 1*b*. A similar mistake, this time in Italian, occurs in *I' vidi in terra*, the last of the Petrarch settings. The word 'soglia' is set as three syllables in the first version, and correctly as two in the second.[1]

EX. 2

The same mistake of treating the diphthong as two syllables occurs in *La Perla*, where 'mia' wrongly appears in this form. In the Hungarian song of farewell, *Isten veled*, the word 'szerelmed ('thy love') is incorrectly set, as if the stress were on the second syllable.

Mistakes of taste in word-setting are more controversial, though Liszt himself gives some authority for adverse criticism, remarking in a letter that 'my earlier songs are mostly too inflated and sentimental, and usually over-padded with accompaniment'. The middle-period revisions usually put this right. It is a lesson in technique to compare the different versions of, among others, *Mignons Lied*, *Im Rhein, im schönen Strome* and *S'il est un charmant gazon.*

I should like to examine one such revised passage in some detail. In *Enfant, si j'étais roi*, there is a passage of somewhat high-flown text which stimulated the young Liszt to a heaven-storming (or barn-storming!) setting; but in the second version, composed fifteen years later, this is reduced in power; after all, this is a

[1] Fischer-Dieskau, interestingly, amends this in performance: LPM 18793.

EX. 3(*a*)

(a) (Andante)
[1st Version: 1844]
loi,
f marcato assai
et le pro-
arpeggiando
ff
tumultuoso
-fond cha - - os aux en - trail - les fé - -
sempre ff e marcato assai
(simile)
mf
- con - - des, l'é - ter - ni té, l'es - -
fs
fff
- pa - - ce et les cieux et les mon - - des
rfs

EX. 3(*b*)

(b) (Quasi Allegro moderato)
[2nd Version: 1860]
loi,
un peu plus animé
f
sfz
rinf.
f
et le pro-fond cha -
sf
rinf.
-os aux en - trail - - les fé -
sf
-con - - des, l'é - ter - - ni -
sf

love-song. The left-hand chromatic broken octaves were originally *ff* crescendo, tumultuoso, three semitones to a beat, culminating in a thunderous tremolando (*fff*) and an upward flourish. Revised, the octaves are marked only *f*, un peu plus animé, two semitones to a beat, while the tremolando is replaced by staccato chords (*ff*) and the final flourish is omitted. The vocal line, too, now avoids the low notes; previously, the song had been for either soprano or tenor, but in the second version the tenor voice, notably weak in the low register, is specified. So Liszt now leaves the idea of depth ('le profond chaos') to be expressed by the piano: the voice must ride above the accompaniment, and the change in the piano's right-hand part is directed towards this end. The substitution of B flat for E flat at the beginning of 'l'éternité' is due to an increased sensitivity to vocal line: it reduces the number of repetitions of E flat and also corresponds pleasantly to the rise of a fourth in the preceding phrase and the succeeding, stepwise fourth leading to the top A. Finally, the broadening out (en élargissant) of the revised version adds the touch of extra weight necessary to tone down the slightly hysterical quality of the earlier setting. The two passages are quoted here in full. (See pp. 227–9.)

Returning to Liszt's own criticism of his earlier songs as 'inflated', we find that repetition of words in them—the only change of text properly considered within a composer's province—is often considerable. There is historical justification for plentiful use of the device; for example, we unhesitatingly accept a whole chorus on 'Dona nobis pacem' from Bach. Nevertheless, Liszt sometimes overdoes it. It is not that musical quality is lacking; rather, the spirit of an intimate lyric simply may not permit such treatment.

This point is well illustrated by one song. Liszt made three versions of Goethe's *Der du von dem Himmel bist*, in 1843, 1856 and 1860; they are respectively 67, 53, and 54 bars long. (The original name of Goethe's poem is *Wanderers Nachtlied*, but Liszt uses the first line as his title.) The poem, dated 1776, is in fact a mere eight lines in length. The last line incorporates a repetition: 'komm, ach komm in meine Brust!'; while the preceding line has simply the words 'Süsser Friede', followed by a comma. Raabe, in the preface to the Collected Edition, rather cruelly spotlights Liszt's treatment of these words. He remarks that when the poet ends, the composer has by no means finished. And so comes 'komm, ach komm in meine Brust, süsser Friede, komm, ach komm, komm, ach komm in meine Brust, komm, ach komm . . .' and so on, with the phrase 'in meine Brust' recurring a further *five* times! In this passage, too, occurs an eccentric interpolation of a new version of the poem's first line: 'Der du im Himmel bist.' Now 'Von dem Himmel' and 'im Himmel' are by no means the same thing, and this gloss of Goethe's text is surely quite unjustifiable—particularly when Liszt marks it 'ritenuto, con somma passione', and thus the climax of the entire song! Such creative passion, as Raabe points out, can only ravage and ruin Goethe's simple nocturnal lyric. Once again, we may profitably study Liszt's second thoughts—and in this case, a third setting still to follow. As we would expect, in the second version the dubious textual gloss disappears and repetition is much reduced, while the accompaniment is lightened. In the third and final setting the last two lines are left exactly as Goethe wrote them.

Line and Texture

Nobody would deny that Liszt was a melodist of great gifts; a glance at (say) the *Consolations* should dispel any doubts. *O lieb*, in spite of its notorious reputation as a piano piece, has a most beautiful vocal line; indeed, were it otherwise it could hardly be so successful in its transcribed form. In its simpler way, *Es muss ein Wunderbares sein* is equally good melodically. Coming closer to recitative, *Gestorben war ich* shows masterly handling of the vocal line, while the discreet but wholly adequate piano part is a model of its kind. True recitative is found at the beginning of *Die Lorelei.* The change in texture and time at the first 'traurig' is utterly right; while the harmony at 'bin'—'(I) am'—expresses to perfection the stab of self-awareness, here at once a grief and an acceptance. The commencement of the piano legato with the 'ich' of 'dass ich so traurig' is no accident: the poet wonders why he feels as he does, and the sustained chord comes as he begins to describe his feeling of sadness.

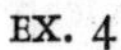

EX. 4

The piano introduction to *Die Lorelei* is noticeably 'Tristanesque'. The song appeared in 1856; while the poem of *Tristan und Isolde* was not begun until the following year, its music being completed in 1859. Perhaps we may permit ourselves this paraphrase of the opening to emphasize the resemblance.

EX. 5

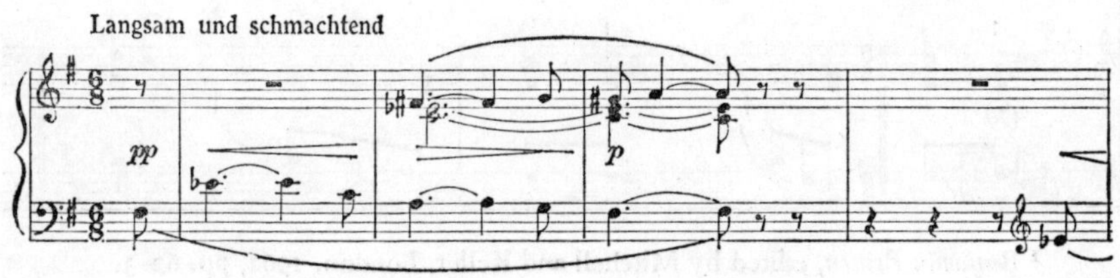

Referring back to Ex. 4, we find the two piano phrases beginning with a leap of the diminished seventh. The voice, however, begins with a fourth, not the expected leap which would echo the piano. And there is good reason. The negative statement—'I don't know'—is followed by a positive one, that 'I am so unhappy'. And it is for that moment that Liszt reserves the more expressive, and indeed passionate and Tristanesque leap of the sixth, identical in enharmonic terms with the piano's diminished sevenths. A final point: there is a delay before the voice enters, a delay haunted by the echo of the piano's 'longing' harmony. Does this not suggest, with the greatest subtlety, the poet-singer's emergence from reverie to voice his thoughts?

Liszt, then, could be sensitive to textual subtleties, and his musical imagination was equal to them. Yet there are pitfalls for the song-writer, and Liszt was sometimes careless. Peter Pears once thoughtfully observed that 'the more realistic the setting of the words becomes, the less interesting does its music tend to be'.[1] In the first version of *Schwebe, schwebe, blaues Auge*, the mere mention of birds in the text prompts Liszt to a miniature orgy of trills and runs; but as we might expect, in the second version these are restrained. Compare Exx. *6a* and *6b*.

EX. 6(*a*)

[1] *Benjamin Britten*, edited by Mitchell and Keller, London, 1962, pp. 62–3.

EX. 6(*b*)

The first version is not exactly dull in itself, but it lacks the musical justification to be compelling in the context of the song.

Simple dullness is something which Wagner warned against in 1851: 'If music subordinates itself to verse, and contents itself with merely contributing fullness of musical tone to its rhythms and its rhymes, it . . . deprives itself of its own sensuous beauty.' In *La Perla*, inspiration is at a low ebb in this passage, though the words are respectfully treated. One wonders whether Liszt felt this, and hoped to improve matters by the 'espress' marking.

EX. 7

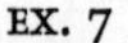

Also in *Jeanne d'Arc au bûcher*, the composer does not rise to the occasion (the last words of the poem): it is, above all, the vocal line which disappoints. In 1881, Liszt referred to this song as 'dürftig'—paltry, inadequate.

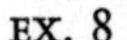

This latter fault is the opposite to that which was pointed out in those early songs, which suffer from *over*-bold musical treatment. Over-boldness and over-caution were Liszt's Scylla and Charybdis in the songs. Fortunately, when his navigational sense is working best, he sails triumphantly between the two dangerous rocks.

National Characteristics

Liszt was something of a cosmopolitan. Yet as such he was all the more interested (and not less) in the characteristic music of different countries; his writings on Jewish and Gypsy music bear this out, and so do his numerous compositions on national themes which range from the *Spanish Rhapsody* to *God Save the Queen*. As a German song composer, Liszt escapes the label of 'nationalist': the long-lasting German hegemony makes us think of that country's composers as somehow having universality, while in fact Richard Strauss is as German as Falla is Spanish. Liszt's national adaptability comes out in the songs, according to which language he is using; and he creates a local atmosphere through appropriateness of style. What could be more naturally Italian than this, the opening of the *Sonetto 47 del Petrarca*?

EX. 9

The sharp fourths of *Isten veled* and *A magyarok Istene*, and their dotted rhythms, are suitably Hungarian. But my own 'East European' favourite, *Die drei Zigeuner*, reveals in no uncertain terms the composer's known enthusiasm for Gypsy music. Surely, before writing *Tzigane*, Ravel knew Liszt's fine setting of Lenau's poem? Here are four short extracts from the piano part.

EX. 10

There is a touch of Spain in a charming setting of Hugo's *Comment, disaient-ils,* prompted by the reference to alguazils;[1] the accompaniment is marked 'quasi Chitarra'. Another setting of Hugo, *Gastibelza,* is a bolero, and the Spanish quality is prominent.

EX. 11

[1] An 'alguazil' is a Spanish warrant-officer.—*Ed.*

Even the rather disappointing, solitary English song seems to show some attempt to capture a national style. This is *Go not, happy day*, a setting of Tennyson written in 1879. There is a certain vague Englishness about the music to the first stanza, which perhaps would be more marked if the triplet rhythm were evened out into equal quavers. The use of high notes for 'rosy' and 'rose' is quite prophetic of the well-known later setting by Frank Bridge. The final piano cadence, echoing the last vocal phrase, ends on a dominant seventh; this is an oddity, even among Liszt's final cadences, of which I shall have more to say. For reasons best known to himself, Liszt provided a miserably sparse accompaniment to this song, which is more effective if the Allegretto un poco mosso marking is interpreted distinctly on the brisk side.

EX. 12

A song which seems particularly Germanic, or perhaps more especially Austrian, in its nostalgia, *Sehnsucht* and *Weltschmerz*, is the lovely *Ich möchte hingehn*. Here, as early as the 1840s, Liszt anticipates not only Wagner, but also Mahler and the Strauss of the 'Four Last Songs'.

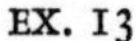

EX. 13

AUTOGRAPH PAGE OF 'DIE LORELEI' (1841)

AUTOGRAPH PAGE OF 'SONETTO 123 DEL PETRARCA' (1861)

A RECITAL ON 18 MARCH 1872, BUDAPEST
Oil Painting by Schams and Lafitte

This is the mood and, at times, nearly the musical language of Mahler's *Der Abschied* and *Ich bin der Welt abhanden gekommen*. The blue heavens, the sunset's glow, the soul weary of life—all are here in this song. Even the reference to harp strings reminds us of the poet's lute in *Der Abschied*. On one copy of the song, Liszt wrote that it was 'the testament of my youth—therefore no better, and also no worse'.

Tonality and Structure

Liszt's use of tonality in the songs is at times so free that the 1890 edition of Grove's Dictionary refers to their 'striking modulations and abrupt transitions'. 'Form', it goes on, 'escapes him' because he 'endeavours to render every word effectively and dramatically'. Einstein is more damning still: 'With Liszt, song lost its form', he says.[1] It is easy to refute Einstein, of whose remarks the most charitable view is that he misread the music. *Die Lorelei*, cited by Einstein in support of his argument, is entirely clear in its strophic shape, even though the music is not repeated for each verse. It may be argued that the absence of exact repetition actually makes the shape of a poem clearer—as well as, most probably,

[1] *Music in the Romantic Era*, London, 1947, p. 195.

its meaning. In a strictly strophic setting of *Die Lorelei* the same music would have to serve for 'so traurig bin' ('am so sad') 'wunderbar' ('wonderful') and 'mit wildem Weh' ('with unrestrained anguish'). Liszt can, and does, do better than that, while still building a perfectly satisfying musical shape. Avoidance of simple repetition allows him to return to the gently caressing music heard in the first stanza. The feeling of recapitulation, denied to the strictly strophic composer, is not only structurally good but reminds us that the events of a poem will no doubt soon be repeated with some other unfortunate victim of the Lorelei's fatal charms.

Another strophic song—with a difference—is *Le vieux vagabond*. The key is E minor; the singer a bass, with a two-octave compass, who is required to sing a long, low E fortissimo and crescendo at the end! There are six stanzas. Each has the same music, but there is, nevertheless, variety. The first, with pauses at the start, sounds almost like a recitative: there is the direction 'declamando'. Verses two, three and four are identical, though without this performing direction, and show the music well under way. Verse five drops a semitone to E flat minor and increases speed. The last verse starts in the same key; but the vocal drop of an augmented seventh (*sic*—at first it is D sharp to E flat, then in verse five, D natural to E double flat) now modifies to a major seventh (D natural to E flat) and we are at once back at the original pitch for the closing lines. This change brings us back to E minor; but it occurs at the right textual point as well, where the destitute old man expresses the wish that he might be allowed to work for the good of his fellow men. Yet the music, even after it has modulated, is still the same, stern and unyielding. The old man will die an outcast of society: 'je meurs votre ennemi'.

Cadences are a feature of Liszt's tonal language offering remarkable variety. His use of harmony can be both free and masterly, his innovations representing genuine advances in language, territory conquered, not mere eccentricity or slapdash thought.[1] If we examine a series of final cadences from the songs, we shall see that they show extraordinary diversity. In the following examples, the layout and rhythm, but *not* the notes, are sometimes simplified for the sake of clarity—for instance, a repetition of a final chord will be omitted. (See Ex. 14.)

[1] With Liszt, harmony could be structurally meaningful as well as a source of colour. The 'Rigoletto' Paraphrase, in D flat major, seems to start in the 'wrong' key of E major, but the initial tonality proves to be the starting-point of a brilliant introductory modulation leading to C sharp major (= D flat major). Liszt is too practical to start in F flat major, which would be theoretically more correct, but whose key-signature would include a double flat! With supreme effectiveness, therefore, he reserves the 'home' key for the start of Verdi's famous 'Quartet' theme.

EX. 14

(a)
'Il m' aimait·tant'
(b)
'Wo weilt er?'
(c)
'Der du von dem Himmel bist'
(1st version)
(d)
'Oh, quand je dors'
(e)
'La tombe et la rose'
(f)
'Was Liebe sei?' (1st version)
8va
(g)
'Pace non trovo' (1st version)
(h)
'Über allen Gipfeln ist Ruh'
8va
(i)
'Der du von dem Himmel bist'
(3rd version).
(j)
'Mignons Lied' (2nd version)
8va
(k)
'Du bist wie eine Blume'
(l)
'Die drei Zigeuner'
(alternative ending)
(m)
'Anfangs wollt ich fast verzagen'
(n)
'Ich möchte hingehn'
(o)
'Wer nie sein Brod mit Tränen ass' (2nd setting)

This lengthy example is, I hope, justified by its interest. A few points are worth comment: (*a*) shows a dominant thirteenth over a tonic pedal, correctly resolved; (*b*) is a dominant chord over a tonic pedal again, but the fifth is chromatically raised and resolves upwards in Tristanesque longing; (*c*) shows a favourite final cadence—a secondary seventh on the supertonic, last inversion, with F sharp and A raised chromatically and C sharp lowered (or, if this is too fussy an analysis, and since neither the resolution not the notation suggests a 'German sixth', here is the flattened sub-mediant, first inversion, plus an A sharp. The notation is admittedly odd, but so was the chord in 1842); (*d*) shows another supertonic seventh, first inversion, C sharp lowered; while (*e*) has again a supertonic seventh, last inversion, in its pure form since this G minor piece ends in the major.

All the cadences so far have included dissonance. The remaining seven do not, but they are hardly conventional. (*f*) approaches the tonic *via* a minor chord on the subdominant, (*g*) *via* a major chord on the mediant, and (*h*) *via* a major chord on the flattened mediant. (*i*) uses the normal (minor) mediant, (*j*) the major chord on the flattened submediant, while (*k*) uses the normal (minor) submediant. (*l*) is a real rarity: the tonic is preceded by the minor chord on the *sharpened* mediant, about the last note one would expect to find in a minor cadence. The use of a second inversion here leads us to the last three cadences. In (*m*), a six-four becomes a root position; in (*n*) the six-four is drawn from a root position to act as a final chord; lastly, in (*o*) the six-four is quite independent —a startling harmonic boldness.

Indeed, the endings of some of the songs are daring in the extreme. *Lasst mich ruhen*, in E major, ends in G sharp major. The second setting of *S'il est un charmant gazon* ends on a dominant seventh with tonic pedal—though a cautious *ad lib* extra pair of bars resolves to the tonic chord. *Go not, happy day* ends on a dominant seventh, second inversion, though this is in my view unconvincing. *J'ai perdu ma force et ma vie* ends on an incomplete diminished seventh; but this *does* seem convincing. The last words of the poem are: 'le seul bien qui me reste au monde est d'avoir quelquefois pleuré.' They are followed by sighing piano appoggiaturas; the final chord could begin the *last but one* of the series, but weariness intervenes and the 'musical' end can only be supplied by a very sympathetic and perceptive ear, and thus the loss of vigour and life described in the title is depicted.[1] To use a musically incomplete ending requires special expressive circumstances and a great deal of judgment. Liszt, when at the top of his form—as he is here—had that judgment in full measure.

[1] The end of Vaughan Williams's Sixth Symphony is similar, for while the tonic chord is eventually reached (but only just) it is nevertheless significantly in its weakest form, a second inversion.

The major-minor progression of (*n*) in Ex. 14 will have been noticed; the same thing happens at the end of *Und wir dachten der Toten*. This song provides an example of the arioso style which is to be found in the songs where Liszt altogether avoids strophic form. *J'ai perdu ma force et ma vie* is held together by subtleties like the recurrent use of a diminished fourth, both in the voice (melodically) and piano (chordally); there is nearly, but not quite, an absence of repetition. The freedom is comparable with that of a Debussy prelude; and the thought is equally masterly in its formal control. *Und wir dachten der Toten* is completely convincing structurally; this last verse of a poem by Ferdinand Freiligrath has received a setting which is both massively expressive and durationally small. Distant 'trumpet calls' on the piano lead to increased movement in the piano's right hand; there is a tremolando over which the voice steadily rises. A slower tempo is now adopted, the tremolando partly changing to sustained chords, for two more bars which lead to the climax. Here, and in the five remaining bars, the harmonies are, to my mind, marvellous. And for the purists, there is even a recapitulation of the distant trumpets at the end. To tell the truth, a proportionately far smaller retrospective glance may be adequate to create a feeling of return at the end of a piece—see, for example, Debussy's *La cathédrale engloutie* or *La sérénade interrompue*.

Interpretation

What are the problems, the special challenges which confront the singer of Liszt's songs? I think the experienced performer of *Lieder*, who no doubt includes in his or her repertory songs as different as Mozart's *Das Veilchen* and Schubert's *Erlkönig*, and also sings Wolf and Strauss, has little to fear. The overall technical and artistic demands of such a repertory are wide, and Liszt will present no fundamentally new difficulty.

A Liszt song recital could have more variety than most recitals devoted to one composer; and the choice of a group of songs for a general programme would be a pleasant task. No particular vocal range has been neglected. Diversity in a sequence of songs could be obtained by contrasting ballads—such as *Le vieux vagabond*, *Die Lorelei* or *Die drei Zigeuner*—with shorter, more intimate lyrics. There are also contrasts available between one language and another, between virtuoso early songs and more austere later ones, and indeed between different versions of the same song.

The composer himself said that artists who performed his songs should be neither coarse nor superficial. The recommendation is like that of Hamlet to the

Player King, which was to 'use all gently', not to 'tear a passion to tatters . . . to split the ears of the groundlings', and yet not to be 'too tame neither'. In other words, extremes are to be avoided: the most vehement song is still melodious, while the most restrained remains expressive. The study of the text, and of its exact relationship to the music, is perhaps the principal recommendation one would wish to make to a singer. The result of such study can only be better, because more meaningful, performance.

Struggles and Achievements

In 1859, Liszt wrote: 'The songs in their present form can stand on their own feet (discounting the inevitable criticism from our ill-tempered and snarling opponents!), and if some singers, neither coarse nor superficial, find the necessary courage to sing songs by the notorious non-composer Franz Liszt, then probably they too will find their public.'

Liszt commonly spoke of the songs with a certain wry humour, even self-doubt. He was pleased to be complimented on *Mignons Lied* by Goethe's friends, who told him that the setting of the phrase 'dahin, dahin' would not have displeased the great poet, and that he had succeeded 'reasonably well'. He told the Princess Wittgenstein of his troubles in setting *Ich scheide*: 'I did three or four different versions, torn up one after another—and, tired out with the struggle, I finished it last night. It's nothing very special—and I certainly swore that I wouldn't get involved like that again.' Yet in the same letter he says that he has started on *Die drei Zigeuner* and 'found the general outline very quickly at the piano. If it goes naturally, so to speak, I'll write it. But otherwise not for the moment, for I was too stupidly bothered for days over that musical inflection twenty times found—and yet remaining unfindable—of Hoffmann's "Scheiden".' Another letter to the Princess tells of *Ihr Glocken von Marling*, 'a little, innocent, dreamy *Lied* . . . which cost me more trouble than I expected. I had to do it three times over . . . If my little "Bells of Marling" tinkle agreeably in Magne's[1] ears that will be a very sweet compensation for me.' A letter to Josef Dessauer is interesting in that it dates from the early 1850s, when there was a break in his output of songs: 'Perhaps you'll put me once again in a song mood, which will prompt me to write in this form. My earlier songs are mostly too inflated and sentimental. . . .'

A glimpse into Liszt's methods, as we have already seen, is provided by the revisions. Even simpler comparison of different solutions to problems is pro-

[1] 'Magne' was Liszt's nickname for the Princess's small daughter Marie.

vided by *ossia* passages, printed together as alternatives for the performer. The first version of *Im Rhein, im schönen Strome* has an *ossia* for piano throughout, 'più difficile'! Also more difficult, indeed, are the *ossia* passages with top D flats in the first versions of *Pace non trovo* and *Benedetto sia 'l giorno*. The for tenor *ossia* at the end of *Die drei Zigeuner* is of quite a different kind—it is an optional continuation of the music, and in fact of the words. That in the piano part at the end of *Ich scheide* is an alternative having nothing to do with difficulty, for the choice is purely musical; and the same is true of the vocal *ossia* near the end of *Die stille Wasserrose*. Most remarkable of all, perhaps, is the end of *Ich liebe dich*. Not content with providing two alternative gentle endings, Liszt writes a third which is fortissimo. But before accusing him of leaving his job as a composer incomplete, we should remember that he is not unique in this. Bartók sometimes provides alternative endings; and present-day composers who do not write any notes at all, but leave them to the performers' discretion, can hardly be critical! Perhaps we should be thankful to a composer who is so generous with his music.

Finally, the achievement of the songs. Principally, I think, it is a method of handling material: a method of infinite structural flexibility: a method which influenced Wagner and through him Strauss and Mahler, even perhaps (in diluted form) composers as different as Debussy, Schoenberg and Britten. 'With Liszt song lost its form'—if Einstein's comment is true, these composers, at any rate, do not seem to have heard about it.[1]

[1] Singers will find several extremely fine songs among those which are so far unmentioned, or only briefly so, in this essay. They include: *Die Vätergruft*, *Wie singt die Lerche schön*, *Vergiftet sind meine Lieder*, *Blume und Duft*, *Die Fischerstochter*, *Sei still*, *Des Tages laute Stimmen schweigen*, *Es muss ein Wunderbares sein*, and the first version of *Der Fischerknabe*.

ROBERT COLLET

Works for Piano and Orchestra

THE works for piano and orchestra form an interesting section of Liszt's output, but as a body they are hardly as important as the solo piano works and the orchestral works. This is less surprising than one might think. The problems of combining satisfactorily the piano and orchestra have troubled many composers, and they have seldom been completely solved; most composers have been content with writing a few specimens, often only one or two. The great exception among the major composers is, of course, Mozart, who was unique both in the number of concertos that he wrote and in the outstanding position that they hold in his output. Mozart succeeded more completely and consistently than any other composer in solving the technical and artistic problems of combining the piano with other instruments, problems that seem almost by their nature to be insoluble; and I am thinking of his piano quartets as much as his concertos.

Throughout the last two hundred years there have been two main tendencies in writing for piano and orchestra: to separate the solo instrument sharply from the orchestra, treating it much as if it were the soloist in an operatic aria; or, by contrast, to integrate it to a high degree into the orchestral texture. The concertos of Field, Chopin and Henselt are extreme examples of the first; Busoni's Concerto and the Sinfonia Concertante of Szymanowski, of the second. Many concertos, including Liszt's, exemplify both trends, which can alternate in the same work.

In spite of Liszt's amazing command of the piano, in which he seems to have anticipated most of the developments of the last hundred years, and of his great knowledge of the orchestra acquired in early middle-life, his output of works for the medium is small. They were all composed before he was forty, although the most important were revised some years later. The revisions gave him so much trouble that he may even have acquired a distaste for the medium.[1] But we should, perhaps, remember the case of Beethoven, who wrote no concertos after producing the 'Emperor' at the age of forty because, presumably, he regarded the medium as unsuited to the style of his later period; the same could be said of Liszt. In Beethoven's case, also, there was the additional factor that his deafness had compelled him to abandon the career of a public performer. Liszt, too, though for different reasons, played little in public after the age of forty. This removed one obvious inducement to write concertos; most successful piano concertos have been written by virtuoso pianists who planned giving the first performances themselves. (It is interesting that this has been rather less true of violin concertos.)

In his two Concertos, especially, Liszt used his 'transformation of themes' technique to special advantage, and it might even be said to have led him on to the discovery of new forms in these works. Liszt actually brought his technique of metamorphosis to perfection during the very period in which the works for piano and orchestra were composed (roughly 1830–60), therefore it is hardly surprising to find in these compositions some splendid illustrations of the device, which, as a matter of historical fact, happens to be an important development in nineteenth-century composition. The kind of thematic transformation one finds, for instance, in the A major piano Concerto, in which the opening theme

EX. 1

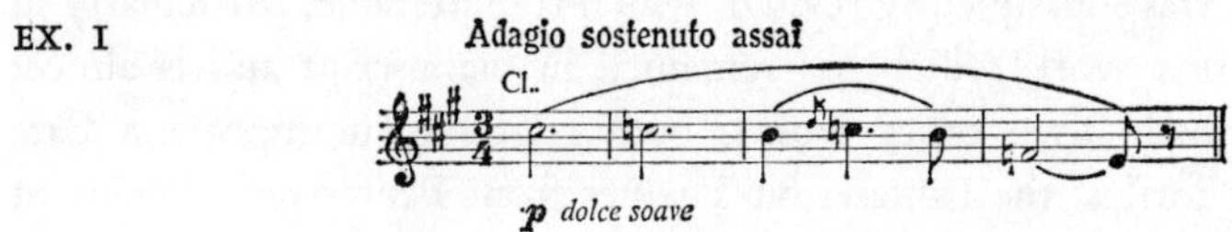

later turns up in this rhapsodic version in the finale,

EX. 2

[1] I regard the whole subject of Liszt's revisions as important and altogether fascinating; his approach was almost the opposite of Beethoven's. With Beethoven, the gestation of a work was often slow, but once completed a work was seldom revised. With Liszt, the gestation was usually rapid but thereafter he felt a frequent need to improve the work, often after an interval of ten years or more.

placed the whole question of structural 'integrity' into a new context which was to have repercussions right down to our own time.[1]

Liszt wrote altogether seven works for piano and orchestra and I want to look at each of them in turn. The best known are the two concertos. The earliest sketches for the E flat Concerto go back as far as 1830; but the work was to undergo many revisions before it reached the final form in which it was published in 1856. The A major Concerto, which was not completed until 1861, went through rather fewer vicissitudes, though Liszt started work on it as early as 1839. In both cases, the dates of the final revisions would lead us to think of them as works of the same period as the 'Faust' Symphony; in all essentials, however, they belong to a much earlier period. The *Totentanz*, in many ways the most original and striking of all the works for piano and orchestra, was completed in an earlier version in 1849, though the version everybody knows dates from 1859. After this, there is nothing further. Although Liszt's style went through the most significant changes in the last twenty-five years of his life, these developments were in the opposite direction from the virtuosity of the Concertos. (I have never heard of any evidence that Liszt planned a work for piano and orchestra during this later period; he almost certainly felt that he had said everything he had to say in the medium.) Two of the other works, the 'Lélio' Fantasy and the so-called 'Malédiction' Concerto, date from the 1830s. Neither of them was subsequently revised, which is regrettable, particularly in the case of the first work which has remained in manuscript and is almost totally unperformed. Two other works, both relatively unimportant, date back to the late 'forties: the Fantasia on Themes from Beethoven's 'Ruins of Athens', and the Fantasia on Hungarian Folk Themes.

Grande Fantaisie Symphonique on themes from Berlioz's 'Lélio' (1834)

The earliest of Liszt's works for piano and orchestra is the Fantasia on Berlioz's *Lélio* (the strangest and least coherent of all Berlioz's works). It has not so far been published. As a curiosity, and for its many individually beautiful touches, it deserves an occasional performance. It is based on two numbers of the original work; the setting of Goethe's Ballade 'Der Fischer' (Ex. 3*a*), originally for tenor with piano accompaniment, and the 'Chorus of Brigands' (Ex. 3*b*).

[1] See Humphrey Searle, pp. 281–83, for a fuller discussion of the 'transformation of themes' technique. Also Louis Kentner, pp. 84–85.—*Ed.*

The orchestral writing is curiously helpless and overloaded, without even a faint foretaste of the mastery that Liszt eventually achieved; but perhaps we should remember that he was only twenty-two when he wrote the work. Still, even in the late forties, he felt unsure of his orchestral technique and sought help from other musicians, notably Joachim Raff. The importance of this help may have been exaggerated;[1] the decisive factor was the direct knowledge of the orchestra that Liszt gained through conducting during his years in Weimar, with all the facilities he had for having his works tried out in rehearsal. In his mature work, Liszt is certainly one of the great orchestrators of the nineteenth century.

There is much that is fascinating in the piano part of this work, but as in other works of the period the technical inventiveness gets out of hand; the young Liszt, at this stage of his career, was interested mainly in developing the resources of the instrument to their extreme limits. There are, consequently, moments when the physical difficulties of the piano writing outweigh its effectiveness in actual performance. The 'Lélio' Fantasy could certainly have gained from being

[1] See Humphrey Searle, pp. 279–80.—*Ed.*

revised; but Liszt either lost interest in the work, or was unable to spare the time. I quote two further examples from the piano part. The alternation of the hands in Exx. 4*a* and *b* is ingenious, but I doubt whether Liszt would have retained it had he revised the work.

EX. 4

Something should be said about the relationship between Berlioz and Liszt as composers, as distinct from their historically important personal friendship. Obviously Liszt's whole conception of the symphony and the symphonic poem was much affected by Berlioz's symphonic works, and the two men shared most of their fundamental musical ideals, although Liszt's extreme eclecticism was quite foreign to Berlioz's temperament and in their actual musical styles they had remarkably little in common. Berlioz's greatest originality lies in a rhythmical freedom and unconventionality that are almost unique in nineteenth-century music and in a very personal gift for extended melody. Both these aspects of his work had little effect on Liszt whose interests, like those of most nineteenth-century composers, were much more harmonic. Even their orchestral styles are quite unalike. The point needs to be made because the bracketing of their names can be very misleading. This does not mean that Liszt's admiration for Berlioz was not sincere. His Berlioz transcriptions, most of which have for many years been out of print, deserve careful study—particularly the daring and resourceful version of the 'Fantastic' Symphony,[1] and a very personal *Andante Amoroso* (virtually an original work) based on the *Idée fixe* theme of the Symphony. The transcriptions of *Harold in Italy* and the *Francs-Juges* overture are also outstanding.

[1] See p. 44. Also the entry 'Berlioz' in the Register of Persons on p. 373.—*Ed.*

'Malédiction' Concerto (1840)

The so-called 'Malédiction' Concerto for piano and strings (the title is not Liszt's) was begun as early as 1830 but it was not completed until some ten years later. It was published posthumously—as recently as 1915—and first acquired its nickname then. The term 'malédiction' (which means 'under a curse') was attached to the work because this was the word Liszt had scribbled over the opening theme (Ex. 5); but it is slightly misleading as Liszt also jotted down other superscriptions in the course of the composition, the second theme (Ex. 6) being marked 'Orgueil' (Pride) and the third theme (Ex. 7*a*) 'Raillerie' (Mockery). One regrets that Liszt never thoroughly revised the work. Like the 'Lélio' Fantasy it is preoccupied with technical inventiveness at the expense of pianistic effectiveness—though perhaps to a lesser degree. The writing for the strings is hardly more than adequate. The composer who, fifteen years later, was producing the mature orchestral works out of the fullness of his experience, could certainly have transformed this into something more impressive.

In spite of some stylistic unevenness, the work has much charm; the mingling of Byronic defiance, great tenderness and a touch of religious sentiment is very characteristic—though no doubt this is precisely what many people dislike in Liszt. From the point of view of its form, the mosaic-like interaction of five or six basic themes (or rather motifs) is characteristic of a technique of construction that turns up frequently in Liszt's later works. Moreover, some of these motifs have connections with other works. The Concerto begins, for instance, with an anticipation of the piano piece *Orage* from the 'Swiss' book of the *Années de Pèlerinage*.

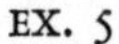
EX. 5

A bit later, we hear a motif which is better known in the *Mephistopheles* movement of the 'Faust' Symphony.

EX. 6

Compare with the 'Faust' Symphony, Ex. 48, p. 309.

Of the remaining themes, the three chief ones are as follows.

EX. 7

molto appassionato ed espressivo

(a)

Piano

poco rit.

ppp

Cello

ppp

non troppo presto

8va

leggierissimo

(b)

Piano un poco più animato

leggiero niente

p

un poco agitato

Cello

dolce espressivo

It is from this small handful of ideas that Liszt builds the entire, mosaic-like structure of the 'Malédiction' Concerto. The work gives us an interesting glimpse into the way in which Liszt's mind was working during this early period—towards the 'transformation of themes' technique which he only properly developed during the Weimar period (1847–61). The structure of 'Malédiction' more than hints at it now and again. The harmonic idiom of the work, also, is quite advanced considering the early date at which it was written. There are bold clashes between the F major triad and the B major triad. In theory, these triads are as far apart as it is possible to get; but like so much that

EX. 8

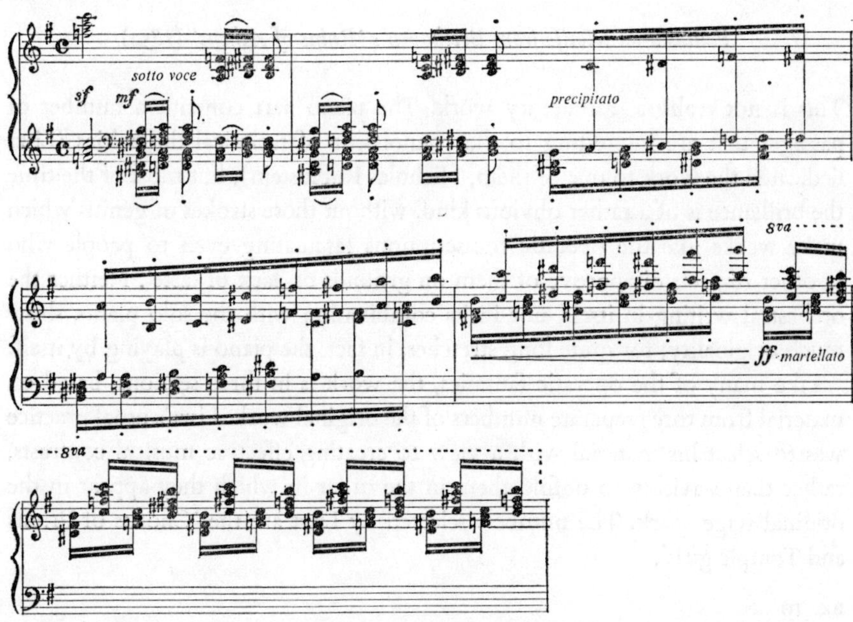

sounds new in Liszt, they are capable of a quite orthodox explanation, being an extension of the use of the major common chord on the flattened supertonic—frequently met with from the seventeenth century onwards in the form of the

Neapolitan sixth. The piano writing, characteristic of early Liszt, contains chords and octaves alternating between the hands (see Ex. 8), and passages in broken octaves, such as the following. Broken octaves play an important part in the writing of the Viennese composers, usually as a pianistic approximation

EX. 9

to the effect of repeated notes on bowed instruments; they have tended to be used less and less by later composers, Liszt being almost the last great composer to employ them.

Fantasia on Motifs from Beethoven's 'Ruins of Athens' (1852)

This is not really a satisfactory work. The piano part contains a number of passages that are interesting to the connoisseur of technical difficulties (Liszt dedicated the work to one of them, Nicholas Rubinstein); but most of the time the brilliance is of a rather obvious kind, without those strokes of genius which make works like the operatic transcriptions fascinating even to people who in other respects disapprove of them on grounds of 'lack of taste'. Neither the orchestral writing in itself, nor in its combination with the solo piano, show much originality; for quite long stretches, in fact, the piano is playing by itself.

Like many of the operatic fantasies, the work is in three sections, based on material from three separate numbers of the original work. Liszt's usual practice was to select his material with a view to creating effective musical contrasts, rather than slavishly to unfold them in the order in which they appear in the original stage work. The numbers selected by Liszt are the 'Chorus of Priests and Temple girls',

EX. 10

AUTOGRAPH PAGE OF SOLO PIANO VERSION OF 'TOTENTANZ'
(c. 1860–65)

LISZT IN ROME (c. 1865)

FRANZ LISZT (c. 1885)

the 'Chorus of Dervishes', and the famous 'Turkish March',

EX. 11

which is first heard on the piano alone and later in an ingenious combination with the 'Chorus of Priests'.

EX. 12

The 'Ruins of Athens' also exists in a version for piano solo.

'Hungarian' Fantasy (1852)

During his lifetime, Liszt's Hungarian Rhapsodies were the most successful of all his works, and he was probably under great pressure to produce versions of them for piano and orchestra. However, only one such work has come down to us—the *Fantasy on Hungarian Folk Melodies.* The work is an extended version of the Hungarian Rhapsody in F minor (No. 14), and the main theme is the Hungarian folk-song 'Mohac's Field'.

EX. 13

A contrasting section, in A minor, marked by Liszt *à la Zingarese*, (in Gypsy style) runs:

EX. 14

Towards the end of the Fantasy we hear a tune of the type played by strolling Gypsy bands, which Liszt probably came across on one of his visits to Hungary.

EX. 15

This brilliant (though to many musicians, vulgar) showpiece is rounded off by a return to 'Mohac's Field' with all the usual pyrotechnics.

Piano Concerto No. 1 in E Flat Major (1830–55)

In spite of its being one of the most hackneyed of all concertos, and despite the distorted and meretricious performances of it one has heard, it seems to me that the E flat major Concerto is an underrated work. An extraordinary number of unpleasant things have been said about it, and even some admirers of Liszt have been distinctly patronizing. I remember many years ago reading in the *Times* a notice of a performance by Cortot, in which the critic[1] pronounced it to be the most vulgar concerto ever written. According to Francesco Berger 'the opening theme of this work is not a theme at all, it is just an empty phrase.' This, of course, sounds devastating, but does it really mean anything? That opening theme in itself is neither vulgar nor distinguished; everything depends on what happens to it later. It is true that the Concerto offers certain opportunities for an exhibitionist approach on the part of the soloist. I did not hear the performance of Cortot that provoked the *Times* critic's remark. But I did hear two unforgettable performances by Liszt's pupil Moriz Rosenthal, memorable for a unique blend of elegance and impetuosity.

Liszt himself gave the first performance of the Concerto in Weimar in 1855 with Berlioz conducting. In many respects the event was an historical one. Liszt had started to sketch the Concerto twenty-five years earlier,[2] and he had

[1] H. C. Colles? In those days, the *Times*'s critics were anonymous.

[2] The earliest sketches for the E flat Concerto date from 1830. There are altogether five versions of the work, the fourth being quite close to the final version. They are all preserved in the Liszt archives at Weimar. It would be expensive, but invaluable, both for pianists and students of composition, to have the material published in a critical edition. In the earliest version the orchestral writing has the same helplessness that we find in the 'Lélio' Fantasy with which it is roughly contemporary. Here are two fragments from the earlier versions.

(a)

This was originally the solo pianist's first entry! Compare with Ex. 20, the final and much simpler version.

(b)

This passage comes from the finale. Compare with Ex. 30, which again is the final, and

worked at it, on and off, ever since. There is much to be learned from a study of its original, 'cyclic' form, which shows conclusively the absurdity of saying that Liszt's music is 'formless'. The work breaks new ground. For while it falls into four quite distinct movements, which are nonetheless thematically linked, it is played without a break, the entire Concerto unfolding more than twenty minutes continuous music. Bartók regarded it as 'the first perfect realization of cyclic sonata form, with common themes treated on the variation principle'—the 'variation principle' being, of course, Liszt's own technique of the 'metamorphosis of themes'.

The Concerto opens in a grandiloquent style with the theme about which Francesco Berger was so scathing.

EX. 16

It is a theme which dominates the entire work and it undergoes several important transformations.[1] Quite frequently it appears in diminution;

EX. 17 

and there is also a very effective occurrence in the cadenza of the third movement where the theme is harmonized with a chain of descending diminished sevenths.

EX. 18

simpler version. These examples sum up Liszt's method of revision, and show the change that occurred round 1845 in his attitude to the piano; in fact the abandonment of the ideal of super-virtuosity. In all his later work, difficult as it may be, we never have the feeling that it is dangerously near the limit of what is physically possible for any player.

[1] Liszt was once asked what was the meaning of this theme. It is said that he sat down at the piano and sang to it the following phrase: 'Das versteht Ihr alle nichte' (This none of you understands). He left no clue as to what he might have meant.

Another of its far-flung derivatives occurs in the finale where the descending chromatic figure is filled in crotchet-wise to produce this theme.

EX. 19

The octave passages at the piano's first entry, and which immediately follow Ex. 16, are less dangerous than they have the reputation of being among pianists, and they can sound very impressive if played in nearly strict tempo.

EX. 20

The chief, contrasting idea in the first movement runs

EX. 21

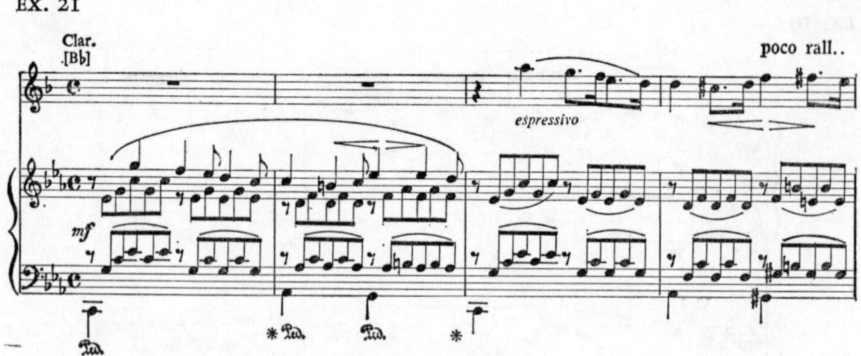

The scoring of this passage, particularly the solo writing for woodwind instruments, is most effective. It is almost chamber musical in style; in fact, it comes as close to genuine chamber music as Liszt ever got, for this was a field he almost totally neglected. When the piano part is not the main centre of attention, Liszt uses it very skilfully as an accompanying instrument (his songs show that he completely understood this use of the piano).

The second movement, Quasi Adagio, opens with a long, Bellini-like melody for piano alone.

EX. 22

This melody offers an excellent illustration of Liszt's 'transformation of themes' technique, for its three main segments (Exx. 22 'x', 'y', and 'z') are all turned into 'contrasting' ideas at later stages in the Concerto. Ex. 22 'x'

EX. 23

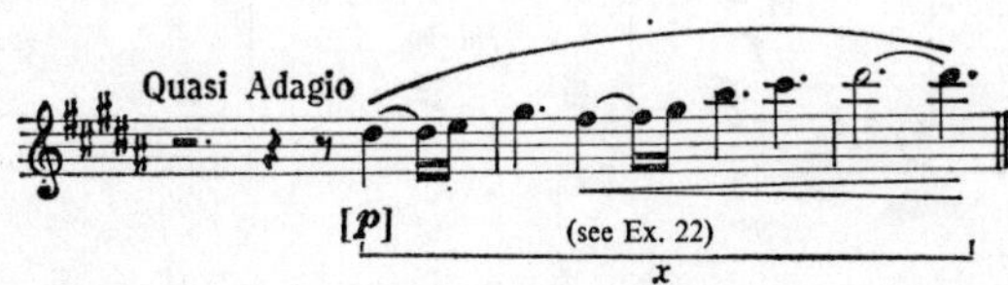

is transformed into a march-tune, the main subject of the finale.

EX. 24

Ex. 22 'y', on the other hand,

EX. 25

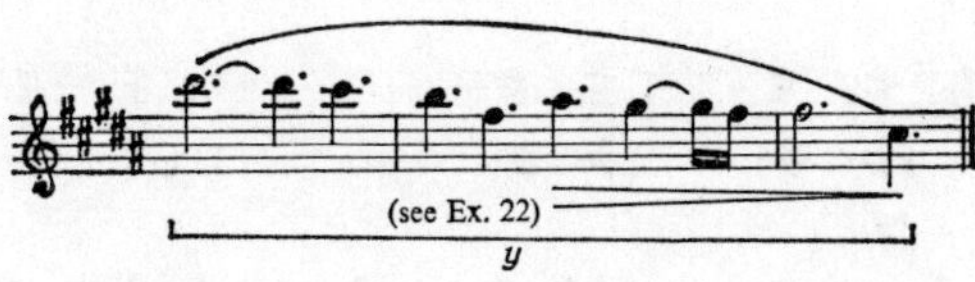

turns up later in the slow movement thus:

EX. 26

while Ex. 22 'z'

EX. 27

is taken up almost immediately and developed into a strikingly original recitative passage.

EX. 28

Later on in the slow movement there is a short episode in C major in which the following new theme appears.

EX. 29

Liszt uses this theme again in the finale in the following transformation.

EX. 30

The third movement is a Scherzo, Mephistophelean in its sardonic wit. Most of Liszt's humour has this character. The use of the triangle in this movement, which so affronted Hanslick when he first heard the Concerto, is a stroke of great originality; it has been criticized in some quarters as an offence against good taste, with the inevitable jokes about 'the eternal triangle' of the two ideas of this section.[1] The first of these ideas (Ex. 31) is composed across the bar-lines, making the triple time sound as if it were duple.

EX. 31

[1] Shortly after Hanslick had cursed the work by calling it the 'triangle concerto', Liszt defended the use of the triangle in a letter to his cousin Eduard Liszt, dated Weimar, 26 March 1857:

'As regards the triangle I do not deny that it may give offence, especially if it is struck too strongly and not precisely. A preconceived disinclination and objection to instruments of percussion prevails, somewhat justified by the frequent misuse of them. . . . Musicians who appear to be serious and solid prefer to treat the instruments of percussion *en canaille* (= as rabble) which must not make their appearance in the seemly company of the symphony. Inwardly, they bitterly deplore that Beethoven allowed himself to be seduced into using the big drum and triangle in the Finale of the Ninth Symphony. Of Berlioz, Wagner and my humble self, it is no wonder that "like draws to like", and, as we are treated as impotent *canaille* amongst musicians, it is quite natural that we should be on good terms with the *canaille* among the instruments. . . . In the face of the most wise proscription of the learned critics I shall, however, continue to employ instruments of percussion, and think I shall win for them some effects little known.' —*Ed.*

The second idea, an off-shoot of the first, runs:

EX. 32

Liszt then proceeds to compose a set of continuous variations on these two themes of ever increasing brilliance. I quote two of their later versions (Exx. 33 *a* and *b*).

EX. 33

Compare these two examples with Exx. 31 and 32.

The finale Allegro marziale animato, contains no fresh thematic material of its own, being created out of metamorphoses of earlier themes—some of them highly ingenious. The movement is best regarded as a gigantic recapitulation to the entire work.

Piano Concerto No. 2 in A Major (1839–61)

The second Concerto, in A major, occupied Liszt for many years. It was composed as early as 1839, but Liszt was dissatisfied with it and it went through several revisions before being finally completed in 1861. The first performance of the Concerto took place in Weimar, in 1857, with Liszt conducting and Hans von Bronsart, one of his highly gifted pupils, playing the solo part. It was finally published in 1863 with a dedication to Bronsart.

The A major Concerto is a less showy, more poetic, work than the one in E flat major, and perhaps this is the reason why it has never attained the same kind of popularity; indeed, it is regarded as a connoisseur's work. I hold what many Lisztians would regard as heretical views about it: that it does not hang together as successfully as the E flat major Concerto—even though it contains finer individual ideas.

Like its predecessor, the A major Concerto is a continuously unfolding 'cyclic' structure, in which Liszt employs his 'metamorphosis of themes' technique to great advantage. Unlike the E flat major Concerto, however, it does not easily lend itself to a division into separate movements; neither does it conform to the opposite kind of structural pattern evinced by the B minor Sonata —a single, long movement constructed on the principles of sonata first-movement form. It is possible that Liszt was here aiming at a type of structure intermediate between the two, and this may explain why the Concerto may seem to have a certain ambiguity of form. In fact, it is possible to divide up the work in different ways, according to how one regards particular sections or subsections.

The opening bars are most romantically suggestive. Unlike so many admirable openings of works, however, whose intrinsic beauty almost seems to rule out significant developments, these bars have possibilities which are exploited with great skill.

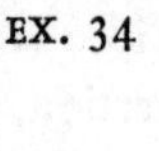

There are two important structural elements: the harmonic progression of the first four bars (bracket 'x'), and the curious melodic twist in bar 3 (bracket 'y'). The second of these two elements is the more fertile, and the way in which it is used is unusually reminiscent of Beethoven. The charge is so often made against Liszt that he did not really understand thematic developments, even though it is grudgingly admitted that he had a certain ingenuity in dressing up his material in varied costumes. The treatment of this small figure in the first seventy bars alone should cause one to re-consider this assertion,

EX. 35

a misleading quarter-truth. This passage becomes increasingly developmental, the solo horn joining in a melodic line which Liszt marks with the unusual term 'träumend' (dreaming) wrapped around with the most delicate, filigree passage-

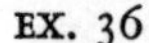
EX. 36

work on the piano. A brilliant cadenza follows, in which the opening idea is alluded to and which leads without a break into the second main section, marked L'istesso tempo. This is one of the most dramatic contrasts in the Concerto.

EX. 37

This in turn, gives way to what is essentially the Scherzo movement of the Concerto. Marked Allegro agitato assai, it starts in B flat minor and ends in C sharp minor. Here is the main theme.

EX. 38

It is later transformed, at the end of the Scherzo, in the following manner. The

EX. 39

D flat major section which follows, although marked Allegro moderato, has so much lyricism and unhurried pace about it as to give it the character of a slow movement. It contains this particularly beautiful metamorphosis of the Concerto's opening idea, played on the cello with the piano accompanying.

EX. 40

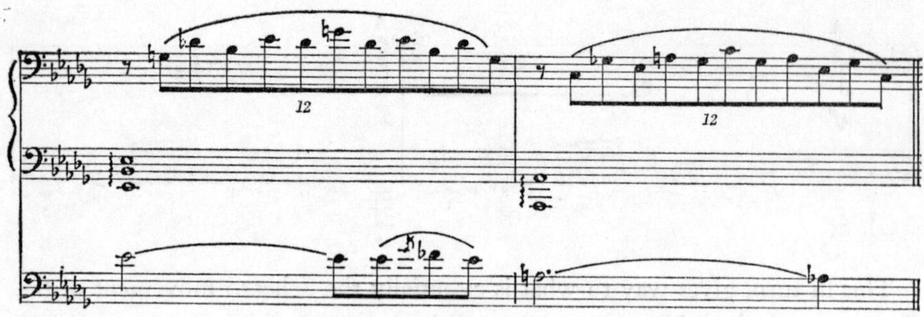

It shows the Italian, *bel canto* element in Liszt at its most uninhibited—one almost says 'unashamed', because it is this element which has shocked so many German and English critics, and even some Lisztians. M. D. Calvocoressi, one of Liszt's most persuasive advocates, obviously thought the Italian influence lay at the root of what he believed to be the weaker side of much of the music. To Busoni, on the other hand, Liszt's Italianism made a deep appeal and he maintained that to enjoy certain works it was best not to have too pure Germanic blood. To me, the Italian side of Liszt seems extremely important, perhaps more important than the Hungarian; few of his works, in any medium, are without some trace of it. As it happens, early nineteenth-century Italian opera is much more generally enjoyed and esteemed than it was sixty years ago, and this has certainly had a positive effect on people's attitude towards Liszt.

This D flat major section leads to what appears to be a new lyrical theme given to the piano, unaccompanied—'con abbandono' (Ex. 41). I think, however, that this theme may well be derived from the motif 'y' of the opening bars (see Ex. 34). Each modified repetition of the bracket 'y' (Ex. 41) makes its derivation from the opening seem more likely. The following quotation makes the point clear.

EX. 41

From this moment on I think that the Concerto begins to deteriorate. The basic weakness is one that can be found in many works of Liszt, even, at moments, in some of his best ones: an excessive employment of sequential repetition (sometimes of quite large units) in an over-mechanical symmetry. One has the feeling that as the canvas is of a pre-determined size it must be covered at all costs. The passage ends with a cadenza, leading on to what I consider to be the Development section—in the same way that one can consider the central section of the B minor Sonata as being one. This section opens in D flat major, Allegro deciso, and it passes through a number of keys, to a pedal-point on E, the dominant of the main key of the work, which stands rather like a 'lead-back' section at the end of a development in a classical sonata. An important feature of this 'Development' is the manner in which Liszt combines two of his earlier themes I quoted earlier. Compare with Exx. 37 and 38.

EX. 42

The remarkable anticipation of the famous passage at the beginning of Tchaikovsky's B flat minor Piano Concerto has been observed many times before.

The closing section of the Concerto is both a finale *and* a recapitulation. No thematic material appears that has not already been used. It begins with a sort of heroic version of the Concerto's opening bars. Compare Ex. 34 with Ex. 43.

EX. 43

This march-like statement of the principal theme Humphrey Searle regards as the Concerto's 'one really weak moment', and it is to my mind, more jarring than anything in the E flat work because it really is out of character with the earlier parts of the composition.[1] The finale's chief 'contrasting' idea is yet another version of the opening theme, much more lyrical in character (see Ex. 2) but somewhat out of style, in my view, with what comes just before and after. Liszt himself suggested that the passage might be cut. Suggestions for cuts occur in quite a number of his works; in a sense they show the practical sense of an immensely experienced concert performer, but they also show a lack of tautness of structure. Cuts of that kind would be unthinkable in Beethoven, and almost so in Chopin. No doubt it is easy to be unjust to the last section of the work precisely because the earliest sections have led one to expect a very great composition.

[1] It may well be that an essential prerequisite to the enjoyment of Liszt's music is a readiness to forgive (not necessarily to approve) these occasional incongruities. If one regards consistency of style as the supreme virtue, and its absence as the unpardonable sin, one will not be attracted towards Liszt. All intelligent admirers of Liszt admit that these moments of weakness exist, and that they are sometimes regrettable; but it is significant they often disagree about which ones matter and which ones don't. Really it isn't a question of separating the sheep from the goats; there are very few works of Liszt that are entirely without blemish, and not many without at least some strikingly individual touches.

As with the E flat Concerto the piano part of the A major was much revised, nearly always achieving equal or greater effectiveness by simpler means. One special feature is the frequent replacement of passages in broken octaves by passages for alternating hands. There would be no point in performing either Concerto in an earlier version; but the piano parts, like the earlier versions of the 'Transcendental' and the 'Paganini' Studies (and like Godowsky's fascinating versions of Chopin's studies) would be of immense interest to virtuoso pianists for study purposes.

Totentanz: Paraphrase on the Dies Irae (1859)

Totentanz occupied Liszt from 1838 to 1859. It consists of a set of variations on the ancient plainchant theme for the dead *Dies Irae*. The first performance of the work was given in 1865 at the Hague, with Hans von Bülow (to whom it is dedicated) playing the solo part.

I think *Totentanz* is one of the most telling and personal of all Liszt's works. It was inspired by the Orcagna fresco *The Triumph of Death* which the 27-year-old Liszt had seen while travelling through Italy with the Countess d'Agoult, and which had made a tremendous impact on him. The fresco portrays a series of ghastly scenes. Death is flying towards her victims swinging a scythe. A heap of corpses lie at her feet. Souls are rising to heaven while others are being dragged down to the flames of hell. There are open graves containing decaying bodies. *The Triumph of Death*, in fact, can be described as a set of variations on the theme of death. Liszt, therefore, put his music into the form of a set of variations on the *Dies Irae* theme. It was not the first time Liszt had encountered *Dies Irae*. Some years earlier he had made a piano arrangement of Berlioz's 'Fantastic' Symphony where this plainchant melody dominates the last movement (see p. 44, Ex. 5), and he may well have had the Berlioz work at the back of his mind when he composed *Totentanz*.[1]

Totentanz begins in the black depths of the keyboard with a pounding ostinato figure against which the orchestra give out the *Dies Irae* melody.

[1] The work exists in two versions. The second is the one generally performed. The first version, the 'Busoni' version, was published by Breitkopf in 1919 in the full score. It was unearthed by Busoni in 1918 from the manuscripts in the possession of the Marquis Casanova. The manuscripts are in a state of some confusion and the reconstruction of the score must have required much patience, skill, and at times the exercise of some degree of personal judgment. There is no reason to suppose, however, that Busoni took liberties with the original. There is also a manuscript of the orchestral parts in Weimar, but without any piano part. As is usually the case in Liszt, the later version is on the whole more satisfying; but the

EX. 44

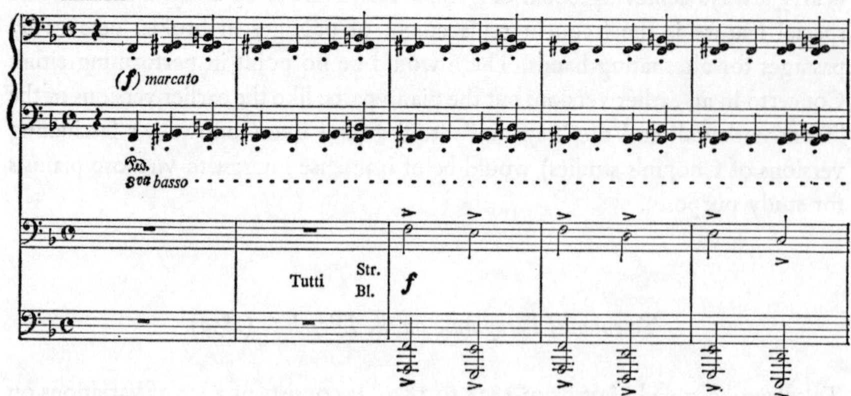

earlier one contains some really striking things that were omitted altogether in the later one. It really deserves an occasional hearing, and in any case the score should be reprinted. It would not be right to combine the two versions.

The final version dates from 1859, ten years later than the Casanova manuscript; the work had first been planned ten years earlier still. The really important things peculiar to the 'Busoni' version are an interlude of Variation VII based on the liturgical melody *de Profundis*, and a D major version of the final section—D minor in the 1859 score. The *de Profundis* motif is first given to a quartet of trombones,

This episode reminds one strongly of the 'Miserere' in *Il Trovatore*, which appeared in 1851, and was the basis of one of Liszt's operatic paraphrases. This chance resemblance may have led to Liszt's decision to remove the whole section in the final version. The following passage, from the final section of the 'Busoni' version, might have come straight from Borodin or Balakirev, who were still in their 'teens at the time this was written.

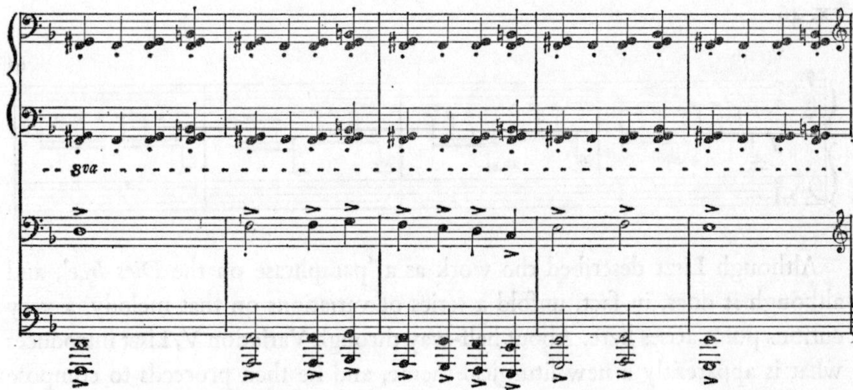

The piano suddenly breaks off with this electrifying cadenza, which sparkles across the entire range of the keyboard.

EX. 45

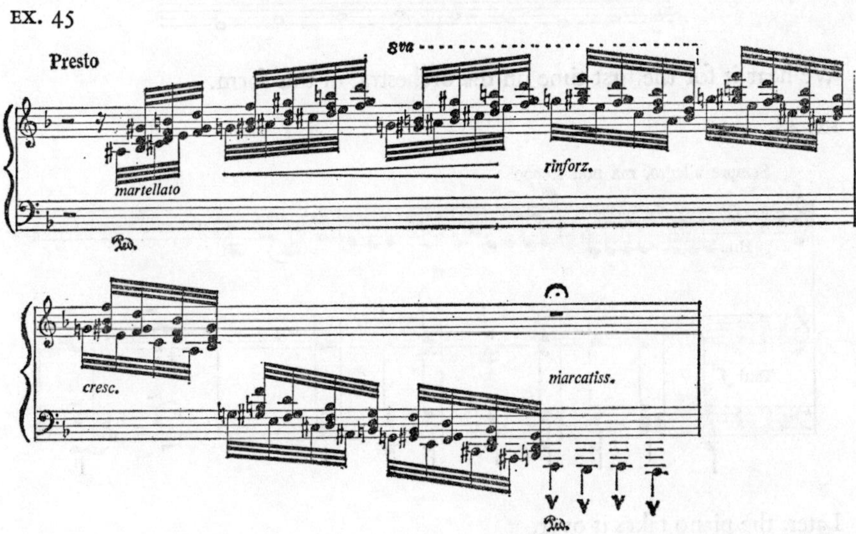

One begins to understand why Liszt's contemporaries used to call him the 'mephisto-Abbé'. This kind of keyboard figuration, highly effective in performance, and lying naturally under the hands, is typical of the very best of Liszt's piano textures. One of the later variations (No. V) reminds one of Liszt's debt to Paganini.

There are many other striking touches in the 'Busoni' version—for example, the first three bars, which are for Tamtam alone. The piano writing is on the whole more difficult and there are traces of the obsessive super-virtuosity of Liszt's early years.

EX. 46

Although Liszt described the work as a 'paraphrase on the *Dies Irae*', and although it does, in fact, unfold a series of variations on that melody, a very curious point arises here. About half-way through Variation V, Liszt introduces what is apparently a new liturgical theme, and he then proceeds to compose variations on it. While it has a marked similarity to the *Dies Irae*, it is definitely a different plainchant melody which begins:

EX. 47

We hear it for the first time on the orchestra, in this form.

EX. 48

Later, the piano takes it over.

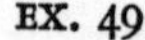

EX. 49

Having two sets of variations on different themes in one work is a most unusual and, on the face of it, rather doubtful procedure, and Liszt himself seems to have had his doubts.[1] He suggested a cut which would have suppressed all these later variations, and much of the preceding section for piano solo, and gone straight to the final section which is again based on the *Dies Irae* theme. I have never heard the work performed with this cut and I do not think that the result would be really satisfactory. It would make the work as a whole too short, besides discarding some of the most original music, more especially the first of these 'new' variations with its sinister horn calls (Ex. 48).

In an address given in 1934, entitled 'Liszt Problems', Bartók has some interesting things to say about this work. After some remarks about the eclectic character of Liszt's style, he says:

> However, there are certain elements that go together ill; for instance, Gregorian music and Italian aria. Such things could not be fused into unity even with all Liszt's art. To quote only one example, there is the *Totentanz* for piano and orchestra. This composition, which is simply a set of variations on the Gregorian melody 'Dies Irae', is startlingly harsh from beginning to end. But what do we find in the middle section? A variation hardly eight bars long, of almost Italianate emotionalism. Here Liszt obviously intended to relieve the overwhelming austerity and darkness with a ray of hope. The work as a whole always has a profound effect upon me, but this short section sticks out so from the unified style of the rest that I have never been able to feel that it is appropriate. In many of Liszt's works we find similar little outbursts breaking up the unity of style.
>
> In the end, however, this is not so important; this fleeting disturbance of the unity is merely external, and is dwarfed into significance beside the wealth of power and beauty that form the essence of the work. But the general public obviously finds it an insurmountable obstacle; they do not perceive nor understand the beauty, and they miss the compensation of dazzling brilliance, which hardly exists in such works as the *Totentanz*, so they drop the whole work.

The passage in question occurs in the final version as a cadenza after the canonic variation, (Variation IV); Liszt himself indicated that the passage could be cut by proceeding straight to the fugato, 41 bars later. One does not lightly disagree with a great musician like Bartók, whose attitude towards Liszt was at

[1] Nonetheless, he repeated the procedure four years later. The *Spanish Rhapsody* (1863) is also a set of variations on two themes, *La Folia* and *Jota Aragonesa*. See pp. 142–44.—*Ed.*

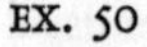

once so warm and so clear-headed. For me, however, this is not one of the really jarring incongruities; I could name several things in Liszt that disturb me far more. In any case, the work has such a phantasmagoric, dream-like quality (a *Walpurgisnacht* as well as a *Totentanz*) that one feels one is in a world in which the strangest things could happen, and no juxtaposition is too bizarre. There are, in any case, far stronger contrasts than this to be found in *Totentanz*.

Liszt did not write much in variation form, although variation technique, of one kind or another, is extremely important in all his larger works. The most important examples of variations by Liszt, apart from *Totentanz*, are 'Weinen, Klagen', the Spanish Rhapsody, and the last of the 'Paganini' Studies which is a set of strict variations on the terse theme of Paganini's Caprice in A minor. Liszt never wrote a set of variations on an extended theme of the type of the 'Goldberg' or 'Diabelli' Variations, or the variation movements in Beethoven's later sonatas and quartets. When one considers how deeply he had studied the later works of Beethoven this may seem surprising; but he must have felt that his natural bent did not lie in that direction.[1]

[1] Is there an alternative explanation? The fact that Liszt wrote fewer sets of variations than almost any other great composer in history is, of course, undeniable. Yet Liszt probably contributed more to variation *technique* than anybody. His method of the 'transformation of themes' dominates all his major works, and many of his minor ones too. Moreover, if one remembers the herculean labours he expended on his revisions (which very often amount to no more than another way of varying the original), to say nothing of his paraphrases of other composers' works, then one begins to see that for Liszt the art of composition and the art of variation were very often one and the same thing. Is it to be wondered at that the task of writing variations in the 'official' manner made little appeal to him? His genius for creating variations had found a far more original outlet.—*Ed.*

HUMPHREY SEARLE

The Orchestral Works

LISZT came late to orchestral writing. In his youth he had composed almost exclusively for solo piano, but in the 1840s he had begun to write songs and choral works. He had, too, performed some of his solo piano works with orchestra, such as the early *Hexameron*, but these had been orchestrated by other hands. However, he was not averse to writing for orchestra, or even worried about the technical side, in cases where there was already a solo instrument like the piano in the score, or a chorus. Thus, a version of the Second Piano Concerto (dated 13 September 1839) shows him already writing for orchestra, and in 1845 he wrote the orchestral part of his first Beethoven Cantata entirely by himself. But he was still somewhat uncertain about writing works for orchestra alone.

At Weimar, where he had had charge of the orchestra since 1843, he was able to try out his orchestral works with the orchestra and revise them considerably as a result. He also had two collaborators who helped him with his scores. The first was August Conradi (1821–73), a composer of farces and operettas. Conradi worked with Liszt at Weimar in 1848–49. He had a first-class technical knowledge of orchestration, but does not seem to have been a man of great imagination. What usually happened was that Liszt made a sketch on a small number of staves with indications of the orchestration, and from this Conradi wrote out a fair score. Liszt then revised this and a new score was often prepared; the whole process might be repeated several times. Liszt respected Conradi very much as a person, and the latter was evidently a glutton for work; but Liszt needed a more imaginative collaborator, and this he found in the composer Joachim Raff (1822–82). Raff came to Weimar in the winter of 1849 and remained as Liszt's assistant till 1854. Though he was technically less experienced than Conradi, he had far more imagination, and was able to give Liszt many helpful suggestions. He seems to have taken a rather inflated view of what Liszt wanted him to do; he was not supposed to teach him orchestration but merely to act as a rather superior copyist. Raff did write out fair copies of many of Liszt's scores, but Liszt invariably made alterations himself, caused by rehearsal experience, and the final printed versions of all Liszt's orchestral works were written by himself.[1] In fact, from 1854 onwards, Liszt did all his own orchestral writing, and never used collaborators again; the only possible exception was in the case of the orchestration of some of the Hungarian rhapsodies in later years, which are announced as being by 'Liszt and F. Doppler'. According to Liszt's English pupil Walter Bache, however, 'Doppler had nothing to do with them'. He was a flute player who had once tried his hand at orchestrating a few of the Rhapsodies. So when Liszt published his own set of six, 'he very generously put Doppler's name on the title out of compliment to him'.[2]

Liszt may have been influenced in his decision to get rid of Raff and other collaborators by a letter which Princess Sayn-Wittgenstein wrote to him on 25 July 1853. In it she says:

> Why do you entrust Raff with the task of orchestrating the march? What painter would content himself with handing over his drawing and leaving the colouring of it to his apprentice? You will say that Raff is not an apprentice. But he is not you! Instrumentation demands individuality and his is heavy-going. I think that you do not put enough emphasis on giving colour to musical thoughts. You content yourself with re-touching. It seems to me that this is entirely not enough, and if I compare it with a

[1] It seems necessary to stress this point.

Peter Raabe in his *Franz Liszt*, vol. 2, has reproduced five sketches which show the evolution of the symphonic poem *Tasso*. In the first there is a sketch by Liszt on three staves of the passage where the funereal theme first appears, at letter B in the score. Liszt has marked the theme to be played on the horn, accompanied by arpeggio figures in three parts on the violins, and single notes on cello and base (as they are in the score today). The next example shows Conradi's copy of this, in which he has simply written out a score according to Liszt's indications, giving the arpeggios to pizzicato strings. This of course is purely a pianistic effect and would not work on the orchestra. The next example shows Raff's orchestration, in which the theme appears on the bass clarinet, accompanied by woodwind and horns; but the latter now play repeated chords instead of arpeggios. The fourth and fifth examples show Liszt's own orchestration of the passage, or rather of the accompaniment to the theme, which remains on the bass clarinet. This is as it appears in the score today, except that in Ex. 4 we have strings and horns only, and Ex. 5 gives the harp part which is added on top. Similarly the Goethe March, which was originally written in 1849 as a piano piece, was orchestrated by Conradi and performed at Weimar on 28 August 1849. Raff then made a new orchestration, which was performed in February 1850; in a letter of the period, Raff says that this was the first time he had heard anything performed which he had orchestrated himself. Raff claimed to have put in the score a lot of things which Liszt 'had never dreamed of', but in fact he added very little new. And in 1857, Liszt completely revised and re-orchestrated the March, so that as we hear it today it is an entirely original work.

[2] *Brother Musicians*, Constance Bache, London 1901, p. 261.

> literary style: correction is never as good as original writing. One can only invent by giving one's thought its first form and first method of expression—a pre-determined outline chains the imagination; to a certain extent it sees a road marked out for it, but it discovers no new paths, no new turnings to round out the new forms of thought which one wishes to express.

Liszt certainly revised and retouched his orchestral works many times, but the final versions of nearly all of them show great originality, both of instrumentation and of actual orchestral writing. They also show a great deal of textual variety, from big *tuttis* down to passages for solo instruments, the so-called 'chamber music for orchestra'. Liszt always avoided the thick texture of many composers who wrote in the second half of the nineteenth century—there are very few doublings, and each instrument is able to make its effect as a soloist.

It is revealing to look at the orchestra Liszt had at his disposal at Weimar. In 1851, the orchestra (which was then led by Joachim) consisted of five first violins, six second violins, three violas, four cellos, three basses, two each of flutes, oboes, clarinets and bassoons, four horns, two trumpets, one trombone, one tuba, and one timpanist. Later in the year Liszt asked the Court for a second and third trombone, harp, organ, and some percussion instruments. This would have brought the orchestra up to the scoring that he used for most of his orchestral works; but the original size of the orchestra would explain why he first wrote the 'Faust' Symphony for an orchestra without trumpets and trombones.

It was during his years at Weimar that Liszt brought to full fruition his revolutionary ideas about musical structure. In particular, the 'transformation of themes' technique, which Liszt may be said to have invented, was fully mastered and there are some striking applications of it in the orchestral works. The technique is essentially that of variation. A basic theme recurs throughout a work, but it undergoes constant transformations and disguises, and is made to appear in several contrasting roles; it may be in augmentation or diminution, or in a different rhythm, or even with different harmonies; but it will always serve the structural purpose of unity within variety. The technique was of supreme importance to Liszt, interested as he was in the 'cyclic' forms and the problem of rolling together several movements into one. There are good examples in most of Liszt's mature works. Consider the following thematic cross-connections, taken from one of his best-known orchestral pieces, *Les Préludes*. The work opens with this idea:

EX. 1

In the next section, it is transformed, thus:

EX. 2

In the quiet section which immediately follows, it takes on yet another form:

EX. 3

and so on, throughout the piece. Towards the end there is a particularly effective 'metamorphosis' into a march.

EX. 4

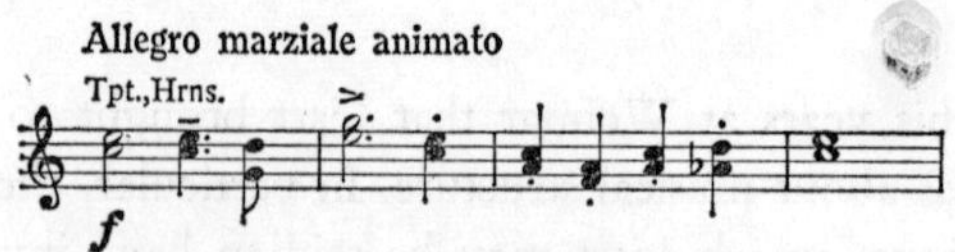

Liszt may have derived the idea from Schubert,[1] whose 'Wanderer' Fantasy (which is also based mainly on a single theme in various forms) he had arranged for piano and orchestra. On the other hand, in his early operatic fantasies, Liszt had often metamorphosed a single theme into various shapes (almost inevitable in the course of an improvisation, which many of the fantasies so often originally were), and this may have suggested the method to him when he came to write

[1] Or even Weber (see John Warrack's book on Weber, London, 1968). Liszt's claim to the 'transformation of themes technique', however, which has often been challenged, rests securely on the indisputable fact that he was the first composer to raise it to the level of a consistent creative policy which governed practically all his middle-period works. The technique is also discussed by Louis Kentner (pp. 84–85), who draws an important distinction between a 'leit-motif' and a 'metamorphosis', and by Robert Collet (pp. 249–50).—*Ed.*

original works later on. Wagner, in his early operas, as Liszt well knew, had associated themes with various characters, but his system of *leit-motivs* did not appear fully developed until *The Ring*, which Wagner began in 1854. By this time, Liszt had completed about eight of the symphonic poems and also made sketches for the 'Faust' Symphony. Though each composer clearly influenced the other, Liszt's method of building up a whole work from metamorphoses of a few short themes is clearly his own original idea, and it may be seen at its most successful in the 'Faust' Symphony. Some of Liszt's procedures, such as the repetition of a whole section a semitone higher, may seem rather artificial; and there are probably too many passages in the symphonic poems which seem to be of an introductory or transitional nature. But nevertheless, Liszt was able to free music from the straightjacket of classical forms, and the idea of a one-movement symphonic poem has lived on into our times.

Symphonic Poems

The term 'Symphonic Poem' was invented by Liszt. It is a convenient one for a work written in a new form and based, to some extent, on literary or pictorial ideas. As we shall see, however, with Liszt the musical aspect was always more important than the pictorial or literary one. This must be borne in mind when considering the symphonic poems. It is true that there are works like *The Procession by Night* and *Les Morts* where the music follows a text fairly closely; but in the Symphonic Poem *Die Ideale*, for instance, though Liszt quotes several passages from Schiller's poem at various places in the score, these are subordinated to the general musical shape which is quite independent of the poem. The programmes printed in the scores were mostly written by Princess Sayn-Wittgenstein and others anyway, and they do not necessarily express Liszt's own thoughts; they usually aim at giving a simple explanation of the content of the music, no more. Liszt is thus nearer to Berlioz than to his successors, such as Smetana, Dvořák, and Saint-Saëns, with their more detailed programmes—to say nothing of Strauss. For the rest, Liszt probably felt that as many of his symphonic poems were written in new forms, some sort of verbal explanation would be welcome to explain their shape—though admittedly the forms are often fairly simple, *e.g. Orpheus* and *Héroïde Funèbre*.

The first twelve of the thirteen symphonic poems were written between 1848 and 1857, a period of enormous productivity when one remembers that at the same time Liszt wrote the two symphonies, the two piano concertos, the piano sonata and many other important piano works. The first one, *Ce qu'on entend sur la montagne*, was based on a poem by Victor Hugo, from *Feuilles d'Automne*. Liszt had played the themes of it through to the Princess Sayn-Wittgenstein as early as 1847 or 1848; the first version may have been scored by Conradi, but the first score which is known to have existed was, in fact, scored by Raff. This was performed at Weimar in February 1850 under Liszt himself.[1] Victor Hugo's poem is prefaced to the score; and in the first edition Liszt made a short synopsis of it in the form of a foreword.

> The poet hears two voices; one immense, splendid, and full of order, raising to the Lord its joyous hymn of praise—the other hollow, full of pain, swollen by weeping, blasphemies, and curses. One spoke of nature, the other of humanity! Both voices struggle nearer to each other, cross over, and melt into one another, till finally they die away in a state of holiness.

Most of the first twelve symphonic poems were published between 1856 and 1858, and as well as Victor Hugo's poem, Liszt inserted in the score of *Ce qu'on entend sur la montagne* a note on the method of interpretation of these works. He recommends sectional rehearsals, the avoidance of regular time-beating, and he calls for the accentuation of the longer periods within the work, and for emphasis on contrast and balance. To a certain extent the music follows the form of Hugo's poem, but Liszt was always inclined to seize on a few simple general ideas rather than to illustrate a poem or story in detail. Thus the Symphonic Poem begins with a rumbling which represents Victor Hugo's 'broad, immense, confused sound', out of which there gradually emerges the first voice, that of Nature. This is done by means of a gradual crescendo and accelerando in which two themes are important, a flowing theme first heard in the oboe, and a fanfare-like figure which appears on clarinets and bassoon (Exx. 5 *a* and *b*).

EX. 5

[1] Another version of 1850 has a score written out by Raff; a third version was written out by Liszt himself, but the Allegro mesto was written out in Raff's hand and inserted in the score. Raff wrote out this third version again and Liszt made corrections to it; this final

At the climax there appears a brief phrase which may be called the voice of Nature.

EX. 6

This hardly seems a strong enough phrase to take the weight of the long build-up to it, but Liszt uses it a great deal during the work. It is developed at some length, and followed by a passionate phrase (Ex. 7*b*) which is strikingly similar to a phrase in the first movement of the 'Faust' Symphony (see (Ex. 39, bar 2). This leads to a violent passage with trumpet fanfares, which finally sinks down with the rumbling theme from the beginning. Then, after two strokes on the tam-tam, comes the second voice, that of Humanity (Ex. 7*a*).

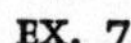
EX. 7

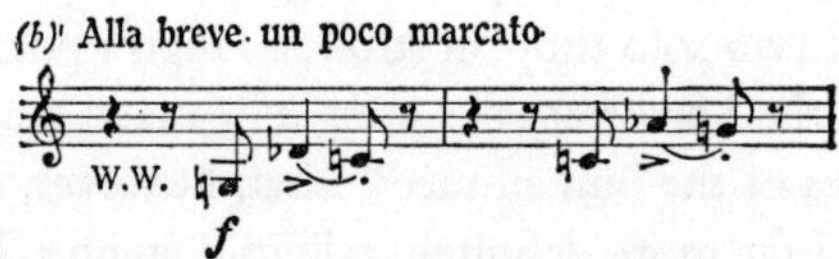

This again is a short phrase, though its continuation on bass clarinet, cellos, and bassoon gives it more importance. It is heard twice, followed by the rumbling theme and then by Ex. 5*a* on solo violin. Then the entire passage is repeated—a common practice of Liszt's, who held that it was necessary for the sake of the public's understanding of the work and also because of 'clarity and the needs of construction'. In this case, as often happens in Liszt, the second half of the passage is repeated a semitone higher than before. Next comes another

---

version was first performed at Weimar on the 7 January 1857, again conducted by Liszt, who was no doubt able to make corrections from rehearsal experience.

violent passage in which two themes already heard (Exx. 7*a* and *b*) seem to be fighting each other. Ex. 5*b* and the trumpet fanfares also return. Ex. 6 returns triumphantly, but the struggle still continues until finally the music again sinks down with the rumbling theme. Now there appears in the trombones and the tuba a chorale described as the 'Song of the Anchorites'. This is repeated by the woodwind, and then by the strings; the latter contains a passage which Wagner seems to have remembered in *Parsifal* many years later.[1]

EX. 8

Andante religioso

Str. *mf*

dim.

This is the central point of the work; from here on, the various themes return in different forms. Then, after a passage for solo woodwind against high string chords, Ex. 7*a* returns menacingly; then the entire section is repeated. Next comes another Allegro, again with Ex. 5*a* and leading to a fortissimo statement of Ex. 6; later Exx. 7*a* and *b* struggle against each other, and development of all the themes leads to a new chorale-like phrase combined with Ex. 5*a*—this however is entirely different from the Anchorite Chorale. The following passages are mostly concerned with, as it were, the triumph of the Voice of Nature, while that of Humanity later puts in a quiet appearance in the low strings. Finally the Anchorite Chorale reappears, and the work ends quietly with Ex. 6 appearing on cello and basses, pizzicato, and two solo timpani strokes. Hugo's poem ended on a note of doubt; 'Why does the Lord eternally mingle in a fatal marriage the song of Nature with the cries of the human race?' Liszt, however, as a practising Catholic, gives the work a far more definitely religious ending. In fact he has really seized on only two ideas from Hugo's poem, the rumbling atmosphere of the beginning and the idea of the contrast between the voice of Nature and the voice of Humanity. The solution of the problem is Liszt's own and not Hugo's.

Ce qu'on entend sur la montagne is not one of Liszt's greatest works; its huge length, nearly forty minutes, prevents it from being performed often, and there

[1] According to a statement made by Liszt to his pupil Göllerich in the last year of his life, Liszt first got to know Victor Hugo's poem in 1830 at the time of the July revolution. The Chorale of the Anchorites refers to the inhabitants of the Carthusian mountain near Grenoble. Hugo's poem, written on 27 July 1829, represents the thoughts of a man who wished to escape from the political turmoil of the time into a solitary contemplation of nature.

is a good deal of repetition in it. Also the themes on the whole are not sufficiently striking to stand up to a framework of this size. However it does contain some striking passages, and is certainly worthy of an occasional revival.

Tasso, the second Symphonic Poem, has been a rather more popular piece than its predecessor. Liszt's first sketch for this work is dated 1 August 1849, and this version was scored by Conradi, as we have seen, and first performed at Weimar on Goethe's centenary (28 August 1849) as an overture to his play *Torquato Tasso*. Conradi's score was later corrected by Liszt, and in 1850–51 Raff produced a new score. Liszt then revised this score entirely and added the central section, and this version was first performed on 19 April 1854, at Weimar, conducted by Liszt. In his preface to the work Liszt refers not only to Goethe's play but to Byron's poem on Tasso; Liszt in fact admits to being considerably influenced by him.[1] Liszt saw Tasso as a kind of symbolic figure, 'the genius who is misjudged by his contemporaries and surrounded with a radiant halo by posterity'. He continues:

> Tasso loved and suffered at Ferrara, he was avenged at Rome, and even today he lives in the popular songs of Venice. These three moments are inseparable from his immortal fame. To reproduce them in music, we first conjured up his great shade as he wanders through the lagoons of Venice even today; then his countenance appeared to us, lofty and melancholy, as he gazes at the festivities of Ferrara, where he created his masterworks; and finally we followed him to Rome, the Eternal City which crowned him with fame and thus paid him tribute both as martyr and as poet.

The main theme is a song to which Liszt heard a Venetian gondolier sing the opening lines of Tasso's *Gerusalemme Liberata*; the work is sub-titled 'Lamento e Trionfo'. The opening Lament begins with a gloomy section based on the triplets which are a feature of the main theme; then follows a violent Allegro, representing Tasso's sufferings at the hands of the Italian princes who did not understand his genius. Then the opening Lento returns briefly and leads to a statement of the main theme on bass clarinet accompanied by pizzicato strings, horns and harp.

[1] Tasso, Torquato (1544–95). Italian poet. Author of *Gerusalemme Liberata*. He was subject to fits of mental instability and was eventually placed in an asylum by the Duke of Ferrara after a stabbing incident at a banquet. His literary genius was finally recognized and Pope Clement VIII planned to crown him laureate in Rome, but Tasso died before this could take place and he was buried with great pomp.

EX. 9

The theme is taken over in turns by violins, trumpet, horn, and finally bursts out Grandioso in E major on two trumpets. Then a kind of recitative passage, based on the triplets from the theme, leads to the middle section, portraying Tasso at the court of Alfonso the Second of Ferrara. This is a minuet, beginning on two solo cellos, and is light and festive in character; as it was not in the original version of the work, it is clear that Liszt inserted it for purely musical reasons, between the gloom of the Lamento and the gaiety of the Trionfo, feeling that a transition of this sort was necessary. The whole atmosphere is light and graceful; later, the original Tasso theme reappears on violins and cellos against the minuet theme on the woodwind. The music gradually accelerates and becomes more passionate until it bursts again into the Allegro strepitoso which portrayed Tasso's sufferings. Then another short Lento passage leads to the final section, representing Tasso's posthumous fame. This begins festively in C major with trumpet and horn calls and diatonic scales on the strings; and then the triplet theme appears mainly on the strings, is taken over by the woodwind, and finally appears fortissimo on the full orchestra. Later, fragments of the original version appear on the trumpets, and finally there is a triumphant statement of it in its complete original form on the woodwind and brass under string arpeggios. This final section, with its triumphal ending, is somewhat bombastic, and does not match either the grave beauty of the first part of the piece, or the gaiety and the fancifulness of the middle section. (The epilogue to *Tasso*, *Le Triomphe Funèbre du Tasse*, is discussed on p. 316 together with the other two *Odes Funèbres*.)

The third Symphonic Poem, *Les Préludes*, is described as 'after Lamartine'; in fact, its origin is very different. It was originally written about 1848 as an overture to a choral work called *The Four Elements* to words by the French poet Joseph Autran. Liszt had met Autran at Marseilles in 1844, at a large banquet organized in Liszt's honour, after which he had set one of Autran's poems, *Les Aquilons*, for mixed chorus. This was performed on the spot by a local choir. During the following year Liszt, while on a tour of Spain, set three further poems by Autran for chorus: *Les Flots*, *Les Astres*, and *La Terre*.[1] The overture seems to have been orchestrated about 1848, and Raff made a new version in 1850, still under the title *The Four Elements*. Later on, this piece is referred to as *Symphonic Meditations*; this was in a letter of Liszt's dating from 1851, but in 1852 Liszt received Autran's *Poèmes de la Mer*, and replied to the poet, referring to the four choruses and the overture, 'We will do something with it one fine day'. Sometime between 1852 and 1854 Liszt revised Raff's score and made an entirely new one; this was first performed on 23 February 1854, at Weimar, conducted by Liszt, under the title *Les Préludes*. This title belongs to a very long meditation by Lamartine, but the only thing it has in common with Liszt's music is that warlike and pastoral elements are closely bound together. It seems uncertain why Liszt should have dropped all mention of Autran and substituted Lamartine; Emile Haraszti, in his *Genèse des Préludes de Liszt*,[2] attributed the change to the influence of Princess Sayn-Wittgenstein. Lamartine was, of course, a much more successful and better-known poet than Autran, and Haraszti thought that the Princess made Liszt change the ascription in order to appear more important, and also perhaps to spite Marie d'Agoult, who was a friend and admirer of Lamartine.[3] This may be far-fetched, but at any rate a good deal of the musical material of *Les Préludes* definitely comes from *The Four Elements*, and the Symphonic Poem is not the philosophical meditation commonly believed, but a description of Mediterranean atmosphere.

The preface to *Les Préludes* was written out four times, twice somewhat incomprehensibly by the Princess and twice by Liszt's pupil von Bülow; the last is the one which now appears in the score, and it begins: 'What is our life but a series of preludes to that unknown song of which death sounds the first and solemn note?' It goes on to describe the various events in life such as love, storms, pastoral quietude, and finally 'the trumpet sounding the signal of alarm'. As we have seen, this is a purely artificial programme, put in to describe the music and to bear a vague relation to Lamartine's poem.

After two quiet pizzicato Cs (which can also be found in *Les Flots*), *Les Préludes* begins with a theme on the strings which is derived from *Les Astres*, and which is the germ cell of the whole work.

[1] These four choruses, orchestrated by Conradi in 1848, have never been published.
[2] *Nouvelle Revue de Musicologie*, December 1953.
[3] Lamartine (1790–1869) was a French poet, writer, and statesman. His volume of poetry *Les Harmonies Poétiques et Religieuses*, which appeared in 1830, was greatly admired by Liszt who wrote a collection of piano pieces with the same title (see p. 137, *Ed.*). Lamartine was a leader of the Revolution of 1848 and chief of the provisional government till overthrown by Louis Napoleon in 1852.

EX. 10

This theme appears throughout the work in all kinds of disguises[1] and is a very typical example of Liszt's method of 'transformation of themes'. It climbs up under wind chords to a climax, and is then heard fortissimo on the trombones and lower strings. (See Ex. 2.) After this it is heard more calmly on cellos and horn (see Ex. 3), and eventually leads to a second theme, on horns and violas, which Liszt took from *La Terre*. This is the section described as 'Love'.

EX. 11

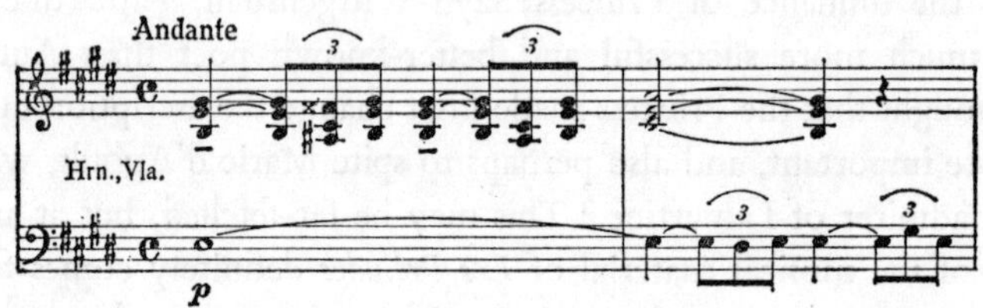

Ex. 10 returns by way of introducing a 'storm' section, at the climax of which we hear a trumpet figure which is derived from *Les Flots*. Next comes the interlude of 'pastoral calm', beginning with a horn solo. Eventually, Ex. 11 reappears on the strings; it is combined with the pastorale theme, and the tempo gradually increases till we reach an Allegro marziale and the return of Ex. 2 on horns and trumpets. Ex. 7 is now transformed into a march,

EX. 12

and the work ends with a peroration similar in mood, if not in actual themes, to that which is found in *Les Aquilons*. *Les Préludes* has always remained one of Liszt's more popular works, chiefly because of its tightness of construction and its lack of the long recitative-like passages which tend to hold up the progress of the music in some of his other symphonic poems. It is not a masterpiece, perhaps, but it is an extremely effective and well-written work.

[1] Some of which I have already drawn attention to. See pp. 281–82.

The fourth Symphonic Poem, *Orpheus*, was written in 1853–54, and was first performed on 16 February 1854, conducted by Liszt, as an introduction to the first Weimar performance of Gluck's *Orpheus.*[1] This work cannot be regarded as programme music of any kind, and does not refer to the story of Eurydice. Liszt wrote a preface to it, in which he says that he was inspired by an Etruscan vase in the Louvre, which represented Orpheus singing to his lyre, and by his music taming the wild beasts and the brutal instincts of mankind—thus he regarded Orpheus as a symbol of the civilizing influence of art. *Orpheus* is a broad and noble work; it is not long, and has the form of a gradual crescendo to a climax and then a quiet ending which returns to the mood of the opening. After a short introduction, mainly for horns and harps, the main theme appears on horns and cellos.

EX. 13

It is repeated in various forms, and later a new figure appears on solo violin.

EX. 14

The rest of the work is quite simple in form. There is an exceptionally beautiful ending, the music dying away with Ex. 14, and this highly original final progression.

EX. 15

[1] Liszt also wrote some closing music on the same themes which was thought to be lost for many years, but was eventually discovered in the Liszt Museum at Weimar. This has not yet been published.

Liszt in his preface to *Orpheus* speaks of the 'civilizing character of music which illumines every work of art, rising gradually like the vapour of incense and enfolding the world and the whole universe as it were in an atmosphere and a transparent cloak of ineffable and mysterious harmony'. Seen in this light the work becomes a piece of orchestral impressionism.

Prometheus was originally written in 1850 as an overture to Herder's dramatic work *Prometheus Unbound*. Liszt gave indications of the orchestration, and from this Raff produced a score which was used at the first performance of the work on the occasion of the unveiling of a monument to Herder on 24 August 1850. In 1855 Liszt entirely revised and rescored both the overture and the choruses, and the symphonic poem *Prometheus* was first performed on 18 October 1855, conducted by Liszt, in Brunswick. It is a short work, but again symbolic in character; here the symbolism is of suffering for the sake of the enlightenment of mankind. It begins with a short Allegro (Ex. 16*a*) which is vaguely similar to the beginning of Liszt's 'Malédiction' Concerto:

EX. 16

then comes a slower passage ending in a recitative-like section. This is followed by the main Allegro section, which is violent and stormy in character, and the themes of the opening Allegro (Ex. 16*a*) and the recitative passage both appear in it. Then another recitative passage leads to a quieter section with a theme that gives a note of hope (Ex. 16*b*). This reaches a climax and dies away; the middle section of the work is a fugue, a rarity in Liszt's work, in this case based on a figure on falling and rising thirds. In it Liszt uses all the classical devices of augmentation and diminution; the opening Allegro themes return, and after a repeat of the recitative passage Liszt indicates an optional cut to the final coda; but in the normal way the Allegro theme returns stormily as before. *Prometheus* is a concise work, and the stormier and more gloomy passages have great character; but Ex. 16*b* does not carry sufficient weight to act as a real contrasting theme.

Mazeppa is based on the story of Ivan Mazeppa (1644–1709), a Polish nobleman who was a page in the court of John Casimir, King of Poland. He had an affair with the young wife of a Podolian count, who had Mazeppa tied naked to a wild horse which was driven into the Ukraine. Eventually the horse collapsed; Mazeppa was rescued and cared for by the Cossacks and in due course became their chief. In the Battle of Pultowa, Mazeppa fought with Charles XII of Sweden against Peter the Great of Russia, and afterwards committed suicide. His story was celebrated by Byron and Victor Hugo in poems, and by Pushkin in the drama *Pultowa*. Liszt's Symphonic Poem is an altered version of the fourth of the 'Transcendental' Studies for piano; the score was written out by Raff from indications given by Liszt in 1851. Liszt revised this after rehearsal experience, and the work was first performed on 16 April 1854 in Weimar, under Liszt. An interesting point is that the fourth 'Transcendental' Study in the 1838 version bore no title, like all the others in the collection; Liszt published *Mazeppa* separately in 1840 with a slightly altered ending to fit the story of Mazeppa, and he retained the title in the 1851 version of the piano studies. So here again, as in *Les Préludes*, we have a case of the music coming first and being afterwards altered to fit a story.

The music begins with a shriek in the woodwind and brass, followed by rushing string passages and rising and descending scales. Then the 'Mazeppa theme' appears in the trombones and lower strings (Ex. 17).

EX. 17

The ride continues with unabated fury until Ex. 17 reappears on woodwind and brass. Later, rising scales lead to a quieter passage in which Ex. 17 appears on cor anglais, trumpets, and lower woodwind. This whole passage is repeated a semitone higher. Then the tempo and the fury increase again; having begun with 6/4 bars, Liszt puts the theme into 3/4 and finally 2/4 metre to increase its tension. We then hear Mazeppa's fall, represented by a chord for the full orchestra and triplet timpani strokes.

The final section of the work, depicting Mazeppa's rescue by the Cossacks, begins with string tremolos and trumpet fanfares. This soon leads to a march, the theme of which Liszt took from his *Arbeiterchor*, a work for bass solo, male chorus and piano written in 1848. The middle section of the march contains an 'oriental' theme, accompanied by triangle and cymbals, which refers, of course, to Mazeppa's new position as leader of the Cossacks. This is repeated fortissimo and combined with the original march theme. Ex. 17 also reappears, and the work ends triumphantly in D major. *Mazeppa*, too, symbolizes the struggles of the artist, for the final section of Victor Hugo's poem begins with a reference to mortal man tied living to the fatal saddle of genius, 'ardent coursier'. And Hugo's poem ends: 'He runs, he flies, he falls, and stands up as King!' *Mazeppa* is an exciting rather than a subtle work, and a great deal of it is extremely bombastic, unfortunately.

Festklänge, which may be translated as 'festive sounds', was composed in 1853 as a kind of pre-celebration of the marriage between Liszt and the Princess Sayn-Wittgenstein which at that time they had both hoped would take place, but which never did. As usual, Liszt revised the work, and the first performance took place on 9 November 1854, at the Court Theatre in Weimar under Liszt.[1] It begins effectively enough with drum-beats and fanfare-like sounds on the woodwind, followed by trumpet notes and rushing scales. The theme announced by clarinets, bassoons, and pizzicato strings is important.

[1] Later, Liszt wrote some variants to the score, which were published in 1861, and these are printed as an Appendix in the Breitkopf Collected Edition of Liszt's Orchestral Works.

EX. 19

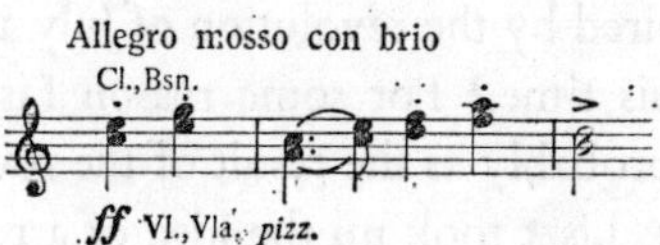

The nature of the event *Festklänge* was composed to celebrate helps to explain the presence, later in the work, of a section in Polonaise rhythm—obviously a tribute to the Polish origin of the Princess.

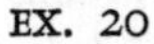
EX. 20

At the end of the Polonaise section Liszt marks an optional cut of forty-five pages. This cut is so big, and the variants he provides for the score, written as afterthoughts, are so numerous that we may ask whether the work is really 'finished' in the conventional sense. The point is of great interest, for there are many works by Liszt where the problem of making a choice among the variants throws an unusual responsibility on to the performer. The fact is, Liszt had flexible views as to what constituted a 'finished' work; and to judge from his compositions, he saw no reason why a composer should not create genuine *alternatives* among which the work might be unfolded. Also, Liszt was rather modest about the value of his own compositions, and he was inclined to take the advice of other people about possible modifications quite seriously, even when, as we have seen, they were hardly qualified to give it. Personally, I feel that the long cut in *Festklänge* rather destroys its shape, but Liszt originally thought of it as a 'Festival Overture' and therefore perhaps he wanted to have a shorter form of it as well as the longer one it eventually became. *Festklänge* can fairly be described as 'effective' music, but without any great originality of invention.

If *Festklänge* hardly shows Liszt at his best, the next Symphonic Poem, *Héroïde Funèbre*, is one of his most interesting and original works. It has a curious history. It was originally intended to be the first movement of a 'Revolutionary' Symphony inspired by the revolution of July 1830, and some of it was even sketched out at this time.[1] For some reason Liszt abandoned the idea. About 1850, however, probably as the result of the revolutionary uprisings all over Europe in 1849–50, Liszt took up the idea of a revolutionary symphony once again; this time it was to be a vast five-movement work in which the first was to be *Héroïde Funèbre*—the only movement, in the event, which Liszt actually finished. Raff scored it in 1850, but Liszt revised it probably about 1854. It was first performed on 10 November 1857 at Breslau under Moritz Schön. In the early 'Revolutionary' Symphony Liszt had shown himself an ardent supporter of the revolutionaries, as may be seen by the programme which he scribbled at the side of his sketches; but by 1850 he took a rather more sanguine view of revolutionary proceedings, and wrote in the preface to *Héroïde Funèbre*:

> In these successive wars and carnages, sinister sports, whatever be the colours of the flags which rise proudly and boldly against each other, on both sides they float soaked with heroic blood and inexhaustible tears. It is for Art to throw her ennobling veil over the tomb of the brave, to encircle with her golden halo the dead and dying, that they may be the envy of the living.

Héroïde Funèbre is, in fact, a vast funeral march which recalls the shape and feeling of many movements in Mahler's symphonies. After a quiet but sinister opening for percussion only, and some fortissimo chords for woodwind and brass, the main theme appears on trombones and trumpets.

EX. 21

It has a distinctly Hungarian flavour. In the trio section there is an idea which reminds one of the Marseillaise. It is interesting that among Liszt's sketches of the 1830 'Revolutionary' Symphony there is a clear reference, both in words and music, to the Marseillaise theme. Here it takes a slightly different form.

[1] I discuss this work more fully in my book *The Music of Liszt*, p. 6 f.

EX. 22

The end of the work is particularly memorable, the music collapsing with this remarkable progression for lower woodwind, brass, and strings.

EX. 23

Héroïde Funèbre certainly deserves to be played more than it is, which at the moment is practically never. It is a fine example of Liszt's mature style.

Hungaria was written in 1854, and is partly based on the Heroic March in the Hungarian Style for piano which Liszt wrote in 1840. Together with some of his other Hungarian works, such as the *Hungaria Cantata* and *Funérailles*, Liszt saw *Hungaria* as his reply to the poem of homage which the Hungarian poet Mihály Vörösmarty had dedicated to him in 1840 on the occasion of his first Hungarian concert tour. *Hungaria* has no programme, and can best be regarded as a Hungarian Rhapsody on an extended scale. It was first performed on 8 September 1856, under Liszt in Budapest at the Hungarian National Theatre, where it achieved an enormous success. There is a short introduction, marked Largo con duolo, and then the main theme of the March in the Hungarian Style appears on clarinets, bassoons, and violas.

EX. 24

In general, this theme and its continuation dominate the whole of the first section of the work, though interrupted at one point by a cadenza for solo violin. The music increases in violence and eventually leads to the second theme.

EX. 25

One of the most typical sections of *Hungaria* is the funeral march based on this second theme. Here, Liszt clearly wished to symbolize both the defeat of Kossuth's revolt of 1848 and the idea that Hungary would one day awake from her bondage and be liberated by her own people. The work ends with a final reference to both themes I have quoted. Though bombastic in places, *Hungaria* contains some fine music and deserves an occasional hearing.

By contrast, *Hamlet*, the next of the symphonic poems, is a remarkable piece of music, and one of Liszt's finest works. *Hamlet* was written in 1858 as a prelude to Shakespeare's play; Liszt tried it out at a rehearsal in Weimar that year, but the first public performance did not take place till 2 July 1876, in Sondershausen under Max Erdmannsdörfer. Liszt saw Bogumil Dawison play Hamlet in Weimar in 1856, and was greatly impressed. He wrote:

> He does not make him into an indecisive dreamer who collapses under the power of his mission, as he is usually regarded since Goethe's theory in *Wilhelm Meister*, but much more as a gifted, enterprising prince with important political views who is waiting for the right moment to complete his work of revenge and come to the aim of his ambition, that is, to be crowned king in the place of his uncle. This goal can naturally not be reached in twenty-four hours and the clever anticipation which Shakespeare has put into the role of Hamlet and the negotiations with England which come clearly to the light of day at the end of the drama according to my view justify Dawison's interpretation, which Herr von Goethe and the aesthetes should not take too badly.

The Symphonic Poem is, therefore, a character sketch of Hamlet rather than an attempt to portray the course of the action in music; and Ophelia, instead of being given an important 'second subject', is only referred to in two short interludes which Liszt added to the score later, marking them 'to be played as quietly as possible and sound like a shadowy picture'. Liszt wrote further about Ophelia:

> She is loved by Hamlet, but Hamlet, like every exceptional person, imperiously demands the wine of life and will not content himself with the buttermilk. He wishes to be understood by her without the obligation of explaining himself to her. She collapses under her mission, because she is incapable of loving him in the way that he must be loved, and her madness is only the de-crescendo of her feeling, whose lack of sureness has not allowed her to remain on the level of Hamlet.

Hamlet opens in a gloomy atmosphere with lower woodwind and timpani strokes.

EX. 26

The tempo increases slightly with a rising figure for the strings, and there are wind chords, echoed by horn and cellos, which seem to reflect the striking of a clock, after which the theme quoted above returns stormily on the strings with chromatic scales. Then the tempo increases again with a variant of this same theme till we reach the Allegro. This begins with a passionately surging theme with the rhythm of Ex. 26 still prominent, till after the figures for woodwind, horns, and trumpets we reach one of Hamlet's main themes.

EX. 27

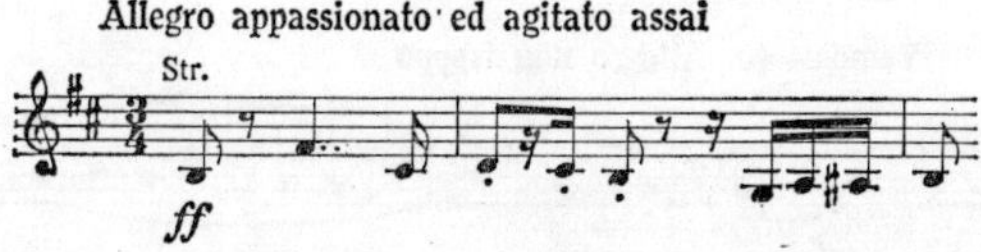

This clearly shows Hamlet in a violent mood, and this mood carries on for some time till it ends with wind chords and string triplets followed by three bars of silence; then we hear the first of the Ophelia interludes for woodwind and solo violin.

EX. 28

The rest of the work is based mainly on Exx. 26 and 27. Nothing is wasted in *Hamlet.* It is a short and concise work (lasting about ten minutes); every point is made with clarity and precision, and a remarkable psychological portrait emerges. Of all Liszt's symphonic poems, this is the one which most merits revival.

In 1855, the Princess sent Liszt a reproduction of the mural *Die Hunnenschlacht* (The Battle of the Huns) by Wilhelm von Kaulbach, which is in a Berlin Museum. This gave Liszt the idea of writing a symphonic poem on the same subject.[1] The story concerns the battle in A.D. 451 on the Catalaunian Fields between the forces of Attila the Hun and the Christian Emperor Theodoric. The legend says that the fighting was so fierce that when dusk fell the spirits of those who had been killed were still to be seen fighting in the sky. Liszt, therefore, intended to start and finish the Symphonic Poem with ghostly, dark sounds. However, using the chorale *Crux Fidelis* to represent the Christian forces, he decided in the end to finish with a treatment of this. The battle, consequently, is over halfway through the work, and the rest of it is a prolonged meditation on, and glorification of, this chorale. The battle begins mysteriously with the main theme, Ex. 29, for bassoons and cellos.

EX. 29

[1] Liszt even thought of a gigantic plan of writing a series of symphonic poems based on Kaulbach's paintings, to be called 'The History of the World in Picture and Music by W. Kaulbach and Franz Liszt'. This was intended to include the Tower of Babylon, Nimrod, Jerusalem, and the Glory of Greece. However, Liszt only completed *Hunnenschlacht* out of the entire grandiose scheme.

This is taken up by the strings and mounts to a high register, though remaining pianissimo, while under it the horns sound their ferocious call.

EX. 30

The whole of this opening section remains quiet and ghostly, but a crescendo leads to a change of a quicker tempo, and now the battle begins in earnest, with a galloping theme on the strings. Ex. 29 predominates in this section, but eventually the music quietens down and an arpeggio theme appears on bassoons and cellos, symbolizing the Christian forces. Again it is attacked by violent chords and soon the chorale theme *Crux Fidelis* is heard on the trombones accompanied by wild string figures.[1]

EX. 31

The battle continues with all the themes so far heard fighting with each other. It is a tremendously exciting battle scene which does not call for detailed description. The Christians eventually win the battle, and between three deafening statements of the arpeggio theme on the full orchestra the organ quietly plays *Crux Fidelis*. *Hunnenschlacht* was first performed on 29 December 1857, under Liszt at Weimar. Liszt made some alterations to the work after the performance and again before its publication in 1861.

The last of the twelve symphonic poems which Liszt composed during his Weimar period, *Die Ideale*, also dates from 1857; it was first performed at a concert on 5 September of that year which was given in honour of the laying of the foundation-stone for a memorial to Goethe's patron the Grand Duke Karl August and the unveiling of memorials to Goethe, Schiller, and Wieland. Liszt printed in the score various extracts from Schiller's poem *Die Ideale* as a

[1] Note bracket 'x' of *Crux Fidelis*, Liszt's 'Cross' motif. See Collet (pp. 322–23, 335 and 343) for a fuller discussion.—*Ed.*

kind of guide to the mood of each section in question. The work was originally conceived as a symphony in three movements, but was later compressed into a three-movements-in-one form akin to that of the B minor Piano Sonata.

Die Ideale begins with a slow introduction; Liszt quotes Schiller's lines, 'Now all ideals and hopes have vanished'. This is expressed by a descending theme on the horn.

EX. 32

Next, comes a section marked 'Aspirations', beginning with a more buoyant theme with the strings. This is the main Allegro section of the work, and it

EX. 33

Ex. 33
Allegro spiritoso
Vlns.
f con impeto
sf
sf

continues forcefully until a third theme is reached, Ex. 34, which is given out by the whole orchestra.

EX. 34

Several other sections follow, each of contrasting mood, and each inscribed with a line from Schiller's poem. It is obvious that the musical construction of the work was of more importance to Liszt than the poetical aspect, for he changed the order of the extracts from Schiller's poem, and towards the end of the work he wrote: 'I have allowed myself to add to Schiller's poem by repeating the motives of the first movement joyously and assertively as an apotheosis.' The work thus has a triumphant ending, a fact otherwise difficult to explain if it is compared too closely with the poem. Because of the way it is conceived, *Die Ideale* tends to be long and episodic; Liszt was to some extent aware of this for he marked a substantial cut which certainly improves the work in performance. Though it is not one of Liszt's best symphonic poems, *Die Ideale* contains many beautiful passages and it is certainly worth an occasional revival.

The thirteenth and last symphonic poem, *From the Cradle to the Grave*, was written many years later than the others, in 1881–2; it was inspired by what is apparently a very bad painting by the Hungarian Count Michael Zichy. It is, however, a very interesting piece. It is divided into three parts: 'The Cradle', 'The Struggle for Existence', and 'To the Grave, the Cradle of the Future Life'. The first part is scored for flutes, harp, violins, and violas only, and it is of tender and delicate character. By this time, Liszt had purified and refined his style, and every note is of importance. There is no longer any question of violence of display for its own sake. After a few introductory bars the main theme, Ex. 35, appears on the violins over a rocking figure on the violas.

EX. 35

This mood continues throughout the whole of the opening section. The second section, 'The Struggle for Existence', begins with this striking phrase:

EX. 36

The figure in the third and fourth bars is derived from 'The Cradle' section. Soon a more flowing figure, marked 'nobilmente', appears on the strings, clarinets, and bassoons, and rises to a climax, interrupted by Ex. 36 on horns. After a fortissimo statement of Ex. 36 on trumpets and trombones, a passage for timpani alone leads to the final section—'To the Grave'. This is the most remarkable part of the work, and one of the most interesting things that Liszt ever wrote. This example gives some idea of its character.

EX. 37

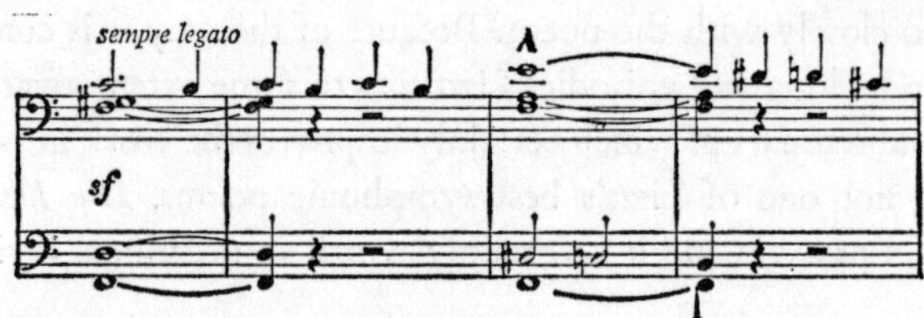

The work ends calmly and peacefully in the higher register of the cellos.

The 'Faust' Symphony (1854)

Liszt got to know the first part of Goethe's *Faust* in 1830, through Berlioz, as the latter relates in his memoirs (Liszt, in fact, dedicated the 'Faust' Symphony to Berlioz). He started sketching it out in the 1840s, during his years as a travelling virtuoso; but it was the performance of Berlioz's *Damnation of Faust* in 1852, in Weimar, which stimulated him to take up the work again. Liszt seems to have had doubts about his task. He commented wryly to one correspondent: 'The worst Jesuit is dearer to me than the whole of your Goethe'. And shortly before he began work on the 'Faust' Symphony he wrote to the Princess: 'Anything to do with Goethe is dangerous for me to handle'. There is also a revealing letter of 1869 in which he contrasts Faust with Manfred.

> In my youth I passionately admired Manfred and valued him much more than Faust, who, between you and me, in spite of his marvellous prestige in poetry, seemed to me a decidedly bourgeois character. For that reason he becomes more varied, more complete, richer, more communicative ... (than Manfred) ... Faust's personality scatters and dissipates itself; he takes no action, lets himself be driven, hesitates, experiments, loses his way, considers, bargains, and is only interested in his own little happiness. Manfred could certainly not have thought of putting up with the bad company of Mephistopheles, and if he had loved Marguerite he would have been able to kill her, but never abandon her in a cowardly manner like Faust.

In spite of his antipathy towards Goethe, however, Liszt produced his masterpiece in the 'Faust' Symphony. The full title of the work is *A Faust Symphony in three character sketches (after Goethe)*: 1. *Faust*; 2. *Gretchen*; 3. *Mephistopheles.* It occupies over 300 pages of full score and lasts more than an hour in perfor-

LISZT'S SYMPHONIC POEM: 'THE MUSIC OF THE FUTURE'

English Caricature of 1869

LISZT AT HIS DESK IN THE HOFGÄRTNEREI

LISZT PRECURSOR OF WAGNER
by Georges Villa

FRANZ LISZT
(in 1839)
Pencil Drawing by Ingres

mance; yet it was composed in the astonishing time of two months, between August and October 1854.

The first movement shows us the conflicting sides of Faust's personality—Faust the thinker, the passionate lover, the striver for higher things, who, when near to victory, falls back into darkness. The movement has all the appearances of a self-portrait, for Liszt identified himself to a large extent with Faust. In the second movement, a portrait of Gretchen, we see all Liszt's love and respect for women. And in the last movement, 'Mephistopheles', we see Liszt's portrayal of an evil power which falsifies and defiles everything great and noble. The version of the 'Faust' Symphony which Liszt wrote in 1854 was very different from the work as we know it today. It was scored for small orchestra, without trumpets, trombones or percussion, and it did not contain the martial music which is to be found in the first and last movements. Raff wrote out a score from Liszt's sketches, and Berlioz was able to study this when he visited Weimar in 1855. Liszt also tried the work out at rehearsal in front of such musicians as Berlioz and later Wagner, as well as members of the Weimar Court and other people who knew very little about music. (Liszt seems to have been a good deal influenced by these people, for he made extensive changes to the work, adding trumpets and trombones, and later the final chorus.) The first performance took place in the already-mentioned concert on 5 September 1857; but this was only a kind of half-way house, for Liszt continued to revise and alter the work. By 1860 there was already a new version of it for two pianos and another one in 1861 for orchestra; in this year, the second 'first performance' of the 'Faust' Symphony took place in August at the 'Composers Meeting' in Weimar. The score appeared shortly afterwards, but Liszt continued to make slight alterations to the work, adding ten bars to the slow movement as late as 1880.

The two principal Faust themes are heard at the beginning of the first movement; the first, on violas and cellos, is the first conscious twelve-note theme ever written and shows, appropriately, Faust as a ponderer and thinker.

EX. 38

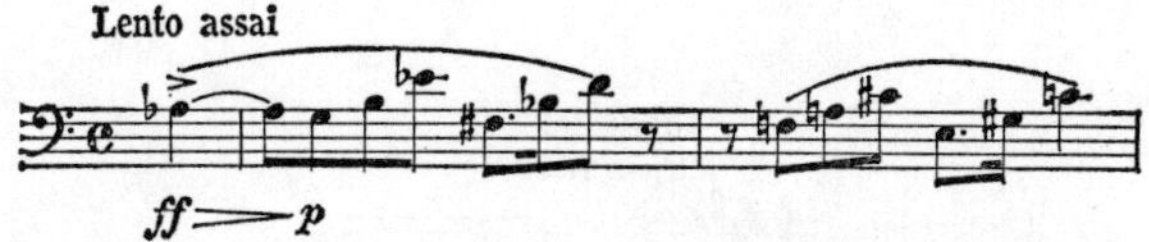

It is immediately followed by a theme on the oboe with a falling seventh which assumes all kinds of shapes during the Symphony.

EX. 39

These themes are heard twice in the Introduction; then, after a short Allegro passage, the third Faust theme appears on the strings. This shows Faust in a mood of passionate intensity.

EX. 40

The theme is repeated by the full orchestra and then leads straight into a new theme for woodwind with a descending scale passage, which is immediately repeated by cellos. There are several episodes during the long Exposition which occupies the first half of the movement. Ex. 39 reappears on horns and woodwind, transformed, showing Faust as a lover.

EX. 41

Then the mood becomes more martial, and leads to Ex. 42 which seems to correspond to Faust's words 'Im Anfang war die Tat' (In the beginning was the deed).

EX. 42

This leads to a climax in which Ex. 38 returns in canon between trombones and trumpets; then Ex. 40 returns on the strings; incidentally, in the original version this theme was written in the experimental time-signatures of 7/4 and 7/8 time. (Compare Exx. 40 and 43.)

EX. 43

A repeat of the slow introduction follows, and a transitional passage which leads to the reprise; this begins with Ex. 40 fortissimo on the full orchestra, and continues more or less as in the Exposition, except that it is very much compressed and this time Ex. 42 begins quietly and works up to a climax. In the Coda, which begins with Ex. 42 on trombones echoed by woodwind, the music finally seems to collapse and dies away.

The scoring of the Gretchen movement is of marvellous delicacy. After a short prelude for woodwind, the main Gretchen theme appears on the oboe accompanied by solo viola.

EX. 44

After a short passage which represents the well-known scene where Gretchen plucks off the petals of a flower, murmuring to herself: 'He loves me—he loves me not—he loves me!' the first Gretchen theme is repeated on the strings and woodwind. A semiquaver passage for violins leads to the second Gretchen theme, in repeated chords, which appears on the strings alone and is repeated by the woodwind.

EX. 45

In the middle section Faust appears on the scene, symbolized by Ex. 39 marked 'patetico'. The flowing theme from the first movement now appears on the cellos at some length under flute arpeggios, and finally Ex. 41 is heard pianissimo on the whole orchestra—a magical moment. It is followed by Ex. 40, now heard 'soave con amore', and then there is a reprise of the Gretchen themes, beginning on four solo violins. At the end Ex. 42 appears quietly on strings and woodwind, symbolizing Faust's contentment and peace.

Mephistopheles is the spirit of negation; he can only destroy, not create. How to represent him in music? Liszt hit upon the ingenious idea of giving him Faust's themes—but in parodied form. Mephistopheles takes possession, as it were, of Faust, whose leading themes now appear distorted and cruelly misshapen. The entire movement is Liszt's finest application of the 'transformation of themes' technique; long as it is, it contains only one new theme, which Liszt borrowed from his own 'Malédiction' Concerto. Here is Faust's main Allegro theme (Ex. 40) mockingly parodied by Mephistopheles.

EX. 46

These two versions of the same theme (Exx. 40 and 46) deserve the closest comparison. Indeed, the whole of *Mephistopheles* should be studied side-by-side with the *Faust* movement, for it represents a major achievement in terms of variation technique. The middle section of *Mephistopheles*, for instance, contains a fugue, based on a remarkable transformation of Faust's 'love theme', now sardonic and twisted.

EX. 47

Compare Ex. 47 with Ex. 41. Liszt prefaced this fugue with a symbolic self-quotation from his 'Malédiction' Concerto.[1]

EX. 48

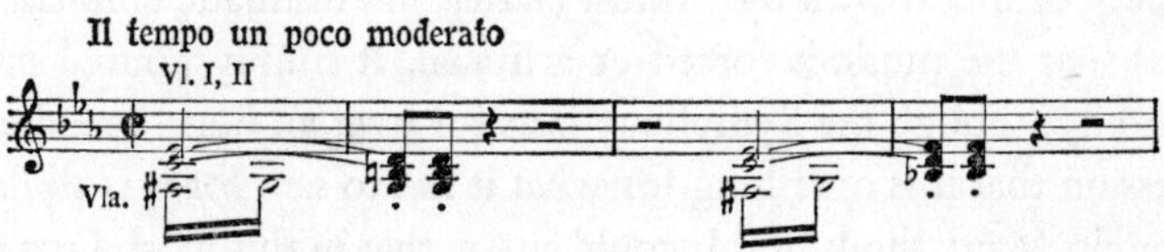

Then Mephistopheles takes hold of Faust's theme 'In the beginning was the deed' (Ex. 42), maliciously tearing it to shreds.

EX. 49

After a series of wild passages, the first Gretchen theme appears in its original form—she alone cannot be parodied or touched by Mephistopheles. Various themes now appear to be fighting for supremacy, and the music rises to an enormous climax. Finally, Mephistopheles is defeated and the music sinks down.

The original ending of the work was purely orchestral; but in a later version Liszt added a Coda in the form of a choral setting of the final *Chorus Mysticus* from the second part of Goethe's 'Faust', and there is no doubt that he was right to do so. The entire work is summed up and given its true perspective by this solemn and triumphal music. The brilliant translation of the almost untranslatable poem is by Louis MacNeice.

Alles Vergängliche	All that is past of us
Ist nur ein Gleichnis;	Was but reflected;

[1] 'Malédiction', of course, means 'under a curse'. Compare Ex. 48 with Ex. 6, on p. 254. —*Ed.*

Das Unzulängliche	All that was lost in us
Hier wird's Ereignis;	Here is corrected;
Das Unbeschreibliche	All indescribables
Hier ist es getan;	Here we descry;
Das Ewig-Weibliche	Woman's divinity
Zieht uns hinan.	Leads us on high.

Liszt was truly inspired when he composed the 'Faust' Symphony. It expresses every variety of mood with the utmost clarity and dramatic emphasis, yet one never feels that the music is forced or artificial. It simply poured out of him quite naturally; though the Symphony lasts for over an hour, one does not get the impression that it is over long for what it has to say, for it is all deeply and genuinely felt. Many think, and I would agree, that in this work Liszt produced his masterpiece.

The 'Dante' Symphony (1856)

Dante was one of Liszt's favourite writers; in the 1830s he often used to read *The Divine Comedy* with Marie d'Agoult. In 1837 he wrote in a letter: 'It would need a Michelangelo to encompass a Dante', and two years later he says: 'Dante had his artistic reflection in Orcagna and Michelangelo; perhaps he will find a musical one some day in a Beethoven of the future'. In fact, by 1837, Liszt himself had already composed the first version of his *Fantasia quasi Sonata* for piano, subtitled *After a Reading of Dante*. In the 1840s he began to think more about the plan of writing a symphony based on 'The Divine Comedy' and in 1847 he was able to play some of the themes of this work to Princess Sayn-Wittgenstein. Liszt at this time had the idea of getting the painter Bonaventura Genelli to design lantern slides which would accompany the music. He also intended to introduce an experimental wind machine for the final passage of the first movement to depict the winds of Hell; but both ideas came to nothing. Liszt attempted to work on the 'Dante' Symphony in 1855, but did not really get going seriously until early in 1856; he finished it in July 1856. It was originally planned as a symphony in three movements representing *Inferno*, *Purgatorio*, and *Paradiso*. However, Wagner wrote Liszt a long letter regarding this plan, in which he said that no human being could express in music the joys of Paradise, and Liszt eventually came round to this view. So now there are only two movements, *Inferno* and *Purgatorio*, the latter closing with a choral Magnificat. This is a pity, for the balance of the Symphony is thereby destroyed; and though

Liszt was certainly more at home in the infernal than the celestial regions, the task should not have been beyond his powers. As it is, the listener is left in the transitional state of Dante at the end of the Purgatorio movement, where he gazes up at the heights of Heaven and hears its music from afar.

The first performance took place on 7 November 1857, in Dresden under Liszt himself, and was a failure. This performance, however, was useful to Liszt, and he was able to make alterations in the score from experience of this and of the previous rehearsals at Weimar. The score was published in 1859, and Liszt sent a copy to Wagner, to whom the work is dedicated, with a flattering private dedication, not intended for publication.

Inferno begins with a musical setting of the words written over the gates of Hell.

Per me si va nella città dolente;
Per me si va nell' eterno dolore;
Per me si va tra la perduta gente . . .
Lasciate ogni speranza, voi ch'entrate.

Through me is the way to the city of weeping;
Through me is the way to eternal torment;
Through me is the way among those that are lost . . .
Abandon hope, all ye that enter here.

The last line, 'Abandon hope, all ye that enter here', is turned into a musical theme which is important in this movement.

EX. 50

Then the musical representation of the descent into Hell begins with a chromatic descending phrase.

EX. 51

The tempo gets faster and faster, and the music becomes stormier all the time (Ex. 52).

EX. 52

At the climax, Ex. 50 is heard again fortissimo in all the brass, and drum-beats, in the same rhythm, lead to the middle section. This represents the story of Paolo and Francesca, whose punishment for their illicit love was to be incessantly driven about by violent winds in the second circle of Hell. (Incidentally, Tchaikovsky in his symphonic poem *Francesca da Rimini* very closely copied not only the form of this movement but also some of the themes.) After an introductory section for flutes, harp, and strings, we hear a theme on the cor anglais to Dante's words:

Nessun maggior dolore	There is no greater pain
Che ricordarsi del tempo felice	Than to recall the happy days
Nella miseria.	In time of misery.

EX. 53

Then a more romantic passage leads to the love theme, played *dolce con intimo sentimento* by two violins in 7/4 time.

EX. 54

The whole section is repeated with fuller orchestration, and then Ex. 50 sounds sinisterly on stopped horn. A harp cadenza leads to the return of the storm, which continues very much as before; it begins with a passage which Liszt wanted to sound 'like mocking laughter, blasphemous, and very sharply accentuated'.

EX. 55

The last section is a kind of Passacaglia which works up to a final statement of Ex. 50.

The second movement, *Purgatorio*, begins with a slow and very beautiful introduction in which Dante, on leaving Hell behind, begins to see the light of the stars and the dawn rising 'like the sapphire of the Orient'. After its repetition a semitone higher, we reach the portrayal of the trials of souls in Purgatory which they must endure in order to reach Heaven. The yearning of these souls for ultimate happiness is depicted by this chorale-like theme on clarinets and bassoons.

EX. 56

Then comes a fugue, the subject of which is closely modelled on Ex. 53.

EX. 57

This works up to a considerable climax, and we hear again the 'souls in Purgatory' passage. But soon the atmosphere lightens, and the women's chorus enters with a setting of the Magnificat. This is simple and rather modal in style; there is only one forte passage towards the end, and the Symphony ends with high ethereal chords.

Although the 'Dante' Symphony may not quite equal the 'Faust' in sustained inspiration, its many fine passages place it among Liszt's best works.

Two Episodes from Lenau's Faust

The two Episodes from Lenau's 'Faust' were both completed by 1860.[1] The first is *The Procession by Night*, and the second is *The Dance at the Village Inn*, better known in its version for piano solo as the first 'Mephisto' Waltz.

The Procession by Night begins with a description of a night, heavy with dark clouds, in the forest. The music begins with dramatic phrases on the lower strings answered by stopped horns. But soon the atmosphere lightens, and Liszt quotes the lines of Lenau about the warm feelings of Spring and the song of the nightingale. This is portrayed by arpeggio-like figures in the strings, and then by bird-calls and trills in the woodwind. The atmosphere is warm and joyful, and builds up to a climax. Now Faust appears, letting his horse saunter quietly on through the night; this is expressed by figures on pizzicato strings and little wind phrases. Next, we hear bells and harp chords; Faust sees lights through the trees and hears distant singing. A religious procession is approaching, and we hear the chorale 'Pange lingua gloriosi corporis mysterium'. The music builds up to a climax as the procession passes and goes away again in the distance. Faust, left alone, thinks of the happiness he has lost and weeps bitterly. The dramatic cello figures from the beginning return and rise to a passionate climax, dying away finally with single notes and low phrases in the lower strings. *The Procession by Night* is one of Liszt's finest works, and its neglect is certainly unintelligible these days.

The second Episode from Lenau's 'Faust' is the well-known 'Mephisto' Waltz —called here in its orchestral version *The Dance at the Village Inn*. Lenau describes a scene where Mephistopheles and Faust approach an inn where a dance is going on; they go in, and finding the music not fiery enough, Mephistopheles seizes a fiddle and makes them all dance. This unleashes a wild orgy of love-making, and Faust, finding a brunette whom he likes, dances with her out into the starry night, where 'they sink in the ocean of their own lust'. After the orgy has spent itself, the song of the nightingale is heard. The orchestral and piano versions of the piece seem to have been written about the same time, though it seems likely that the orchestral version is slightly the later of the two, for some of the passages towards the end are developed in a more complete manner. It was dedicated to Liszt's pupil Carl Tausig, one of the greatest pianists of his day. This would seem to confirm that the work was originally intended to be a piano piece.

[1] Nikolaus Lenau (1802–50) was a Hungarian poet who wrote chiefly in German. His version of the Faust legend, which dates from 1836, differs considerably from Goethe's. Lenau visited the U.S.A. in 1832 and went mad in 1844.

In later years, Liszt wrote three more 'Mephisto' waltzes: one for orchestra, and two for piano. These do not represent any particular story, but they show the same combination of diabolical and sensual elements as the first one. The second 'Mephisto' Waltz, which is the other one for orchestra, was written in 1880 and first performed the following year in Budapest, after which Liszt subjected it to considerable alteration. It is dedicated to Saint-Saëns—a rather doubtful compliment when one considers how much more violent its expression is than that of Saint-Saëns' own *Danse Macabre*, which Liszt, it will be remembered, had already transcribed for piano.

Three Funeral Odes

The three Funeral Odes are among Liszt's most interesting works. The first, *Les Morts* (The Dead), was composed in 1860, the year after the death of Liszt's only son Daniel at the age of twenty. It is called an 'oration for orchestra', and in the score is written a prose passage by Lamennais. This begins:

> They too have lived on this earth; they have passed down the river of time; their voices were heard on its banks, and then were heard no more. Where are they now? Who shall tell? But blessed are they who die in the Lord.

The last three sentences recur like a refrain from time to time, and each time a male chorus enters with the words 'Beati mortui qui in Domino moriuntu'. The words were written in merely as a guide to the musical thought, but the work has been performed in modern times with the words declaimed, with very moving effect. It begins gloomily on lower strings and bassoons; the phrases 'Where are they? Who will tell us?' are heard as a horn theme. Before the entry of the chorus the strings have a beautiful quiet phrase which is repeated several times during the work. The next section, mainly for brass, is concerned with the riches and vanity of the world. It ends with the same refrain; and then, in the subsequent section, a Cross appears like a ray of light. After the refrain, the next section begins dramatically with the words 'In an unknown place where the river is lost to sight'. This rises to a climax for the full orchestra with the words 'We praise Thee, We bless Thee, O Lord'. After choral Hosannas the music breaks off abruptly, and the final section goes back to the quiet mood of the beginning with the words: 'And we too shall go there whence come those cries, those songs of victory.' The final choral refrain is extended into a beautiful quiet passage which ends the work. The choral part, incidentally, was added six years after the rest of the work, but it undoubtedly makes it more effective.

The second funeral ode, *La Notte*, was written in 1864, two years after the death of Liszt's elder daughter Blandine. The main part of it is an orchestration of *Il Penseroso* from the *Years of Pilgrimage*.[1] This is prefaced by four bars with the timpani rhythm based on that of the piece itself. The main theme is given to the horns in the first statement, accompanied by woodwind and strings; it is repeated by the violins and violas. At the end, a solo for clarinet leads to a new middle section prefaced by Virgil's words 'Dulces moriens reminiscitur Argos' ('Dying he remembers sweet Argos'). This refers to the death in Italy of Antores, an Argive companion of Aeneas, who was killed in battle by a spear aimed at his leader; Liszt was living in Rome at the time he wrote this work, and he too felt that he might die far from his native country. In fact, he wrote in the score that he wished *La Notte*, together with *Les Morts*, to be played at his funeral, the former 'because of the Hungarian cadence'.

EX. 58

Liszt's wish was not fulfilled, and both works remained unperformed till 1912 and unpublished till 1916. The middle section is quiet and restrained, and the dynamics do not rise above forte. It dies away on higher violin octaves. Then *Il Penseroso* returns after the timpani introduction; this time the theme is accompanied by tremolos in the strings. Part of the original theme is replaced with a passage for the first violins in arpeggios partly based on the Hungarian scale. At the end of *Il Penseroso* another 'Hungarian' phrase brings the work to a quiet and sad conclusion.

Le Triomphe Funèbre du Tasse is described as an epilogue to the symphonic poem *Tasso*.[2] It was written in 1866 and first performed in March 1877 in New

[1] See p. 122, Ex. 61.—*Ed.*

[2] It is partly based on Ex. 9.

York under Leopold Damrosch, to whom Liszt dedicated it. Damrosch had been a member of the Weimar Orchestra as a violinist for many years, and was an early supporter of Liszt's music. Liszt wanted Abbot Pier-Antonio Serassi's account of Tasso's splendid funeral printed in the programme, which was done at the first New York performance, and it is also printed in the score of the collected edition. This work is again autobiographical in nature. Liszt felt that he, like Tasso, would only be really appreciated after his death, and this in fact has come to pass.

*

Liszt's other works for orchestra need little discussion. They consist mostly of marches written for various ceremonial occasions; the earliest is the *Goethe March*, originally composed in 1849 for the centenary of Goethe's birth, and performed as an interlude in Goethe's *Tasso* on that day. The *Schiller March* contains a theme from *Die Ideale* (Ex. 34). Three of the marches are in Hungarian style, one being an arrangement of the well-known Rákóczy March. Liszt had originally arranged this tune in the fifteenth Hungarian Rhapsody for piano; in fact, the earliest version pre-dates Berlioz's well-known arrangement of the same theme in *The Damnation of Faust*. However, Liszt naturally did not want to compete with Berlioz, and his orchestral version was not made until 1865, when he conducted the first performance of it in Budapest the same year. It is an effective arrangement, but it has nothing like the power and brilliance of Berlioz's version. Six of the Hungarian rhapsodies were arranged for orchestra by Liszt, possibly in collaboration with Franz Doppler, as we have already seen (p. 280). Liszt also made an orchestral version of the two Legends for piano, of which his pupil Göllerich possessed the manuscript, but these have never been published. In addition, Liszt made an excellent arrangement for orchestra of four of Schubert's piano duet marches.

ROBERT COLLET

Choral and Organ Music

OF all the branches of Liszt's work, the Choral Music is the least known; many generally knowledgeable musicians would be hard put to name half-a-dozen works, and I have even heard a musician say 'I didn't know there were any'. Liszt wrote a great deal of music for Chorus in various forms, and the range and variety is rather bewildering. The best things, and the best are very good indeed, are to be found dispersed through a large number of works rather than concentrated in a small number of masterpieces; consequently selection is both essential and at the same time difficult. It is not usually enough that the conductor should be an excellent musician and of the highest technical competence; in most cases a high degree of sympathetic insight is needed and this has been rare among English conductors. Beecham could be a very fine Liszt conductor and he gave some splendid performances of some of the choral works; but his advocacy of Liszt, though at times effective, was a bit intermittent. Even the works that employ small forces need unusually careful rehearsal, and the large-scale works, the ones most likely to have a wide appeal, are expensive to produce. To this must be added the very strong anti-Lisztian tradition in England, which again links up with religious attitudes. Many Englishmen prefer Protestant simplicity and austerity to Catholic pomp and flamboyance, and on the strength of their acquaintance with other aspects of Liszt's music, they are ready to assume that if Liszt wrote religious music it must exhibit these latter qualities in an extreme form. Consequently, they have no incentive to study the works and to find out if this is really true. It is not accidental that the opposition to Liszt's music, both informed and uninformed (the dislike is frequently, but not always, based on ignorance), has been much the strongest in Protestant countries, especially England and North Germany. In England, at least, the climate of opinion has changed much in the last forty years, and the time is surely ripe for a reappraisal of the choral music which has not, up till now, benefited from the general growth of interest in Liszt's music.

Liszt had very early conceived the ideal of a new kind of church music. An essay 'On the future of Church Music' dates from 1834—when he was only twenty-three years of age. He wanted a religious music that would unite 'on a colossal scale, the theatre and the Church'. How far he succeeded is still a matter of debate. But the desire to reform the music of the church never left him. Even in his late sixties, Liszt was still attempting to evolve a style of composition which employed all the resources of secular music while being intended for liturgical use. He was ideally placed for this project. During his Weimar years he had acquired much experience in choral conducting and handling voices with orchestra. From 1862, he was the regular guest of the Dominican friars at the monastery of the Madonna del Rosaria on the Monte Mario near Rome; and it was in this peaceful retreat that Liszt worked on most of his religious compositions. It was his habit to rise before dawn, attend mass, and then compose for several hours before lunch. For some years, he never varied this routine. Pope Pius IX became his personal friend and used to call Liszt 'my dear Palestrina', an indication of the high regard in which he held him. On one occasion Pius visited Liszt at his retreat and asked Liszt to play to him. Liszt improvised, and after the music had died away the Holy Father, who was obviously moved, turned to him and said:

> The law, my dear Palestrina, ought to employ your music . . . in order to lead hardened criminals to repentance. Not one could resist it, I am sure; and the day is not far distant, in these times of humanitarian ideas, when similar psychological methods will be used to soften the hearts of the vicious.

It was against this ecclesiastical background that Liszt conceived much of his choral music. I have called this background ideal. So it must be regarded as one of the greatest tragedies of Liszt's life that his religious music never 'caught on'. The last twenty-five years of his life saw stupendous exertions on his part—he left more than sixty compositions in this field, most of them for liturgical use. But even as he wrote it the tide was turning against him, and the purist movement towards a less 'showy' form of music in church—indeed, towards no form of music at all—became stronger. Through no fault of his own a major portion of Liszt's output has, for all practical purposes, vanished, buried by the vicissitudes of the Catholic Church, instead of becoming a living part of its tradition, as he had hoped.

I now want to consider some of this music in more detail. The two works with which my essay is chiefly concerned are the large-scale 'concert' oratorios *St. Elisabeth* and *Christus*. But I shall also have something to say about the 'Gran' Mass (one of Liszt's masterworks), the highly effective setting of Psalm Thirteen, some of the simpler liturgical compositions, and *Via Crucis: Fourteen Stations of the Cross*, one of the most original compositions of Liszt's old age.

*

The two oratorios *The Legend of St. Elisabeth* and *Christus* were planned quite differently from one another. The first, set to a German text, is really a concert opera on a sacred, or semi-sacred subject, and having a high degree of thematic unity. It shows pretty clearly what Liszt's strengths and weaknesses would have been if he had written works for the stage—as he often planned to do. *Christus*, on the other hand, is really a succession of musical tableaux based on episodes from the life of Christ, from the Annunciation to the Resurrection. There is nothing operatic about the work, in a good or a bad sense, and the separate numbers are seldom thematically linked. The text is in Latin, based partly on the Vulgate, partly on Medieval Latin poems. There is a further curious antithesis between these two Oratorios. It is not really possible to perform *St. Elisabeth* except as a complete work; consequently, its weaknesses tell against it very seriously. *Christus*, on the other hand, on account of its episodic character, could well be performed in sections, and in some cases even separate numbers could be given by themselves. *Christus* also contains a higher proportion of Liszt's best music. Despite this, it is almost as completely neglected as *St. Elisabeth* for reasons that are much harder to fathom.

Apart from these two oratorios, there is a third, unfinished one, called *St. Stanislaus* based on the life of a Polish saint. A good deal of the music is still in manuscript and I have been unable to see it. An orchestral interlude *Salve Polonia* has been published, and it is occasionally performed.

The Legend of St. Elisabeth (1856–62)

The oratorio *St. Elizabeth* has been very much neglected and is, unfortunately, likely to remain so. This is probably inevitable. It is a work which contains many beauties of detail, but in a composition of such length (it unfolds nearly three hours' music) these are not really enough to outweigh serious structural weaknesses. Basically, one feels, Liszt was not quite certain what kind of a work

LISZT IN ROME (c. 1865)

Below PERFORMANCE OF THE 'GRAN' MASS (PARIS, 1866)

AUTOGRAPH PAGE OF 'THE BEATITUDES' (PART II OF THE ORATORIO 'CHRISTUS', 1867)

he was writing. Sometimes, it has the character of a Concert Opera, while at others it has the essentially static character associated with Oratorio.[1]

The story of the work is based on the life of *St. Elisabeth*, one of the national saints of Hungary. As presented here, the story departs in a number of places from historical fact. The actual text of the work does not make the sequence of events at all clear. This would matter less to a Hungarian, or even to a German, audience to whom the story could be presumed to be familiar; an English audience, however, would depend very much on some form of commentary to grasp what is happening. The action, for instance, is spread over a good many years, and this is an obvious source of bewilderment; in one case, where several years have elapsed, there is not even a break in the music. But all this is to some extent explained by the fact that the Oratorio was inspired by the frescoes on the life of St. Elisabeth by the German painter Moritz von Schwind. These frescoes were installed in the Wartburg, the old castle of the Kings of Thuringia, in 1855. Liszt saw them there and commenced work on his Oratorio the following year. The six sections of *St. Elisabeth* correspond to these six frescoes of von Schwind, and Liszt probably expected his listeners to be familiar with them. But how many are?

Here is a summary of the main events of the story. Elisabeth, the daughter of Andrew II, King of Hungary, was born in 1207. At the age of four she was betrothed to Ludwig IV, Margrave of Thuringia. From an early age she devoted herself to religion and to works of charity. She acquired great influence over her husband, although at first he forbade her extravagant gifts to the poor. One day, returning from the hunt, he meets his wife on her way back from the Wartburg with a heavy basket filled with bread. To avert suspicion she tells him she has been gathering roses. On his command she opens the basket and he sees there a mass of red roses. The miracle completed his conversion. In 1227, Ludwig died on a Crusade. According to history, Elisabeth was deprived of the Regency by Ludwig's brother Henry and mercilessly driven from her home in complete destitution. In the Oratorio, however, Elisabeth is persecuted by her mother-in-law, the Landgravine Sophie. She is eventually given asylum in the house of her uncle, the Bishop of Bamberg; she spends the rest of her life in severe penances and in ministrations to the sick. Elisabeth died in 1231. Four years later she was canonized by the Pope on account of the miracles performed at her tomb.

Musically, the work is characterized by an all-pervading thematic unity, to

[1] But whatever one calls it, it would be wrong to call it a genuine opera. A staged version was, in fact, mounted in Weimar in 1881, but it was undertaken against Liszt's wishes and he refused to be present.

which the obvious parallels are to be found in Wagner's music dramas.[1] At the end of the score, Liszt himself wrote out in full the four main themes from which the rest of the Oratorio is metamorphosed.

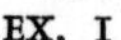

EX. 2

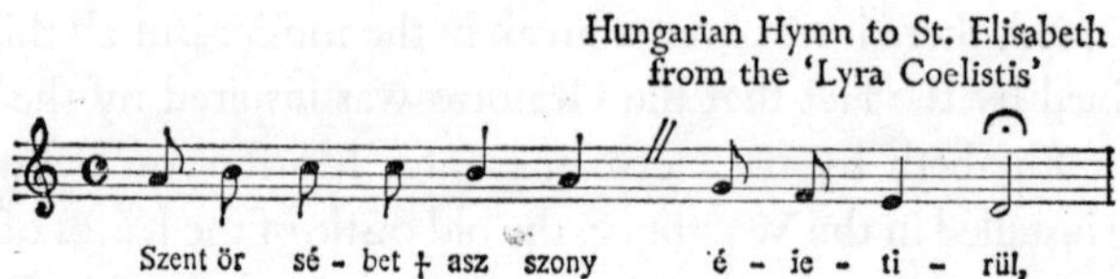

EX. 3

EX. 4

In addition, Liszt makes a most interesting comment about the use of the figure

EX. 5

which occurs frequently in Gregorian chant. He gives a list of examples of its use in his own compositions—the Fugue of the Gloria of the 'Gran' Mass, the final

[1] When Liszt started work on *St. Elizabeth*, in fact, he knew the score of *Die Walküre*, and in the course of the six years he spent composing it he got to know *Tristan* and the first two acts of *Siegfried* as well.

chorus of the 'Dante' Symphony, and the Symphonic Poem *The Battle of the Huns.*[1] This motif, in fact, is an unconscious, stylistic 'fingerprint' which recurs throughout Liszt's life, and I shall later give examples of its use in the 'Gran' Mass and in *Via Crucis*. In *St. Elisabeth*, according to Liszt, it is used as a symbol of the Cross, and it occurs in the Chorus of the Crusaders and in the March of the Crusaders.

The most important idea in the Oratorio is the plainchant melody (Ex. 1) which dominates the work. Here are two of its derivatives.

EX. 6

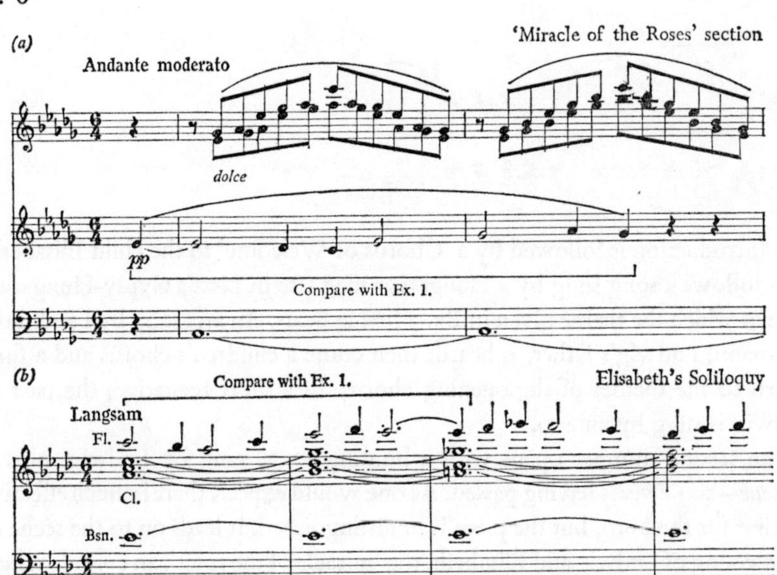

The other basic ideas (Exx. 2, 3, and 4) are of less importance, Ex. 2, for instance appearing quite late in the work.

St. Elisabeth divides into two parts, each consisting of three sections, the six numbers corresponding to the six frescoes of von Schwind. The first number is preceded by an orchestral introduction, very beautifully scored, which could just possibly be performed as a separate work in the concert hall. The opening, in E major,[2] (Ex. 7) is scored for three flutes alone. One wonders if the opening

[1] It occurs in the chorale *Crux Fidelis* which Liszt quotes in *The Battle of the Huns* where it symbolizes the Christian forces in the battle scene. (See Humphrey Searle, p. 301, Ex. 31.) Oddly enough, Liszt seems to have overlooked the important role of this motif in his B minor Sonata, notably in the D major second subject marked 'Grandioso'.

[2] The key of E major is one which seems to have been associated in Liszt's mind with serene religious feeling. Among other examples, one thinks of *Sposalizio* and *St. Francis walking on the waters;* and there is much E major music in *Christus*.

of any other work is scored like this. Note the connection with the plainchant theme (Ex. 1).

EX. 7

The Introduction is followed by a 'Chorus of Welcome' to the child Elisabeth; then follows a song sung by a Hungarian magnate in Liszt's Gypsy-Hungarian style in which the theme given in Ex. 3 first appears. An aria sung by Landgrave Hermann, Ludwig's father, is heard; then come a children's chorus and a final return to the themes of the opening chorus. In a short recitative, the part of Ludwig is sung by an alto.

The second number opens with a hunting song, sung by Ludwig, now a *baritone*—some years having passed. As one would expect, there is much effective writing for the horn, but the piece is undistinguished. It leads on to the scene of the meeting of Ludwig and Elisabeth, the 'miracle of the roses', an episode which is most revealing. It is one of the more obviously operatic sections of the work, and it gives one a chance to consider Liszt's potentialities and limitations as an opera composer. More than anything else, a composer's operatic powers are tested by his skill in setting dialogue in a style that is expressive of the words, musically alive, and above all, producing a feeling of dramatic movement. The music in these sections of *St. Elisabeth* is often very beautiful indeed, but they lack the kind of dramatic movement and tension that one finds, for example, in so many of the recitatives in Bach's Passions.[1]

The episode of the 'miracle of the roses' follows, scored with great delicacy, the melody being given to horn and cellos with supporting chordal figures

[1] We have probably lost something through Bach never having written an opera, and we have probably lost nothing through Liszt never having done so. I do not think this statement is a paradox. What people call the 'theatricality' in Liszt's music is something which has little or nothing to do with the theatre.

from flutes, clarinets and *divisi* violins. This episode has been praised even by unsympathetic critics, but I believe there are more important things in the work; it is rounded off by a chorus in E major, based on the plainchant melody (Ex. 1).

The third number opens with the Chorus of Crusaders, in which the 'Cross' motif (Ex. 5) plays a great part. Ludwig has decided to set out on the Crusades, and in a dialogue with her husband Elisabeth expresses her sorrow and her fears; Ludwig begs her to show fortitude. The following passage from this scene is a fair example of Liszt's more 'operatic' vocal writing.

EX. 8

The March of the Crusaders, choral in the later part, has two principal themes: the first based on the 'Cross' motif (Ex. 9).

EX. 9

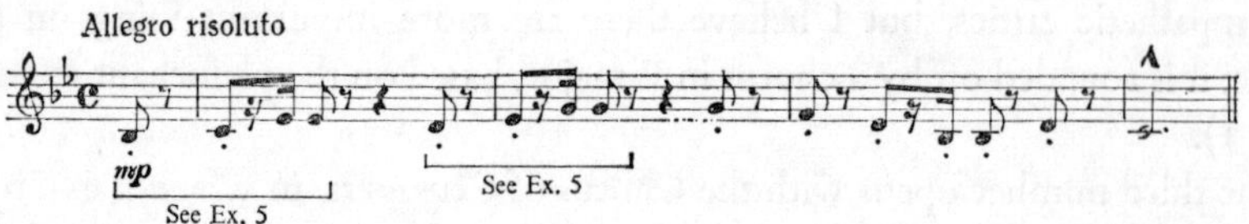

The second is the 'Pilgrim's' theme (stated in full, this time) of which the opening bars are quoted in Ex. 4. Apart from the orchestral introduction at the opening of the work, and the Interlude preceding the final number, this March is almost the only piece in the whole Oratorio really suitable for separate performance. It brings Part I to a close.

Part II opens with a tumultuous scene between the Landgravine Sophie, Ludwig's mother, her Seneschal, and Elisabeth. Sophie, who has heard of the death of her son on the Crusade, decides to throw Elisabeth out, despite her passionate pleadings and the timid remonstrances of the Seneschal. This scene is, superficially at least, the most 'dramatic' in the work; the music given to Sophie is forceful if rather stagey; she is in the line of mezzo-soprano villainesses.

Elisabeth, with her children, is finally driven out; a violent storm breaks and Sophie's castle is struck by lightning. The storm music has a degree of chromaticism that most people would call Wagnerian.

EX. 10

The storm eventually subsides; the number continues without a break to the next scene, the penultimate number of the Oratorio. This scene, taking place several years later, is a long soliloquy by Elisabeth. She knows her life is nearing its end, and gives thanks to God for the happiness as well as the suffering of her life, and asks for special blessings for her children and her native land.[1]

The style is arioso; there is a great sensitiveness in detail in the vocal writing as well as in the orchestration. The total effect is rather too much that of a lengthy improvisation. But this is largely a performing problem. With a very intelligent and sympathetic singer, and a conductor with the same approach, it could be convincing. The part of Elisabeth needs a dramatic soprano, but one with an unusual command of *pianissimo* shading. Elisabeth's solo is followed by a short, very quiet, orchestral interlude leading to a new section: a 'Chorus of the Poor' whom Elisabeth has always helped. This chorus, sung *sotto voce* almost throughout, is based on the old Hungarian hymn to St. Elisabeth (Ex. 2). It is followed by another solo for Elisabeth, at the end of which she dies.

The final scene, the burial of Elisabeth, opens with an oration by the Emperor Frederick II, rather in a style which suggests pastiche Spontini and Meyerbeer. The actual music of the funeral procession begins with orchestral figures based on the theme of Ex. 2, the 'Chorus of the People' which is to follow later. There are sections sung by the Hungarian bishops in unison, later by the German bishops. These sections, which one could describe, not unfairly, as ecclesiastical rhetoric are, in a way, impressive, but not as totally convincing as the simpler and quieter 'Chorus of the Poor'. *St. Elisabeth* ends as it began, in E major, with a passage recalling the orchestral Introduction at the beginning.

Christus (*1855–67*)

I consider *Christus* to be one of Liszt's most important works. It may not be entirely convincing as an integrated, large-scale work like the 'Faust' Symphony or the B minor Sonata. But that is not especially important here. Liszt deliberately conceived the structure of *Christus* as an essentially episodic one, and this makes it possible to perform any of its three Parts, or even some of its individual numbers, as separate pieces. (*St. Elisabeth*, conceived as it was, as a thematic whole, is a far trickier problem to solve from the performing standpoint.) Moreover, this is a positive advantage when one considers the very great length of *Christus* (which would make complete performances rare, anyway), and also the fact that a few of these autonomous sections contain some of Liszt's very finest music—which makes it all the more desirable to hear them in the concert hall. Despite this, however, *Christus* has had few performances in any country,

[1] Appropriately, her prayers are in F sharp major, a key which had strong mystical associations for Liszt. See John Ogdon, p. 156n.

even in part. It is as if musicians and critics had tacitly agreed to pre-judge the work and dismiss it. If this is true, it is a major critical blunder.

Christus is based on selected episodes from the life of Jesus, from the Annunciation by the Angel to the Shepherds, to the Resurrection. It consists of a series of lyrical and descriptive tableaux with no consistent narrative thread, and little real drama. And mainly because the events are spread over such a long period of time, the Oratorio has none of the dramatic concentration of the Bach Passions. The text is in Latin. There are fourteen numbers, four of them being settings of mediaeval Latin poems, the rest being taken from the Vulgate. The choral writing is generally more effective than in *St. Elisabeth*, even though it has the same basically homophonic character, the frequent six-part writing sometimes being in a rather low tessitura. Despite these weaknesses, the numbers for chorus with organ accompaniment, particularly the settings of the *Beatitudes* and the *Lord's Prayer*, are among the most moving things Liszt ever wrote. The writing for solo voices is effective and very singable, even though it is never really adventurous. The orchestral writing has great refinement and sureness of touch. In a sense it is the summit of Liszt's orchestral technique; the music gives a feeling of being more truly orchestrally conceived than is the case even in such great works as the two Symphonies. After *Christus*, in fact, Liszt did not write a great deal for the orchestra, and the evolution of his orchestral technique can be said to finish with this work.

Part I of *Christus* is called 'Christmas Oratorio'. It is one of the few works of Liszt showing traces of the stylistic influence of Berlioz—the Berlioz of the *Childhood of Christ*. The great charm of much of the pastoral music is, in my view, spoilt by its excessive length and an undue amount of music in 6/8 and 12/8 time—which are, admittedly, the traditional pastoral metres. The first number is a purely orchestral introduction headed by a quotation from Isaiah, ch. 45, v. 8.

> Drop down, ye heavens, from above, and let the skies pour down righteousness.

The Introduction divides into two parts: an Andante Sostenuto in a highly modalized D minor in 6/4(3/2) time; and a longer 12/8 section mostly in G major. Both passages are based on motifs from the plainsong melody 'Angelus ad pastores ait' (see Ex. 13). This melody reappears in an extended form at the beginning of the second number. The Andante opens in the following manner, suggestive of Fugue without being truly fugal. It is scored for muted strings, with intermittent support from solo woodwind instruments. The effect is quite

EX. 11

ethereal, reminding one of Berlioz's overture to 'The Flight to Egypt'. The second number, 'Pastorale and Annunciation of the Angel' follows without a break. I quote the first nine bars in full; they give a good example of Liszt's writing for woodwind.[1]

EX. 12

[1] I consider Liszt, particularly in the work of his late middle period, to be one of the most successful composers in dealing with the difficult problem of woodwind ensemble. The

It is worth making the point that here, as elsewhere, Liszt uses the cor anglais as an 'unusual' instrument (as indeed it was at the time of his middle period) reserved for special effects, and seldom, like Wagner, in *Tristan* and the *Ring*, as a normal element in the woodwind ensemble. This cor anglais theme, of course, is a variant of the 'Angelus ad pastores' plainchant. At the end of the movement the opening bar of the main theme appears in a rhythm anticipating its full statement in the next number. This final form of the plainsong melody is given here, and it is interesting to compare Liszt's metrical version with the form given in the 'Liber Usualis'.[1]

EX. 13

The harmony of this number is mostly simple and diatonic, suggesting a study of the less contrapuntal works of the sixteenth century. The short episode in E major which follows is a good example of those unexpected stylistic contrasts (or discrepancies, according to your taste) which are so often remarked on in Liszt. The number ends with a beautiful passage scored for flutes, clarinets, and solo violins.

The third number of *Christus* is a setting for chorus and organ of the anonymous mediaeval poem 'Stabat mater speciosa'. The organ part (and this is typical of Liszt) is fingered very carefully, even in the full score; and in its role of supporting instrument, Liszt shows both tact and resourcefulness. The number closes with a very original final cadence which is worth quoting.

---

essential difficulty arises from the diversity of timbre of the instruments, as compared with the homogeneity of the strings and brass. The heterogeneity of the woodwind can be either deliberately exploited or deliberately played down. Liszt knew how to do both. What is always perilous is to forget it.

[1] The problem of the correct interpretation of the rhythm of plainsong has never been finally settled, despite prolonged, and sometimes acrimonious argument, and in all probability it never will be. Essential documentation is lacking. Liszt had a deep feeling for Gregorian plainsong, as well as for sixteenth-century church music. But in neither case was his knowledge at all scholarly; he had neither the time, nor the temperament, for research. Some experts on plainsong could well hold that Liszt's metrical version is as near to the mediaeval manner of performance as the unmetrical speech-rhythm of the Solesmes school. I am not qualified to express an opinion on the matter either way.

EX. 14

One of Liszt's most effective orchestral movements is to be found in the fifth number of *Christus*: the 'March of the three Holy Kings'. It could well be performed as a separate piece, and it has all the makings of a popular concert work, but it has suffered from the neglect of the Oratorio as a whole; most conductors do not even know of its existence. In a sense, it is a counterpart to the 'March of the Crusaders' in *St. Elisabeth* and it is the better of the two pieces. The March opens very quietly in C minor, reminding one slightly of the March in the same key near the beginning of Berlioz's *Childhood of Christ*. The principal theme is stated by the lower strings *pizzicato*.

EX. 15

The second main theme appears in D flat major.

EX. 16

This section, in contrast to the delicate, almost chamber-musical, scoring in some of the earlier numbers, is a splendid example of Liszt's handling of full orchestral sonorities; it never falls into coarseness or loses clarity of texture. With this March, Part I of *Christus* ends.

Part II has the general title 'After the Epiphany'. It begins with a setting of 'The Beatitudes' whose text, of course, comes from the Gospel of St. Matthew, and which was composed in 1855—a good deal earlier than most of the Oratorio. It is set for baritone solo and chorus with organ accompaniment, and it opens with a short introduction for organ. For most of the time the solo voice, quite unsupported (Ex. 17*a*) is used antiphonally to the chorus (Ex. 17*b*), which is given direct support from the organ. The key is E major, whose religious associations for Liszt have already been mentioned.

EX. 17

This example, with its frequent five- and six-part chords, is very characteristic of Liszt's choral style. It is strange that this beautiful piece, remarkable equally for its intensity and its restraint should be so little known; it could be performed separately in the concert hall.

The eighth number of *Christus* is called 'The Foundation of the Church'. It opens with a figure of four notes

EX. 18

to the words 'Thou art Peter and on this rock I build my Church'. Liszt had a deep veneration for the institution of the Catholic Church, a veneration quite independent of his religious beliefs, about which there is some uncertainty. His religious feelings were undoubtedly complex, and in some of his religious music the word 'mystical' could be used. Here I think that 'ecclesiastical' is the right one; music full of pomp, without being pompous.[1]

The next number, 'The Miracle', is an orchestral piece describing the miracle of Jesus walking on the waves. It would require analysis in the greatest detail to give an adequate idea of this music; until its final section it is very un-thematic, and could easily be regarded as just one more in the succession of 'storm pieces' with chromatic scales in all the usual combinations of minor thirds and diminished sevenths. But the piece succeeds because all the apparent 'effects' are so placed that they form part of an entirely logical whole. At the climax of the storm the voices of the disciples cry out 'Lord, we perish!'; there is a dramatic silence and the voice of Jesus answers, unaccompanied: 'How fearful ye are, O ye of little faith'. This is followed by a final, quiet section, containing some of Liszt's most serene music.

EX. 19

[1] This piece also exists as a work for organ called *Der Papsthymus* written at the time when Liszt was living in Rome and had become personally acquainted with Pius IX.

The final number of Part II is 'The Entry into Jerusalem'. I quote the opening.

EX. 20

Part III of *Christus* opens with a setting of the words 'Tristis est anima mea' ('My soul is exceeding sorrowful even unto death'). This I consider to be one of the summits of Liszt's entire work, and one of the most moving of all the pieces inspired by the Agony in the Garden. It is one of those works of Liszt in which one finds all the things that one is usually most ready to criticize: repetition of longish sections in different keys; the constant use of sequence and the rather mannered chromaticism of much of the thematic material. Yet here one feels these things scarcely matter, or rather that everything is emotionally and structurally right, and that what might well be a *cliché* elsewhere is here natural and inevitable. The orchestration is as remarkable as in the 'Miracle Scene'. Through large parts of this number, the orchestra is on its own; the piece is almost a Symphonic Poem with bass solo. The sparing use of the voice gives tremendous force to its entries. The number opens with a long orchestral introduction rather like the opening of the third act of *Tristan*, and it works up

EX. 21

to a great orchestral climax ending in complete calm with an orchestral Epilogue after the words 'Not what I will but what Thou wilt'.

The remainder of *Christus* consists of a setting of the Stabat Mater and the Easter Hymn 'O fillii et fillia'; it ends with 'The Resurrection' on a note of great exultation.

'Gran' Mass (1855–58)

The neglect of this important and impressive work is not easy to explain. It was written for the consecration of the cathedral at Esztergom in western Hungary. Among German-speaking peoples the city is known as Gran.

The work as a whole is of the extrovert kind which befits an important ceremonial occasion; yet, as happens in so many settings of the Mass, the most musically satisfying as well as the most moving sections are the Kyries, the Qui tollis, the Sanctus, Benedictus, and Agnus dei. The music of the more dogmatic sections of the text is relatively conventional. There is a very high degree of formal unity in the Gloria and the Credo, both of which are planned on the scale of symphonic movements.

The 'Gran' Mass is scored for four soloists, chorus, large orchestra, and organ. At the foot of the full score is Liszt's own piano arrangement of the work, which even contains his own fingerings; it is well worth careful study, and it is a model of what can and should be done in this difficult art.

The Kyrie opens quietly, but impressively, with a figure of four notes (Ex. 22, bracket 'x') which is developed in an almost Beethovenian fashion.

The Gloria is a piece of dazzling sonority. It contains a particularly effective fugue in B major to the words 'Cum sanctu spiritu'. The reader will be struck by its resemblance to the 'Grandioso' second subject of the B minor Sonata. Observe, also bracket 'x', the 'Cross' motif, one of Liszt's musical fingerprints (see p. 323).

EX. 23

It is true of this fugue, as of virtually all Liszt's fugues, that its theme is full of character; but the absence of a clearly defined counter-subject means that it does not quite fulfil the expectations aroused at the opening. This is also true of the fugue in the B minor Sonata and in the 'Mephistopheles' movement of the 'Faust' Symphony, though in both cases there are imaginative strokes of fugal procedure.

One of the most effective sections is the Crucifixus. At the words 'judicare vivos et mortuos' there occurs this passage for brass.

EX. 24

It is easy to say that any composer with sufficient orchestral recourses at his disposal can produce an effective representation of the Last Trump. This passage seems to look back to Berlioz's *Requiem* and forward to Verdi's—who may well not have known Liszt's work. But the listener and critic should hear this passage open-mindedly before falling back on stock phrases about 'theatricality' and 'insincerity'.

I see no reason, apart from prejudice, and the strange ill-luck that seems to follow so many works of Liszt, why this remarkable work should not establish itself in the choral repertory. But climates of opinion can change; compare, for instance, the number of performances of Berlioz's *Requiem* in England during the past twenty years with those of the preceding twenty. Apart from its grandeur and expressiveness, the 'Gran' Mass is unique among nineteenth-century masses in its thematic unity, though striking parallels are to be found in those of the sixteenth century.

Hungarian Coronation Mass (1867)

The Hungarian Coronation Mass, like the 'Gran' Mass, was composed for a ceremonial occasion, in this case for the coronation of the Austrian Emperor Franz-Josef as King of Hungary at Budapest in 1867, an event which inaugurated the 'Dual Monarchy' which lasted until the end of the 1914–18 War. The work was written at tremendous speed, being completed in the remarkably short time of three weeks. Liszt himself travelled to Budapest for the first performance, and to attend the coronation celebrations; while he was there a banquet was given in his honour, and among the tributes to him was a toast by the entire assembly—delivered in Latin.

It is easy to dismiss the Coronation Mass as a less convincing repeat of the 'Gran' Mass; but this view would be hard to justify because by this time Liszt had moved away from the ideal of an elaborate and highly coloured style of church music, which he held in the 'fifties, towards the far simpler and more austere style of his later works. But the Coronation Mass has certain special features, among them the frequent use of the 'Hungarian' idiom—in the special Lisztian sense. The Credo, too, is unusual, being written entirely in a neo-plainsong style,[1] the voices singing mostly in octaves or unison, occasionally doubled in thirds or sixths.

EX. 25

There is a long violin solo in the Benedictus, obviously inspired by the Benedictus of Beethoven's *Missa Solemnis*. As in all the choral works, there are exceptionally beautiful lyrical passages—with the same curious and unfortunate

[1] See p. 330n for more comment on Liszt's interest in plainsong.—*Ed.*

result that while they at once strike any sensitive musician who has the time to familiarize himself with the scores, they could pass almost unnoticed if he only had the opportunity to hear the work once.

Psalm Thirteen (1855)

The setting of the Thirteenth Psalm, 'Lord, how long wilt Thou forget me?', for tenor, chorus, and orchestra, was completed in 1855. It is the only choral work of Liszt's that is fairly well known. It was a favourite with Beecham who conducted it from time to time. Like *St. Elisabeth* and parts of the 'Gran' Mass, it is essentially an application to choral music of the principles of thematic metamorphosis as we find them exemplified in the Symphonic Poems. The theme given out at the very beginning dominates the work.

EX. 26

Among the several important derivatives of this idea, there is a particularly effective chorus

EX. 27

The Thirteenth Psalm is a work which could well have a popular appeal. It communicates with real conviction the spirit of the words, both their anguish and their serenity, reaching heights of great expressiveness.

Smaller Choral Works

The sacred works written for chorus, with organ accompaniment, are an important part of Liszt's output, and one of the most completely neglected. In contrast to the large-scale 'concert' pieces I have discussed, they are definitely planned for liturgical use. They employ modest forces, and they are relatively short. Despite this, they have never been accepted—either within the Church, or without.

Liszt fully supported the revived study of Gregorian music and the church music of the sixteenth century. He also seems to have had a knowledge of composers like Palestrina and Lassus. That this music both moved and stimulated him is unquestioned; but it hardly influenced him. Since his death, the movement towards a simpler style in church music has developed rapidly; there are now many Catholics to whom even a Palestrina mass smacks too much of 'a concert in church', distracting attention from the act of worship. Liszt's liturgical music inevitably falls under the same censure, even though when he composed it listeners were surprised by its spareness and simplicity. Nor are those who attack a work like the 'Gran' Mass for its flamboyance and theatricality necessarily impressed by the restraint of Liszt's liturgical works; this very restraint seems to them a more subtle form of attitudinizing. Either way, Liszt loses.

There are three liturgical masses that I want, briefly, to mention. The first is the *Mass for Male Voices*, which Liszt composed as early as 1849. It received its first performance at Weimar in 1852 to celebrate the birthday of the President of the French Republic—later the Emperor Napoleon III! Liszt published a revised edition of the piece in 1870. This is an unusual and austere work in which the singers effectively declaim, not sing, parts of the Credo. The melodic line of the Gloria reveals the influence of plainchant. Note the appearance of the 'Cross' motif (bracket 'x').[1]

EX. 28

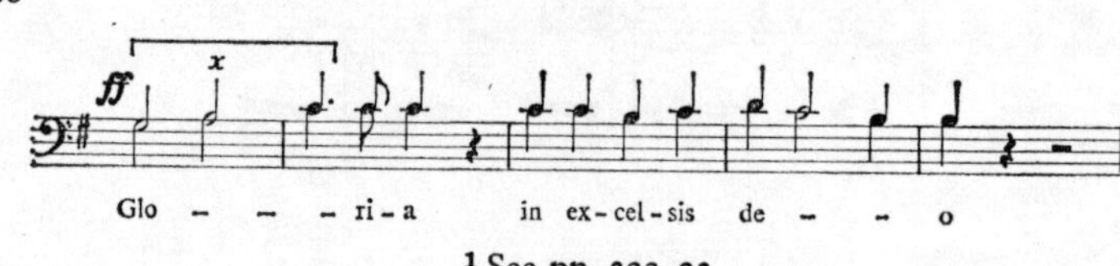

[1] See pp. 322–23.

The second of these liturgical masses, the *Missa Choralis*, is an important composition. It dates from 1865 about the time Liszt received the tonsure of the Catholic Church. Few works of Liszt have so little chromaticism, so little Romantic rhetoric. It is scored for mixed chorus and organ. The Kyrie shows great harmonic austerity, as if Liszt were trying to return to the language of the sixteenth century.

EX. 29

One of the most ambitious of the liturgical is works the *Requiem Mass* completed in 1868. It employs male voice choir and organ; in the Dies Irae and the Sanctus there are optional parts for brass and timpani. We are a long way removed from the serenity of thc *Missa Choralis*. There is an extreme chromaticism reminiscent of some of the more anguished moments in *Parsifal* (which Wagner had not yet begun).

EX. 30

Among the smaller choral works there remains an important group of three pieces which has a most curious and revealing history. The three pieces, *Via Crucis*, the *Seven Sacraments*, and a sequence of short choral pieces called *Rosario*, were sent in 1884 by Liszt to the publisher Pustet, at Regensburg in Bavaria—the chief centre of the revival of Catholic church music in Germany. Liszt was ready to have the works published without any payment, only asking to be given a hundred complimentary copies. Astonishingly, the works were rejected by the publisher.[1] This was two years before Liszt's death, and there is some evidence that he felt the blow severely. These works carried to its natural conclusion the whole line of development begun years earlier with the Mass for Male Voices and continued with the other works I have discussed in this section. Liszt felt he had put his very best into these late works, in which his ideal of a reformed church music had steadily become clearer. The rejection, coming at the end of his life, was a final confirmation of what he must have known for a long time: that his religious music, when not completely misunderstood, had failed to achieve any real recognition. But before one condemns Pustet as an exceptionally stupid man, one should remember that many Lisztians shared his low opinion of the choral works,[2] and with far less excuse: they, at least, should have taken the trouble to discover what, exactly, Liszt was trying to achieve. Of the three works, *Via Crucis* is unquestionably the most significant. Liszt completed it in 1879. It received its first performance fifty years later in Budapest on Good Friday, 1929. Scored for mixed chorus, soloists, and organ, it consists of a Prelude, followed by fourteen short pieces each describing one of the Stations of the Cross; some of these are vocal and some are played by the organ alone. The texts were arranged by the Princess Sayn-Wittgenstein from the Bible and from various hymns and chorales, including 'O sacred head sore wounded'.

[1] They were not published until 1918.
[2] This is particularly true of Peter Raabe, Liszt's chief biographer.

The solo voices represent Jesus, Pilate, and the other leading personalities in the story of the Crucifixion. The titles of the fourteen Stations are:

1. *Jesus is condemned to death*
2. *Jesus takes up his Cross*
3. *Jesus falls for the first time*
4. *Jesus meets his blessed Mother*
5. *Simon of Cyrene helps Jesus to carry the Cross*
6. *St. Veronica wipes Jesus' face with her veil*
7. *Jesus falls for the second time*
8. *The women of Jerusalem mourn for Jesus*
9. *Jesus falls for the third time*
10. *Jesus is stripped of his clothing*
11. *Jesus is nailed to the Cross*
12. *Jesus dies on the Cross*
13. *Jesus is taken down from the Cross*
14. *Jesus is laid in the Tomb.*

The work begins with a Prelude *Vexilla Regis prodeunt* ('The Royal banners forward go, the Cross shines forth in mystic glow').

EX. 31

The 'Cross' motif (bracket 'x') recurs several times; and the style of the music veers between the bareness and austerity of Ex. 31, to the most advanced chromaticism not very far removed from atonality (Ex. 32).

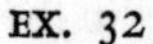

Altogether, I think *Via Crucis* is unclassifiable. It is unlike anything else that Liszt ever wrote.

This essay must, of necessity, remain somewhat superficial; the field is much more extensive than is generally recognized, and it could well form the subject of a book. The tendency of most writers on Liszt has been to treat it as the least important part of his output. To those of them who are hostile to Liszt, his religious music is suspect anyway; and even to many Lisztians the great importance that he himself attached to it seemed a supreme example of the frequent tendency of creative artists to go wrong in judging their own work.

My own belief is that Liszt's choral works contain some of the most underrated music in the whole literature. But one does not help to a real understanding of it by mere assertions. Musicians should study these works for themselves, and draw their own conclusions.

*

From time to time, I have touched on Liszt's use of the organ as an accompanying instrument. I now want to say something about Liszt's *solo* organ works. They are not numerous; but they tend to be significant because Liszt was one of the few Romantics to compose for the instrument. Indeed, he did much more than this. He literally dragged the organ out of church and into the concert hall. The two solo works I shall consider demand, in fact, a virtuoso technique to do them full justice.

Liszt and the Organ

As early as 1836 Liszt had revealed an astonishing mastery over the organ. He was living in Geneva at that time with the Countess d'Agoult. During the summer they had organized a holiday excursion to the village of Chamonix where they were joined by George Sand and one or two other guests. Every day they would set out on a ramble across the beautiful countryside, eating a picnic lunch under the trees or by a mountain stream. It was during one of these excursions that the exhausted party arrived at Fribourg and entered the church of St. Nicholas. There, Liszt saw a particularly fine organ built by the famous Mooser. He sat down and astounded everybody by improvising for several hours, during which he worked up a tremendous fantasy on the *Dies Irae*. His concentration was so intense he appeared to be in a trance, and the impact of his playing was so great that the company grew frightened and withdrew. They had witnessed something unique, and it was an event none of them ever forgot.[1]

Liszt played the organ a good deal in middle and later life, and we know that he practised on the pedal piano. His organ works show great insight into the instrument. They have been criticized for reflecting too strongly the nineteenth-century tendency to be concerned mainly with the *power* of the organ, a power which enabled it to produce massive effects rivalling those of the orchestra; to be, in fact, a one man orchestra. But we must remember that the whole trend of organ building during the nineteenth century was determined by this outlook. It was the Romantics who turned the organ into the 'King of Instruments', and we can hardly be surprised at the result when the King of Pianists wrote for it. Liszt's works for the organ are not numerous, but one or two are really important and they have secured a firm place in the repertory.

Liszt's chief work, perhaps the most important organ composition to come out of the nineteenth century, is the Fantasy and Fugue on the chorale *Ad nos, ad Salutarem undam* from Meyerbeer's opera *Le Prophète*. Its scale is gigantic, unfolding about thirty minutes' continuous music, and it exploits every

[1] Adolphe Pictet, one of the party, later described the event in his book *Un Voyage à Chamonix*.—*Ed.*

conceivable tonal resource of the organ. *Ad nos* falls into three sections. The opening is an extended fantasy in which the chorale theme is developed.

EX. 33

An Adagio section follows, which begins with a complete statement of the chorale. This chorale is by Meyerbeer himself and is not a traditional tune as some musicians think. It comes from the first act of *Le Prophète* where it is sung by the three Anabaptists who urge the people to be re-baptized in the healing waters.[1]

EX. 34

[1] Liszt transposed it into the 'mystical' key of F sharp major. See John Ogdon, p. 156 n.

A brilliant cadenza-like passage follows the Adagio and ushers in the Fugue.

EX. 35

Although it shows considerable contrapuntal ingenuity, the Fugue (it is, in fact, a double fugue) is far removed from the academic conception of the form and unfolds almost like a grand improvisation—as, indeed, it possibly was. It reaches a brilliant climax and the work ends with a triumphant statement of the chorale theme.

Liszt completed *Ad nos* in 1850 and dedicated it to Meyerbeer who was, apparently, considerably impressed with the result.[1] Given the right combination of circumstances—a resonant building, a good organ, and above all a virtuoso organist—*Ad nos* can sound overwhelming.

Liszt's other major work for the organ is his Prelude and Fugue on B.A.C.H. He composed it in 1855, five years after *Ad nos*, and dedicated it to the German organist Alexander Winterberger who gave the first performance at Merseberg the following year. Ever since Bach in his *Art of Fugue* introduced a musical theme on the letters of his own name, composers have been attracted to this idea as the basis for a composition. Liszt had a great veneration for Bach, and his B.A.C.H. Prelude and Fugue is to be regarded as a musical tribute to him. Humphrey Searle sees in it 'the beginning of that sliding chromaticism which eventually weakened the tonal system . . . to such an extent that tonal analysis hardly became possible any more', and a little later he writes that 'this Prelude and Fugue may be regarded as a more or less direct link between Bach and Schoenberg'.[2] All this is true enough, but for me the work is somewhat marred by its excessive use of the chord of the diminished seventh. Many examples could be quoted; I confine myself to one.

EX. 36

[1] See Meyerbeer's letter quoted on p. 169.—*Ed.*

[2] In German, of course, 'B' stands for B flat, while 'H' is used for B natural. The name 'Bach', then, produces the following motif

Sixteen years after completing the B.A.C.H. Prelude and Fugue, Liszt made an effective piano transcription of it in which form it has become deservedly well known, especially among pianists. This transcription is dealt with elsewhere in this volume.

There are a small handful of other organ pieces, but nothing on the scale of the two works I have discussed. But on the strength of *Ad nos* and the B.A.C.H. Prelude and Fugue alone, Liszt has a secure place in the organ repertory. They are among the most significant compositions for the instrument between Bach and Reger.

ALAN WALKER

Liszt and the Twentieth Century

THE picture Liszt's contemporaries had of him during his final years was that of an eccentric, idling away at the keyboard, producing pieces which were an embarrassment to his friends and a source of considerable amusement to his enemies. Liszt himself was now regarded as something of a joke, and in Vienna, especially, the torrent of criticism and personal abuse which rained on him—it came chiefly from people like Hanslick and Essler—would have wrung a reply from a lesser man.[1] But Liszt remained silent. For one thing, he had boundless confidence in his musical 'after-life', as he used to call it. For another, he was well aware that to debate publicly the pros and cons of his recent music with somebody of Hanslick's persuasion was a waste of time.

The question arises: who was Liszt addressing in these last works?

In a letter written to Princess Wittgenstein Liszt once confessed that his only remaining ambition was to hurl a lance as far as possible into the boundless realm of the future. These words are significant, and the princess grasped their meaning: 'Generations will pass before he will be perfectly understood; he has hurled his lance much further into the future than Wagner. (That she was right is beyond dispute; and in this essay I shall try to show that many of the twentieth century's most treasured 'discoveries' were already anticipated by Liszt.) On another occasion, the seventy-four-year-old Liszt once turned to his pupil August Stradel and remarked: 'The time will yet come when my works are appreciated. True, it will be late for me because then I shall no longer be with you'. The conclusion is inescapable. Liszt was deliberately setting himself to address listeners as yet unborn. One of his favourite observations whenever his

[1] 'After Liszt, Mozart is like a soft spring breeze penetrating a room reeking with fumes' (Hanslick). Such remarks would be considered almost libellous today. Critics have become much more respectful towards the avant-garde.

music met with blank incredulity was: 'I can wait; meanwhile, my shoulders are broad.'[1]

Towards Impressionism

It was Liszt's compulsive involvement with musical experiment of all kinds which, in his last years, not only cut him off from his wider public, but from a great many serious musicians as well, some of whom must have wondered what he was trying to achieve. Consider for instance his penchant for abandoning a work in 'mid-air', leaving it floating on unfinished harmonies.

EX. 1

Fourth Valse Oubliée [1885]

EX. 2

Nuages Gris [1881]

A later generation was to call such effects 'impressionistic'. Dissonance is quitted as if it were consonance. A centuries-old barrier here begins to crumble.

In 1884 the young Debussy heard Liszt play in Rome. The experience made a deep impact on him. Liszt had just published several impressionistic pieces, including the famous *Les jeux d'eaux à la Villa d'Este*, and there is something strangely moving about the thought of the ageing Abbé performing his musical sound-picture of those splashing fountains before the astonished ears of the young rebel who, years later, was to emerge as 'the father of modern music'. When we hear such passages as this, however, based on a descending chain of secondary sevenths, we are entitled to ask who the 'father' really was.

[1] They had to be. Liszt was everybody's whipping-boy. One of the most sanctimonious utterances in the history of criticism came from Sir George Macfarren, Principal of the Royal Academy of Music, who piously declared that Liszt was 'working a great evil upon music'. Anxious, no doubt, to protect his students against Liszt's pernicious influence, he tried to dissuade them from listening to his music lest it corrupt them. This was an extreme measure, but, as he put it: 'Were you to preach temperance at a gin-shop door, and let your congregation taste the poison sold therein that they might know its vileness, they would come out drunkards.' This kind of twaddle, a typical piece of contemporary Liszt criticism, was endured by Liszt for a quarter of a century or more.

EX. 3

As Busoni put it, the piece still remains today the model for all musical fountains which have flowed since then.[1] Ravel took it as the starting-point for his own *Jeux d'eau*. Historically the work is one of the most important Liszt ever composed. In it, he paved the way almost single-handed for the French Impressionists. There is, incidentally, an unmistakable likeness between the main idea of *Les Jeux d'Eaux à la Villa d'Este* and that of Debussy's *L'Isle Joyeuse*. Compare Exx. 4 and 5.

EX. 4

EX. 5

[1] *The Essence of Music*, p. 138, London, 1956.

THE VILLA D'ESTE
Oil Painting by Edward Lear

AUTOGRAPH PAGE OF 'CZARDAS OBSTINE' (1884)

Debussy's use of bare consecutive fifths often landed him in difficulties with the establishment. It is a salutary reminder of Liszt's questing spirit that Debussy was only nineteen when the 70-year old wizard defiantly threw out the following passage.

EX. 6

It was after hearing this piece (which contains a deliberate distortion of the *Dies Irae*)[1] that August Göllerich, a somewhat conservative Liszt pupil, exclaimed: 'Is it allowed to write such a thing? Is it allowed to listen to it?'[2]

All his life, Liszt had a great fondness for the augmented triad. One of his favourite ways of using the chord, especially in his younger days, was at cadence-points where it led him to create one of his most characteristic 'fingerprints'. An example which immediately springs to the ear is the closing bars of the *Petrarch Sonnet 104*.

EX. 7

[1] See p. 165, Ex. 51.

[2] The *Czárdás Macabre* (1881) was not published until 1951. As Szabolcsi says, there seems to have been a 'conspiracy of silence' surrounding Liszt's late works. They were familiar only to a small circle of Liszt's admirers, who held back from publishing them for fear of exacerbating still further Liszt's poor relationship with the critics.

Another occurs at the end of the well-known *Funérailles.*

EX. 8

Dozens of other examples clamour to be heard. In fact, it is impossible to enjoy even a limited acquaintance with Liszt's music without such progressions ringing in the mind's ear long after the music, so to speak, has stopped. But the augmented chord gradually came to have a far deeper significance for Liszt than that of a mere 'colour effect'. He eventually came to the conclusion that it was the way into modern harmony[1] (later confirmed by the French Impressionists), and he audaciously proceeded to exploit the consequences, chief among them the suspension of tonality.

EX. 9

Liszt stood head and shoulders above his contemporaries in this kind of thing. One can draw a straight line from Ex. 9 to the twentieth century; indeed, the textbooks refer to such harmonies as 'functional chords'—that is, chords whose structure remains unchanged with changing pitch—and they attribute its invention to Debussy.

Towards Atonality

The augmented triad is derived artificially from the whole-tone scale which, by definition, is keyless. Very few nineteenth-century composers interested

[1] In 1853 a Berlin musician C. F. Weitzmann published a book on the augmented triad(!). Liszt, who knew him well, became familiar with his theories and they might well have influenced his thinking at this time.

themselves in the whole-tone scale, but as early as 1840 Liszt had written the following passage in his seventh Hungarian Rhapsody.[1]

EX. 10

The effect came to have a great hold over him, and such passages are a commonplace in Liszt's music.

A commonplace? I do not use the term in a pejorative sense. All composers repeat themselves; but the great ones vary what they repeat. Unlike mediocrities, they are not reduced to forging their own signatures. Ex. 10 could not be further removed from Ex. 11, either in sound or in spirit. Yet it, too, is based on the whole-tone scale. But whereas the one is spirited sound, the other is sounding spirit.

EX. 11

This quotation, from the climax of *Sursam Corda*, is one of the most telling moments in all Liszt; and if it is not generally recognized as such, it is only because those pianists who 'know Liszt' are almost certainly fewer than those who say that they do. The weakening, and eventual break-up, of tonality towards the end of the nineteenth century had its origins in such passages which, in their day, must have sounded revolutionary.

The logical outcome of Liszt's whole-tone experiments came in 1860. His

[1] It is not true, as the textbooks sometimes have it, that Dargomijsky (1813–69) invented the whole-tone scale. It was known to theorists considerably earlier, although its first appearance in a piece of music seems to have been in Mozart's *A Musical Joke*. Liszt was the first to exploit it seriously.

remarkable 'monodrama' *Der Traurige Mönch* for voice and piano is based entirely on the consistent use of the whole-tone scale—perhaps the first such piece in musical history. Liszt himself described *Der Traurige Mönch* as a 'Melodrama'. It is a setting for voice and piano of words by Nicholas Lenau.

EX. 12

An astonishing thing about it is that the words are *declaimed*, not sung. The piece thus paves the way for the Schoenbergian device of 'sprechstimme'—and Szabolcsi's remark that 'Liszt threw open the gates of the twentieth century' here takes on a new meaning. Liszt was understandably nervous of the reactions this piece would provoke. He feared that its 'keyless discords would prove impossible of performance'. And he had good reason to feel apprehensive. For years Liszt's 'experiments' had provoked hostile comment. *Mazeppa*, for instance, had been greeted with catcalls in Leipzig.[1] An even more humiliating defeat occurred at Dresden in 1857 with the failure of the 'Dante' Symphony; for years, in fact, Dresden remained closed to Liszt as a result of that *débâcle*. The crunch came in 1860 when Liszt opened the newspaper *Das Echo* and read there a violent manifesto directed against his music and signed by Brahms and Joachim among others. The document referred to the theories of composition associated with Liszt and Wagner as 'contrary to the innermost spirit of music, strongly to be deplored and condemned'. Wagner sat down, dipped his pen in vitriol, and proceeded to expand his malicious essay 'The Jews in Music' into a book, with its barbed shafts aimed at Joachim. (Joachim bore a lifelong grudge. Later, when he became director of the Hochschule in Berlin, he refused admission to a Liszt pupil until he had repudiated Liszt's doctrines.) Liszt, on the other hand, maintained silence.[2] His 'reply', as we have seen, was to continue

[1] His standing had always been low in that city. The main opposition came from a group of reactionary professors at the Leipzig Conservatory, Rietz, Hauptmann, and Ferdinand David, who complained that the bulk of Liszt's orchestral pieces were 'needlessly and gratuitously ugly'. Hauptmann, especially, attacked Liszt for his 'impure' harmony. All his life Liszt retained a predilection for harmonic experiment and it was this that Wagner had in mind when he good-humouredly grunted: 'Give him white bread and he'll sprinkle red pepper upon it'.

[2] It is difficult to find any redeeming feature in the affair for Brahms. He owed much more

to compose music which anticipated the twentieth century. He was, nevertheless, deeply concerned about his loss of following, and it had serious psychological consequences for him. It is still a little-known fact that after 1860 Liszt actually went out of his way to *discourage* performances of his music. He became highly sensitive to negative criticism and in moments of extreme despair he could take measures to protect himself against it. He wrote to the conductor von Herbeck in Vienna:

> On my advice, von Bulöw will not play my A major Concerto, *nor any other compositions of mine* ... My intimate friends know perfectly well that it is not my desire to push myself into any concert programme whatsoever. (My italics)

By 1864 his hyper-sensitivity had become chronic. He wrote to von Herbeck:

> With regard to performances of my work generally, my disposition and inclination are more than ever completely in the negative ... *It seems to me, now, high time that I should be somewhat forgotten*, or at least placed very much in the background. My name has been frequently put forward; many have taken umbrage at this, and been needlessly annoyed by it.
> (My italics)

Reading between the lines, it is not difficult to see that Liszt had drunk his cup of bitterness to the very dregs during those years of petty rivalries and jealous bickerings which formed the sickening backdrop to his Weimar period. Musicians generally are so used to thinking of Liszt as a showman, basking in the full glare of an adoring public, that it comes as a shock to learn about his

---

to Liszt than he ever acknowledged, especially in his use of the technique of metamorphosis. Here are two examples.

In his First Piano Sonata (C major, Op. 1) Brahms quite clearly derives the first subject of the last movement from that of the first.

Similarly, the second subject of the Intermezzo in B flat minor is a 'metamorphosed' version of the first.

Is the structural principle here disclosed 'contrary to the innermost spirit of music, strongly to be deplored and condemned?' One can only charitably assume that Brahms's aggressiveness towards Liszt was his unconscious way of repaying his debts.

setbacks.[1] A year later, in 1865, he was writing in a similar vein to Mme Jessie Laussot:

> Knowing by experience how little favour my works meet with, I have been obliged to force upon myself *a sort of compulsory disregard of them and a passive resignation*. Thus during the years of my foreign activity in Germany I constantly observed the rule of never asking anyone whatsoever to have any of my works performed; more than that, I really dissuaded many persons from doing so who showed some intentions of the kind, and I shall do so elsewhere.
>
> (My italics)

All the evidence seems to point to the fact that Liszt had fallen into a condition of acute mental apathy concerning the immediate fate of his own music. But its ultimate fate, its 'after-life' as he called it, was a different matter and he had great faith in its survival value. It says much for his artistic integrity that he remained inflexibly committed in his search for the new, even though he knew this meant he was virtually alienated from all but a close circle of his admirers.

This search for the new took many forms. That Dresden audience was not hostile for nothing when Liszt affronted its ears with the 'Dante' Symphony. He took many calculated risks in that work, not least in writing his second subject in seven-four time. Even today, with our streamlined orchestral ensembles, such passages need careful rehearsing. In Liszt's day, this passage must have been in continual jeopardy. Incidentally, is this the first example in music of 7/4 time?[2]

[1] There is a story that Liszt once went to have his portrait painted by a second-rate French artist Ary Scheffer. Liszt sat down and assumed his usual expression. Whereupon Scheffer snapped angrily: 'Don't put on the airs of a man of genius with me; you know well enough that I am not impressed by them.' To which Liszt gently replied: 'You are perfectly right, my dear friend. But you must try to forgive me; you cannot realize how it spoils one to have been an infant prodigy.' Liszt's youthful triumphs must indeed have made his later setbacks seem, by comparison, like catastrophic disasters to him.

[2] Oddly enough, the 'Faust' Symphony, which had appeared three or four years earlier, originally had *its* second subject in 7/4 time, but Liszt eventually decided to notate it more cautiously in alternating 4/4 and 3/4 bars, thus

See also Humphrey Searle, p. 307.

EX. 13

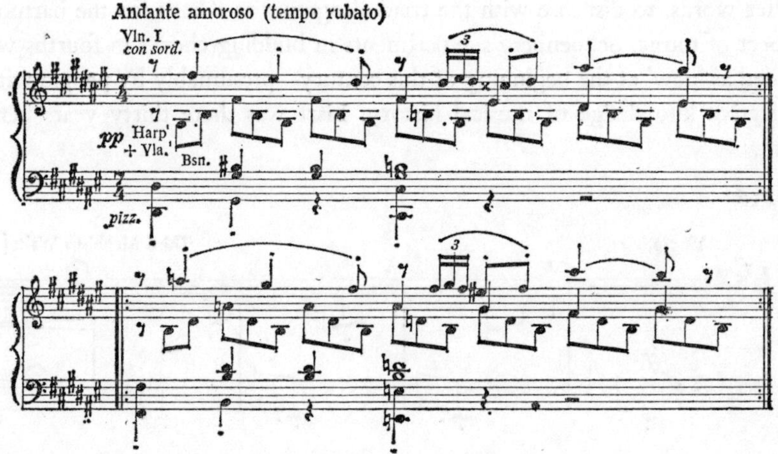

Equally new was Liszt's interest in the nature of chord-structure. Until the end of the nineteenth century the triad reigned supreme and few thought to question the fact that other kinds of chord might be possible.

One advance Liszt made was in the simultaneous use of major and minor thirds. This kind of thing,

EX. 14

in which the major and minor third are struck together, turns up with increasing frequency. Here is a typical application of the device, from the *Czárdás Obstiné*.

EX. 15

Another advance was in building chords in intervals other than thirds—in other words, to dispense with the triad altogether as a basis for the harmonic aspect of music. Schoenberg's experiments in building chords in fourths were hailed as 'new' at the beginning of this century—presumably by people with a defective knowledge of musical history. Liszt was there thirty years before him.

EX. 16

The basic chord in this passage

EX. 17

is difficult to explain in terms of traditional harmonic theory; it is, in fact, derived from the following chord—built in fourths—in its last inversion.

EX. 18

Nor is this an isolated case. A similar attempt to construct chords in fourths is seen in the Seventeenth Hungarian Rhapsody (1883).

EX. 19

But perhaps the most remarkable case of all, remarkable because of its unique 'sound-effect', occurs in *Via Crucis* (1879).

EX. 20

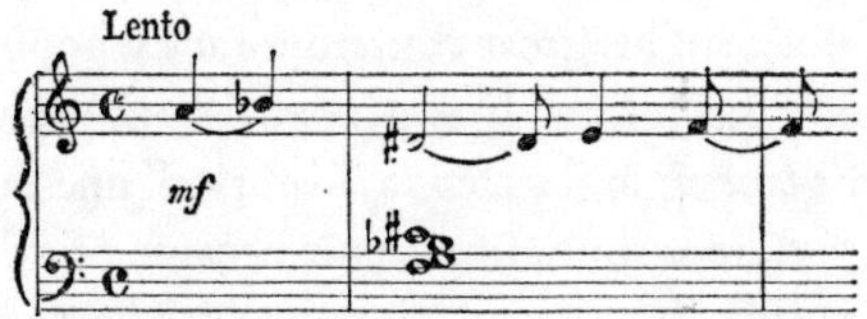

This forward-looking harmony is impossible to analyse from any orthodox point of view. It can only be regarded as a derivative from the following 'fourths' chord.

EX. 21

These examples remain unknown to theorists generally for the obvious reason that the works themselves are never played. But one wonders whether we are so blinkered by our mentors that it would now make all that much difference even if they were. One of the most popular works in the entire piano repertory is Liszt's First 'Mephisto' Waltz. Its popularity has deafened us to its originality. How many musicians have stopped to consider what historical precedents there were for the striking pile-up of fifths with which the work begins?[1]

EX. 22

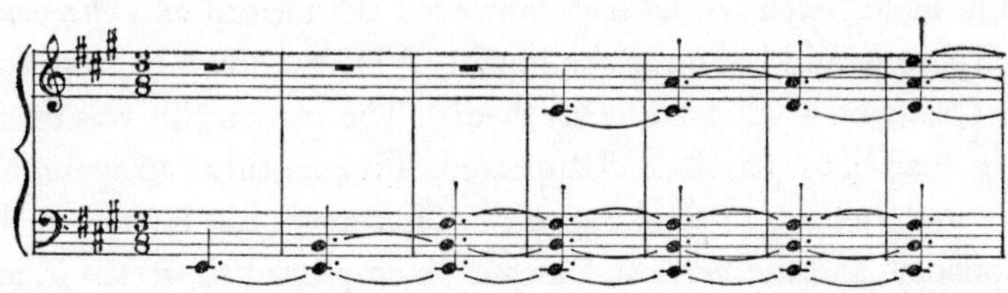

These examples would not be out of place in a textbook of twentieth-century harmony. Indeed, they help to explain why textbooks on twentieth-century harmony came to be written at all. If Liszt had not existed, it would probably be necessary for historians to invent him.

[1] See pp. 101–2, where this remarkable passage is quoted in full.

The historical Liszt, then, is of the utmost significance. And however long the argument continues about the *intrinsic* value of his music, there can be no doubt that its striking originality often led to the most important *historical* consequences. This is what Liszt meant by 'hurling a lance into the future'. In this, he was the exact opposite of his great contemporary Chopin, who could hardly have cared less about the future. It is a neat debating-point this, whether a particular composer's true significance is a 'historical' one or an 'intrinsic' one—whether, that is to say, he is more important because of what he is, or because of what he helped to bring about—and it is one which happens to be fundamental to a philosophy of musical aesthetics. I have no doubt as to what the answer to this question is, but I must admit that the essence of the 'historical' case, involving as it does the very evolution of the language of music, is undeniably strong—particularly when applied to Liszt.

One of Liszt's most remarkable glimpses into the future of music is the keyless opening of the 'Faust' Symphony.

EX. 23

The sound is almost Schoenbergian. Actually, the passage is renowned for being one of the earliest twelve-note rows in musical history. It appeared seventy years before Schoenberg officially announced the discovery of twelve-note technique. Nor was this the only time that Liszt cheated history, so to speak, by stealing ideas from the twentieth century. As early as the 1830s, while he was still in his twenties, he had conceived the idea of an *ordre omnitonique* whose purpose would be to replace tonality.[1] He is known to have composed a *Prélude Omnitonique* illustrating his theory. The manuscript was exhibited in London in 1904 but it has since disappeared. If it ever turns up again, historians may have some serious re-thinking to do. Liszt never lost interest in the problem of tonality, and the ways and means he employed to stretch it, and, on a few remarkable occasions, to anticipate the future by suspending it altogether, form an unwritten chapter of musical history. It is a great pity that Liszt's treatise on modern harmony was never finished, and that even the sketches

[1] Liszt may have got the idea from Fétis, the theorist, whose lectures on the aesthetics of music he attended during the winter of 1832. Fétis was renowned for his speculations on the future of harmony. See entry 'Fétis' in Register of Persons, p. 375.

appear to have disappeared. We know that Liszt kept returning to this manuscript and that he still possessed it as late as 1885. Arthur Friedheim, who was a pupil of Liszt's at that time, tells of seeing it among Liszt's papers at Weimar.[1]

> In his later years the Master had formed the habit of rising at five o'clock in the morning, and I paid him many a solitary visit at that hour, even playing to him occasionally. Jokingly, he would inquire whether I were still up, or already up. On the last of these matutinal visits I found him poring over books and old manuscripts. With his permission I joined him in this very interesting occupation. Catching sight of one manuscript which particularly drew my attention I picked it up saying: 'This will make you responsible for a lot of nonsense which is bound to be written someday'. I expected a rebuke for my remark, but he answered very seriously: 'That may be. I have not published it because the time for it is not yet ripe'.
>
> The title of this little book was *Sketches for a Harmony of the Future.*

Meanwhile, other manuscripts of Liszt have continued to turn up and make nonsense of our conventional notions about the origins of modern music. Here is a recently-discovered example from his old age: the *Bagatelle without Tonality (1885)*.[2]

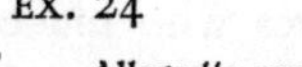
EX. 24

[1] *Life and Liszt*, p. 161, New York, 1961.

[2] The title is Liszt's own. The manuscript turned up in Weimar in 1956. It was originally conceived as the Fourth 'Mephisto' Waltz.

The astonishing fact is that Liszt here approaches atonality some twenty-five years before Schoenberg felt 'the air of another planet'.[1] Of course, the Bagatelle is not atonal in the strict Schoenbergian sense of the term, for Liszt does not entirely succeed in eradicating all feeling of tonality. But the work is not in a key, and therefore it is of vital interest when we come to consider the origins of modern music. It would be interesting to have old Göllerich's reaction; unfortunately, it has not come down to us. As for Liszt, I believe he would have approved Schoenberg's aphorism: 'the ear is the musician's sole brain.'

*

I do not think that Liszt has yet received the credit he deserves for his modernity. He 'hurled his lance into the future' and unconcernedly left it for posterity to pick up. Unfortunately, there is so much prevailing ignorance surrounding Liszt's last works that few modern composers know from which direction that lance was thrown. It is necessary to ask ourselves who made modern music modern. Bartók, as a young man, made a deep study of Liszt and was profoundly influenced by him. In his autobiography he wrote:

> The great artist's true significance was revealed to me at last. I came to recognize that, for the continued development of musical art, his compositions were more important than either Wagner's or Strauss's.

I am convinced that Liszt has yet to come into his own. Constant Lambert once described him as the greatest composer to come out of the nineteenth century, and while I disagree with this evaluation, I begin to see what he meant. Liszt was a tremendous historical force. He was the true father of modern music. Everything seems to have flowed from him. His experiments in harmony, his audacious handling of form, his unparalleled ability to draw strange sonorities from the piano, all confirm that his is one of the most revolutionary personalities in the entire history of music.

[1] Schoenberg's first venture into atonality occurs in the last movement of his Second String Quartet (1908) where the soprano voice enters on Stefan George's lines: 'I feel the air of another planet'.

SACHEVERELL SITWELL

A Biographical Summary of Liszt's Life

1811, 22 October. Franz Liszt is born at Raiding, on the Austrian estates of Prince Esterházy.

1817–18. Liszt receives his first piano lessons from his father.

1820. Gives his first concert at Sopron.

1821. Taken to Vienna by his father. Studies piano under Czerny and theory under Salieri.

1822. Makes début in Vienna, 1 December. Meets Schubert.

1823 Visit to Beethoven. Second concert in Vienna, 13 April. Moves to Paris, December.

1824. Visits England, and plays to George IV at Carlton House.

1825. He returns to England, plays to George IV at Windsor Castle, and gives a concert at Manchester. On 17 October his opera *Don Sanche* is performed at the Academie Royale in Paris.

1826. Tours France and Switzerland.

1827. Visits England again. His father dies at Boulogne in August. Suffers nervous strain and experiences longings to become a priest.

…9. Falls in love with Caroline de Saint-Cricq, one of his pupils, to the …pproval of her parents. Nervous breakdown. He is reported dead and his …bituary notice is published in Paris.

1830. The July Revolution. Meets Berlioz.

1831. Liszt hears Paganini on 9 March and experiences an artistic re-awakening.

1832. Hears Chopin for the first time on 26 February.

1833. Witness at wedding of Berlioz and Harriet Smithson.

1834. Forms a liaison with Countess d'Agoult.

1835. Elopes to Switzerland with Countess d'Agoult. Their daughter Blandine is born at Geneva on 18 December. Liszt is appointed to the Geneva Conservatoire.

1836. George Sand visits them. Liszt returns to Paris in December in order to compete with Thalberg.

1837. Returns to Italy with Countess d'Agoult. Their second daughter, Cosima, is born at Como on 25 December.

1838. Plays in Vienna, on behalf of the victims of the Danube flood.

1839. He spends some months in Rome, where his son, Daniel, is born, 9 May. In November he temporarily separates from Countess d'Agoult and returns to Vienna and to his native Hungary. This is the start of his career as a virtuoso.

The Years of Transcendental Execution (1839–47)

1840. He gives concerts in Vienna and elsewhere, to raise money for the Beethoven Monument at Bonn. He visits London again. He plays to Queen Victoria at Windsor Castle. Tours England and Ireland.

1841. He visits England once more, playing at the Royal Philharmonic Society's concert on 14 June. This is his last visit to England until 1886.

1842. His Russian tour. Appointed Music Director at Weimar. Holidays at Nonnenworth with Countess d'Agoult and the children.

1843–44. Tours Russia, Turkey, Danubian Principalities, Poland, Denmark, etc. Parts from the Countess d'Agoult.

1844. Concert tours extended to Spain and Portugal. Meets Caroline de Saint-Cricq once more.

1845. More concerts in Germany, Switzerland, and France. Visits Bonn for the Beethoven Festival.

1846. Tours Hungary and Rumania. Studies Gypsy music. The Countess d'Agoult publishes her novel *Nélida*, a fictional account of her relationship with Liszt.

1847. He meets Princess Carolyne Sayn-Wittgenstein at Kiev. He gives his last public concert at Elizabetgrad in Southern Russia. Henceforward he does not earn a single farthing by playing, teaching or conducting.

The Weimar Period (1848–60)

1848. The Princess Carolyne Sayn-Wittgenstein joins Liszt in Weimar and they make their home together at the Villa Altenberg.

1849. The Tsar Nicholas I refuses the Princess permission to divorce. Liszt conducts *Tannhäuser* at Weimar. Friendship with Wagner develops.

1850. Liszt conducts the first performance of *Lohengrin* at Weimar, 28 August.

1851. Liszt completes the revision of his *Transcendental Studies*. Hans von Bülow becomes his pupil.

1852. Performs Berlioz's *Benvenuto Cellini* at Weimar during a Berlioz week at which the composer is present. Piano Sonata in B minor written.

1853. Visits Wagner in Switzerland where the latter is living in exile.

1854. 'Faust' Symphony composed.

1855. 'Dante' Symphony begun. Berlioz visits Weimar and conducts the first performance of the Concerto in E flat major with Liszt at the piano.

1856. 'Dante' Symphony finished. Bülow becomes engaged to Cosima.

1857. First performance of the 'Faust' Symphony at Weimar. Bülow gives first performance of B minor Sonata in Berlin. Cosima and Bülow are married in Liszt's presence on August 18.

1858. Liszt resigns from Weimar.

1859. Death of his son Daniel, aged twenty.

1860. Liszt makes his will.

The Roman Period (1861–68)

1861. His marriage to the Princess, arranged to take place in Rome on his fiftieth birthday, is suddenly postponed. He lives chiefly in retirement, and composes numerous religious works, *Legend of St. Elizabeth, Christus,* etc.; hoping to be given an official position as musical director to the Vatican, but this does not materialize.

1862. Death of his elder daughter, Blandine, aged twenty-seven.

1863. Withdraws into semi-religious retirement. Enters the oratory of the Madonna del Rosario in Rome where he is visited by Pope Pius IX.

1865. 25 April, Liszt receives minor orders in the Roman Church and becomes an Abbé.

1866. His mother dies in Paris, 6 February.

1867. 'Hungarian Coronation Mass' given in Budapest for the crowning of Franz-Josef. Quarrels with Wagner who has eloped with Cosima.

1868, July. Commences theological studies at Grottammare. Then moves to the Villa d'Este.

LISZT ON HIS DEATH-BED (AUGUST, 1886)

LISZT'S TOMB

The 'Vie' Trifurquée (1869–86)

1869. He emerges from retirement and returns for a part of each year to Weimar, living in the Hofgärtnerei and giving lessons to numerous pupils. The 'vie trifurquée' begins, between Rome (Villa d'Este), Weimar, and Budapest. Owing to the troubles over the Olga Janina episode, Liszt avoids Rome for a time and only returns regularly to the Villa d'Este after 1873–74.

1870. Bülow divorces Cosima who now marries Wagner.

1871. Lives, from now on, between Rome, Weimar, and Budapest. Elected a Royal Hungarian Councillor.

1872. The quarrel with Wagner is patched up. Wagner and Cosima visit Liszt at Weimar.

1873. November, Liszt visits Budapest to celebrate the fiftieth anniversary of his career as a pianist.

1875. July, Liszt visits Bayreuth and attends the rehearsals for the production of Wagner's *Ring*.

1876. Death of Countess d'Agoult and George Sand. His pupils at this time include Eugène d'Albert, Moriz Rosenthal, Siloti, Frederic Lamond, and Emil Sauer.

1879. He is made Canon of Albano and is now entitled to wear a cassock.

The Final Period

1880–85. Liszt travels on an ever-increasing scale of activity, giving his services wherever they can help any useful purpose. He also enters a final and interesting period of composition including: *Nuages Gris*, *Czárdás Macabre*, *La Lugubre Gondola*, and *Am Grabe Richard Wagners*.

1886. Liszt died 31 July. His last tour is in celebration of his forthcoming seventy-fifth birthday. He returns to Paris, and visits London, once again, after a lapse of forty-five years. He spends a triumphant two weeks in England in April; his orchestral works are played under Sir Alexander Mackenzie, and he performs himself on more than one occasion. He plays to Queen Victoria at Windsor Castle, attends a reception in his honour at the Grosvenor Gallery, and goes to a gala performance of *Faust* at the Lyceum with Henry Irving.

He leaves London and spends Holy Week at Antwerp, returning to Paris on 5 May. *St. Elizabeth* is performed with great success. He returns to Weimar, then to Bayreuth for the wedding of his granddaughter Daniela. In July, he stays with the painter Munkácsy at his Castle of Colpach in Luxembourg, and returns to Weimar on 20 July. Attends festival performance of *Tristan* at Bayreuth, develops pneumonia, and dies there on 31 July.

1887, February. Princess Sayn-Wittgenstein finishes the twenty-fourth, and last volume of the *Causes Intérieures*, on which she has worked for twenty-five years, and dies a fortnight later.

ALAN WALKER

Register of Persons

d'Agoult, Countess Marie (1805–76), born de Flavigny. Liszt's first mistress and the mother of his three children, Blandine, Cosima, and Daniel. Her grandparents were members of the wealthy Bethmann family who were bankers in Frankfurt; Marie thus enjoyed considerable private means. In 1827 she married Comte Charles d'Agoult, a minister in the court of Charles X and some twenty years her senior. There were two children of the marriage.

Marie was first introduced to the twenty-two-year-old Liszt by George Sand in 1834 and quickly fell under his spell. While she was not particularly beautiful she was intelligent and idealistic, qualities that immediately appealed to the young Liszt; and in the depth of her reading and general culture she was more than a match for him. Some people found her too serious and prudish. George Sand once described her as: 'Straight as a candle; white as a sanctified wafer.' Despite the obvious hazards, she deserted her husband and eloped with Liszt to Geneva in 1835, taking her young family with her —an onerous responsibility for Liszt, but one which he shouldered philosophically. For the next four years they lived together in Switzerland and Italy, during which period Marie bore Liszt three children. In the summer of 1839 relations between the pair became strained and the Countess returned to Paris. From this time, Liszt's children were brought up there by his mother. The final break between Marie and Liszt came in 1844, after which she became increasingly embittered against him. She finally took her revenge by publishing, in 1846, a biographical novel called *Nélida* under the pseudonym of Daniel Stern. Its central character, Guermann, was a thinly disguised portrayal of Liszt, and the book exposed to the world such intimate nuances of their relationship that Liszt's reputation was damaged. It is hardly surprising that Liszt harboured a life-long resentment against Marie for what he regarded as a stab in the back, and he became seriously alarmed when, in 1866, he learned that his old lover was preparing her memoirs. He went out of his way to see her again in Paris after a lapse of many years to try to discover what she was plotting. The meeting must have been extremely disagreeable for both of them, but the memoirs remained in manuscript. It was not until 1927 that Marie's grandson Daniel Ollivier had the memoirs published. They were used as a basis for Ernest Newman's study *The Man Liszt* (1934), in which they were employed as a stick with which to give the composer one of the biggest beatings any biographer can have meted out to his subject.

Alkan, Charles (1813–88). French pianist. His real name was Charles Henri Valentin Morhange and he was one of the more colourful eccentrics who graced the musical scene in Paris during the nineteenth century.

As a child prodigy, Alkan was so precocious that the Paris Conservatoire was obliged to admit him as a student when he was only six; thereafter, he took as of right practically every piano prize that august establishment had to offer. By the time he was seventeen, Alkan was firmly established as a virtuoso and was the possessor of a formidable piano technique. After a short visit to London in 1833 he returned to Paris where he settled down as a teacher and composer, concentrating on the creation of a body of piano music which, in technical difficulty, is rivalled perhaps only by Liszt's. His greatest achievement is the set of Studies in all the major and minor keys opp. 35 and 39 which contain such significant works as the Piano Symphony in four movements and the Variations called *Le Festin d'Ésope*. The writing is surprisingly modern. A proper evaluation of Alkan is one of the more urgent tasks still facing musical criticism. Liszt had a high opinion of Alkan and visited him frequently whenever he was in Paris.

Alkan's performing career was blighted by an introverted personality which forced him to withdraw almost completely from public life while still relatively young. For the last forty years he lived like a hermit. Frederick Niecks, the scholar, once tried to see Alkan in 1880. The concièrge, who was very well drilled, told him that Alkan was not in. Niecks persisted: 'When *will* he be in?' The concièrge drew himself up to his full height. 'Never!'

His death was original. He tried to reach for a copy of the Talmud on the top shelf of his bookcase which toppled over and crushed him to death.

Altenburg, The. Liszt's official residence in Weimar where he lived from 1847 to 1859. See p. 66.

Apponyi, Count Rudolph. Austro-Hungarian ambassador to Paris and one of the young Liszt's patrons. He helped to organize the subscription fund which enabled the Liszt family to travel from Esterháza to Vienna where the twelve-year-old Liszt took lessons from Carl Czerny. Liszt dedicated his *Grand Galop Chromatique* to him.

Apponyi, Count Albert (1846–1933). Hungarian patriot and nobleman whose memoirs contain some vivid accounts of Liszt (see p. 70n). He pleaded his country's cause before the League of Nations when the map of Europe was being re-drawn after the first World War. Liszt had a great affection for the young aristocrat whom he regarded as one of the more worthwhile of his country's 'jeunesse doré'—that is, privileged youth or 'idle rich'.

Bache, Walter (1842–88). An English disciple of Liszt. He studied with Liszt in Rome from 1862 onwards. After his return to England he settled in London and was instrumental in arranging a steady stream of performances of Liszt's works, many of which had never been played in this country. It was largely due to Bache's efforts that the Liszt Scholarship was established at the Royal Academy of Music in 1886.

When Liszt paid his last visit to England in the spring of 1886 Walter Bache gave him a magnificent reception in the Grosvenor Gallery at which master and pupil played the finale of Schubert's 'Divertissement à la hongroise' and Liszt played his Hungarian Rhapsody in A minor. A few months later, when Liszt died, Walter Bache was chosen as one of the pallbearers.

His sister, Constance Bache, translated and edited two volumes of Liszt's correspondence which were published in 1894.

Belgiojoso, Princess Christine (1808–1871). Italian-born aristocrat who, together with her husband Prince Belgiojoso, ran one of the most fashionable *salons* in Paris. She organized frequent concerts for charity; it was at one of these occasions that she brought together Liszt and Thalberg for their famous keyboard duel. She also inspired the idea of the 'Hexameron' Variations (in which six composers, headed by Liszt, each contributed a variation on a theme from Bellini's *I Puritani*) which is dedicated to her. Liszt had a brief flirtation with her and then wisely abandoned her for fresh pastures. The Princess was definitely eccentric. When one of her lovers died she had his corpse mummified and kept it at home in a cupboard.

Bellini, Vincenzo (1801–35). Italian operatic composer. He settled in Paris in 1833. The March from his opera *I Puritani* was used by Liszt as the basis of the so-called 'Hexameron' Variations (see entry above). Bellini's two greatest masterpieces, *La Sonnambula* and *Norma*, were written when he was only twenty-nine. Liszt paraphrased both works for solo piano, his

Réminiscences de Norma (1841) being a model of its kind. See pp. 184–91.

Berlioz, Hector (1803–69). Liszt and Berlioz were on terms of intimacy during the 1830s when both men were living in Paris. Liszt was a witness at Berlioz's marriage to Harriet Smithson, the Irish actress, in 1833; later that year, the bond between the two musicians was sealed when Liszt brought out his arrangement of the 'Fantastic' Symphony—a pianistic *tour de force*, the value of which Berlioz was quick to recognize: Liszt's score was for some years the only published version of the work, and it formed the basis of all the critical praise (and abuse) heaped upon Berlioz's masterpiece which meanwhile remained largely unperformed and largely unperformable. Berlioz was a great admirer of Liszt's piano playing and publicly defended him in the *Gazette Musicale* when Liszt ran into hostile criticism, about the time of his contest with Thalberg in 1837, describing him unequivocally as 'the pianist of the future'. Liszt in turn fought for Berlioz's music. He organized two Berlioz festivals during his years at Weimar, the first in 1852 when he conducted the first performance of 'Benvenuto Cellini', and the other in 1855 when Berlioz himself conducted the 'Fantastic' Symphony and the first performance of Liszt's Piano Concerto in E flat major with Liszt as soloist.

Brahms, Johannes (1833–97). Brahms's attitude towards Liszt, uneasy at first, became openly hostile after 1860. He had travelled to Weimar in 1853 with a letter of introduction from Joachim (Liszt's former orchestral leader there) but had blotted his copy-book by dozing off during a performance by Liszt of the latter's Sonata in B minor. Unsympathetic to Liszt's views on music, he refused to be associated with his 'New German' School of composition. In 1860 Brahms drafted his famous 'Manifesto' against the Weimar group and their philosophy of music; he canvassed Germany for signatures, but the plan went off at half-cock when the Berlin newspaper *Das Echo* got hold of a copy and published it prematurely with only four signatories, including Brahms. Liszt refused to be drawn into debate; but it is significant that he never played a Brahms work in public. Whatever Brahms thought of Liszt's music, he respected his piano playing. 'We others can play the piano, but we all of us have only a few fingers of his hands.'

Breitkopf and Härtel. German firm of music publishers. Between the years 1901 and 1936 they published a Complete Edition of Liszt's music in thirty-four volumes. This edition is described as the 'Grand Duke Carl Alexander Edition' after Liszt's patron at Weimar.

Bülow, Hans Guido von (1830–94). German pianist and conductor. Liszt's son-in-law and one of his leading champions. Bülow's early training was under Friedrich Wieck, father of Clara Schumann. After studying law at Berlin University, he abandoned a legal career in order to perfect his piano playing under Liszt at Weimar. He was with Liszt from 1851 to 1853 and was, with the possible exception of Tausig, Liszt's most brilliant pupil. Liszt entrusted to him the first performance of the Sonata in B minor which he gave in 1857 in Berlin. Bülow had a prodigious memory and he carried the largest repertoire of any pianist of his generation. His powers of assimilation were such that he is once reputed to have mastered an unfamiliar score during a railway journey and to have played it in public the next day from memory. In 1857 Bülow married Liszt's second daughter Cosima, a disastrous mistake which led to a divorce in 1870, Cosima having become the mistress of Richard Wagner. It was after this that Bülow embarked upon an international conducting career which brought him to England on several occasions. He re-married, in 1882, a German actress Marie Schanzer. In 1894 ill-health forced him to seek a warmer climate. He travelled to Egypt and died in Cairo on 12 February.

Busoni, Ferruccio Benvenuto (1866–1924). Italian pianist and composer. Busoni was one of the foremost Liszt exponents of his generation. He was also a member of the Editorial Committee of the Collected Edition of Liszt's works, and he was personally responsible for the volume of piano studies to which he wrote a lengthy introduction dated 'Berlin, 1910'.

The only occasion Busoni ever heard

Liszt play was in 1877, when he was eleven. Unfortunately, a few days earlier, Liszt had damaged the second finger of his left hand. He played Beethoven's 'Emperor' Concerto and was definitely below form; the young Busoni appears to have been disappointed in his idol. In later life, after a profound study of Liszt's music, he came to revere Liszt as he revered no other composer with the possible exception of Bach. His essay on Liszt (in *The Essence of Music*) remains a classic. Busoni was frequently criticized for including so much Liszt in his recitals, and he defended himself vigorously in an 'Open Letter about Liszt' published in 1916, in which he declared: 'We are all descended from Liszt radically, without excepting Wagner, and we owe to him the lesser things that we can do. César Franck, Richard Strauss, Debussy, the penultimate Russians, are all branches of his tree.' Referring to Liszt's skill in transcribing other composers for the keyboard, and the ingenuity of some of his technical solutions, he said: 'It can compromise no pianist if he shows himself to be of the same opinion as Liszt, otherwise it must follow that he excels Liszt as a musician and pianist. Such a pianist, up to now, is not known to me. I am myself respectfully conscious of the distance which separates me from his greatness.' Busoni's own transcription for piano of Liszt's organ Fantasy and Fugue on *Ad Nos ad Salutarem Undam* is one in which Liszt himself would undoubtedly have revelled.

Cherubini, Luigi (1760–1842). Italian composer. He settled in Paris in 1788 and eventually became the Director of the Paris Conservatoire, a post for which he was eminently suited owing to his somewhat academic cast of mind. 'Beethoven makes me sneeze,' he once remarked. Cherubini refused the young Liszt admittance to the Conservatoire on the grounds that the rules did not allow foreigners to study there. The rules, apparently, were bent for Directors.

Chopin, Frédéric (1810–49). Although Chopin's name is often linked with Liszt's, the notion of any romantic friendship between the two composers is a legend inherited from the 'popular' biographies of the nineteenth century. Temperamentally, they were incompatible. Chopin admired Liszt as a pianist ('How I wish I could steal from him the way to play my own Études') but was suspicious of his music which he found vulgar and showy. In particular, he disliked Liszt's habit of tinkering around with the text ('He can't keep his hands off anything,' he once burst out) especially when it was done merely for effect. Chopin did not settle in Paris until 1831; Liszt left the city in 1835. This four-year period, during which they rubbed shoulders frequently, is the main extent of their personal friendship which in fact ended in estrangement (see pp. 58–65). After Chopin's death, when it became known that Liszt was writing a book about him, Chopin's family were unhelpful and refused to return to Liszt the questionnaire he sent them, which was filled out by Chopin's pupil Jane Stirling instead.

Cornelius, Peter (1824–74). German composer and author. After a period of study in Berlin, Cornelius became a pupil of Liszt at Weimar in 1852. He had an active pen and for a time he was Liszt's secretary. He wrote a number of articles for the *Neue Zeitschrift für Musik* in which he expounded the principles of the 'New German' School which Liszt headed at that time. This made him a target for criticism from those who disapproved of Liszt's ideas. When his opera *Barber of Bagdad* was produced by Liszt at Weimar in 1858, it got such a hostile reception from the audience that it precipitated Liszt's resignation from the city.

Czerny, Carl (1791–1857). Austrian pianist and pedagogue. Composer of countless piano exercises and studies, the best-known set being the 'School of Velocity'. An iron disciplinarian, Czerny became Liszt's teacher when the boy was eleven. 'It was evident at once', said Czerny, 'that nature had intended him as a pianist.' Teacher and pupil clashed violently in the early stages of instruction, Liszt finding Czerny's insistence on basic technical matters irksome. Later, Liszt saw his lessons with Czerny as a significant turning-point which placed his technique on solid foundations. Liszt retained a great respect for Czerny, and in 1851 he dedicated to his former master his revised set of Twelve 'Transcendental' Studies.

Damrosch, Leopold (1832–85). German-American violinist, conductor, and composer. Liszt appointed him leader of the Weimar court orchestra in 1857. He eventually moved to New York in 1871 and lived in America for the rest of his life. He conducted several first performances of Liszt's music in the States, including *Le Triomphe funèbre du Tasse* which is dedicated to him. Father of Walter Damrosch.

Delacroix, Eugène (1798–1863). French painter. He was a keen music-lover and a member of Liszt's circle of friends in Paris around 1831. His portrait of Chopin is probably the best ever done of that composer.

Dreyschock, Alexander (1818–69). Born in Bohemia, Dreyschock studied with Tomašek in Prague until he was twenty; he then began a brilliant career as a travelling virtuoso, almost rivalling that of Liszt, which eventually took him to Russia and a professorship at the St. Petersburg Conservatory. (See p. 42.) Dreyschock was famous for his highly developed left hand with which he performed astonishing feats of dexterity. When J. B. Cramer heard him in Paris he exclaimed: 'The man has no left hand! Here are two right hands!'

Érard, Sébastien (1752–1831). Alsatian-born piano manufacturer domiciled in Paris. His most notable contribution to the development of the piano was the invention of the 'double-escapement' action, which made it possible to re-iterate single notes at high speed. A piece such as Liszt's *La Campanella* would be unthinkable and unplayable without Érard's invention.

Esterháza. The vast estates in Austria and Hungary owned by the Esterházy family whose patronage of music was long and distinguished. Haydn was their Kapellmeister for nearly 30 years. He was succeeded by Hummel, the piano virtuoso, who held the post from 1804 until 1811. Liszt's grandfather and father were both stewards on the Esterháza estates, and Liszt himself was born there in the village of Raiding.

Fay, Amy (1844–1928). An American pupil of Liszt. Her book *Music-Study in Germany* is a classic; it contains the best description of Liszt's Weimar master classes during the 1870's that has come down to us. (See pp. 33–35.)

Fétis, François Joseph (1784–1871). Belgian musicologist, teacher and composer. From 1821, he was a professor at the Paris Conservatoire, teaching counterpoint and fugue. In February 1827 he brought out the first issue of *Revue Musicale*; he was also a joint musical editor of *Le Temps*. Fétis's fame rests almost entirely on his theoretical writings, which dominated nineteenth-century musical education. Liszt attended a course of lectures Fétis gave on musical aesthetics in Paris during the winter of 1832, and he was much impressed by them. One of the main harmonic theories Fétis outlined was his 'omnitonique' system which showed that any harmonic combination of notes could be resolved into any key or mode, an idea far in advance of its day. For the rest of his life, Liszt harboured the notion of a possible 'ordre omnitonique' which might replace tonality, and he even composed a 'Prelude omnitonique' to illustrate the theory. The M.S. of this work, which is now lost, was last seen at a London exhibition in 1904.

Field, John (1782–1837). Irish pianist born in Dublin. He was apprenticed to Clementi in his youth who taught him the piano in return for public demonstrations at his piano warehouse in London. Spohr met him there, and described him in his autobiography as 'a pale, melancholy youth, awkward and shy . . . but who had only to place his hands on the keys for all such drawbacks to be forgotten'. In 1802, he settled in St. Petersburg and became a fashionable teacher. He toured Europe in 1832 when both Liszt and Chopin heard him play. He died in Moscow in conditions of pitiful privation. Liszt wrote an interesting pamphlet on Field which was published in 1859; he also brought out an edition of his Nocturnes.

Gregorovius, Ferdinand (1821–91). A Roman Catholic priest. His *Roman Journal* contains some vivid descriptions of the Abbé Liszt during his 'Roman' period. (See pp. 14–15.)

Grieg, Edvard Hagerup (1843–1907). As a young man, struggling to establish himself in his native Norway, Grieg received powerful encouragement from Liszt who persuaded him to visit his classes at Weimar. Grieg brought with him the manuscript of his A minor Piano Concerto which Liszt, much to Grieg's amazement, read through at sight, singing the orchestral parts as he went along.

Halévy, Fromental (1799–1862). Popular French opera composer of the day. One of his best-known operas was *La Juive*. Liszt composed his *Réminiscences de La Juive* in 1835 which was among his first attempts at the operatic paraphrase.

Hallé, Sir Charles (1819–95). English pianist and conductor born in Germany. He went to Paris in 1836 to study the piano under Kalkbrenner and there met Liszt, Chopin, and Berlioz whose music he was one of the first conductors to champion. He once heard Liszt play his own piano arrangement of Berlioz's *Marche au Supplice* immediately after the orchestral version had been conducted by Berlioz. 'Such marvels of executive skill and power I could never have imagined. One of the transcendent merits of his playing was the crystal-like clearness which never failed for a moment, even in the most complicated and to anybody else impossible passages; it was as if he had photographed them in their minutest detail upon the ear of the listener.' (See p. 43.) Hallé was the first pianist to play the complete cycle of Beethoven sonatas in public, in 1861.

Hanslick, Eduard (1825–1904). Viennese music critic. He lectured in aesthetics and musical history at the University of Vienna from 1861, and became a full professor there in 1870. By training and by inclination, Hanslick was a fundamentalist with a highly conservative cast of mind. His enmity towards the music of Liszt and Wagner is well-known; so is his championship of Brahms. Hanslick was a brilliant writer whose literary products were noted for their elegance, wit and cogent logic. He spoke his mind fearlessly, and sometimes recklessly. 'The violin is beaten black and blue', he wrote of Tchaikovsky's Violin Concerto. 'After Liszt, Mozart is like a soft spring breeze penetrating a room reeking with fumes', was another of his darts. Wagner took a lot of punishment from Hanslick, but repaid him in full by satirizing him in the character of Beckmesser in his opera *Die Meistersinger*. Hanslick's most important book was his *Vom Musikalisch-Schönen* (1854) in which he may be said to have founded a new school of musical aesthetics by arguing, for the first time, the 'integrity' of musical structure. His 'closed world' view of a work of art, in which that work of art is its own meaning, has powerfully influenced twentieth-century music criticism.

Heine, Heinrich (1797–1856). German poet. Member of the artistic circle in Paris which included Chopin, Liszt, and Delacroix. Heine had a sharp tongue. His witticisms about his contemporaries are legend. He once described the nose of Johann Pixis, which was admittedly somewhat large, as 'one of the curiosities of the musical world'. After hearing Kalkbrenner, who was famed for his detachment, play at a concert in 1843, Heine came away and wrote: 'On his lips there still gleamed that embalmed smile which we recently noticed on those of an Egyptian pharaoh, when his mummy was unwrapped at the museum here.'

Henselt, Adolf (1814–89). German pianist and composer. Pupil of Hummel. Owing to a shy disposition he rarely performed in public. He was a phenomenal player, however, and trained observers such as Schumann placed him in the very top rank. When he played in St. Petersburg in 1838 he created such a sensation that he was appointed Court Pianist on the spot. For years, Henselt was virtual dictator of all things concerning the piano in Russia. He visited England in 1867 and was prevailed upon to play before a select audience at Broadwood's. 'His playing was glorious, faultless,' wrote Hipkins. Liszt knew Henselt and held him in great esteem; he dedicated to him his *Grosses Konzertsolo*, originally composed for the piano competition at the Paris Conservatoire in 1850.

Herz, Henri (1803–88). Austrian pianist and composer. He contributed a variation to Liszt's 'Hexameron' Variations.

Hiller, Ferdinand (1811–85). German

pianist, conductor, and composer. Pupil of Hummel. Settled in Paris in 1828, after which he became on close terms with the young Liszt. He felt a special affinity with Beethoven whose music he tried to make better known in France. He gave the first performance of Beethoven's 'Emperor' Concerto in Paris.

Hofgärtnerei. The house at Weimar in which Liszt lived and conducted his master classes during his second Weimar period, roughly 1869–1886.

Hohenlohe, Gustav von, Cardinal (1823–1896). A close friend of Liszt in his old age. He received Liszt into the priesthood of the Roman Catholic Church. Through his influence, Liszt was able to spend several months of each of his last years at the Villa d'Este. The Cardinal's brother, Prince Constantine Hohenlohe, married Marie Sayn-Wittgenstein, the daughter of Princess Carolyne.

Hummel, Johan Nepomuk (1788–1837). Hungarian pianist and composer. When he was a child of seven he was taken to Vienna where Mozart was so impressed with him that he took him into his household for two years and gave him lessons free of charge. Afterwards, Hummel's prestige as a teacher was enormous; his treatise on piano playing (published 1828) became a classic. Liszt nearly studied with him, but his fees were too high so he went to Czerny instead. Hummel was a severe critic of Liszt's brand of pianism which he considered undisciplined. By a curious coincidence, Hummel's chief post—Court Kappelmeister at Weimar—was also Liszt's; and he held it for nearly twenty years until his death in 1837. When Liszt took over his job shortly afterwards, the Hummel family were firmly against it and let it be known that in their view Liszt was responsible for the decline of 'the true art of piano playing'. Hummel's widow lived in Weimar for the rest of her long life, dying as late as 1883. Her hostile presence cannot have been particularly pleasant for Liszt. It was worse for the widow herself, however, who lived to see her husband's work completely eclipsed by Liszt's masterclasses.

Ingres, J. D. (1780–1867). French artist. One of the best drawings we have of the young Liszt was produced by Ingres (see plate facing p. 305). For a time he was director of the French school in the Villa Medici; Liszt saw a lot of him during his 'Italian' period around 1839. It was Ingres who introduced him to the great masters of Italy including Raphael, Michelangelo, and Leonardo, the results of which are to be seen in some of the titles of the pieces in the second, 'Italian', Volume of the *Années de Pèlerinage.*[1]

Janina, Olga (b. circa 1850; d. ?). Practically all we know about her origins comes from her highly coloured autobiographical novels *Souvenirs d'une Cosaque* and *Souvenirs d'une pianiste*. If only a fraction of the episodes she there relates were true, her chequered career would make that of Lucrezia Borgia pale into insignificance. She married at fifteen, horsewhipped her husband after the wedding night, tried to kill herself and her baby daughter (by a previous union), failed, and eventually enrolled as a student at the Kiev Conservatoire where one of her pet tigers bit the Principal who promptly contracted gangrene and expired. Olga then got herself an introduction to Liszt, whose path she crossed in 1870, and who lived to curse the day he ever became involved with her. She literally threw herself into Liszt's arms who, more used to chasing than being chased, fled from Rome to Budapest with Olga in hot pursuit. There, he realized the futility of resistance and succumbed to her passions. She was with Liszt in Hungary throughout the summer of 1871. The couple were visited by Monseigneur Hohenlohe who took Olga to task for some suggestive remarks she made to him about the sexual undertones of the Old Testament verses 'The Song of Song's which is Solomon's'. The Monseigneur uttered a suitable rebuke and, turning to Liszt, inquired whether Olga had been paraphrasing the text for him in view of her intimate acquaintance with it. Olga's retort has gone down in history. 'The Abbé, my dear Monseigneur, prefers the real thing.'

The *coup de grâce* occurred when Olga created a scene in Liszt's apartments; she burst in brandishing a revolver and threatened to shoot him and take poison. Liszt saw the writing on the wall and, somewhat late in the day, broke with her.

Eventually, she avenged herself on him by publishing under the pseudonym 'Robert Franz' the above-mentioned novels in which no detail of her escapades with Liszt is spared.

Born in the Ukraine, Olga is sometimes jocularly known among Lisztians as 'the Cossack Countess'. There is no evidence that she was of aristocratic descent, however, although she herself did lay claim to the title 'Countess' and had it entered into her passport.

Joachim, Joseph (1831–1907). Hungarian-born violinist. Liszt's orchestral leader at Weimar from 1850 to 1852. Joachim later reacted against the 'New German' School, and allied himself with Brahms and Schumann. He was one of the signatories to the 'Manifesto' (1860) drawn up by Brahms and directed mainly against Liszt and Wagner.

Kalkbrenner, Friedrich (1785–1849). German-born piano pedagogue. Taught by his father. He lived in London between 1814 and 1823, and then settled in Paris as a member of the piano firm of Pleyel. He cultivated a 'quiet' manner at the keyboard while nonetheless producing some dazzling effects; his deliberately restrained approach to the instrument placed him at the opposite pole from Liszt who thought him old-fashioned. Chopin had a high opinion of him, however, and nearly took lessons from him: 'It is difficult to describe to you his "calm", his enchanting touch, the incomparable evenness of his playing and that mastery which is obvious in every note. . . .' (See entry under Heine.)

Kapp, Julius (b. 1883). His biography of Liszt first appeared in 1909; it went through nineteen editions, the last appearing in 1924. For its day the book was unusual. It ignored the idealized portrait of Liszt handed down to us by his disciples and worshippers; it took, instead, an objective stand based only on the evidence. In his preface, Kapp defended himself, thus: 'I forbore', he said, 'to write Liszt's life as it *might* have been; I made no scruple about demolishing many a halo that had been created by friendly hands or illegitimately maintained by an adroit use of tradition; I tried to construct, instead of an ideal figure bathed in incense, a figure of flesh and blood just as it walked the earth, illuminated by the nobility of its own being, but also burdened with human weaknesses.' Kapp's book has the reputation of being one of the most reliable in the Liszt literature.

Klindworth, Karl (1830–1916). German pianist, composer, and conductor. Pupil of Liszt from 1852. He was appointed professor of piano at Moscow Conservatoire in 1868. His name is well-known through his critical edition of Chopin.

Lager, Anna (1791–1866). Liszt's mother. A native of Lower Austria. She married Adam Liszt in 1810; their son was born in the following year. Once the family had settled in Paris, in 1823, Anna lived there for the rest of her life. She was widowed in 1827, Adam dying of typhoid fever in Boulogne whilst on tour with the young Liszt, and she was thereafter supported entirely by her son who at that time was only fifteen. She later brought up his three children, by Marie d'Agoult, and they lived with Anna until they were in their 'teens.

La Mara (1837–1927). German writer on music, personally acquainted with Liszt. She collected and published Liszt's correspondence in eight volumes between 1893 and 1905. Her real name was Marie Lipsius.

Lamartine, Alphonse de (1790–1869). French poet. Liszt was first introduced to his poetry by Carolyne de Saint-Cricq, his first love. One of Liszt's best-known orchestral works *Les Préludes* is subtitled 'after a reading from Lamartine', while the piano piece *Bénédiction de Dieu dans la Solitude* was inspired by Lamartine's poem of the same name. In 1845, Liszt proposed to Lamartine's niece, the Countess Valentine Cessiat, and was turned down.

Lammenais, Felicité Robert de, Abbé (1782–1854). Religious philosopher, priest, and teacher. After the death of Liszt's father, Liszt (who was 15) experienced a religious crisis lasting some three or four years. He sought religious instruction from Lammenais whom he loved as a second father, and who became, in Guy de Portalès's phrase, 'the general of his conscience'. He spent much time at the Abbé's Brittany retreat of La Chênaie, filling his mind with religious literature. Lammenais held advanced views and was regarded as a renegade by Rome with whom he had several times taken issue on matters ecclesiastical. George Sand has told us that in an unguarded moment Liszt once confessed to her (1834) that he had never been greatly drawn to anyone but the Abbé Lammenais.

Lamond, Frédéric (1868–1948). One of the last surviving pupils of Liszt. In March 1886, he gave a recital in St. James's Hall, London, in the presence of Liszt which set the seal on his career as a performer. He later made a great reputation as a Beethoven interpreter. Until the Second World War he preferred to live in Germany; then, being unable to accept the Nazi regime, he returned to England.

Liapunov, Sergei Mikhailovitch (1859–1924). Russian pianist and composer. Professor at the St. Petersburg Conservatory. He left Russia shortly after the Revolution and settled in Paris. His training as a concert pianist brought him into close touch with the music of Liszt. He composed a set of 12 Transcendental Studies 'dedicated to the memory of Liszt' which completes the circle of keys begun and left unfinished by Liszt in his own set of 12 transcendental studies. (See p. 105.)

Liszt Family. Liszt himself said that the family name was originally 'List' and this is how his own surname was entered in the baptismal register at Raiding. His father later changed the spelling to 'Liszt' to avoid the Magyar pronunciation 'Lischt'. The family may originally have been of noble origin; both Adam and Franz believed this to be the case (their family name occurs as far back as the sixteenth century). Unfortunately, the Holy Roman Emperor Francis II disagreed. When he was petitioned in 1840 for a patent of nobility for Liszt, by several of the leading magnates of Hungary, it was turned down.

Liszt Society. Formed in 1950. The founder members included Constant Lambert, Ralph Hill, Humphrey Searle, and Edward Dent (the first President). The objective of the Society is to promote the republication, recording, and performance of works by Liszt, especially those which are difficult of access. Mr. Louis Kentner is now the President, and Dr. Barry Goalby is the Chairman.

Menter, Sophie (1846–1918). 'No woman can touch her,' Liszt once said of his favourite female pupil. She visited London in 1890 and Bernard Shaw wrote of her: 'She produces an effect of magnificence which leaves Paderewski far behind'—and this at a time when Paderewski had made his first tremendous impact on the British capital.

Meyendorff, Baroness Olga (1841?–d. ?). Born Princess Gortschakoff. Her husband was the Russian ambassador to the Weimar Court. He died in 1871 and the thirty-year-old Baroness, a woman of great good looks, promptly attached herself to Liszt. Her attentions do not appear to have been unwelcome to him. She was a woman of considerable culture and a gifted pianist; Liszt saw a good deal of her whenever he was in Weimar. He kept up a vast correspondence with her almost to the end; 380 of his unpublished letters to her were put up for sale at Sotheby's in April 1934.

Meyerbeer, Giacomo (1791–1864). German composer and member of a wealthy banking family. He was first trained as a pianist, and had some lessons from Clementi, but eventually turned to composition, producing a steady stream of operas. He settled in Paris where he became a pillar of the establishment. His opera *Robert le Diable* (1831) created a sensation; Liszt paraphrased the work for piano and it became one of his popular war-horses. The King of Prussia made him General Music Director in Berlin; he travelled twice to London, the last occasion being in 1862 when he was the official representative of German music at the International Exhibition. Liszt's most important organ work, the Fantasy and Fugue on *Ad Nos ad Salutarem Undam* is based on the Chorale of the Anabaptists in Meyerbeer's opera *Le Prophète*. (See p. 169.)

Montez, Lola (1818–61). Half Andalusian, half Irish, Lola Montez was a danceractress of European notoriety, with fire in her veins, who became Liszt's mistress in the early 1840's. The affair set the seal on his break with Countess d'Agoult and its attendant publicity did Liszt considerable harm. Liszt had difficulty in breaking off with Lola who refused to be jilted. She pursued him to Bonn, where he had journeyed for the banquet to celebrate the unveiling of the Beethoven Monument, and jumped on the table to execute one of her famous dances, dumbfounding the all-male assembly. See p. 68, footnote for further revelations.

Moscheles, Ignaz (1794–1870). Born in Prague, Moscheles was an infant piano prodigy. Trained in the Clementi tradition, he was launched on the career of a travelling virtuoso by the time he was nineteen, and was soon hailed as the foremost pianist of his time. He taught the young Mendelssohn in 1824, who retained such a high opinion of him in later life that he invited him to become the first piano professor of the Leipzig Conservatoire, in 1846, under his aegis. Moscheles appears to have been out of sympathy with the Romantics, and he could write of Chopin's Studies in 1833: 'My thoughts, and consequently my fingers, ever stumble and sprawl at certain crude modulations, and I find Chopin's productions on the whole too sugared, too little worthy of a man and an educated musician, though there is much charm and originality in the national colour of his motives.'

Mosonyi, Mihály (1815–70). Hungarian composer, writer, and virtuoso double-bass player. Liszt thought highly of him, both as a man and as a musician; it was for Mosonyi that Liszt wrote the double-bass solo in the Agnus Dei of his *Messe solennelle*. In 1856, Liszt tried to stage at Weimar Mosonyi's opera 'Kaiser Max' but the project fell through. Mosonyi possessed a melancholy disposition which forced him to abandon composition during his last years. He then supported himself by teaching and writing, his articles becoming an important rallying-point for the developing nineteenth-century Hungarian Nationalist School. Liszt left him a fine memorial in the last of his 'Hungarian Historical Portraits'.

'New German' School. The school of composers centred around Weimar, with Liszt and Wagner at its head, including such lesser figures as Raff and Cornelius. The term was coined to distinguish the work of these musicians (which in its time was considered avant-garde) from that of their contemporaries—Brahms, Mendelssohn and, to a lesser extent, Schumann, who drew their inspiration from classical models.

Nicholas I, Tsar of Russia (1796–1855). This was the monarch to whom Liszt delivered a public rebuke after he had made a noisy entrance to one of his recitals. Nicholas: 'Why have you stopped playing?' Liszt: 'Music herself should be silent when Nicholas speaks!' As Sacheverell Sitwell put it, this was probably the first time that 'music herself' had answered back, and the retort probably cost Liszt a medal. Nicholas was later to prove a thorn in the flesh to Liszt; he sequestrated the property of Princess Sayn-Wittgenstein after she had joined Liszt in Weimar, and for many years he successfully blocked all her attempts to secure a divorce from her Russian husband. There are many Lisztians who believe that he thereby did Liszt a considerable favour.

Paer, Ferdinando (1771–1839). Born in Parma. Prolific opera composer. Settled in Paris in 1807 as Napoleon's Kapellmeister. He became the young Liszt's composition teacher in 1823 when Liszt was turned away from the Paris Conservatoire.

Paganini, Niccolò (1782–1840). Italian violinist. His early childhood was marked by privation. Paganini's mother was fond of relating a dream in which she claimed to have been visited by an angel who had declared that her son was destined to become the greatest violinist in the world. Anxious, no doubt, to reap the financial benefits of this disclosure as quickly as possible, Paganini's father set to work with a will and nearly wrecked everything with his rigorous training methods, which included the administration of generous doses of corporal punishment each time the lad produced a wrong note. From about the age of seven, however, Paganini was a pupil of Giacomo Costa, *maestro di cappella* of the Cathedral of San Lorenzo, under whose guidance he made such rapid progress that in 1793 he made his début, aged nine. Two years later, there occurred the famous encounter with Rolla, one of Italy's foremost violinists. Paganini had travelled with his father to

Parma to visit the distinguished fiddler who, apparently, was ill in bed. He was ushered into an adjoining room and spotting Rolla's violin lying on the table, together with a copy of his latest concerto, Paganini picked up the music and read it through at sight. The therapeutic effect on Rolla was remarkable. He leaped out of bed and rushed to the other room, anxious to greet 'the master violinist' who had just despatched his difficult new work; on discovering an eleven-year-old boy instead, he was thunderstruck and is reported to have said that he, Rolla, could teach him nothing. After a suitable interval had elapsed he was prevailed upon to change his mind, and Paganini remained with Rolla for several months.

Such tales are part and parcel of the Paganini legend. He was the supreme violinist who could do anything. Soon, people, unable to account for his miraculous powers, had to invent a reason, and the rumour spread that he was in league with the Devil. Paganini, who was a superb showman, did nothing to deny it, and throughout his professional life the man and his violin were shrouded in mystery and associated with the sinister and the macabre.

Paganini began his travels in earnest in 1828, by playing in Vienna; the newspapers talked about little else for two months. Three years of subsequent travel through Poland, Prussia, Bavaria and Austria finally brought him to Paris, where, on 9 March, 1831, he played before a vast audience in the Opéra House amidst scenes of wild enthusiasm. Liszt was in the audience and the memory of that evening remained with him for life; he took Paganini as his chief model and transcribed some of his more difficult violin pieces for the piano. (See pp. 44–51.)

Paganini built a large fortune out of his concerts, much of it in landed estates. On his death he left his son Achillino 2 million Lire (about £80,000).

Pixis, Johann Peter (1788–1874). German pianist and composer. He was a noted piano teacher, and lived for some time in Paris. One of the contributors to the 'Hexameron' Variations. (See entries under Princess Belgiojoso and Heine.)

Pohl, Richard (1826–96). German critic. Propagandist of the 'New German' School, writing mainly about Liszt and Wagner. He wrote the first analysis of 'Tristan' and upset Wagner by showing that the opera was influenced by Liszt. (See p. 73.)

Raabe, Peter (1872–1945). For many years, he was Director of the Liszt Museum at Weimar. His book *Franz Liszt* (1931) remains a standard biography on the composer, and it contains the first complete catalogue of Liszt's music.

Raff, Joseph Joachim (1822–82). Swiss composer. In 1850 he settled in Weimar to be near Liszt, and remained there as his assistant for two or three years. He helped Liszt towards an understanding of orchestration and gave him a great deal of critical advice. His opera 'King Alfred' was produced at Weimar under Liszt's direction in 1851.

Ramann, Lina (1833–1912). The official biographer of Liszt. Her three-volume biography of the composer *F. Liszt als Künstler und Mensch* was spread across fourteen years (vol. 1, 1880; vol. 2, 1887; vol. 3, 1894). It has been the source of much confusion and error. Ramann was assisted in the preparation of her book by the Princess Sayn-Wittgenstein, a somewhat biassed guide, particularly with regards to Liszt's early years and his liaison with the Countess d'Agoult. The result is a book which attempts to whitewash Liszt rather than to understand him, although Ramann was admittedly in a delicate position as her first volume, covering Liszt's most notorious years, was published during both his and the Princess's lifetimes.

Reményi, Eduard (1830–98). Hungarian violinist of strong, nationalistic leanings. He took part in the 1848 insurrection against Austria and had to flee the country when it was crushed. He toured Germany with Brahms in 1852–53 and visited Liszt at Weimar who at once recognized his outstanding qualities. Liszt started to write a violin concerto for him which, alas, was never finished; the sketches are in the Liszt Museum at Weimar. There was a dramatic, gypsy-like quality about his playing which won acclaim wherever he went, although his critics sometimes accused him of 'playing to the gallery'. Undoubtedly, his most extravagant gesture came in 1898 when he dropped dead on the concert platform in San Francisco.

Ricordi, Giovanni (1785–1853). Founder of the music publishing firm which bears his name, and a great admirer of Liszt. His introduction to Liszt happened by chance. Liszt found himself in Milan in 1838, and passing Ricordi's shop walked in and started playing one of the pianos in the showrooms. Ricordi, who was sitting in his office, rushed out shouting: 'This must be Liszt or the Devil.' Having established that it was not the Devil, Ricordi was kindness itself to Liszt, opening his sumptuous villa at Brianza for the pianist and placing at his disposal his famous library of 1500 musical scores.

Rossini, Gioacchino Antonio (1792–1868). By the time Liszt had embarked on his career as a travelling virtuoso, Rossini was already the lion of the operatic stage. It is hardly surprising, then, that Liszt should have paraphrased one of the master's most popular operas *William Tell* and toured Europe with it. Rossini's sense of humour was legend. When Liszt visited him in his house in Paris in the Chausée d'Antin, after an absence of many years, Rossini embraced him and then ran his hands through Liszt's hair inquiring if it was his own. Liszt assured him that it was, whereupon Rossini removed his wig and pointed to his balding pate. 'And soon,' he said, 'I shall have no teeth and legs, either.'

Rubenstein, Anton (1829–94). Russian pianist and composer of German-Polish descent. He received his early training in Moscow; in 1840, he visited Paris and worked for a time under Liszt's supervision. Liszt followed his career with interest. 'That is a clever fellow—the most notable musician, pianist, and composer who has appeared from among the younger lights.' He founded the St. Petersburg Conservatory in 1862, becoming its first Principal. Rubinstein's brand of pianism was of the 'thunder and lightning' variety, and he could produce an enormous range of sound. His pupils tried to emulate him. Liszt good-humouredly called them 'the young matadors of the keyboard' and privately hoped (in vain) that history wouldn't hold him personally responsible for their piano-smashing tendencies. Rubinstein was a great Bach-lover. Appropriately, Liszt dedicated to him his Variations on the ground bass from Bach's *Weinen, Klagen* cantata.

Saint-Cricq, Carolyne de (1812(?)–1872). She was a pupil of the young Liszt and his first real love. Her father, who was a minister to Charles X, brutally squashed the affair almost as soon as it had begun, as a result of which Liszt suffered a nervous breakdown. But he never forgot Carolyne. Years later, long after she had married, he went out of his way to see her again at Pau where he was giving a recital; and when he drew up his Will he left Carolyne a ring.

Saint-Simonists. A humanitarian movement of enlightened social views which took as its creed the teachings of the Comte de Saint-Simon (1760–1825). Broadly speaking, the Saint-Simonists stood for State control of property and the distribution of produce, believing such measures to be the only ones likely to alleviate individual human suffering. Liszt came under their influence in his late 'teens, and he even attended some of their meetings. Their teachings remained with him for life.

Salieri, Antonio (1750–1825). Italian opera composer. He spent most of his life in Vienna and became court Kapellmeister there in 1788. Salieri was so widely respected as a theorist and a teacher that even the mature Beethoven sought advice from him. The young Schubert was Salieri's pupil for four years (1813–17) after his first teacher had declared 'the boy knows everything already; he has been taught by God.' Salieri, apparently, had no qualms about taking over from the Almighty. By the time Liszt's family moved to Vienna, in 1821, Salieri enjoyed a European reputation and he was an obvious choice of teacher for the eleven-year-old Franz who took theory lessons from him for a period of eighteen months.

Sand, George (1804–76). Author, social reformer, and mistress of Chopin. Unhappily married at eighteen to Baron Casimir Dudevant, she soon became bored by the deadly dull routine of it all. Resolved to cast off her yoke she made for Paris, and the independent life, in 1831 aged twenty-seven. 'George Sand' was the pen-name she adopted for the publication of her novels which soon attracted notoriety for their advanced ideas, particularly on the emancipation of women. She wore men's clothing, smoked cigars, and demanded to be treated as an equal. In 1833–34 she had an affair with the poet Alfred de Musset which was the scandal of the season; then she met Chopin for whom she formed a lasting attachment. Her attitude towards Liszt was ambivalent. She knew him far better in the early days than later on. Perhaps they were on closest terms during 1836–37 when she joined Liszt and Marie d'Agoult for a holiday in Chamonix and invited them in turn to visit her at Nohant. Here she worked on her novel *Mauprat* while Liszt arranged Schubert's songs for the piano. 'When Franz plays I am comforted. . . . Mighty artist, sublime in great things, always superior in small ones, and yet sad, gnawed by a secret wound . . .' Of this period, Liszt later wrote: 'We had then three months of intellectual life the memory of whose moments I have kept religiously in my heart.' Not only 'intellectual life', either. They were almost certainly infatuated with each other for a time, although Marie d'Agoult seems to have turned a blind eye.

Sayn-Wittgenstein, Princess Carolyne (1819–87). Liszt's mistress. Born Iwanowski, the daughter of a wealthy Polish landowner, she married at seventeen Prince Nicholas Sayn-Wittgenstein who was a millionaire and an adjutant to the Tsar. The marriage was doomed from the start; the Princess later claimed that she was forced into it (this was one of the chief propositions in her plea to the Vatican to have the marriage annulled) and within a short time they agreed upon a permanent separation. There was one child of the union, a daughter called Marie, born in 1837. As the Princess had inherited all her father's lands, she was a wealthy woman in her own right, and she established herself at Woronince on the family estates where she held dominion over 30,000 serfs.

Carolyne had pronounced intellectual interests. She spoke perfect French. She possessed an enormous library and she read voraciously, often far into the night. She also had literary pretensions. In later life, she became a religious bigot and got bogged down in the *minutiae* of theology. Her *magnum opus* was her *Interior Causes of the Exterior Weakness of the Roman Catholic Church* in 24 volumes (sic) which she completed only two weeks before she died. She had a liking for strong black cigars, which she indulged to the full. With her powerful personality, and her well-stocked mind, she could dominate most conversations and usually did—a fact for which Wagner never forgave her. Ernest Newman described her as a 'half-cracked blue-stocking'.

Liszt first met the Princess in February 1847 when she turned up at one of his charity concerts in Kiev. She invited him to Woronince shortly afterwards, and within a few months their fate was sealed. Liszt was soon to take up his appointment at the Weimar Court, and as they both believed that Carolyne's divorce was imminent, it was arranged for her to follow Liszt to Weimar where they would marry when convenient. Neither of them bargained for the intractability of the husband who not only refused to countenance the idea but secured a powerful ally in the Tsar who banished the Princess from Russia and sequestrated all her lands. Liszt and the Princess now began a 12-year battle to have her marriage annulled, but owing to the machinations of the Tsarist court (the Tsar was head of the Russian Orthodox Church) it came to nothing. Meantime, they had established their household in Weimar at the Altenburg where they lived as man and wife until 1859. Carolyne's daughter, Marie, was brought up there; Liszt was so deeply attached to her he regarded her as his own child. His nickname for her was 'Magnolette', and she is mentioned frequently in his correspondence. (In 1859, Marie married Constantine Hohenlohe, the brother of Monseigneur Hohenlohe, who owned the Villa d'Este and from whom Liszt later received the tonsure of the Roman Catholic Church.)

In May 1860, the Princess left Weimar for Rome, hoping to expedite her divorce through the personal intervention of the Pope. Liszt, having resigned his post at the Weimar Court, followed her the following year, and they made plans to marry on 22 October 1861, Liszt's fiftieth birthday. On the eve of the wedding, however, an emissary from the Vatican informed them that the Wittgenstein family had raised fresh technicalities and that the marriage must therefore be postponed. Liszt might well have been relieved. Cosima said that he looked forward to the ceremony 'as to a burial service'. At any rate, there was no further talk of marriage between them, and from this time they went their separate ways. Carolyne lived in Rome for the next twenty-five years, a lonely and tragic figure, and died there on 8 March 1887. She was discovered dead in bed by her daughter and the Cardinal Hohenlohe who had come to visit her.

Schlesinger, Adolf Martin (d. 1839). Founder of a famous firm of music publishers in the nineteenth century. He was not only an enterprising business man, but also a man of ideals. He brought out a full score of Bach's St. Matthew Passion shortly after Mendelssohn's revival in 1828 'for the honour of the house'.

Schlesinger, Maurice Adolf (d. 1871). Son of the above. Following his father's example he started in 1834 a music publishing firm in Paris which brought out the very first 'complete' editions of Weber, Hummel, and Beethoven. His 'house journal' was the famous *Gazette Musicale* which appeared for the first time in January 1834 and which served as a platform for any and every deserving musical cause until its expiry in 1880. Liszt wrote several articles for Schlesinger including 'On the position of artists' (1835), and 'On the future of Church music' (1834).

Schumann, Robert (1810–56). As young men in their twenties, full of Romantic ideals, Schumann and Liszt enjoyed a respectful friendship towards each other. Unfortunately, as time wore on, it cooled to a point where they were hardly on speaking terms. When they first met (in 1840) Schumann said that 'it was as if we had known one another for twenty years'. They had, in fact, already had a cordial correspondence and Schumann had sent Liszt some of his compositions, including *Carnaval*, *Kinderscenen* and the C major Fantasy, op. 17, which Schumann had dedicated to him. 'The Fantasy', wrote Liszt, 'is a work of the highest kind—and I am really rather proud of the honour you have done me in dedicating to me so grand a composition.' Nevertheless, he never played the work in public. Maybe he was disappointed with Schumann's review of his first Dresden concert (1840), part of a tour to raise funds for the Beethoven Monument, in which as a gesture to Schumann he had included a performance of *Carnaval*. He got little thanks for his trouble; Schumann seems to have been difficult to please with this work. Towards 1850, their friendship deteriorated rapidly; it was apparent that they stood for different artistic aims. Clara Schumann did not help matters; she hated everything Liszt represented, and declared him to be a 'smasher of pianos'. Eventually, Schumann moved from Leipzig to Dresden, while Liszt settled down in Weimar; as both men were influential enough to attract powerful support from other musicians, the situation gradually hardened into two rival schools—the Leipzig–Dresden axis versus Weimar. The Leipzig–Dresden coterie included at first Schumann and Mendelssohn (until his death in 1847), together with the academics from the Leipzig Conservatoire, Rietz, Hauptmann, and Ferdinand David; at Weimar there was Liszt, Cornelius, Raff, and (closely associated with them) Richard Wagner—the so-called 'New German' School. In 1852, Joachim, who had been Liszt's orchestral leader at Weimar, defected to Leipzig. Brahms hovered between the two Schools for a short time and then closed ranks behind Schumann. Liszt often referred to the goings-on at Leipzig as 'Leipzigerisch'; the Leipzigers retaliated by booing 'Mazeppa' when Liszt (in a vain effort to let bygones be bygones) favoured them with a performance of the work in 1857.

It says much for Liszt's breadth of vision that the row between Leipzig and Weimar did not prevent him from performing several of Schumann's works at the Weimar Court Theatre. He wrote to Schumann in 1849 expressing the wish to stage Schumann's 'Scenes from Faust' for the Goethe Centenary celebrations; but Schumann sulked and refused to give him a satisfactory answer. Liszt staged it anyway. He also produced *Manfred* and the opera *Geneviève*, the performances of which Schumann declined to attend. A final peace offering from Liszt came in the form of the dedication of his B minor Sonata to Schumann. By this time, however, Schumann had already entered that mental decline to which he eventually succumbed, and a reconciliation never materialized.

Behind the controversy, which is not easy to disentangle, lay the troubled history of the *Neue Zeitschrift für Musik* which Schumann had founded in 1834 and edited for ten years. In 1844, Schumann had resigned the editorship which passed to Paul Brendel a disciple of Liszt and the 'New German' School. The magazine thus began to champion the cause of Weimar. Schumann was appalled, but had no power to intervene; he saw the organ which he himself had created turned against his own party. Schumann never lived to see the final outcome of the quarrel which was almost unique in the annals of musical history: the publication in 1860 of the 'Manifesto' against the 'New German' School, by Brahms and Joachim, which was drawn up in direct response to the Liszt propaganda of the *Zeitschrift*.

Stasov, Vladimir (1824–1906). A leading Russian critic. His writings were influential in gaining recognition for 'The Five' whose cause he made it his life's work to champion. When Liszt visited St. Petersburg for the first time in 1842, Stasov, then a young student, was in the audience. He left one of the best accounts of Liszt that we have during this period.

Strelezki, Anton. Pupil of Liszt. In 1887, he published a book of reminiscences called *Conversations with Liszt* which contains a number of anecdotes about Liszt's Weimar masterclasses. He was an Englishman; his real name was Burrand and he was born in Croydon.

Tausig, Carl (1841–1871). Liszt's favourite pupil. Born in Poland, his father took him to Liszt when he was only fourteen. Liszt and his friends were taken aback when he sat down at the piano to play. 'He dashed into Chopin's A flat Polanaise and knocked us clean over with his octaves,' said Cornelius. Liszt took the boy into his household at Weimar where he lived as one of the family while receiving instruction. Later on, he moved to Berlin and opened a highly successful piano academy. He gave frequent recitals in that city; his Chopin programmes were epoch-making. Liszt described his technique as 'infallible'. He died of typhoid fever before he was thirty. This was a tragedy for the history of piano playing. Had he enjoyed a normal life-span he would have survived into the twentieth century and the age of the gramophone.

Thalberg, Sigismond (1812–71). Born in Geneva. He later settled in Vienna and became a pupil of Hummel. He was one of Liszt's most serious rivals. Their famous contest took place in 1837, when Liszt was declared the winner by public acclaim (see pp. 55–58). Thalberg's brand of pianism was much admired, particularly among connoisseurs. He had a 'quiet' demeanour at the keyboard (in marked contrast to Liszt's 'storm and stress') as befitted a pupil of Hummel, and he could produce a remarkably fine singing tone on the old-fashioned Viennese-action pianos which he always preferred to play. 'If anybody were to criticize Thalberg, all the girls in Germany, France, and the other European countries would rise up in arms,' said Schumann, whose 1841 notice of Thalberg's Leipzig concert is full of praise. Thalberg's trick of bringing out a melody in the middle of the keyboard, and surrounding it with decorative accompaniment, creating the impression of three hands, earned him the nickname of 'Old Arpeggio'.

Urhan, Chrétien (1790–1845). French violinist. Leader of the Paris Opera Orchestra in the 1830's. Urhan was a mystic whose religious beliefs had a powerful effect on the young Liszt. For a time, he was Liszt's closest friend. (See footnote, p. 46.)

Villa d'Este. The Villa was originally a Benedictine convent. In 1550, Cardinal d'Este was installed there as Governor; he was responsible for starting the gardens, which rank among the most magnificent in the world, and the Villa has borne his name ever since. It eventually passed into the hands of the Hapsburg family and is today owned by the Italian government.

Situated at Tivoli, near Rome, Liszt spent much of the last twenty years of his life at the Villa d'Este. Through the influence of his friend Cardinal Hohenlohe he had a suite of rooms set aside for him which he could use whenever he wished. The gardens of the Villa d'Este, with their famous cypress trees and hundreds of fountains, inspired Liszt to compose some of the best music of his old age. Liszt once described the Villa d'Este as his 'El Dorado'. (See plate facing p. 352.)

Wagner, Richard (1813–83). The friendship between Wagner and Liszt was one of the most fruitful in musical history. At first, the two men were on cool terms. They met in Paris in 1840 and failed to get on. Later, they became closer through their vast correspondence when Liszt got to know *Tannhäuser* and decided to stage the opera at Weimar. The turning-point in their relationship came in 1848–49 when Wagner fled the Dresden uprising with a price on his head and sought sanctuary from Liszt, who not only sheltered him but also helped him financially. At that time, Liszt was practically the only musician in Germany who believed in Wagner. He quite early came to see in Wagner the hope for the music of the future. 'There is in the art of our day a name already glorious, and which will be more and more glorious still: Richard Wagner. His genius has been a lighted torch to me; I have followed in his footsteps, and my friendship with him has all the character of a noble passion.' Wagner, for his part, was well aware of the debt he owed to Liszt, even if he was unduly sensitive about it, and towards the end of his life he publicly discharged it. At a reception in Bayreuth, given in 1876 to mark the occasion of the first performance of *The Ring*, Wagner delivered a speech before 700 guests. 'There sits the man who believed in me first of all, when no one as yet knew anything about me, the one without whom you might never have heard one note of my music, my very dear friend Franz Liszt.' The friendship was marred by their historic quarrel over Cosima whom Wagner enticed from her husband Hans von Bülow and lived with, against Liszt's wishes, for some years before they eventually married. The whole complex story is dealt with in a masterly fashion by William Wallace in his book *Liszt, Wagner and the Princess.*

The question of who influenced whom is, as Humphrey Searle puts it, rather like the proverbial problem of the chicken and the egg. Musical history, nonetheless, has tended to view the question mainly from Wagner's side and has assumed that he influenced Liszt far more than Liszt influenced him. The opposite may very well be the case, and one of the tasks still awaiting the historian is to put this problem into perspective.

Wohl, Janka (1846–1901). Hungarian pianist and pupil of Liszt. Her book *Souvenirs d'une compatriote* (1887) is full of information on Liszt which his later biographers have found indispensable.

BIBLIOGRAPHY

d'Agoult, Comtesse Mémoires 1838–54 (Paris, 1927)
—— Meine Freundschaft mit Franz Liszt (Dresden, 1930)
—— Correspondence de Liszt et de Madame d'Agoult (Paris, 1933)
Apponyi, Count Albert Memoirs (London, 1935)
Bache, Constance (ed.) Liszt's Letters (London, 1894)
—— Letters of Liszt and von Bülow (London, 1898)
—— Brother Musicians (London, 1901)
Bartha, Dénes von Franz Liszt, 1811–1886 (Leipzig, 1936)
Beckett, Walter Liszt (Master Musician Series) (London, 1956)
Ben, O. Franz Liszt in tara noastra (Sibin, 1934)
Bergfeld, Joachim Die formale Struktur der symphonischen Dictumgen Franz Liszts (Eisenach, 1931)
Boissier, Valérie Liszt pédagogue: leçons de piano données par Liszt à Mlle V Boissier à Paris en 1832 (Paris, 1928)
Bory, Robert La vie de Franz Liszt (Paris, 1937)
—— La vie de Franz Liszt par l'image (Geneva, 1936)
—— Liszt et ses enfants Blandine, Cosima et Daniel (Paris, 1936)
—— Une Retraite romantique en Suisse (Geneva, 1930)
Bourguès, L. & Dénéréaz, A. La Musique et vie intérieure de Liszt (Paris, 1921)
Calvocoressi, M. D. Liszt (Paris, 1906)
Chantavoine, Jean Franz Liszt (Paris, 1950)
—— Liszt (Paris, 1928)
Chop, Max Franz Liszts symphonische Werke (Leipzig)
Cooper, Martin Liszt as a song writer (M. &. L, XIX, 1938)
Corder, Frederick Ferencz Liszt (London, 1933)
Csapo, Wilhelm von (ed.) Franz Liszts Briefe an Baron Anton Augusz (Budapest, 1911)
Csatkai, André Versuch einer Franz Liszt-Phonographie (Eisenstadt, 1936)
Danckert, Werner Liszt als Vorläufner des musikalischen Impressionismus (Die Musik, XXI, 1929)
Day, Lillian Paganini of Genoa (New York, 1929; London, 1966)
Dobiey, Herbert Die Klaviertechnik des jungen Franz Liszt (Berlin, 1932)
Engel, Hans Franz Liszt (Potsdam, 1936)
—— Franz Liszt, l'artiste, le clerc: documents inédits, ed. by Jacques Vier (Paris, 1950)
Fay, Amy Music Study in Germany (London, 1893; New York, 1965)
Franz Robert (Olga Janina) Souvenir d'une Cosaque (1874–75)
Friwitzer, Ludwig Chronologisc-systematisches Verzeichnis sämtlicher Tonwerke Franz Liszts (Vienna, 1887)
Galston, G. Studienbuch (Munich, 1926)
Gardonyi, Zoltan Die ungarischen Stileigentümlichkeiten in den musikalischen Werken Franz Liszts (Berlin, 1931)
Göllerich, August Franz Liszt (Berlin, 1908)
Gray, Cecil The Heritage of Music, vol. 2 (Oxford, 1934)
Gregorovius Roman Journal (London, 1911)
Grunsky, K. Franz Liszt (Die Musik, Vol. XV, Leipzig)
Habets, A. Letters of Liszt and Borodin (ed. Rosa Newmarch, London, 1895)

Hallé, Sir Charles Life and Letters (London, 1896)
Haraszti, Emil Le Problème Liszt (Acta musicologica, Dec. 1937)
Harsányi, Zsolt von Hungarian Melody, trans. by Lynton Hudson (London, 1936)
Hervey, Arthur Franz Liszt (London)
Hevesy, André de Liszt, ou le roi Lear de la musique (Paris, 1936)
Hill, Ralph Liszt (London, 1936)
Howard, Walther Franz Liszt, Rhapsodie no. 5: ein Kapitel Romantik (Berlin, 1932)
—— Liszts Bearbeitung des *Cujus animam* aus dem Stabat Mater von Rossini (Berlin, 1935)
Hueffer, Francis (ed.) Correspondence of Wagner and Liszt (London, 1888)
Hugo, Howard, E. (ed.) Letters of Franz Liszt to Marie zu Sayn-Wittgenstein (Harvard, 1963)
Huneker, James Liszt (London, 1911)
Kapp, Julius Franz Liszt (Berlin, 1909, 7th ed. 1918
—— Liszt und Wagner (Berlin, 1909)
Koch, Lajos Liszt Ferencz: Biografiai kisérlet (Budapest, 1936)
Kokai, Rudolf Franz Liszt in seinen frühen Klavierwerken (Leipzig, 1933)
La Mara (ed.) An der Schwelle des Jenseits: Letzte Errinerungen an die Fürstin Carolyne Sayn-Wittgenstein, die Freundin Liszts
—— Bilder und Briefe aus dem Leben der Fürstin K. Sayn-Wittgenstein (1906)
—— Briefe hervorragender Zeitgenossen an Franz Liszt (Leipzig, 1895)
—— Briefwechsel zwischen Franz Liszt und Hans von Bülow (Leipzig, 1898)
—— Franz Liszts Briefe (8 vols., Leipzig, 1893–4)
—— Franz Liszts Briefe an seine Mutter (Leipzig, 1918)
Liszt, Eduard Ritter von Franz Liszt (Vienna, 1937)
Mackenzie, Sir Alexander A Musician's Narrative (London, 1918)
Mesa, R. Liszt, su vida y sus obras (Paris, 1929)
Meyer, W. Charakterbilder grosser Tonmeister. Vol. 3: Liszt, Wagner (Bielefeld, 1927)
New Hungarian Quarterly Liszt–Bartók issue (Budapest, 1962)
Newman, Ernest The Man Liszt (London, 1934)
Nowak, Leopold Franz Liszt (Vienna, 1936)
Ollivier, Blandine Liszt, le musicien passionné (Paris, 1936)
Ollivier, Daniel Autour de Mme d'Agoult et Liszt: . . . Lettres (Paris, 1941)
Philipp, I. La Technique de Franz Liszt. 5 vols. (Paris, 1932)
Pohl, Richard Franz Liszt (Leipzig, 1883)
Pourtalès, Guy de La vie de Franz Liszt (Paris, 1926)
—— Liszt et Chopin (Paris, 1929)
Prod'homme, J. G. Franz Liszt (Paris, 1910)
Raabe, Peter Franz Liszt: Leben und Schaffen, 2 vols. (Stuttgart, 1931)
—— Grossherzog Karl Alexander und Liszt (Leipzig, 1918)
—— Wege zu Liszt (Ratisbon, 1944)
—— Weimarer Lisztstätten (Weimar, 1932)
Ramann, Lina Franz Liszt als Künstler und Mensch (1880), 1st vol. only trans. by E. Cowdrey (London, 1882)
Reboux, Paul Liszt, ou les amours romantiques (Paris, 1940)
Rellstab, Ludwig F. Liszt (1842)
Revue Musicale (Special Liszt number) (Paris, 1928)
Robert, P. L. Études sur Boieldieu, Chopin et Liszt (Rouen, 1913)
Ruach, Walter Franz Liszt: Années de pèlerinage (Bellinzona, 1934)
Ruess, E. F. Liszt: ein Lebensbild (1898)
—— F. Liszts Lieder (1907)
Salaman, Charles Recollections of Liszt (Blackwood's Magazine) (London, 1901)
Salles, A. Le Centenaire de Liszt—Liszt à Lyon (Paris, 1911)
Sand, George Lettres d'un voyageur
Schnapp, Friedrich Verschollene Kompositionen Franz Liszts (Leipzig, 1942)
Schrader, Bruno Franz Liszt (Berlin, 1927)

Searle, Humphrey Liszt's Final Period (Proc. Roy. Musical Assn. LXXVIII, 1951–52
—— The Music of Liszt (London, 1954)
—— Article 'Liszt' in Grove V. (London, 1954)
Simoni, Dario Un soggiorno di Francesco Liszt a San Rossore (Pisa, 1936)
Sitwell, Sacheverell Liszt (London, 1934; rev. ed. 1955)
Stern, Adolf (ed.) Franz Liszts Briefe an Carl Gille (Leipzig, 1903)
Stradal, August Erinnerungen an Franz Liszt (Berne, 1929)
Szabolcsi, Bence The Twilight of Liszt (Budapest, 1956)
Strelezki, Anton Personal recollections of chats with Liszt (London, 1893)
Taddei, A. La divina commedia di F. Liszt (1903)
Tibaldi, Chiesa Maria Vita romantica di Liszt (Milan, 1937)
Trifonof Esquisse biographique (London, 1887)
Wagner, Cosima F. Liszt (Munich, 1911)
Wallace, William Liszt, Wagner and the Princess (London, 1927)
Wessem, C. van Franz Liszt (The Hague, 1927)
—— Liszt: romantische jaren van een pianist (Masstricht, 1931)
Westerby, Herbert Liszt, Composer, and his Piano Works (London, 1936)
Wetz, R. Franz Liszt (Leipzig)
Wohl, Janka François Liszt (London, 1887)
Zorelli, Sylvia (Olga Janina) Les amours d'une Cosaque—par un ami de l'abbé X
—— Le Roman du pianiste et de la Cosaque (1874–5)

COMPLETE CATALOGUE OF LISZT'S WORKS

To compile a complete catalogue of Liszt's works is a daunting task. He was one of the most prolific of composers, and there are many hundreds of items—literary as well as musical—to be accounted for.

It was in 1931 that Peter Raabe published the first exhaustive Liszt catalogue, but this gradually fell out of date as new works came to light and more accurate information became available. Humphrey Searle took on the task of compiling a fresh catalogue and the results were published in the fifth edition of *Grove's Dictionary* in 1954. Mr. Searle recently updated his catalogue[1] and this still remains the most reliable guide in Liszt musicography.

When the question first arose of providing a General Catalogue for the present volume, I was faced with a difficult problem. The easy solution would have been to re-print Mr. Searle's catalogue and have done with it. But on reflection it seemed to me that this would not suit the needs of the reader of this book. The lay-out of Mr. Searle's catalogue was imposed upon him by the curious 'house style' governing all the catalogues published in *Grove V*, which in Liszt's case makes it irksome to unearth information quickly and painlessly—particularly that relating to the solo piano music, the best known of all Liszt's output—and I thought it better, therefore, to compile what is, in effect, a new catalogue, containing as it does a completely fresh set of index numbers and a different disposition of the main categories. I have also provided a 'Key' to the catalogue for easier reference. My thanks are due to Mr. Searle for raising no objections to this idea and for so generously allowing me to make the fullest use of his researches. Each entry is, of course, cross-indexed both with the Searle and the Raabe numbers.

Liszt was one of the greatest arrangers in musical history. Well over half his entire output consists of arrangements of his own or other composers' music. A general catalogue of his compositions, then, is bound to contain many cross-references showing the creative connections between different works. But the matter is further complicated by the fact that after finishing one composition, Liszt would frequently steal ideas from it (maybe just a single theme) for use in another. The resulting cross-references are indicated in two chief ways.

[1] Gregg Press, 1966

(a) When Liszt has arranged the work in question for a different medium, the indication is: e.g.

CAT. NO.	TITLE
129	Concerto no. 1, in E flat major for two pianos, **634**

This type of entry is, I hope, self-explanatory. The E flat major Concerto (Cat. no. **129**) exists in another version for two pianos (Cat. no. **634**). There are many such entries, for Liszt transcribed a great number of his works in this fashion.

(b) When Liszt has taken thematic material from one composition and reworked it in the body of another, the indication is, e.g.:

CAT. NO.	TITLE
126	'Malédiction' Concerto, with string orchestra. See **161**

This type of entry means that the 'Malédiction' Concerto (Cat. no. **126**) has a thematic connection with the 'Faust' Symphony (Cat. no. **161**). Where more detailed information about the precise nature of this kind of connection is sought (and it can vary widely from one work to another), I refer the reader to *Grove V*.

Alan Walker

Key to the Complete Catalogue of Liszt's Works

(A) *Original Works*

(B) *Arrangements*

Appendix

COMPLETE CATALOGUE OF LISZT'S WORKS

(A) ORIGINAL WORKS

1. Piano Solo

(a) Studies

CAT. NO.	TITLE	DATE OF COMPOSITION	AGE	DATE OF PUBLICATION	DEDICATION	SEARLE	RAABE
1	'Étude en 48 exercices dans tous les tons majeurs et mineurs'. See **2–4.** (Only 12 were composed)	1826	15	1827	Mlle Lydie Garella	136	1
2	'24 Grandes Études' 1st version of the *Transcendental Studies*. See **3, 4.** (Only 12 were composed; from **1**)	1838	26	1839	Carl Czerny	137	**2*a***
3	'Mazeppa'. See **4,** 4. (From **2,** 4)	1840	29	1847	Victor Hugo	138	**2*c***
4	'Études d'exécution transcendante' 1. Preludio 2. A minor 3. Paysage 4. Mazeppa (from **3**) 5. Feux follets 6. Vision 7. Eroica 8. Wilde Jagd 9. Ricordanza 10. F minor 11. Harmonies du soir 12. Chasse-neige (From **2**)	1851	39	1852	Carl Czerny	139	**2*b***
5	'Études d'exécution transcendante d'après Paganini'. See **6.** 1. G minor (Tremolo Study)	1838	26	1840	Clara Schumann	140	3*a*

CAT. NO.	TITLE	DATE OF COMPOSITION	AGE	DATE OF PUBLICATION	DEDICATION	SEARLE	RAABE
	1. ***Piano Solo (cont.)***						
	(*a*) *Studies*						
	2. E flat major (Scale and Octave Study)						
	3. La campanella*						
	4. E major (Arpeggio study)						
	5. La Chasse						
	6. A minor (Theme and variations)						
	(*Uses same theme as **396**)						
6	'Grandes Études de Paganini' (from **5**)	1851	39	1851	Clara Schumann	141	3*b*
7	'Morceau de salon, étude de perfectionnement'	1840	29	1841		142	4*a*
	Written for Fétis's 'Méthode des méthodes'. See **8**						
	(Contains a theme from Les Préludes, see **150**)						
8	'Ab Irato. Étude de perfectionnement de la Méthode des méthodes' (from **7**)	1852	41	1852		143	4*b*
9	'3 Études de Concert'	*c.* 1848		1849	Eduard Liszt	144	5
	1. A flat major (*Il lamento*)						
	2. F minor (*La leggierezza*)						
	3. D flat major (*Un sospiro*)						
10	2 Concert Studies	1862–63	52	1863	Dionys Pruckner	145	6
	1. Waldesrauschen						
	2. Gnomenreigen						
11	Technical Studies (12 books)	*c.* 1868–80	57–69	1886		146	7
	(b) Various Original Works						
12	Variation on a Waltz by Diabelli	1822	11	1823		147	26
13	'Huit Variations'	*c.* 1824	13	1824–25	Sébastien Érard	148	27
14	'Sept Variations brillantes sur un thème de G. Rossini' (theme from 'La donna del lago')	*c.* 1824	13	1824	Mme Panckoucke	149	28

15	'Impromptu brillant sur des thèmes de Rossini et Spontini' (themes from 'La donna del lago', 'Armida' } Rossini; 'Olympie', 'Ferdinand Cortez' } Spontini)	1824	13	c. 1824	Countess Eugénie de Noirberne	150	29
16	'Allegro di bravura'	1824	13	1825	Count Thaddeus Amadé	151	30
17	'Rondo di bravura'	1824	13	1825		152	31
18	Scherzo in G minor	27 May 1827	13	1896		153	19
19	'Harmonies poétiques et religieuses'. See **39**	1834	23	1835 7 June, (Supp. 'Gazette Musicale')	Lamartine	154	13
20	'Apparitions'	1834	23	1835		155	11
	1. Senza lentezza quasi allegretto				1. Comtesse Clara de Rauzan		
	2. Vivamente				2. Vicomtesse Frédéric de Larochefoucauld		
	3. Molto agitato ed appassionato				3. Mme la marquise de Camaran		
21	'Album d'un voyageur'. See **22** & **25**	1835–36	24–25	Complete: 1842		156	8
	I. Impressions et poésies			I. 1840 (as Vol. I of Années de pèlerinage—'Suisse')			
	1. Lyon				1. Mr. de L. (Lamennais)		
	2a. Le Lac de Wallenstadt						
	2b. Au bord d'une source				2b. Ferd. Denis		
	3. Les Cloches de G . . .				3. Blandine (L's daughter)		
	4. Vallée d'Obermann				4. Étienne Pivert de Senancour		
	5. La Chapelle de Guillaume Tell				5. Victor Schölcher		
	6. Psaume						
	II. Fleurs mélodiques des Alpes			1840	II. Mad. H. Reiset		
	7a. Allegro, C major						
	7b. Lento, E minor, G major						

CAT. NO.	TITLE	DATE OF COMPOSITION	AGE	DATE OF PUBLICATION	DEDICATION	SEARLE	RAABE
	1. Piano Solo (cont.)						
	(b) Various Original Works						
	7c. Allegro pastorale, G major 8a. Andante con sentimento, G major 8b. Andante molto espressivo, G minor 8c. Allegro moderato, E flat major 9a. Allegretto, A flat major 9b. Allegretto, D flat major 9c. Andantino con molto sentimento, G major						
	III. Paraphrases 10. Improvisata sur le Ranz de Vaches de Ferd. Huber 11. Un Soir dans les montagnes. Nocturne sur le chant montagnard d'Ernest Knop 12. Rondeau sur le Ranz de Chèvres de Ferd. Huber			1836	10. Mme Adolphe Pictet 11. Countess Marie Potocka 12. Count Theobald Walsh		
22	'Fantaisie romantique sur deux mélodies suisses'. See **21**, 7b	1835	24	1836	Valérie Boissier	157	9
23	'Tre sonetti del Petrarca' (1st version; from **273**). See **26**, 4–6	1839(?)	28	1846		158	10*b*
24	'Venezia e Napoli' (1st version). See. **149** & **27** 1. Lento 2. Allegro 3. Andante placido 4. Tarantelles napolitaines	1840	29	unpublished		159	10*d*
25	'Années de pèlerinage' Première Année: Suisse 1. Chapelle de Guillaume Tell	1848–54	37–43	1855		160	10*a*

	2. Au lac de Wallenstadt						
	3. Pastorale						
	4. Au bord d'une source						
	5. Orage						
	6. Vallée d'Obermann						
	7. Églogue	7: 1836	25				
	8. Le Mal du pays						
	9. Les Cloches de Genève (from **21**)						
26	'Années de pèlerinage' Deuxième Année: Italie	Completed by 1849	38	1858		161	10*b*
	1. Sposalizio						
	2. Il Penseroso						
	3. Canzonetta del Salvator Rosa						
	4. Sonetto 47 del Petrarca						
	5. Sonetto 104 del Petrarca						
	6. Sonetto 123 del Petrarca						
	7. Après une lecture du Dante: fantasia quasi sonata (4–6 from **23**)						
27	'Venezia e Napoli'. Supplément aux Années de pèlerinage, 2nd volume	1859	48	1861		162	10*c*
	1. Gondoliera						
	2. Canzone						
	3. Tarantella (from **24**)						
28	'Années de pèlerinage' Troisième Année	Completed by 1877	66	1883		163	10*e*
	1. Angelus! Prière aux anges gardiens				Daniela von Bülow		
	2. Aux cyprès de la Villa d'Este, thrénodie I						
	3. Aux cyprès de la Villa d'Este, thrénodie II						
	4. Les Jeux d'eaux à la Villa d'Este						
	5. Sunt lacrymae rerum, en mode hongrois				Hans von Bülow		

CAT. NO.	TITLE	DATE OF COMPOSITION	AGE	DATE OF PUBLICATION	DEDICATION	SEARLE	RAABE
	1. Piano Solo (cont.)						
	(b) Various Original Works						
	6. Marche funèbre				In memory of Maximilian I of Mexico		
	7. Sursum corda						
29	'Albumblatt' (E major) (from **77**)	1841	30	1841		164	**64, 1**
30	'Feuilles d'album' (A flat major)	1841	30	1844	Gustave Dubousquet	165	**62**
31	'Albumblatt' in waltz form. See **79**	1842	31	1908		166	63
32	'Feuille d'album' (A minor) (from **277**)	*c.* 1843	32	1843		167	64, 2
33	'Élégie sur des motifs du Prince Louis Ferdinand de Prusse'	1842	32	1843(?)	The Princess of Prussia	168	75
34	'Romance' (from **305**) for piano and viola, or violin, or cello **355**	1848	37	?	Mme Josephine Koscielska	169	66*a*
35	Ballade No. 1, in D flat major	1845–48	34–37	1849	Prince Eugen Wittgenstein	170	15
36	Ballade No. 2, in B minor	1853	42	1854	Count Charles de Linange	171	16
37	Madrigal. See **38**, 5	1845	34	unpublished		171a	—
38	'Consolations' (Six Nos.)	1849–50	38–39	1850		172	12
39	'Harmonies poétiques et religieuses'	1847–52	36–41	1853	Jeanne Élisabeth Carolyne (Princess Sayn-Wittgenstein)	173	14
	1. Invocation						
	2. Ave Maria (from **193**)						
	3. Bénédiction de Dieu dans la solitude	3. sketched 1845	34				
	4. Pensée des morts (from **19**)						
	5. Pater noster (from **194**)						
	6. Hymne de l'enfant à son réveil (from **192**)						
	7. Funérailles, Oct. 1849						
	8. Miserere d'après Palestrina						

	9. Andante lagrimoso						
	10. Cantique d'amour						
40	'Berceuse'						
	1st version	1st ver. 1854	43	1854		174	57*a*
	2nd version	2nd ver. 1862	51	1862	Princess M. Czartoryska		57*b*
41	'Légendes' 1. St. François d'Assis. La prédication aux oiseaux 2. St. François de Paule marchant sur les flots	1863	51	1866	Cosima von Bülow	175	17
42	Grosses Konzertsolo for 2 pianos, **136** for piano and orchestra, **555**	*c.* 1849	38	1851	Adolf Henselt	176	18
43	Scherzo and March	1851	40	1854	Theodor Kullak	177	20
44	Sonata in B minor	1852–53	41–42	1854	Robert Schumann	178	21
45	'Weinen, Klagen, Sorgen, Zagen' (Prelude after J. S. Bach). See **46**	1859	48	1863	Anton Rubinstein	179	23
46	Variations on a theme of Bach (Basso continuo of the 1st mov. of the cantata 'Weinen, Klagen, Sorgen, Zagen'): for organ, **658**	1862	51	1864	Anton Rubinstein	180	24
47	Sarabande and Chaconne from Handel's opera 'Almira'	1879	68	1880	Walter Bache	181	25
48	'Ave Maria' for the pf. school of Lebert and Stark, 'The Bells of Rome'	1862	51	1863		182	67
49	'Alleluja et Ave Maria' (d'Arcadelt)	1862	51	1865		183	68
50	'Urbi et orbi. Bénédiction papale'	1864	53	unpublished		184	69
51	'Vexilla regis prodeunt' for orchestra, **659**	1864	53	unpublished		185	70
52	'Weihnachtsbaum. Arbre de Noël'. See **594** 1. Psallite 2. O heilige Nacht! for chorus and organ, **222** 3. Die Hirten an der Krippe ('In dulci jubilo')	1874–76	63–65	1882	Daniela von Bülow	186	71

CAT. NO.	TITLE	DATE OF COMPOSITION	AGE	DATE OF PUBLICATION	DEDICATION	SEARLE	RAABE
	1. Piano Solo (cont.)						
	(b) Various Original Works						
	4. Adeste fideles (Marsch der hl. drei Könige)						
	5. Scherzoso						
	6. Carillon						
	7. Schlummerlied						
	8. Altes provençalisches Weihnachtslied						
	9. Abendglocken						
	10. Ehemals! (Jadis)						
	11. Ungarisch						
	12. Polnisch						
53	'Sancta Dorothea'	1877	66	1927		187	73
54	'In festo transfigurationis Domini nostri Jesu Christi'	1880	69	1927		188	74
55	Pianoforte piece in A flat major Later became 'Romance Oubliée'. See **355**	May 1866	54	unpublished		189	—
56	'La Marquise de Blocqueville. Portrait en musique.'	1868	56	14th April, 1886, in 'Figaro'		190	65
57	'Impromptu'	1872	61	1877	Baroness Olga von Meyendorff	191	59
58	5 Little piano pieces (for Baroness von Meyendorff)	1865–79	54–68	1928		192	60
59	'Klavierstück in F sharp major'	in Liszt's later years		1928		193	61
60	'Mosonyis Grabgeleit. Mosonyi gyázmenete.'	Nov. 1870	59	1871		194	110
61	'Dem Andenken Petöfis. Petöfi Szellemének' for piano duet, **595**	1877	66	1877		195	111
62	First Elegy (from **353**)	1874	63	1875	In memory of Marie Mukhanov	196	76

63	Second Elegy for piano and violin, or cello **354**	1877	66	1878	Lina Ramann	197	77
64	Toccata	1879	68	unpublished		197a	—
65	'Wiegenlied (Chant du berceau)'. See **160** and **356**	18 May 1881	69	unpublished	Arthur Friedheim	198	58
66	'Nuages gris'	1881	70	1927		199	78
67	'La lugubre gondola' 1st version 6/8 2nd version 4/4 (from **357**)	Dec. 1882 (both versions)	71	1916		200	81
68	'R. W.—Venezia.' After Wagner's death	1883	71	1927		201	82
69	'Am Grabe Richard Wagners'	22 May 1883	71	1952		202	85
70	'Schlaflos, Frage und Antwort' (Nocturne after a poem by Toni Raab)	March 1883	71	1927		203	79
71	'Recueillement'	in Liszt's last years		1884		204	86
72	7 Hungarian Historical Portraits 1. Széchenyi István (see **73**) 2. Eötvös József 3. Vörösmarty Mihály 4. Teleki László 5. Deák Ferenc 6. Petöfi Sándor (from **61**) 7. Mosonyi Mihály (from **60**)	1885	74	1956		205	112
73	'Trauervorspiel und Trauermarsch' (from **72**, 1)	1885	73	1887	August Göllerich	206	83, 84
74	'En rêve. Nocturne'	1885	74	1888	August Stradal	207	87
75	'Unstern. Sinistre. Disastro'	in Liszt's last years		1927		208	80

(c) **Works in Dance Forms**

76	'Grande Valse di bravura', 1st version (2nd version **81**, 1)	1836	25	1836	Peter Wolf	209	32*a*
77	'Valse mélancolique'. 1st version (2nd version **81**, 2). See **29**	1839	28	1840		210	33*a*
78	'Ländler in A flat'	1843	32	1921		211	34

1. *Piano Solo (cont.)*

(*c*) *Works in Dance Forms*

CAT. NO.	TITLE	DATE OF COMPOSITION	AGE	DATE OF PUBLICATION	DEDICATION	SEARLE	RAABE
79	'Petite Valse favorite'. See **80** & **31**	1842	31	1843	Marie von Kalergis	212	35
80	'Valse impromptu' (from **79**)	*c.* 1850	39	1852		213	36
81	'Trois Caprices—Valses' 1. from **76** 2. from **77** 3. from **376**	*c.* 1850	39	1852		214	32*b*
82	Carousel de Mme Pelet-Narbonne	1879	68	unpublished		214a	—
83	4 valses oubliées	1881–85	70–74	1881–85		215	37
84(a)	Mephisto Waltz No. 1 for orchestra, **163**, 2	1859–60	48–49	1860	Carl Tausig	514	181
84(b)	Mephisto Waltz No. 2 for orchestra, **164**	1881	70	1881	Camille Saint-Saëns	515	182
84(c)	Mephisto Waltz No. 3	1883	72	1883	Marie Jaëll	216	38
85	Mephisto Polka	1883	72	1883	Lina Schmalhausen	217	39
86	Bagatelle sans Tonalité	1885	74	1956		216a	—
87	Galop in A minor	Jan. 1841	29	1928		218	40
88	'Grand Galop chromatique' for piano duet, **597**	1838	27	1838	Count Rudolph Apponyi	219	41
89	'Galop de Bal'	*c.* 1840	29			220	42
90	'Mazurka brillante'	1850	39	1850	Antoine Koczuchow-ski	221	43
91	Mazurka in A flat major	?	?	unpublished		222	—
92	2 Polonaises 1. C minor 2. E major	1851	40	1852		223	44
93	'Csárdás macabre'	1881–82	70–71	1951		224	46
94	2 Csárdás 1. Allegro 2. Csárdás obstiné for piano duet, **599**	1884	73	1886		225	45
95	'Festvorspiel—Prélude' for orchestra, **670**	1856	45	1857		226	47

96	'Festmarsch zur Saecularfeier von Goethe's Geburtstag' (1st version). See **168**	1849	36	1849	Grand Duke Carl Friedrich of Saxe-Weimar	227	46a
97	'Huldigungsmarsch' for orchestra, **671**	1853	42	1858	Grand Duke Carl Alexander	228	49
98	'Vom Fels zum Meer. Deutscher Siegesmarsch' for orchestra, **672**	1853–56	42–45	1865	William I of Prussia	229	50
99	'Bülow-Marsch' for piano duet, **601**	1883	72	1884	The Meiningen Court Orchestra	230	52
100	'Heroischer Marsch im ungarischen Styl' for orchestra, **156**	1840	29	1840	King Ferdinand of Portugal	231	53
101	'Seconde Marche hongroise' (1st version). See **172**	1843	32	1843	Count Sándor Teleky	232	54a
102	'Ungarischer Geschwindmarsch. Magyar Gyors induló'	1870	59	1871		233	56

(d) Works on National Themes

	Austrian						
103	'Tyrolean Melody'. See **750**	?	?			233a	—
104	*Czech* 'Hussitenlied' of the 15th *c.*: for piano duet, **602**	1840	29	1840	Count Chotek of Chotkowa and Wognin	234	100
	English						
105	'God Save the Queen'	1841	30	1841		235	98
	French						
106	'Faribolo Pastour' and 'Chanson du Béarn'	1844	33	1845	Caroline d'Artigaux	236	93, 94
107	'La Marseillaise'. See **705, 155**			1872		237	95
108	'La cloche sonne'	*c.* 1850	39	unpublished		238	96
109	'Vive Henri IV'	*c.* 1870–80	59–69	unpublished		239	97
	German						
110	'Gaudeamus igitur'. Concert paraphrase	1843	32	1843		240	99
	Hungarian						
111	2 Movements of Hungarian character	1828(?)	17	unpublished		241	107

CAT. NO.	TITLE	DATE OF COMPOSITION	AGE	DATE OF PUBLICATION	DEDICATION	SEARLE	RAABE
		1. Piano Solo (cont.)					
		(d) Works on National Themes					
112	**A** 'Magyar Dallok. Ungarische National-melodien'	1839–47	28–36	1840–47	1–6. Count Leo Festetics	242	105 *a–c*
	Book I						
	1. Lento, C minor						
	2. Andantino, C major						
	3. Sehr Langsam, D flat major						
	4. Animato, C sharp major See **113**, 2						
	5. Tempo guisto, D flat major See **113**, 1						
	6. Lento, G minor See **114**, 5						
	Book II						
	7. Andante cantabile, E flat major See **114**, 4				Count Casimir Esterházy		
	Book III						
	8. Lento, F minor						
	9. Lento, A minor						
	Book IV						
	10. Adagio sostenuto, D major See **114**, 15						
	11. Andante sostenuto, B flat major. See **113**, 3 & **114**, 3 & 6						
	B 'Magyar Rhapsodiák, Rhapsodies hongroises'						
	Book V						
	12. Mesto, E minor (Héroïde élégiaque). See **114**, 5						
	Book VI						
	13. Tempo di marcia, A minor. See **114**, 15						

	Book VII						
	14. Lento a capriccio, A minor. See **114**, 11				Baron Fery Orczy		
	Book VIII						
	15. Lento, D minor. See **114**, 7				Baron Fery Orczy		
	Book IX						
	16. E major. See **114**, 10				Béni Egressy		
	Book X						
	17. Andante sostenuto, A minor. See **114**, 13						
	C 18. Adagio, C sharp minor, C major. See **114**, 12			unpublished			
	19. Lento patetico, F sharp minor. See **114**, 8			unpublished			
	20. Allegro vivace, G minor. Ed. Busoni *c.* 1900 as 20th Rhapsody. Published as 'Rumanian Rhapsody' in 1936. See **114**, 6 & 12			1936			
	21. Tempo di marcia funèbre, E minor. See **114**, 14			unpublished			
113	'Ungarische Nationalmelodien'. See **114**, 6	*c.* 1840	29	*c.* 1840	Count A. Apponyi	243	105*d*
	1. D flat major (**112**, 5)						
	2. C sharp major (**112**, 4)						
	3. C sharp/B flat (see **112**, 11)						
114	Hungarian Rhapsodies						
	1. Lento, quasi Recitativo, C sharp minor	1846	35	1851	E. Zerdahélyi	244	106
	2. Lento a capriccio, C sharp minor	1847	36	1851	Count László Teleky		
	3. Andante, B flat major (from **112**, 11)			1853	Count Leo Festetics		
	4. Quasi Adagio, altieramente E flat major (from **112**, 7)			1853	Count Casimir Esterházy		
	5. 'Héroïde-Élégiaque' Lento con duolo, E minor (from **112**, 12). See **673**, 5 and **603**, 5			1853	Count Sidonie Revicsky		
	6. Tempo giusto, D flat major (from **112**, 4, 5, 11, 20). See **115**, **673**			1853			
	7. Lento, D minor (from **112**, 15)			1853	Baron Fery Orczy		

CAT. NO.	TITLE	DATE OF COMPOSITION	AGE	DATE OF PUBLICATION	DEDICATION	SEARLE	RAABE
	1. Piano Solo (cont.)						
	(d) Works on National Themes						
	8. Lento a capriccio, F sharp minor			1853	Baron Anton Augusz		
	9. 'Pester Karneval'. Moderato, E flat major. See **673**, 6; **603**, 6 and **698**			1st ver. 1848 2nd ver. 1853	H. W. Ernst		
	10. 'Preludio', E major (from **112**, 16)			1853	Béni Egressy		
	11. Lento a capriccio, A minor (from **112**, 14)			1853	Baron Fery Orczy		
	12. Mesto, C sharp minor (from **112**, 18 and 20)			1853	Joseph Joachim		
	13. Andante Sostenuto, A minor (from **112**, 17)			1853	Count Leo Festetics		
	14. Lento quasi marcia funèbre, F minor (from **112**, 21). See **673**				Hans von Bülow		
	15. Rákóczy March						
	Allegro animato, A minor						
	1st ver. (from **112**, 10 and 13)						
	2nd version (from 170)			1871			
	simplified ver. (from 1st ver.)			1852			
	16. Allegro in A minor. See **604**	1882	71	1882	Michael Munkácsy		
	17. Lento, D minor			1886			
	18. Lento, F sharp minor. See **605**	1885	74	1885			
	19. Lento, in D minor	1885	74	1886			
	20. Allegro vivace in G minor known as 'Rumanian' Rhapsody			1936			
115	5 Hungarian Folk Songs, transcribed for piano	1873	62	1873		245	108
116	'Puszta-Wehmut. A Puszta Keserve' (from a poem by Lenau). See **700**(b)	in Liszt's last years		1885		246	113
	Italian						
117	'La Romanesca'	1839	28	1840	Mme Herminie Seghers	247	91

118	'Canzone napolitana'	1842	31	1843	Mlle Claire de Groeditzberg	248	92
	Polish						
119	'Glanes de Woronince' 1. Ballade d'Ukraine (Dumka) 2. Mélodies polonaises (Chopin's 'Mädchens Wunsch'). See **456**, 1 3. Complainte (Dumka)	1847–48	36–37	1849	Princess Marie Sayn-Wittgenstein	249	101
	Russian						
120	'Deux Mélodies russes. Arabesques' 1. Le Rossignol, air russe d'Alabieff 2. Chanson bohémienne	1842	31	1842		250	102
121	'Abschied. Russisches Volkslied'	1885	74	1885	Alexander Siloti	251	104
	Spanish						
122	'Rondo fantastique sur un thème espagnol' ('El contrabandista')	1836	25	1837	George Sand (inspired by her story 'Le Contrebandier')	252	88
123	'Grosse Konzertfantasie über spanische Weisen'	Feb. 1845	33	1887	Lina Ramann	253	89
124	'Rhapsodie espagnole. Folies d'Espagne et Jota aragonese'	*c.* 1863	52	1867		254	90

2. Piano and Orchestra

125	'Grande Fantaisie Symphonique' on themes from Berlioz' *Lélio*	1834	23	unpublished		120	453
126	'Malédiction', with string orchestra. See **152** and **161**	1830–40	19–29	1915		121	452
127	Fantasia on themes from Beethoven's 'Ruins of Athens' for piano solo, **364** and **363**; for two pianos, **633**	1848–52	37–41	1865	Nicholas Rubinstein	122	454
128	Fantasia on Hungarian Folk Tunes (from **114**, 14)	1852	41	1864	Hans von Bülow	123	458
129	Concerto No. 1, in E flat major for two pianos, **634**	1830–56	29–45	1857	Henry Litolff	124	455
130	Concerto No. 2, in A major for two pianos, **635**	1839–61	28	1863	Hans von Bronsart	125	456

CAT. NO.	TITLE	DATE OF COMPOSITION	AGE	DATE OF PUBLICATION	DEDICATION	SEARLE	RAABE
	2. Piano and Orchestra (cont.)						
131	'Totentanz'. Paraphrase on the *Dies irae* for piano solo, **502**; for two pianos, **636**	1838–59	27–48	1865	Hans von Bülow	126	457
	3. Other Keyboard Works						
	(a) Piano Duet						
132	'Festpolonaise'	15 Jan. 1876	64	1908	for the marriage of Princess Marie of Saxony	255	296
133	Variation on the 'Chopsticks' theme for the 2nd ed. of the collection of pieces on this theme by Borodin, Cui, Liadov and Rimsky-Korsakov	1880	69	1880		256	297
134	Notturno in E major (from **23**—Sonnet **104**). Authenticity doubtful	?	?	?		256a	—
	(b) Two Pianos						
135	'Grosses Konzertstück über Mendelssohn's *Lieder ohne Worte*'	1834	23	unpublished		257	355
136	'Concerto pathétique' (from **42**). See **555**	1856		1866	Ingeborg von Bronsart	258	356
	(c) Organ						
137	Fantasy and Fugue on the choral *Ad nos, ad salutarem undam*. See **607**	1850	39	1852	Giacomo Meyerbeer	259	380
138	'Prelude and Fugue on the name B.A.C.H.' See **506**	1st. ver. 1855 2nd. ver. 1870	44 59	1855 1870	Alexander Winterberger	260	381
139	'Pio IX. Der Papsthymnus'. See **175, 649, 675, 507** & **608**	1863(?)	52	1865		261	391
140	'Andante religioso'				Dr. Karl Gille	261a	
141	'Ora pro nobis. Litanei'	1864	53	1865	Cardinal Prince G. Hohenlohe	262	383

143	'Missa pro organo lectarum celebrationi missarum adjumento'. See **180** and **193**	1879	68	1880	Princess Sayn-Wittgenstein	264	384
144	'Gebet'	1879	68	?		265	386
145	'Requiem für die Orgel' (from **184**)	1883	72	1885		266	385
146	'Am Grabe Richard Wagners'. See **69** and **358**	1883	72	?		267	387
147	'Zwei Vortragsstücke'						
	1. Introitus	1884	73	1887		268	390
	2. Trauerode (Les Morts, **165**, 1)	1860	59	1890			

4. Orchestral Works

(a) Symphonic Poems

148	'Ce qu'on entend sur la montagne (Berg-symphonie)' (after Victor Hugo)	Three vers. 1. 1848–9 2. 1850 3. 1854	37–43	1857	Princess Sayn-Wittgenstein	95	412
149	'Tasso, Lamento e trionfo' (after Byron). See **165**, 3; **24**, 1	Four versions 1849–54	38–43	1856	,, ,,	96	413
150	'Les Préludes (d'après Lamartine)'. See **252**, **7**, **308**	1848 rev. before 1854	37–43	1856	,, ,,	97	414
151	'Orpheus' for piano duet, **573** for two pianos, **622**	1853–54	42–43	1856	,, ,,	98	415
152	'Prometheus' for two pianos, **623**. See **241**, **126**	1850 rev. 1859	39–48	1856	,, ,,	99	416
153	'Mazeppa' (after Victor Hugo) (expanded from the piano study 'Mazeppa' **4**, 4) for piano duet, **575**; for two pianos, **624**	1851 rev. 1854	40–43	1856	,, ,,	100	417
154	'Festklänge' (intended as a celebration of his forthcoming marriage with Princess Sayn-Wittgenstein): for piano duet, **576**; for two pianos, **625**	1853	42	1856	,, ,,	101	418

CAT. NO.	TITLE	DATE OF COMPOSITION	AGE	DATE OF PUBLICATION	DEDICATION	SEARLE	RAABE
	4. Orchestral Works (cont.)						
	(a) Symphonic Poems						
155	'Héroïde funèbre' (from the first mov. of the 'Revolutionary' Symph., **705**) for two pianos, **626**	1848–50 rev. 1854	37–39	1857	Princess Sayn-Wittgenstein	102	419
156	'Hungaria' (from the 'Heroischer Marsch im ungarischen Stil', **100**): for piano duet, **577**; for two pianos, **627**	1854	43	1857	,, ,,	103	420
157	'Hamlet' for piano duet, **578**; for two pianos, **628**	1858	47	1861	,, ,,	104	421
158	'Hunnenschlacht' (after Kaulbach) for two pianos, **629**	1857	46	1861	,, ,,	105	422
159	'Die Ideale' (after Schiller) for two pianos, **630**	1857	46	1858	,, ,,	106	423
160	'From the Cradle to the Grave' for piano solo, **489**; for piano duet, **579**. See **65**	1881–2	70–71	1883	Count Michael Zichy	107	424
	(b) Other Orchestral Works						
161	A Faust Symphony in three character pictures (after Goethe) 1. Faust 2. Gretchen 3. Mephistopheles, and final chorus: for two pianos, **631**; 'Gretchen' for piano solo, **490**	1854	43	1861	Hector Berlioz	108	425
162	A Symphony to Dante's 'Divina Commedia' 1. Inferno 2. Purgatorio and Magnificat	1855–56	44–45	1859	Richard Wagner	109	426

	2. Der Tanz in der Dorfschenke (1st Mephisto Waltz): for piano duet, **580**; 2. for piano solo, 84(a)			2. 1866			
164	Second Mephisto Waltz: for piano solo, **492**; for piano duet, **581**	1881	69	1881	Camille Saint-Saëns	111	428
165	'Trois Odes funèbres' 1. Les Morts (Lamennais) (Oration for full orchestra with male chorus) for piano solo, **493**; for piano duet, **582**; for organ, **147**, 2	1860	49	1916	Cosima von Bülow	112	429
	2. La notte (after Michelangelo) for piano solo, **714**; for piano duet, **583**; for violin and piano, **696**	1864	52	1916			
	3. Le Triomphe funèbre du Tasse (epilogue to **149**) for piano solo, **494**; for piano duet, **584**	1866	54	1877	Leopold Damrosch		
166	'Salve Polonia'. Interlude from the Oratorio 'St. Stanislas' (**703**)' for piano solo, **495**; for piano duet, **585**	1863	52	1884		113	430
167	'Kunstlerfestzug zur Schillerfeier' 1859 for piano solo, **497**; for piano duet, **586**	1857	46	1860		114	432
168	'Festmarsch zur Goethejubiläumsfeier' for piano solo, **498**; for piano duet, **587**	1849–57	38–45	1859		115	433
169	'Festmarsch nach Motiven von E.H.z S.-C.-G' (Ernst Herzog zu Sachsen-Coburg-Gotha from his opera 'Diana von Solange'): for piano solo, **499**; for piano duet, **588**	1859	48	1860		116	436
170	Rákóczy March, symphonic arrangement for piano solo, **114**, 15; for piano duet, **589**	1865	53	1871		117	439
171	'Ungarischer Marsch zur Krönungsfeier in Ofen-Pest am Juni 1867': for piano solo, **500**; for piano duet, **590**	1870(!)	59	1871		118	438

CAT. NO.	TITLE	DATE OF COMPOSITION	AGE	DATE OF PUBLICATION	DEDICATION	SEARLE	RAABE
		4. Orchestral Works (cont.)					
		(b) Other Orchestral Works					
172	'Ungarischer Sturmmarsch', rev. from **101** for piano solo, **501**; for piano duet, **591**	1875	64	1876	Count Sándor Teleky	119	437
		5. Vocal Works					
		(a) Opera					
173	'Don Sanche, ou Le Château d'Amour'	1824–25	12–13	unpublished		1	476
		(b) Sacred Choral Works					
174	'Die Legende von der heiligen Elizabeth'	1857–62	46–51	1867	King Ludwig II of Bavaria	2	477
175	'Christus' Oratorio on texts from the Holy Scripture and the Catholic Liturgy. S.A.T. Bar. B. solos, chorus, orch., and organ I. Christmas Oratorio 1. Introduction 2. Pastorale and Annunciation 3. Stabat mater speciosa 4. Shepherd's song at the manger* 5. The three holy kings (March)* II. After Epiphany 6. The Beatitudes 7. Peter noster 8. The foundation of the Church†‡ 9. The Miracle 10. The Entry into Jerusalem III. Passion and Resurrection	1855–66	44–45	1872		3	478

	13. O filii et filiae 14. Resurrexit *for piano duet, **560**; †for organ, **649**: ‡for chorus and organ, **209**)						
176	'Cantico del sol di San Francesco d'Assisi'. Bar. solo, Male chorus, orch. and organ for piano solo, **476**	1862	51	1884	Dr. Arnold Freiherr Senfft von Pilsach	4	479
177	'Die heilige Cäcilia. Legende, gedichtet von Mad. Émile de Girardin'. M-S solo, chorus, and orch.	1874	63	1875	Ludwig Haynald, Archbishop of Kálocsa	5	480
178	'Die Glocken des Strassburger Münsters' (Longfellow) 1. Vorspiel: Excelsior! for piano solo, **477**; and piano duet, **561** 2. Die Glocken	1874	63	1875	H. W. Longfellow	6	482
179	'Cantibus organis. Antifonia per la festa di Sta. Cecilia'. Solo, chorus, and orch.	1879 (for a Palestrina festival in Rome)	68	1880		7	481
180	'Missa quattor vocum ad aequales concinenete organo'. Male chorus and organ. See **143**	1. 1848 2. 1869	37 58	1853 1869	1. Pater Albach	8	485
181	'Missa solennis zur Einweihung der Basilika in Gran.' S.A.T.B. solos, chorus, and orch.	1855	44	1859		9	484
182	'Missa choralis, organo concinente'. Mixed chorus and organ	1865	54	1869		10	486
183	'Hungarian Coronation Mass'. S.A.T.B. solos, chorus, and orch. Benedictus and Offertorium for piano solo, **478**; for piano duet, **562**; for vln. and organ, **663**; for vln, and pf, **699**. Benedictus for vln. and orch., **676**. Offertorium for organ, **652**	1867 (for the coronation of Franz Josef as King of Hungary)	55	1869		11	487
184	Requiem. T.T.B.B. solos, male chorus, organ and brass. See **145**	1867–68	56–57	1869		12	488

5. *Vocal Works (cont.)*

(*b*) *Sacred Choral Works*

CAT. NO.	TITLE	DATE OF COMPOSITION	AGE	DATE OF PUBLICATION	DEDICATION	SEARLE	RAABE
185	Psalm XIII. 'Lord, how long?' T. solo, chorus and orch.	1855 rev. 1859			Peter Cornelius	13	489
186	Psalm XVIII. 'Coeli enarrant'. Male chorus with orch. or organ or woodwind and brass	Aug. 1860	48	1871	Princess Sayn-Wittgenstein	14	490
187	Psalm XXIII. 'The Lord is my shepherd' 1. T. (or S.) solo, harp (or pf.), and organ (or Harm.) 2. Do., with male chorus (*ad lib.*)	1859 rev. 1862	48	1. 1864 2. unpublished		15	491
188	Psalm CXVI. 'Laudate Dominum'. Male chorus and pf. Added to **183** as Gradual	1869	58	?		15a	
189	Psalm CXXIX. 'De Profundis' 1. Bar. solo, Male chorus and organ 2. B. (or A.) and pno. Later added to St. Stanislas, **703**	Nov. 1881	70	1. Supp. to N.Z.f.M. 2. 1883		16	492
190	Psalm CXXXVII. 'By the waters of Babylon'. S. solo, women's chorus, vln. solo, harp, and organ	1859 rev. 1862	48	1864		17	493
191	Five choruses with French texts 1. Qui m'a donné 2. L'Éternel est son nom (Racine) 3. Chantons, chantons l'auteur 4. (A mj., without text) 5. Combien j'ai douce souvenance (Chateaubriand)	1840s 1. for 3 equal voices 2–5. for mixed voices 5. Melody by Chateaubriand	30s	unpublished		18	506
192	'Hymne de l'enfant à son réveil' (Lamartine). Women's chorus, harm. (or pf.), and harp (*ad lib.*). for piano solo, 39, 6	*c.* 1845 rev. 1862 and 1874	*c.* 34	1875	The Liszt Choral Society in Budapest	19	508

	1. Chorus and organ (B flat mj.)	1. 1846	35	1. 1846		20	496
	2. 'Quattor vocum concinente organo' (A mj.)	2. *c.* 1852	41	2. 1852	2. Pater Albach		
	for piano solo, **39**, 2; for organ, **143**						
194	'Pater Noster' II						
	1. Male chorus, unaccomp.	1. 1846	35	1. 1846		21	518*a*
	'Pater Noster quattor vocum adaequales concinente organo secundum rituale SS. ecclesial Romanea'	2. *c.* 1848	*c.* 37	2. 1852	2. Pater Albach		518*b*
195	'Pater Noster' IV. Mixed chorus and organ	1850	39	unpublished		22	520
196	'Domine salvum fac regem'. T. solo, male chorus, and organ	1853	42	1936		23	504
197	'Te Deum' II. 'Hymnus SS. Ambrosii et Augustini'. Male chorus and organ	1853(?)	42(?)	1936		24	—
198	'Die Seligkeiten'. Bar. solo, mixed chorus, and organ (*ad lib.*)	1855–59	44–48	1861	Princess Sayn-Wittgenstein	25	529
199	'Festgesang zur Eröffnung der zehnten allgemeinen deutschen Lehrerversammlung' (Hoffmann von Fallersleben). Male chorus and organ (*ad lib.*)	1858	46	1859	The German Schoolteacher's Association	26	505
200	'Te Deum' I. Mixed chorus, organ, brass, and drums (*ad lib.*)	1859(?)	48(?)	1936		27	533
201	'An den heiligen Franziskus von Paula. Gebet.' Male voices (solos and chorus), harm. or organ, 3 trombones, and timps. (*ad lib.*). See **41**, 2	1860 at latest rev. 1874	49	1875		28	494
202	'Pater Noster' I. Mixed chorus and organ.	1860 at latest	49	1864		29	519
203	'Responses and Antiphons'. Mixed chorus and organ	1860	49	1936		30	526
204	'Christus ist geboren' I ('Weinachtslied von Theophil Landmesser')	1863(?)	52(?)	1865		31	
	1. Mixed chorus and organ						536*a*
	2. Male chorus and organ						536*c*[1]
205	'Christus ist geboren' II (Theophil Landmesser)	1863(?)	52(?)	1865		32	
	1. Mixed chorus and organ						536*b*

5. *Vocal Works (cont.)*

(*b*) *Sacred Choral Works*

CAT. NO.	TITLE	DATE OF COMPOSITION	AGE	DATE OF PUBLICATION	DEDICATION	SEARLE	RAABE
	2. Male chorus, unaccomp., with organ postlude						536*c*[2]
	3. S.S.A. unaccomp. See **479**						536*d*
206	'Slavimo Slavno Slaveni!' Male chorus and organ for piano solo, **480**; for organ, **653**	1863	51	1936		33	531
207	'Ave maris stella'					34	499
	1. Mixed chorus and organ	1865–66	54–55	1870			
	2. Male chorus and organ or harm. See **483**	1868	57	1868			
208	'Crux! Hymne des marins avec Antienne approbative de N.T.S.P. Pie IX. Paroles de M. Guichon de Grandpont, Commissaire Général de la Marine' 1. Male voices unaccomp. 2. Female voices and pf.	1865	54	1865		35	501
209	'Dall' alma Roma'. 2-part chorus and organ. From **175**, 8	after 1867	56	unpublished		36	502
210	'Mihi antem adhaerere'. Male chorus and organ	1868	57	1871		37	513
211	'Ave Maria' II. Mixed chorus and organ: for pf. or harm., **481**; for voice and organ or harm., **680**	1869	58	1870	Mme Jessie Laussot	38	497
212	'Inno a Maria Vergine'. Mixed chorus, harp; organ or piano duet and harm.	1869	58	1936		39	510
213	'O salutaris hostia' I. Female chorus and organ	*c.* 1869	57–58	1871	F. X. Haberl	40	516*a*
214	'Pater noster' III						
	1. Mixed chorus and organ (F mj.)	1869	58	1871		41	521*a*
	2. Male chorus and organ or harm. or	1869	58	1936			521*b*

215	Tantum ergo 1. Male chorus and organ 2. Female chorus and organ	1869	58	1871	F. X. Witt	42	532
216	'O salutaris hostia' II. Mixed chorus and organ	*c.* 1870(?)	59(?)	1871		43	516*b*
217	'Ave verum corpus'. Mixed chorus and organ (*ad lib.*)	1871	60	1871		44	500
218	'Libera me'. Male chorus and organ	1871	60	1871		45	511
219	'Anima Christi sanctifica me'. Male chorus and organ	1st ver. June 1874 2nd ver. *c.* 1874	62	1936 1882	Pater Joseph Mohr	46	495
220	'Sankt Christoph'. Legend for Bar. solo, female chorus, pf., harm., and harp (*ad lib.*)	Planned 1874	63	unpublished		47	483
221	'Der Herr Bewahret die Seelen seiner Heiligen. Festgesang zur Enthüllung des Carl-August-Denkmals in Weimar am 3. September 1875'. Mixed chorus, organ, and wind.	1875	63	1887		48	503
222	'Weihnachtslied (O heilige Nacht)'. T. Solo, female chorus, and organ or harm. From **52**, 2	after 1876	65	1882		49	535
223	Chorales						
	1. Es seqne uns Gott. Mixed chorus and organ 2. Gott sei uns gnädig (Meine Seel' erhebet'). Mixed chorus and organ 3. Nun ruhen alle Wälder. Unacc. chorus 4. O Haupt voll Blut. Unacc. chorus 5. O Lamm Gottes. Unacc. chorus 6. Was Gott tut. Unacc. chorus 7. Wer nur den lieben Gott. Unacc. chorus 8. Vexilla regis. Unacc. chorus 9. Crux benedicta. Unacc. chorus 10. O Traurigkeit. Unacc. chorus	probably 1878–79	67–68	1936 (1–7 only) 8–12 unpublished		50	72

CAT. NO.	TITLE	DATE OF COMPOSITION	AGE	DATE OF PUBLICATION	DEDICATION	SEARLE	RAABE
	5. *Vocal Works (cont.)* ***(b) Sacred Choral Works***						
	11. Nun Danket alle Gott. Unacc. chorus 12. Jesu Christe ('Die fünf Wunden'). Unacc. chorus. 4 and 8–10 are also used in 'Via Crucis' **226**; 11 was extended to **234**, and 2 to **224**, 5 for piano duet, **563**						
224	'Gott sei uns gnädig und barmherzig. Kirchensegen' (Meine Seel' erhebet den Herrn!). Mixed chorus and organ	1878	67	unpublished		51	507
225	'Septem Sacramenta. Responsoria cum organo vel harmonio concinendo' 1. Baptisma 2. Confirmatio 3. Eucharistia 4. Poenitentia 5. Extrema unctio 6. Ordo 7. Matrimonium M.-S., Bar. solos, mixed chorus, and organ	1878	67	1936		52	530
226	'Via Crucis. Les 14 Stations de la Croix pour Chœur et Soli, avec accompagnement d'orgue (ou Pianoforte)'	1878–79	67–68	1936		53	534
227	'O Roma nobilis'. Mixed chorus and organ (*ad lib.*) or solo voice and organ	1879	68	1936		54	514
228	'Ossa arida'. Male chorus (unis.) and organ duet, or piano duet	1879	68	1936		56	517
229	'Rosario' 1. Mysteria gaudiosa 2. Mysteria dolorosa 3. Mysteria gloriosa (1–3: for mixed chorus and harm. or organ)	Nov. 1879	69	1936		56	527

	4. Pater noster. Bar. solo or male chorus (unis.) and organ or harm. 1–3 for organ, **655**						
230	'In domum Domini ibimus'. Mixed chorus, organ, brass, and drums prelude for piano solo, **482**; organ, **656**	in Liszt's last years		1936		57	509
231	'O sacrum convivium'. A. solo, female chorus (*ad lib.*), and organ or harm.	in Liszt's last years		1936		58	515
232	'Pro Papa' 1. Dominus conservet eum. Mixed chorus and organ 2. Tu es Petrus. Male chorus (unis.) and organ	*c.* 1880		1881		59	523
233	'Zur Trauung. Geistliche Vermählungsmusik' (Ave Maria III). Organ or harm. and female chorus (unis.) (*ad lib.*) (from 'Sponsalizio', **26**, 1)	1883	72	1890		60	498
234	'Nun danket alle Gott'. Mixed or male chorus, organ, brass, and drums	1883	72	1884		61	408
235	'Mariengarten (Quasi cedrus)'. S.S.A.T. and organ	1884 at latest	73	1936		**62**	**512**
236	'Qui seminant in lacrimis'. Mixed chorus and organ	1884	73	1936		63	525
237	'Pax vobiscum!' Male voices and organ (*ad lib.*)	1885	74	1885–6	The Strasbourg Male Choir and its conductor Herr Hilpert	64	522
238	'Qui Mariam absolvisti'. Bar. solo, mixed chorus, unaccomp.	1885	74	1886		65	524
238(*a*)	'Salve Regina' Mixed chorus, unaccomp.	1885	74	1936		66	528

(c) Secular Choral Works

239	'Festkantate zur Enthüllung des Beethoven-Denkmals in Bonn'. S.S.T.T.B.B. solos, chorus, and orch. Text by O.L.B. Wolff. The second	1845	34	unpublished		67	537

5. *Vocal Works (cont.)*

(*c*) *Secular Choral Works*

CAT. NO.	TITLE	DATE OF COMPOSITION	AGE	DATE OF PUBLICATION	DEDICATION	SEARLE	RAABE
	part contains an arr. of the Adagio from Beethoven's Trio in B flat major, op. 97 (see **240**)						
	for piano solo, **565**						
240	'Zur Säkularfeier Beethovens' (2nd Beethoven Cantata). Text by Adolf Stern, with some verses by Ferdinand Gregorovius. S.A.T.B. solos, chorus, and orch. Introduction is an orchestration of the Adagio from Beethoven's Trio in B flat major. (See **239**)	1869–70	68–69	1870	Grand Duchess Sophie von Sachsen-Weimar	68	538
241	'Chöre zu Herders entfesseltem Prometheus'. S.A.T.T.B.B. solos, chorus, and orch. See **485**	1850	39	1855		69	539
242	'An die Künstler' (Schiller). T.T.B.B. male chorus and orch.	1st. ver. June 1853	42				
		2nd. ver. end of 1853	43	1854		70	540
		3rd. ver. 1856	45	1856			
243	'Gaudeamus igitur. Humoreske'. Solos (*ad lib.*), mixed or male chorus and orch.	1869	58	1871	Justizrat Dr. Carl Gille	71	541
	for piano solo, **486**; for piano duet, **567**						
244	Four-part male choruses (for the benefit of the Mozart-Stiftung)	1841	30	1843		72	542
	1. Rheinweinlied (Herwegh), with piano				J. Lefebvre		
	2. Studentenlied aus Goethes Faust. Unaccomp.				W. Speier		
	3. Reiterlied (Herwegh), 1st ver. with piano				Count Sándor Teleky		
	4. Reiterlied, 2nd ver. Unaccomp.						

245	'Es war einmal ein König' (from Goethe's 'Faust'). B. solo, male chorus pf. and,			unpublished		73	543
246	'Das deutsche Vaterland' (Ernst Moritz Arndt). Four-part male chorus					74	545
		1st ver. 1841		1843	Frederick William IV of Prussia		
		2nd ver. ? ?		unpublished	The students of Berlin, Vienna, Königsberg, Breslau, Halle, and Jena		
247	'Über allen Gipfeln ist Ruh' (Wanderers Nachtlied: Goethe). Male chorus					75	544
	1st ver. unaccomp.	1st ver. 1842	39	1844	Prince F. W. C. von Hohenzollern-Hechingen		
	2nd ver. (with 2 horns)	2nd ver. 1849	38	1849			
248	'Das düstre Meer umrauscht mich'. Male chorus and pf.	1842	31	1844		76	546
249	'Die lustige Legion' (Bucheim) Male chorus and pf. (*ad lib.*)	1846	35	1848		77	551
250	'Trinkspruch'. Male chorus and pf.	1843	32	'Zeitschrift für Musik' June 1929		78	550
251	'Titan' (Schober) Bar. solo, male chorus and pf.	1842	31	unpublished		79	549
252	'Les Quatre Élémens' (Autran) 1. La Terre 2. Les Aquilons 3. Les Flots 4. Les Astres Male chorus and pf. See **150**	1844–45	33–34	unpublished		80	547
253	'Le Forgeron' (Lamennais). Male chorus and pf.	1845	34	unpublished		81	548
254	'Arbeiterchor'. B. solo, male quartet, and chorus, pf. Similar to the march from Mazeppa, **153** for piano solo, **487**; for piano duet, **568**	1848	37			82	552
255	'Ungaria-Kantate' (Schober). Bar. solo, mixed chorus, and pf.	1848	37	unpublished		83	553

CAT. NO.	TITLE	DATE OF COMPOSITION	AGE	DATE OF PUBLICATION	DEDICATION	SEARLE	RAABE
		5. Vocal Works (cont.)					
		(*c*) *Secular Choral Works*					
256	'Licht, mehr Licht' (?Schober). Male chorus and brass	1849	38	1849		84	554
257	Chorus of Angels from Goethe's 'Faust'. mixed chorus and harp or pf.	1849	38	1849		85	555
258	'Festchor zur Enthüllung des Herder-Denkmals in Weimar' (Schöll)	1850	39	*Leipziger Illustrierte Zeitung*, Nov. 1850		86	556
259	'Weimars Volkslied' (Cornelius) from the trio of the 'Huldigungsmarsch', **671** for piano solo, **519**; for piano duet, **569**; for organ, **657**; for solo voice and piano, **317**	1857	46	1857		87	557
260	'Morgenlied' (Fallersleben). Women's chorus unaccomp.	1859	48	1861		88	558
261	'Mit klingendem Spiel'. Children's voices	*c.* 1859	48	1860		89	559
262	'Für Männergesang'	1842–1859	46	1844–1861		90	560
	1. Vereinslied (Fallersleben)						
	2. Standchen (Ruckert) with T. solo						
	3. Wir sind nicht Mumien (Fallersleben)						
	4. Vor der Schlacht } 'Geharnischte Lieder'	1845 (with piano accomp.)			Dr. C. Brenner		
	5. Nicht gezagt } 'Geharnischte Lieder'				Herr A. Müller		
	6. Es rufet Gott } 'Geharnischte Lieder'				Herr Architekt Heimlicher		
	for pf. solo, **488**						
	7. Soldatenlied aus Goethes 'Faust'. (Tpts and timps *ad lib.*)						
	8. Die alten Sagen kunden (with solo quartet)						
	9. Saatengrün (Uhland)						
	10. Der Gang um Mitternacht (Herwegh) with T. solo						

	11. Festlied zu Schillers Jubelfeier (10 Nov. 1859) (Dingelstedt) with Bar. solo. 12. Gottes ist der Orient (Goethe)						
263	'Das Lied der Begeisterung'. 'A lelkesedés dala'	1871	60	1871	The Hungarian Choral Society	91	561
264	'Carl August weilt mit uns. Festgesang zur Enthüllung des Carl-August-Denkmals in Weimar am 3 Sept. 1875'. Male chorus, brass, drums, and organ (*ad lib.*)	1875	64	1887		92	562
265	'Ungarisches Königslied'. 'Magyar Királydal' (Abrányi). See **344**	1883	72	1884		93	563
266	'Gruss'. Male chorus	1885(?)	74	1885	The Riga Liedertafel	94	564

(d) **Miscellaneous**

267	'Ave Maria' IV. Voice and organ (or harm. or piano)	1881	70			341	640
268	'Le Crucifix' (Hugo). Alto and piano or harm.	1884	73	1884		342	642
269	'Sancta Caecilia'. Alto and organ or harm.	in Liszt's last years		1936		343	643
270	'O Meer im Abendstrahe' (Meissner). S.A. and piano or harm.	*c.* 1880	69	1883		344	637
271	'Wartburg-Lieder' from 'Der Braut Wilkomm auf Wartburg' (Scheffel) 1. Introduction and mixed chorus 2. Wolfram von Eschenbach (Bar.) 3. Heinrich von Ofterdingen (T.) 4. Walter von der Vogelweide (T.) 5. Der tugenhafte Schreiber (Bar.) 6. Biterolf und der Schmied von Ruhla (2 Bar.) 7. Reimar der Alte (T.)	1872	61	1873		345	638

CAT. NO.	TITLE	DATE OF COMPOSITION	AGE	DATE OF PUBLICATION	DEDICATION	SEARLE	RAABE
	6. Songs						
272	'Angiolin dal biondo crin' (Bocella). Two versions: 1st ver. for piano solo, **508**, 6	1st ver. 1839 2nd ver. ?	28	1843 1856		269	593*a* 593*b*
273	'Tre Sonetti di Petrarca' 1. Pace non trovo (No. 104) 2. Benedetto sia'l giorno (No. 47) 3. I vidi in terra angelici costumi (No. 123) 1st ver. for piano solo, **23** 2nd ver. for piano solo, **26**, 4–6	1st ver. 1838–1839 2nd ver. 1861	27–28 50	1846 1883		270	578*a* 578*b*
274	'Il m'aimait tant' (Delphine Gay) for piano solo, **510**	*c.* 1840	29	1843		271	566
275	'Am Rhein' (Heine). Two versions 1st ver. for piano solo, **508**, 2	1st ver. *c.* 1840 2nd ver. *c.* 1856	29	1843 1856	Princes Augusta of Prussia	272	567*a* 567*b*
276	'Die Lorelei' (Heine). Two versions 1st ver. for piano solo, **508**, **1** 2nd ver. for piano solo, **509**; with orch., **686**	1st ver. Nov. 1841 2nd ver. *c.* 1856	30 45	1843 1856	Countess d'Agoult	273	591*a* 591*b*
277	'Die Zelle in Nonnenwerth' (Prince Felix Lichnowsky). Two versions 1st ver. for piano solo, **511** and **32** 2nd ver. for piano solo, **511**; for piano and violin (or cello), **701**(a)	1st ver. 1841 2nd ver. 1860	30 49	1843 1860	Countess d'Agoult Emilie Genast	274	618*a* 618*b*
278	'Mignons Lied' (Goethe). Three versions 1st ver. for piano solo, **508**, 3 3rd ver. with orch., **687**	1st ver. 1842 2nd ver. 1856 3rd ver. 1860	31 45 49	1843 1856 1863		275	592*a* 592*b* 592*c*
279	'Comment, disaient-ils' (Hugo). Two versions 1st ver. for piano solo, **512**	1st ver. 1842	30	1844		276	570*a*

		c. 1859					
280	'Bist du' (Prince Elim Metschersky)	1843 rev. 1877–78	32	1844 rev. 1879		277	625
281	'Es war ein König in Thule' (Goethe). Two versions					278	
	1st ver. for piano solo, **508**, 4	1st ver. 1842	31	1843			594*a*
		2nd ver. 1856	45	1856			594*b*
282	'Der du von dem Himmel bist' (Goethe). Four versions	1st ver. 1842	31	1843	Princess Augusta of Prussia	279	568*a*
		2nd ver. *c.* 1856	45	1856			568*b*
		3rd ver. *c.* 1860	49	1860			568*c*
		4th ver. in Liszt's last years		1918			568*d*
283	'Freudvoll und leidvoll' (Goethe). Two settings	1st setting *c.* 1844		1847	Ary Scheffer	280	579*a*
		rev. *c.* 1860		1847			579*c*
		2nd setting *c.* 1848		1860			579*b*
284	'Die Vätergruft' (Uhland) with orch., **688**	1844	33	1860		281	601
285	'O quand je dors' (Hugo). Two versions. 1st ver. for piano solo, **513**	1st ver. 1842	31	1844		282	569*a*
		2nd ver. *c.* 1859	48	1859			569*b*
286	'Enfant, si j'étais roi' (Hugo). Two versions 1st ver. for piano solo, **514**	1st ver. *c.* 1844	33	1844		283	571*a*
		2nd ver. *c.* 1859	48	1859			571*b*
287	'S'il est un charmant gazon' (Hugo). Two versions	1st ver. *c.* 1844	33	1844		284	572*a*
	1st ver. for piano solo, **515**	2nd ver. *c.* 1859	48	1859			572*b*
288	'La tombe et la rose' (Hugo) for piano solo, **516**	*c.* 1844	33	1844		285	573
289	'Gastibelza, Bolero' (Hugo) for piano solo, **517**	*c.* 1844	33	1844		286	574
290	'Du bist wie eine Blume' (Heine)	*c.* 1842–43	31–32	1844		287	607

CAT. NO.	TITLE	DATE OF COMPOSITION	AGE	DATE OF PUBLICATION	DEDICATION	SEARLE	RAABE
	6. Songs (cont.)						
291	'Was Liebe sei' (Charlotte von Hagn). Three settings	1st setting *c.* 1843	42	1844	Grand Duchess Sophie of Weimar	288	575*a*
		2nd setting *c.* 1855	44	1921			575*b*
		3rd setting *c.* 1878	67	1879			575*c*
292	'Vergiftet sind meine Lieder' (Heine)	1842	31	1844		289	608
293	'Morgens steh' ich auf und frage' (Heine).	1st ver. 1843	32	1844		290	576*a*
	Two versions	2nd ver. *c.* 1855	44	1859			576*b*
294	'Die tote Nachtigall' (Kaufmann).	1st ver. 1843	32	1844		291	577*a*
	Two versions	2nd ver. 1878	67	1879			577*b*
295	Songs from Schiller's 'Wilhelm Tell' 1. Der Fischerknabe 2. Der Hirt 3. Der Alpenjäger					292	
	Two versions	1st ver. 1845	34	1847			582*a*
	2nd ver. with orch., **689**	2nd ver. *c.* 1859	48	1859			582*b*
296	'Jeanne d'Arc au bûcher' (Dumas). Two versions	1st ver. 1845	34	1846		293	586*a*
	2nd ver. with orch., **690**	2nd ver. 1874	63	1876			586*b*
297	'Es rauschen die Winde' (Rellstab). Two versions	1st ver. *c.* 1845	34	1921			596*a*
		2nd ver. *c.* 1860	49	1860			596*b*
298	'Wo weilt er?' (Rellstab)	*c.* 1845	34	1860		295	598
299	'Ich möchte hingehn' (Herwegh)	*c.* 1845	34	1859		296	606
300	'Wer nie sein Brot mit Tränen ass' (Goethe). Two settings	1st setting *c.* 1845	34	1847		297	609*a*
		2nd setting *c.* 1860	49	1860			609*b*
301	'O lieb, so lang du lieben kannst' (Freili-	*c.* 1845	34	1847		298	589

303	'Le Juif errant' (Béranger)	1847	36	unpublished		300	585
304	'Kling leise, mein Lied' (Nordmann). Two versions	1st ver. 1848 2nd ver. *c.* 1860	37 59	1918 1860		301	580*a* 580*b*
305	'Oh pourquoi donc' (Mme Pavloff)	1848	37	unpublished	Mme Pavloff	301a	
306	'Die Macht der Musik' (Duchess Helen of Orleans). Orch. by Conradi and by Raff	1848–49	37–38	1849	Grand Duchess Maria Pavlovna	302	583
307	'Weimars Toten, Dithyrambe' (Schober). Orch. by Conradi	1848	37	1849		303	584
308	'Le vieux vagabond' (Béranger) foreshadows Les Préludes, **150** and 'Dante' Symphony, **162**	1848	37	1918		304	565
309	'Schwebe, schwebe, blaues Auge' (Dingelstedt). Two versions	1st ver. 1845 2nd ver. *c.* 1860	34 49	1918 1860		305	581*a* 581*b*
310	'Über allen Gipfeln ist Ruh' (Goethe). Two versions 1st version for male chorus, **247**	1st ver. *c.* 1848 2nd ver *c.* 1859	37 48	? 1859		306	610*a* 610*b*
311	'Hohe Liebe' (Uhland) for piano solo, **518**	*c.* 1849	38	1850		307	587
312	'Gestorben war ich' (Uhland) for piano solo, **518**	*c.* 1849	38	1850		308	588
313	'Ein Fichtenbaum steht einsam' (Heine). Two settings	1st setting *c.* 1855 2nd setting *c.* 1860	44 49	1860 1860		309	599*a* 599*b*
314	'Nimm einen Strahl der Sonne (Ihr Auge)' (Rellsteb)	*c.* 1855	44	1860		310	
315	'Anfangs wollt' ich fast verzagen' (Heine)	1856 rev. 1880	45	1860		311	602
316	'Wie singt der Lerche schön' (Fallersleben)	*c.* 1856	45	1856		312	595
317	'Weimars Volkslied' (Cornelius). **259**	1857	46	1857		313	597
318	'Es muss ein Wunderbares sein' (Redwitz)	1857	46	1859		314	590
319	'Ich liebe dich' (Rückert)	1857	46	1860		315	617

CAT. NO.	TITLE	DATE OF COMPOSITION	AGE	DATE OF PUBLICATION	DEDICATION	SEARLE	RAABE
	6. Songs (cont.)						
320	'Muttergottes-Straüsslein zum Mai-Monate' (Müller) 1. Das Veilchen 2. Die Schlüsselblumen	1857	46	1895		316	603
321	'Lasst mich ruhen' (Fallersleben)	*c.* 1858	47	1859		317	604
322	'In Liebeslust' (Fallersleben)	*c.* 1858	47	1859		318	605
323	'Ich scheide' (Fallersleben)	1860	49	1860		319	611
324	'Die drei Zigeuner' (Lenau) for violin and piano, **701**(b); with orch., **691**	1860	49	1860	Emilie Merian-Genast	320	612
325	'Die stille Wasserrose' (Geibel)	*c.* 1860	49	1860		321	613
326	'Wieder möcht' ich dir begegnen' (Cornelius)	1860	49	1860		322	614
327	'Jugendglück' (Pohl)	*c.* 1860	49	1860		323	615
328	'Blume and Duft' (Hebbel)	*c.* 1860	49	1860		324	616
329	'Die Fischerstochter' (Coronini)	1871	60	1879		325	619
330	'La Perla' (Princess Therese von Hohenlohe)	1872	61	?		326	623
331	'J'ai perdu ma force et ma vie (Tristesse)' (De Musset)	1872	61	1879		327	620
332	'Ihr Glocken von Marling' (Kuh)	1874	63	1879	Princess Marie von Hohenlohe	328	621
333	'Und sprich' (Biegeleben)	1874	63	1879	Princess Sayn-Wittgenstein	329	622
334	'Sei still' (Nordheim)	1877	66	1879		330	634
335	'Gebet' (Bodenstedt)	*c.* 1878	67	1879		331	628
336	'Einst' (Bodenstedt)	*c.* 1878	67	1879		332	629
337	'An Edlitam' (Bodenstedt)	*c.* 1878	67	1879		333	630
338	'Der Glückliche' (Wilbrandt)	*c.* 1878	67	1879		334	631
339	'Go not, happy day' (Tennyson)	1879	68	1880		335	626
340	'Verlassen' (Michell)	1880	69	1880		336	632
341	Des Tages laute Stimmen schweigen'	1880	69	1922	Princess Marie von Hohenlohe	337	633
342	'Und wir dachten der Toten' (Freiligrath)	*c.* 1884	73	1922		338	634
343	'Ungarns Gott. A magyarok Istene' (Petöfi)	1881	70	1881		339	635

	dal (Ábrányi) for piano solo, **521**; for piano duet, **609**; for chorus and orch., **265**						

7. Recitations

345	'Lenore' (Bürger) with piano	1858 rev. 1860	47	1860		346	**654**
346	'Vor hundert Jahreu' (Halm) with orch.	1859	48	unpublished		347	**655**
347	'Der traurige Mönch' (Lenau) with piano	1860	49	1872	Franziska Ritter (born Wagner)	348	**656**
348	'Des toten Dichters Liebe. A holt költö szerelme' (Jókai) with piano	1874	62	1874		349	**657**
349	'Der blinde Sänger' (Tolstoy) with piano	1875	63	1875		350	**658**

8. Chamber Music

350	Duo (Sonata), violin and piano. Based on Chopin's Mazurka in C sharp minor, op. 6, no. 2	*c.* 1851	40	1964		127	**461**
351	'Grand Duo Concertant sur la Romance de M. Lafont, *Le Marin*', violin and piano	*c.* 1835 rev. 1849	24	1852		128	**462**
352	'Epithalam zu E. Reményis Vermählungsfeier', violin and piano: for piano solo, **503**; for piano duet, **592**	1872	61	1873		129	**466**
353	'Elegie'	1874	63		In memory of Countess Marie Moukhanoff	130	**471**
	1. Cello, piano, harp, and harmonium			1875			
	2. Cello and piano			1875			
	3. Vln and piano for piano solo, **62**; piano duet, **593**			1876			
354	Second Elegy. Piano and violin, or cello for piano solo, **63**	1877	66	1878	Lina Ramann	131	**472**
355	'Romance Oubliée'. Piano and viola, or violin, or cello for piano solo, **504**	1880	69	1881	Hermann Ritter	132	**467**

CAT. NO.	TITLE	DATE OF COMPOSITION	AGE	DATE OF PUBLICATION	DEDICATION	SEARLE	RAABE
	8. Chamber Music (cont.)						
356	'Die Wiege'. 4 Violins	1881	70	unpublished		133	475
357	'La lugubre gondola'. Piano and violin, or cello for piano solo, **67, 2**	1882	71	unpublished		134	468
358	'Am Grabe Richard Wagners'. String Quartet and harp: for piano solo, **69**; for organ, **146**	1883	72	1952 (Liszt Society)		135	474

(B) ARRANGEMENTS

9. Piano Solo

(a) Paraphrases, Operatic Transcriptions, etc.

CAT. NO.	TITLE	DATE OF COMPOSITION	AGE	DATE OF PUBLICATION	DEDICATION	SEARLE	RAABE
	Alabieff, see **120**						
359	'Mazurka pour piano composée par un *amateur de St. Petersbourg*, paraphrasée par F.L.'	1842	31	1842		384	115
	Auber						
360	'Grande Fantaisie sur la Tyrolienne de l'opéra La Fiancée'	1829	18	1829	Chopin	385	116
361	'Tarantelle di bravura d'après la Tarantelle de La Muette de Portici' (Masaniello)	1846	35	1847	Marie Pleyel	386	117
362	2 piano pieces on themes from 'La Muette de Portici' (one on the 'Berceuse')			unpublished		387	118
	Beethoven						
363	'Capriccio alla turca sur des motifs de Beethoven' (Ruines d'Athènes)	1846	35	1847		388	125
364	'Fantasia on Beethoven's Ruins of Athens' for piano and orch., **127**			1865	Nicholas Rubinstein	389	126
	Bellini						
365	'Réminiscences des Puritains'	1836	25	1837	Princess Belgiojoso	390	129

	Grandes Variations de Bravoure sur le Marche des Puritains' (with Thalberg, Pixis, Herz, Czerny, and Chopin) for two pianos, **368**						
368	'Fantaisie sur des motifs favoris de l'opéra La Sonnambula' for piano duet, **610**	1839	28	1842	The Princess of Prussia	393	132
369	'Réminiscences de Norma' for piano duet, **639**	1841	30	1844	Mme Pleyel	394	133
	Berlioz						
370	'L'Idée fixe. Andante amoroso' (On a theme from Symphonie Fantastique)	1833	22	1833		395	135
371	'Bénédiction et Serment, deux motifs de Benvenuto Cellini' for piano duet, **611**	1852	41	1854		396	141
	Donizetti (Gaetano)						
372	'Réminiscences de Lucia de Lammermoor' (based on the Sextet)	1835–36	24–25	1840	Mme Vanotti	397	151
373	'Marche et cavatine de Lucia de Lammermoor' (intended as part of **372** but separated by the publisher)	1835–36	24–25			398	152
374	'Nuits d'Eté à Pausilippe' 1. Barcajuolo 2. L'Alito di Bice 3. La Torre di Biasone	1838	27	1839	Mme la marquise Sophie de Medici	399	153
375	'Réminiscences de Lucrezia Borgia' 1. Trio du second acte 2. Fantasie sur des motifs favoris de l'opéra; Chanson à boire (Orgie)—Duo—Finale	1840	29	2. 1841–42 both parts 1848		400	154
376	'Valse à capriccio sur deux motifs de Lucia et Parisina'	1842 (1st ver. see **81**, 3)	31	1842		401	155
377	'Marche funèbre de Dom Sébastien'	1844	33	1845	Queen Maria da Gloria of Portugal	402	156

9. *Piano Solo (cont.)*

(*a*) *Paraphrases, Operatic Transcriptions, etc.*

CAT. NO.	TITLE	DATE OF COMPOSITION	AGE	DATE OF PUBLICATION	DEDICATION	SEARLE	RAABE
	Donizetti (Guiseppe)						
378	'Grande Paraphrase de la marche de Donizetti composée pour Sa Majesté le sultan Abdul Medjid-Khan' *E.H. z. S-C-G* (Ernst Herzog zu Sachsen-Coburg-Gotha)	1847	36	1848		403	157
379	'Halloh! Jagdchor und Steyrer' from the opera 'Tony'	1849	38	1849		404	159
	Erkel, Franz						
380	'Schwanengesang and March from Hunyadi László'	1847	36	unpublished	Fräulein Sophie Bohrer	405	160
	Glinka						
381	'Tscherkessenmarsch from Russlan and Ludmila' for piano duet, **612**	1843	32	1843	Count A. Kutuzoff	406	164
	Gounod						
382	'Valse de l'opéra Faust'	1861	50	1861	Baron Alexis Michels	407	166
383	'Les Sabéennes. Berceuse de l'opéra. La Reine de Saba'	*c.* 1865	54	1865		408	167
384	'Les Adieux. Rêverie sur un motif de l'opéra Roméo et Juliette'	*c.* 1868	57	1868		409	169
	Halévy						
385	'Réminiscences de La Juive'	1835	24	1836	Clémence Kautz	409a	170
	Mendelssohn						
386	'Wedding March and Dance of the Elves from the music to Shakespeare's "A Midsummer Night's Dream"'	1849–50	38–39	1851	Fräulein Sophie Bohrer	410	219

	Mercadante						
FF 387	'Soirées italiennes. Six amusements sur des motifs de M.' 1. La primavera 2. Il galop 3. Il pastore svizzero 4. La serenata del marinaro 5. Il Brindisi 6. La zingarella spagnola	1838	27	1839	Archduchess Elizabeth of Austria	411	220
	Meyerbeer						
388	'Grande Fantaisie sur des thèmes de l'opéra Les Huguenots'	1836	25	1837	Countess Marie d'Agoult	412	221
389	'Réminiscences de Robert le Diable. Valse infernale' for piano duet, **613**	1841	30	1841	Mme la princess de Soutzo	413	222
390	'Illustrations du Prophète 1. Prière, hymne triomphale, marche du sacre 2. Les Patineurs, scherzo 3. Chœur pastoral, appel aux armes (4 is **137**)	1849–50	38–39	1849–50		414	223
391	'Illustrations de l'Africaine' 1. Prière des matelots 2. Marche indienne	1865	54	1866	Alfred Jaëll	415	224
392	'Le Moine' (a song)	1841	30	1842	Baron Ziegesar	416	225
	Mosonyi, Michael						
393	'Fantaisie sur l'opéra hongrois Szép Ilonka'	1867	56	1868	Michael Mosonyi	417	227
	Mozart						
394	'Réminiscences de Don Juan' for two pianos, **640**	1841	30	1843	King Christian VIII of Denmark	418	228
	Pacini						
395	Divertissement sur la cavatine 'I tuoi frequenti palpiti' (Niobe)	1835–36	24–25	1836	Countess Miramont	419	230
	Paganini						
396	'Grande Fantaisie de bravoure sur la Clochette' (on 'Campanella' theme)	1831–32	20–21	1834		420	231

9. *Piano Solo (cont.)*

(*a*) *Paraphrases, Operatic Transcriptions, etc.*

CAT. NO.	TITLE	DATE OF COMPOSITION	AGE	DATE OF PUBLICATION	DEDICATION	SEARLE	RAABE
	Raff						
397	Andante finale and March from the opera 'König Alfred' for piano duet, **614**	1853	42	1853	Karl Klindworth	421	233
	Rossini						
398	'La Serenata e l'Orgia. Grande Fantaisie sur des motifs des soirées musicales'	1835–36	24–25	1837	Mme Jenny Montgolfier	422	234
399	'La pastorella dell'Alpi e Li marinari. 2me Fantaisie sur des motifs des Soirées musicales'. (See **400**, 6 and 12)	1835–36	24–25	1837	Hermine de Musset	423	235
400	'Soirées musicales'	1837	26	1838	Countess Julie Samoyloff	424	236
	1. La promessa						
	2. La regata Veneziana						
	3. L'invito						
	4. La gita in gondola						
	5. Il rimprovero						
	6. La pastorella dell'Alpi						
	7. La partenza						
	8. La pesca						
	9. La danza						
	10. La serenata						
	11. L'orgia						
	12. Li marinari						
	Schubert						
401	'Mélodies hongroises (d'après Schubert)'	1838–39	27–28	1840	Count Gustav Neipperg	425	250
	1. Andante						
	2. Marcia						
	3. Allegretto						

402	Schubert's 'Märsche für das Pianoforte Solo'. Nos. 1–3 (from the 4-hand marches, opp. 40 and 121): for orch., **677**	1846	33	1847	Fräulein Flore Freiin von Kadelka	426	251
403	'Soirées de Vienne (9). Valses caprice d'après Schubert'	1852	41	1852–53	Simon Löwy	427	252
	Cadenzas to 6 and 9	1883	72	1883			
	Sorriano						
404	'Feuille morte. Élégie d'après Sorriano'	*c.* 1845	34	1845		428	258
	Tchaikovsky						
405	Polonaise from Eugene Onegin	1880	69	1880	Karl Klindworth	429	262
	Végh, János						
406	Concert Waltz after the 4-hand waltz suite	?		1889		430	263
	Verdi						
407	'Salve Maria de Jérusalem' ('I Lombardi')	1848	37	1848	Marie von Kalergis (later Countess Mukhanov)	431	264
408	Concert paraphrase on 'Ernani' (different from **409**)	June 1847	35	unpublished		431a	293
409	'Ernani. Paraphrase de concert'	1849	38	1860		432	265
410	'Miserere du Trovatore'	1859	48	1860		433	266
411	'Rigoletto. Paraphrase de concert'	1859	48	1860		434	267
412	'Don Carlos. Transcription. Coro di festa e marcia funèbre'	1867–68	56–57	1868		435	268
413	'Aïda. Danza sacra e duetto final'	1871–79	60–68	1879	Toni Raab	436	269
414	'Agnus Dei de la Messe de Requiem'	1877	66	1879		437	270
415	'Réminiscences de Boccanegra'	Dec. 1882	71	1883		438	271
	Wagner						
416	'Phantasiestück' on themes from 'Rienzi'	1859	48	1861		439	272
417	Spinning chorus from 'The Flying Dutchman'	1860	49	1861	Louis Jungman	440	273
418	Ballad from 'The Flying Dutchman'	before 1873	?	1873		441	274
419	Overture to 'Tannhäuser'	1848	37	1849		442	275
420	Pilgrims' chorus from 'Tannhäuser' for organ, **661**	1st ver. *c.* 1861	50	1st ver. 1865		443	276
		2nd ver. 1862	51	2nd ver. 1885			

CAT. NO.	TITLE	DATE OF COMPOSITION	AGE	DATE OF PUBLICATION	DEDICATION	SEARLE	RAABE
	9. Piano Solo (cont.)						
	(*a*) *Paraphrases, Operatic Transcriptions, etc.*						
421	'O du mein holder Abendstern' for cello and piano, **700**(a)	1849		1849	Grand Duke Carl Alexander	444	277
422	Two pieces from 'Lohengrin' and 'Tannhäuser' 1. Entry of the guests on the Wartburg 2. Elsa's bridal procession to the minster	1852	41	1853	Hans von Bülow		
423	From 'Lohengrin' 1. Festival and bridal song 2. Elsa's dream and Lohengrin's rebuke	1854	43	1854		446	279
424	'Isolda's Liebestod' from 'Tristan and Isolda'	1867	56	1868			**280**
425	'Am stillen Herd' from 'Meistersinger'	1871	60	1871	Freifrau Marie von Schleinitz (later Countess Wolkenstein)	448	
426	'Valhalla' from 'The Ring of the Nibelung'	1878–80	67–69	1876		449	**282**
427	'Solemn march to the Holy Grail' from 'Parsifal'	1882	71	1883		450	**283**
	Weber						
428	'Freischütz' Fantasy	1840–41	29–30	unpublished		451	284
429	'Leyer and Schwert'	1846–47	35–36	1848	The Princess of Prussia	452	285
430	'Einsam bin ich, nicht alleine' from the music to 'Preciosa'	1848	37	1848	Mme Pauline Bérard	453	286
431	'Schlummerlied von C. M. von Weber mit Arabesken'	1848	37	1848	Franz Kroll	454	287
432	'Polonaise brillante'	*c.* 1851	40	between 1851–1853	Adolf Henselt	455	460
	Zichy, Count Géza						
433	'Valse d'Adèle. Composée pour la main gauche seule. Transcription brillante à deux mains'	*c.* 1877	66	1877		456	**292**

No.	Title	Composed	Vol.	Published	Dedication	No.	No.
	Unknown						
434	Piano piece on Italian operatic melodies			unpublished		458	**294**
435	Three short pieces on themes by other composers			unpublished		459	
436	'Kavallerie-Geschwindmarsch'			1883		460	295

(b) Partitions de Piano, Instrumental Transcriptions, etc.

No.	Title	Composed	Vol.	Published	Dedication	No.	No.
	Allegri and Mozart						
437	'A la Chapelle Sixtine. Miserere d'Allegri et Ave verum corpus de Mozart'	1862	51	1865		461	**141**
	Arcadelt (see **49**)						
	Bach						
438	Six organ preludes and fugues 1. A minor 2. C major (4/4) 3. C minor 4. C major (9/8) 5. E minor 6. B minor	1842–50	31–39	1852		462	**119**
439	Organ Fantasy and Fugue in G minor	before 1872	?	?		463	**120**
	Beethoven						
440	'Symphonies de Beethoven. Partitions de Piano' 1. C major 2. D major 3. E flat major ('Eroica') 4. B flat major 5. C minor 6. F major ('Pastorale') 7. A major 8. F major 9. D minor ('Choral') for two pianos, **641**	5–7: 1837; Marcia funèbre of 3, 1843; rest and revision of others 1863–64	26–53	5 6, & 7, 1840 Marcia funèbre of 3, 1843 Complete, 1865	Complete version Hans von Bülow	464	**128**
441	'Grand Septuor' (op. 20): for piano duet, **617**	1841	30	1842	Grand Duchess Maria Pavlovna	465	**127**

9. *Piano Solo (cont.)*

(*b*) *Partitions de Piano, Instrumental Transcriptions, etc.*

CAT. NO.	TITLE	DATE OF COMPOSITION	AGE	DATE OF PUBLICATION	DEDICATION	SEARLE	RAABE
442	'Adelaide' (op. 46)	1839	28	1840	Marquise Martellini	466	121
443	'Six geistliche Lieder' (Gellert) (op. 48) 1. Gottes Macht und Versehung 2. Bitten 3. Busslied 4. Vom Tode 5. Die Liebe des Nächsten 6. Die Ehre Gottes aus der Natur	1840	29	1840	Mlle Zoé de la Rue	467	122
444	'Beethoven's Lieder von Goethe' (from opp. 75, 83, 84) 1. Mignon 2. Mit einem gemalten Bande 3. Freudvoll und leidvoll 4. Es war einmal ein König 5. Wonne der Wehmut 6. Die Trommel gerühret	before 1849	?	1849		468	123
445	'An die ferne Geliebte.' Song-cycle (op. 98)	1849	38	1850		469	124
	Berlioz						
446	'Épisode de la vie d'un artiste. Grande Symphonie fantastique. Partition de Piano.' (New transcription of mov. 4 'Marche au supplice' *c.* 1864–65)	1833	22	1834		470	134
447	'Ouverture des Francs-Juges'	1833	22	1845		471	137
448	'Harold en Italie. Symphonie en quatre parties avec un alto principal. Partition de piano (avec la partie d'alto)'	1836	25	1879		472	138
449	'Marche des Pèlerins de la sinfonie Harold en Italie. Transcrite pour le piano'	*c.* 1836	*c.* 25	1866		473	139
450	'Ouverture du Roi Lear.'	1836	25	unpublished		474	140
451	'Danse des Sylphes de La Damnation de Faust'	*c.* 1860	49	1866		475	142

	Berlin, Louise						
452	'Esmeralda. Opéra en quatre actes. Accompagnement de piano'	1837	26	1837		476	
453	'Air chanté par Massol (from 'Esmerelda') arrangé pour le piano'	1837	26	1837		477	
	Bulhakov						
454	'Russischer Galopp'	1843	32	1843		478	143
	von Bülow						
455	'Dante's Sonnet "Tanto gentile e tanto onesta"'	1874	63	1875		479	144
	Chopin						
456	'Six chants polonais' (op. 74) 1. Mädchens Wunsch. (See **119**, 2) 2. Frühling 3. Das Ringlein 4. Bacchanal 5. Meine Freuden 6. Heimkehr	1847–60	36–59	1860	Princess Marie zu Hohenlohe	480	145
	Conradi						
457	'Le Célèbre Zigeunerpolka'	*c.* 1847	36	1849		481	146
	Cui						
458	'Tarantelle'	1885	74	1886		482	147
	Dargomizhsky						
459	'Tarantelle, transcrite et amplifiée pour le piano à deux mains'	1879	68	1880	Nadine Helbig	483	148
	David, Ferdinand						
460	'Bunte Reihe', op. 30	1850	39	1851		484	149
	Dessauer						
461	'Lieder' 1. Lockung 2. Zwei Wege 3. Spanisches Lied	1847	36	1847		485	150
	Draeseke						
462	Cantata, Der Schwur am Rütli, Pt. 1, piano reduction	1870	59	unpublished		485a	

9. *Piano Solo (cont.)*

(*b*) *Partitions de Piano, Instrumental Transcriptions, etc.*

CAT. NO.	TITLE	DATE OF COMPOSITION	AGE	DATE OF PUBLICATION	DEDICATION	SEARLE	RAABE
	Egressy and *Erkel*						
463	'Szózat und Ungarischer Hymnus'	not before 1870	?	1873	Count Julius Andrássy	486	**158**
	Festetics, Count Leo						
464	'Spanisches Ständchen'	1846	35	unpublished		487	**161**
	Franz						
465	'Er ist gekommen in Sturm und Regen'	1848	37	1849	Mlle Jousselin	488	**162**
466	'Lieder'	1848	37	1849		489	**163**
	I. Schilflieder, op. 2						
	1. Auf geheimen Waldespfaden						
	2. Drüben geht die Sonnescheiden						
	3. Trübe wird's						
	4. Sonnenuntergang						
	5. Auf dem Teich						
	II. Three lieder (from opp. 3 & 8)						
	6. Der Schalk						
	7. Der Bote						
	8. Meerestille						
	III. Four lieder (from opp. 3 & 8)						
	9. Treibt der Sommer						
	10. Gewitternacht						
	11. Das ist ein Brausen und Heulen						
	12. Frühlung und Liebe						
	Goldschmidt, Adalbert von						
467	'Liebesszene und Fortunas Kugel' from 'Die sieben Todsünden'	1880	69	1881		490	**165**
	Gounod						
468	'Hymne à Sainte Cécile'	1866	55	unpublished		491	**168**

469	'Tanzmomente'	1869	58	?	Princess Marie zu Hohenlohe-Schillingsfürst	492	171
	Hummel						
470	Septet, op. 74	1848	37	1849		493	172
	Lassen						
471	'Löse Himmel meine Seele'	1861	50	1866		494	173
472	'Ich weil, in tiefer Einsamkeit'	?	?	1872	Baroness Olga von Meyendorff	495	174
473	From the music to Hebbel's 'Nibelungen' and Goethe's 'Faust' I. Nibelungen 1. Hagen und Krunhild 2. Bechlarn II. Faust 1. Osterhymne 2. Hoffest. Marsch und Polonaise	1878–79	67–68	1878–79	Baroness Ingeborg von Bronsart	496	176
474	'Symphonisches Zwischenspiel' (Intermezzo) zu Calderons Schauspiel 'Über allen Zauber Liebe'	not before 1882	?	1883		497	175
	Lessmann						
475	Three Songs from J. Wolff's 'Tannhäuser' 1. Der Lenz ist gekommen 2. Trinklied 3. Du schaust mich an	*c.* 1882	*c.* 71	1882		498	177
	Liszt						
476	'Cantico del Sol di San Francesco', **176**	1881	70	unpublished		499	191
477	'Excelsior! Preludio zu den Glocken des Strassburger Münsters', **178**	*c.* 1875	64	1875		500	see 337
478	'From the Hungarian Coronation Mass', **183** 1. Benedictus 2. Offertorium	1867	56	1871		501	192
479	'Weihnachtslied' II, **205**	*c.* 1864	*c.* 53	1865		502	197
480	'Slavimo Slavno Slaveni!', **206**	*c.* 1863	*c.* 52	?		503	196

9. *Piano Solo (cont.)*

(*b*) *Partitions de Piano, Instrumental Transcriptions, etc.*

CAT. NO.	TITLE	DATE OF COMPOSITION	AGE	DATE OF PUBLICATION	DEDICATION	SEARLE	RAABE
481	'Ave Maria' II, **211**					504	193
	1st ver. (D major)	*c.* 1870	*c.* 59	1871			
	2nd ver. (D flat major)	*c.* 1872	*c.* 61	1872			
482	'Zum Haus der Herrn ziehen wir', **656** (Prelude to **230**)	?	?	unpublished		505	178
483	'Ave maris stella', **207**, 2	*c.* 1868	*c.* 57	1871		506	195
484	70 bars on themes from the first Beethoven Cantata, **239**	*c.* 1847	*c.* 36	1847		507	198
485	'Pastorale. Schnitterchor aus dem Entfesselten Prometheus', **241**	1861	50	1861		508	199
486	'Gaudeamus igitur. Humoreske,' **243**	*c.* 1870	59	1871	Justizrat Dr. Gille	509	200
487	'Marche héroïque', **254**	*c.* 1848	37	unpublished		510	201
488	'Geharnischte Lieder', **262**, 4–6	before 1861	?	1861		511	202
489	'Von der Wiege bis zum Grabe', **160**	1881	70	1883		512	179
490	'Gretchen', 2nd movement of the Faust Symphony, **161**	1874	63	1876		513	180
491	'Der Tanz in der Dorfschenke' (1st Mephisto Waltz), **163**, 2	1859–60	48–49	1862	Carl Tausig	514	181
492	'Second Mephisto Waltz', **164**	1880–81	69–70	1881	Camille Saint-Saëns	515	182
493	'Les Morts', **165**, 1	1860	49	1908		516	183
494	'Le Triomphe funèbre du Tasse', **165**, 3	1866	55	1878	Leopold Damrosch	517	184
495	'Salve Polonia', **166**	after 1863	?	1884		518	185
496	'Deux Polonaises de l'oratorio St. Stanislaus', **703**	1870's	?	unpublished		519	186
497	'Künstlerfestzug zur Schillerfeier', **167**	1857–60	46–49	1860		520	187
498	'Festmarsch zur Goethejubiläumsfeier', **168**	1857	46	1859		521	48*b*
499	'Festmarsch nach Motiven von, E.H. zu S-C-G', **169**	*c.* 1859	*c.* 48	1860		522	51
500	'Ungarischer Marsch zur Krönungsfeier in Ofen-Pest', am 8 Juni 1867, **171**	1870(!)	59	1871		523	55

	172				Teleky		
502	'Totentanz', **131**	*c.* 1860–65	49–54	1865	Hans von Bülow	525	188
503	'Epithalam zu Eduard Reményis Vermählungsfeier', **352**	*c.* 1872	*c.* 61	1872		526	189
504	'Romance oubliée', **355**	1880	69	1881		527	66*b*
505	'Festpolonaise', **132**	1876	65	unpublished		528	191
506	'Fantasie und Fuge über das Thema BACH', (2nd version), **138**	1871	60	1871		529	296
507	'L'Hymne du Pape. Inno del Papa. Der Papsthymnus', **139**	*c.* 1864	53	1865		530	190
508	'Buch der Lieder für Piano allein'	*c.* 1843	32	1844		531	209
	1. Lorelei, **276**, I						
	2. Am Rhein, **275**, I						
	3. Mignon, **278**, I						
	4. Es war ein König in Thule, **281**, I						
	5. Der du von dem Himmel bist, **282**, I						
	6. Angiolin dal biondo crin, **272**, I						
509	'Lorelei' (2nd version), **276**	1861	50	1862		532	209
510	'Il m'aimait tant', **274**	*c.* 1843	32	1843		533	203
511	'Die Zelle in Nonnenwerth. Elégie', **277**	*c.* 1843	32	1844	Prince Felix Lichnowsky	534	213
512	'Comment, disaient-ils', **279**, I	1847(?)	36(?)	unpublished		535	204
513	'O quand je dors', **285**, I	1847(?)	36(?)	unpublished		536	210
514	'Enfant, si j'étais roi', **286**, I	1847(?)	36	unpublished		537	205
515	'S'il est un charmant gazon', **287**, I	1847(?)	36	unpublished		538	206
516	'La tombe et la rose', **288**	1847(?)	36	unpublished		539	207
517	'Gastibelza', **289**	1847	36	unpublished		540	208
518	'Liebesträume'. 3 Notturnos, **311**, **312** and **301**	*c.* 1850	*c.* 39	1850		541	211
519	'Weimars Volkslied', **259**	1857	46	1857		542	212
520	'Ungarns Gott', **343**	1881	70	1881		543	214
521	'Ungarisches Königlised', **344**	1883	72	1884–85		544	215
522	'Ave Maria IV', **267**	1881	70	unpublished		545	194
523	'Der blinde Sänger', **349**	1878	67	1881		546	216

9. *Piano Solo (cont.)*

(*b*) *Partitions de Piano, Instrumental Transcriptions, etc.*

CAT. NO.	TITLE	DATE OF COMPOSITION	AGE	DATE OF PUBLICATION	DEDICATION	SEARLE	RAABE
	Mendelssohn						
524	'Lieder', (from opp. 19, 34 & 47)	1840	29	1841	Frau Cécile Mendelssohn	547	217
	1. Auf Flügeln des Gesanges 2. Sonntagslied 3. Reiselied 4. Neue Liebe 5. Frühlingslied 6. Winterlied 7. Suleika						
525	'Wasserfahrt' and 'Der Jäger Abschied' (from op. 50)	1848	37	1849		548	218
	Meyerbeer						
526	'Festmarsch zu Schillers 100-Jähriger Geburtsfeier'	1860	49	1860		549	226
	Mozart						
527	'Confutatis' and 'Lacrymosa' from the Requiem	?	?	1865		550	229
	Pezzini						
528	'Una stella amica'. Mazurka					551	232
	Rossini						
529	'Ouverture de l'opéra Guillaume Tell'	1838	27	1842		552	237
530	'Deux Transcriptions'	1847	36	1848		553	238
	1. Air du Stabat Mater (Cujus animam) 2. La Charité For organ and trombone, **664**; for voice and organ, **681**						
	Rubinstein						
531	Two Songs	?	?			554	239
	1. O! wenn er doch immer so bliebe			1881	Mme Rubinstein		
	2. Der A...			188...			

532	'Danse macabre', op. 40	1876	65	1876	Sophie Menter	555	**240**
	Schubert						
533	'Die Rose' ('Heidenröslein')	1833 rev. 1838	24 27	1835 rev. 1838	Mme la comtesse d'Apponyi	556	**241**
534	'Lob der Tränen'	1838	27	1838		557	**242**
535	12 Lieder 1. Sei mir Gegrüsst 2. Auf dem Wasser zu singen 3. Du bist die Ruh 4. Erlkönig 5. Meeresstille 6. Die junge Nonne 7. Frühlingsglaube 8. Gretchen am Spinnrade 9. Ständchen (Hark! Hark!) 10. Rastlose Liebe 11. Der Wanderer 12. Ave Maria	1838	27	1838	1–11. Comtesse Charles d'Aragon 12. Mme d'Agoult	558	**243**
536	'Der Gondelfahrer', op. 28	1838	27	1838		559	**244**
537	'Schwanengesang' 1. Die Stadt 2. Das Fischermädchen 3. Aufenthalt 4. Am Meer 5. Abschied 6. In der Ferne 7. Ständchen ('Leise flehen') 8. Ihr Bild 9. Frühlingssehnsucht 19. Liebesbotschaft 11. Der Atlas 12. Der Doppelgänger 13. Die Taubenpost 14. Kriegers Ahnung	1838–39	27–28	1840	Archduchess Sophie	560	**245**

9. *Piano Solo (cont.)*

(*b*) *Partitions de Piano, Instrumental Transcriptions, etc.*

CAT. NO.	TITLE	DATE OF COMPOSITION	AGE	DATE OF PUBLICATION	DEDICATION	SEARLE	RAABE
538	'Winterreise'	1839	28	1840	Princess Elenore Schwarzenberg	561	246
	1. Gute Nacht						
	2. Die Nebensonnen						
	3. Mut						
	4. Die Post						
	5. Erstarrung						
	6. Wasserflut						
	7. Der Lindenbaum						
	8. Der Leyermann						
	9. Täuschung						
	10. Das Wirtshaus						
	11. Der Stürmische Morgen						
	12. Im Dorfe						
539	'Geistliche Lieder'	1840	29	1841		562	247
	1. Litaney						
	2. Himmelsfunken						
	3. Die Gestirne						
	4. Hymne						
540	'Sechs Melodien'	1846	35	1846		563	248
	1. Lebewohl						
	2. Mädchens Klage						
	3. Das Sterbeglöcklein						
	4. Trockene Blumen						
	5. Ungeduld (1st ver.)						
	6. Die Forelle (1st ver. see **541**)						
541	'Die Forelle' (2nd ver. see **540**)	1846	35	1846	Fräulein Rosalie Spina	564	248
542	'Müllerlieder'	1846	35	1847		565	249
	1. Das Wandern						
	2. Der Müller und der Bach						
	3. Der Jäger						

	5. Wohin?						
	6. Ungeduld (2nd ver.)						
	Schumann						
543	'Liebeslied (Widmung)'	1848	37	1848		566	253
544	'An den Sonnenschein' and 'Rotes Röslen'	?	?	1861		567	255
545	'Frühlingsnacht (Überm Garten durch die Lüfte)'	?	?	1872		568	256
546	'Lieder von Robert and Clara Schumann'	?	?	1872		569	257
	A. (Robert, from opp. 79 and 98A)						
	1. Weihnachtslied						
	2. Die Wandelnde Glocke						
	3. Frülings Ankunft						
	4. Des Sennen Abschied						
	5. Er ist's						
	6. Nur wer die Sehnsucht kennt						
	7. An die Türen will ich schleichen						
	B. (Clara)						
	1. Warum willst du Andere fragen?						
	2. Ich hab' in Deinem Auge						
	3. Geheimes Flüstern						
547	'Provençalisches Minnelied'	1881	70	1882		570	254
	Spohr						
548	'Die Rose. Romanze'	?	?	1877		571	259
	Szabady						
549	'Revive Szegedin. Marche Hongroise transcrite d'après l'orchestration de J. Massenet'	1879	68	1892	Armand Gouzien	572	260
	Széchényi, Count Imre						
550	'Einleitung und Ungarischer Marsch. Bevezetés és magyar induló'	?	?	1878	Count Széchényi	573	261
	Weber						
551	Overture, 'Oberon'	1843	32	1847		574	288
552	Overture, 'Der Freischütz'	1846	35	1847		575	289
553	'Jubelouvertüre'	1846	35	1847		576	290

9. *Piano Solo* (*cont.*)

(*b*) *Partitions de Piano, Instrumental Transcriptions, etc.*

CAT. NO.	TITLE	DATE OF COMPOSITION	AGE	DATE OF PUBLICATION	DEDICATION	SEARLE	RAABE
	Wielhorsky, Count Michael						
554	'Autrefois. Romanze'	1843	32	1843		577	291

10. Piano and Orchestra

CAT. NO.	TITLE	DATE OF COMPOSITION	AGE	DATE OF PUBLICATION	DEDICATION	SEARLE	RAABE
	Liszt						
555	'Grand Solo de Concert', **42, 136**	*c.* 1850	*c.* 39	unpublished		365	
	Schubert						
556	'Fantasia in C major', op. 15 ('Wanderer') symph. arr.	1851	40	1857		366	459
	Weber						
557	'Polonaise brillante', op. 72	*c.* 1851	*c.* 40	1851–53	Adolf Henselt	367	460

11. Other Keyboard Works

(a) Piano Duet

CAT. NO.	TITLE	DATE OF COMPOSITION	AGE	DATE OF PUBLICATION	DEDICATION	SEARLE	RAABE
	Field						
558	Nocturnes Nos. 1–9, 14, 18 and Nocturne Pastorale in E	?	?	?		577a	
	Liszt						
559	Four pieces from 'St. Elizabeth', **174** 1. Prelude 2. March of the Crusaders 3. Storm 4. Interlude	*c.* 1866	*c.* 55	1868		578	334
560	Two orchestral pieces from 'Christus', **175** 1. Hirtenspiel 2. Die heiligen drei Könige	1866–73	55–62	1873		579	335
561	'Excelsior!', **178**	*c.* 1875	*c.* 64	1876		580	337

562	'Benedictus' and 'Offertorium' from the 'Hungarian Coronation Mass', **183**	1869	58	1871	581	338
563	'O Lamm Gottes, unschuldig', **223**, 5	1878–79	67–68	unpublished	582	350
564	'Via Crucis', **226**	1878	67	unpublished	583	339
565	'Festkantate zur Enthüllung des Beethoven-Denkmals in Bonn', **239**	1845	34	1846	584	340
566	'Pastorale. Schnitterchor aus dem Entfesselten Prometheus', **241**	1861	50	1861	585	341
567	'Gaudeamus igitur. Humoreske', **243**	1870–72	59–61	1872	586	342
568	'Marche Héroïque', **254**	*c.* 1848	37	unpublished	587	343
569	'Weimars Volkslied', **259**	1857	46	1857	588	344
570	'Ce qu'on entend sur la montagne', **148**	1874	63	1875	589	315
571	'Tasso', **149**	*c.* 1858	*c.* 47	1859	590	316
572	'Les Préludes', **150**	*c.* 1858	*c.* 47	1859	591	317
573	'Orpheus', **151**	*c.* 1858	*c.* 47	1859	592	318
574	'Prometheus', **152**	*c.* 1858	67	1862	593	319
575	'Mazeppa', **153**	1874	63	1875	594	320
576	'Festklänge', **154**	1854–61	43–50	1861	595	321
577	'Hungaria', **156**	1874(?)	63(?)	1875	596	322
578	'Hamlet', **157**	1874	63	1875	597	323
579	'From the Cradle to the Grave', **160**	1881	70	1883	598	324
580	Two episodes from Lenau's 'Faust', **163**	1861–62	50–51	1862	599	325
581	Second Mephisto Waltz, **164**	1881	70	1881	600	326
582	'Les Morts', **165**, 1	1860	49	unpublished	601	327
583	'La Notte', **165**, 2	1866	55	unpublished	602	328
584	'Le Triomphe Funèbre du Tasse', **165**, 3	1866–69	55–58	unpublished	603	329
585	'Salve Polonia', **166**	1863	52	1884	604	330
586	'Künstlerfestzug zur Schillerfeier', **167**	1859	48	1860	605	331
587	'Festmarsch zur Goethejubiläumsfeier', **168**	*c.* 1858	47	1859	606	302
588	'Festmarsch nach Motiven von E.H. zu S-C-G', **169**	*c.* 1859	*c.* 48	1860	607	303
589	'Rákóczy March', **170**	1870	59	1871	608	310
590	'Ungarischer Marsch zur Krönungsfeier in Ofen-Pest', **171**	1870	59	1871	609	306
591	'Ungarischer Sturmmarsch', **172**	1875	64	1876	610	305
592	'Epithalam', **352**	1872(?)	61(?)	1872(?)	611	332
593	'Elegie', **353**	1874	63	1875	612	333

CAT. NO.	TITLE	DATE OF COMPOSITION	AGE	DATE OF PUBLICATION	DEDICATION	SEARLE	RAABE
	11. Other Keyboard Works (cont.) *(a) Piano Duet*						
594	'Weihnachtsbaum', **52**	*c.* 1876–82	65–71	1882		613	307
595	'Dem Audenken Petöfis'	1877	66	1877		614	313
596	'Grande Valse di Bravura', **76**	1836	25	1844	Peter Wolff	615	298
597	'Grand Galop Chromatique', **88**	1838	27	1838		616	299
598	'Csárdás macabre', **93**	1882	71	unpublished	Johann von Végh		
599	'Csárdás obstiné', **94**, 2	1884(?)	73(?)			618	300
600	'Vom Fels zum Meer', **98**	?	?	unpublished		618*a*	
601	'Bülow-Marsch', **99**	*c.* 1883	*c.* 72	1884		619	304
602	'Hussitenlied', **104**	1840	29	*c.* 1840		620	308
603	Hungarian Rhapsodies (from the orchestral version, **673**) 1. **114**, 14; 4. **115**, 2; 2. **114**, 12; 5. **114**, 5 3. **114**, 6; 6. **114**, 9	1874	63	1875		621	309
604	16th Rhapsody **114**, 16	1882	71	1882		622	311
605	18th Rhapsody **114**, 18	1885	74	1885		623	312
606	19th Rhapsody					623*a*	
607	'Fantasy and Fugue on *Ad Nos*', **137**	1850	39	1852		624	314
608	'Der Papsthymnus', **139**	*c.* 1865	*c.* 54	1865		625	336
609	'Ungarisches Königslied', **344**	*c.* 1884	*c.* 73	*c.* 1884		626	345
610	'Sonnambula' Fantasy, **368**	*c.* 1852	*c.* 41	1876		627	348
611	'Bénédiction et Serment de Benvenuto Cellini', **371**	1853(?)	42(?)	1854		628	349
612	'Tscherkessenmarsch', **318**	1843	32	1843		629	351
613	'Réminiscences de Robert le Diable', **389**	1841–43	30–32	1843		630	352
614	Andante Finale and March from 'King Alfred', **397**	1853(?)	42(?)	1853(?)		631	353
615	'Vier Märsche von Franz Schubert': **401**; 2; **402**	after 1860			Willi and Louis Thern	632	354
616	'A la Chapelle Sixtine', **437**	*c.* 1865	*c.* 54			633	346
617	'Grand Septuor de Beethoven', **441**	1841(?)	30(?)	1842(?)		634	347
	Mozart						
618	Adagio from 'The Magic Flute'	?	?	unpublished		634*a*	

(b) Two Pianofortes

Liszt

619	'Ce qu'on entend sur la montagne', **148**	1854–57	43–46	1857		635	357
620	'Tasso', **149**	*c.* 1854–56	43–45	1856		636	358
621	'Les Préludes', **150**	*c.* 1854–56	43–45	1856		637	359
622	'Orpheus', **151**	*c.* 1854–56	43–45	1856		638	360
623	'Prometheus', **152**	1855–56	44–45	1856		639	361
624	'Mazeppa', **153**	1855	44	1856		640	362
625	'Festklänge,' **154**	*c.* 1853–56	42–45	1856		641	363
626	'Héroïde funèbre', **155**	*c.* 1854–56	42–45	1856		642	364
627	'Hungaria', **156**	*c.* 1854–61	43–50	1861		643	365
628	'Hamlet', **157**	*c.* 1858–61	47–50	1861		644	366
629	'Hunnenschlacht', **158**	1857	46	1861	Wilhelm von Kaulbach	645	367
630	'Die Ideale', **159**	1857–58	46–47	1858		646	368
631	A Faust Symphony, **161**	1856 rev. 1860	45	1863		647	369
632	A Symphony to Dante's 'Divina Commedia', **162**	1856–59	45–48	1859		648	370
633	Fantasy on themes from Beethoven's 'Ruins of Athens', **127**	after 1852	after 41	1865		649	371
634	Piano Concerto No. 1, in E flat major, **129**	1853	42	1857		650	372
635	Piano Concerto No. 2, in A major, **130**	1859	48	1862		651	373
636	'Totentanz', **131**	1859–65 (Liszt transcribed the work *twice*, by mistake!)	48–54	1865		652	374
637	'Wanderer' Fantasy, **556**	after 1851	after 40	1862		653	375
638	'Hexameron', **367**	after 1837	after 26	1870		654	377
639	'Réminiscences de Norma', **369**	after 1841	after 40	1874		655	378
640	'Réminiscences de Don Juan', **394**	after 1841	after 40	1877		656	379
641	Beethoven's Ninth Symphony	1851 latest	40	1851		657	376
642	See **787**!						

11. *Other Keyboard Works (cont.)*

(c) Organ

CAT. NO.	TITLE	DATE OF COMPOSITION	AGE	DATE OF PUBLICATION	DEDICATION	SEARLE	RAABE
	Allegri and Mozart						
643	'Evocation à la Chapelle Sixtine', **437**	*c.* 1862	51	1865	A. W. Gottschalg	658	400
	Arcadelt						
644	'Ave Maria'	1862	51	1865	A. W. Gottschalg	659	401
	Bach						
645	'Einleitung und Fuge aus der Motette "Ich hatte viel Bekümmernis" und Andante "Aus teifer Not"'	1860	49	1862(?)	Johann Gottlob Töpfer	660	402
646	'Adagio from the 4th violin sonata'	only the last 5 bars arr. by Liszt; the rest by Gottschalg	?	?		661	403
	Chopin						
647	Preludes Op. 28, Nos. 4 & 9	?	?	?		662	404
	Lassus						
648	'Regina coeli laetare'	1865	?	?		663	405
	Liszt						
649	'Tu es Petrus', **175**, 8	July 1867	55	?		664	391
650	'San Francesco. Preludio per il cantico del sol di San Francesco', **176**	1880	69	unpublished		665	392
651	'Excelsior! Preludio zu den Glocken des Strassburger Münsters', **178**	after 1874	after 63	?		666	393
652	'Offertorium' from the Hungarian Coronation Mass', **183**	after 1867	after 56	?		667	411*b*
653	'Slavimo Slavno Slaveni!', **206**	1863	52	?		668	397
654	'Zwei Kirchenhymnen', 1. Salve Regina 2. Ave maris stella, **207**	after 1868	57	1880	Cardinal Prince G. von Hohenlohe-Schillingsfürst	669	394
655	'Rosario', **229**, 1–3	1879	68	unpublished		670	396
656	'Zum Haus des Herren ziehen Wir' (Prelude to **230**). See **482**	1884	73	1908		671	395

657	'Weimars Volkslied', **259**	1865	54	1873		672	398
658	'Weinen, Klagen' Variations, **46**	1863	52	1865		673	382
659	'Ungarns Gott', **343**	*c.* 1881	70	1882		674	399
	Nicolai						
660	'Kirchliche Festouvertüre über den Choral "Ein feste Burg ist unser Gott"'	1852	41	1852		675	406
	Wagner						
661	'Chor der jüngeren Pilger aus "Tannhäuser"', **420**	1st ver. 1860 2nd ver. 1862	49 51	1864		676	407

(d) Organ with other instruments

662	'Hosannah', for organ and trombone from **176**	1862	51	1867		677	409
663	'Offertorium and Benedictus' from the Hungarian Coronation Mass, **183**: for violin and organ	*c.* 1871	*c.* 60	?		678	411*a*
664	Aria 'Cujus animan' from Rossini's 'Stabat Mater' for organ and trombone, **530**	1860's	50's	1874(?)	Eduard Grosse	679	410

12. Orchestral Works

	Bülow						
665	'Mazurka-Fantasie', Op. 13	1865	54			351	446
	Cornelius						
666	Second Overture to 'The Barber of Bagdad' (completed by Liszt from Cornelius' sketches)	1877		unpublished		352	447
	Egressy and Erkel						
667	'Szózat and Hymnus' (2 patriotic songs of Vorösmarty and Kölcsey)	1870–73	59–62	1878	Count Andrássy	353	448

CAT. NO.	TITLE	DATE OF COMPOSITION	AGE	DATE OF PUBLICATION	DEDICATION	SEARLE	RAABE
	12. *Orchestral Works* (*cont.*)						
	Liszt						
668	Two Legends, **41** 1. San Francesco d'Assisi 2. San Francesco di Paola	1863	52	unpublished		354	440
669	'Vexilla Regis prodeunt', **51**	1864	53	unpublished		355	442
670	'Festvorspiel', **95**	1857	46	1857		356	431
671	'Huldigungsmarsch zur Huldigungsmarsch (28 Aug. 1853) S. K. H. des Grossherzogs Carl Alexander von Sachsen-Weimar', **97, 259**	1857	46	1859		357	434
672	'Vom Fels zum Meer. Deutscher Siegesmarsch', **98**	1860	49	?	King Wilhelm I of Prussia	358	435
673	Hungarian Rhapsodies, **114**, arr. by Liszt and Franz Doppler					359	441
674	'A la chapelle Sixtine', **437**			unpublished		360	445
675	'Der Papsthymnus', **139**			unpublished		361	443
676	Benedictus from the Hungarian Coronation Mass, **183**, for violin and orchestra	1875	63		August Kömpel	362	444
	Schubert						
677	4 Marches from opp. 40, 54 and 121 see **401–2**	1859–60	47–48			363	449
	Zarembski						
678	'Danses galiciennes'	1881	69			364	450
	13. Vocal Works						
679	'Ave maris stella', **207** Voice and piano, or harm.	1868	57	1868		680	641
680	'Ave Maria' II, **211** Voice and organ, or harm.	1869	58	1936		681	639
681	'Cujus animam' from Rossini's 'Stabat Mater', T. and organ, **530**	?	?	1874		682	—

682	Serbisches Lied ('Ein Mädchen sitzt am Meerestrand"), in Musik gesezt von F. W. C. Fürst von Hohenzollern-Hechingen, mit Pianoforte-Begleitung von F. L.'	?	?		'Orpheon-Album (Göpel, Stuttgart) Vol. 4, No. 137	—	—
683	'Barcarole vénitienne de Pantaleoni, avec accompagnement de pianoforte par F. L.'	?	?	1842	Mme. Thérèse de Bacheracht	684	644
684	'Es hat geflammt die ganze Nacht' (Grand Duchess Maria Pavlovna), with piano accomp. by L.			unpublished			

14. Songs with Orchestra

	Korbay						
685	2 songs	1883	71	prob. unpublished		368	653
	Liszt						
686	'Die Lorelei', **276**, 2	1860	49	1863		369	647
687	'Mignons Lied', **278**, 3	1860	49	1863		370	648
688	'Die Vätergruft', **284**	1886	74	1886		371	649
689	Three Songs from Schiller's 'Wilhelm Tell', **295**	*c.* 1855				372	645
690	'Jeanne d'Arc au Bûcher', **296**, 2	1858 rev. 1874	46	1877		373	646
691	'Die drei Zigeuner', **324**	1860	49	1872		374	650
	Schubert						
692	6 Songs 1. Die junge Nonne 2. Gretchen am Spinnrade 3. Lied der Mignon 4. Erlkönig 5. Der Doppelgänger 6. Abschied	1860	49	1–4 1863 5 & 6 unpublished		375	651
693	'Die Allmachte' (T. or S. solo, male chorus and orch.)	1871	60	1872		376	652
	Géza Zichy						
694	'Die Zaubersee'. Ballad	?	?	unpublished		377	451

CAT. NO.	TITLE	DATE OF COMPOSITION	AGE	DATE OF PUBLICATION	DEDICATION	SEARLE	RAABE
	15. Recitation						
	Draeseke						
695	'Helges Treue' (Strachwitz)	1860	49	1874	Bogumil Davison	686	659
	16. Chamber Music						
696	'La Notte' **165**, 2 vl. and pf.	1864–66	52–54	unpublished		377a	—
697	'Angelus', **28,** 1						
	1. Harmonium	1877	66	1883	Daniela von Bülow	378	389
	2. String quartet	1880	69	1883			473
698	'Pester Karneval', **114**, 9	?	?	?		379	470
699	'Benedictus and Offertorium' from the Hungarian Coronation Mass, **183** vl. and pf.	1869	58	1871		381	465
700(a)	'O du mein holder Abendstern' from 'Tannhäuser', **421**	1852	49	unpublished		380	—
700(b)	'Puszta-Wehmut', **116** vl. and pf.	?	?	unpublished		379a	—
701(a)	'Die Zelle in Nonnenwerth', **277** pf. and vl. or cello	prob. not arr. by Liszt		unpublished		382	463
701(b)	'Die drei Zigeuner', **324** vl. and pf.	1864	52	1896	Eduard Reményi	383	469
	17. Unfinished Works						
702	'Sardanapale'. Opera in three acts. Text after Byron by Rotondi (?)	1846–51	35–40	unpublished		687	670
703	'Die Legende von heiligen Stanislaus'. ORATORIO. Text after Lucien Siemienski by Princess Sayn-Wittgenstein (?), Cornelius, and K. E. Edler	1873–85	62–74	mostly unpublished		688	671
704	'Singe, wem Gesang gegeben'. Male	c. 1847	c. 36	unpublished		689	672

705	Revolutionary Symphony. Orchestra. See **155**	1830 rev. 1848	19 37	1916 unpublished		690	667
706	'De Profundis. Psaume instrumental'. Piano and Orch. see **131**	*c.* 1834		unpublished	Abbé Lammenias	691	668
707	Violin Concerto	1860	49	unpublished	for Reményi	692	669
708	2 Hungarian Piano Pieces 1. B flat minor 2. D minor	*c.* 1840	*c.* 29	1954		693	662
709	Fantasia on English themes	*c.* 1840	*c.* 29	unpublished		694	(98)
710	Piano piece in F major (4/4)	July 1843 (?)	31	unpublished		695	663
711	4th Mephisto Waltz. Piano	March 1885	73	1952		696	661
712	Fantasy on two themes from 'Figaro' (completed by Busoni, 1912)	1842	30	1912		697	660
713	'La Mandragore. Ballade de l'opéra Jean de Nivelle de L. Delibes'	after 1880	after 68	unpublished		698	666
714	'La Notte', **165**, 2. Piano	1864–66	52–54	unpublished		699	664
715	'Carnaval de Venise' (Paganini) for piano			unpublished		700	665
716	'Den Felsengipfel steig ich einst hinan'. Voice and piano	?	?	unpublished		701	673

APPENDIX

1. Doubtful or Lost

Sacred Choral Works

717 Tantum ergo. 1822. (Lost) 702
718 Psalm 2 for T. solo, mixed chorus and orchestra, 1851. (Prob. part of **705**) 703
719 Requiem on the death of the Emperor Maximilian of Mexico (?) 704
720 The Creation. (?) 705
721 Benedictus, for mixed chorus and organ. Pub. 1939, New York. (Doubtful) 706
722 Excelsior, **178**, 1 for M-S. or Bar. solo, male chorus and pf. ? (not arr. by L.) 707

Secular Choral Works

723 Rinaldo (Goethe) for T. solo, male chorus and pf. ? (not by L.) 708
724 A patakhoz (Garai). 1846. (Lost. (?)) 708*a*

For Orchestra

725 Boze cos Polske. Also for pf., **166** 709
726 Funeral March. (?) 710
727 Czárdás macabre, **93** (?) 711
728 Romance oubliée, **355** for viola and orch. (Not arr. by L.) 712

4. *For Piano and Orchestra*

729 Two concertos. 1825. (Lost) 713
730 Concerto in the Hungarian style. (?) 714
731 Concerto in the Italian style. (?) 715
732 Grande Fantaisie Symphonique in A minor. (?) 716

Other Instrumental Works

733 Trio. 1825. (Lost) 717
734 Quintet. 1825. (Lost) 718
735 The Seasons, for string quartet. (?) 719
736 Allegro moderato in E major for violin and piano. (?) 720
737 Violin prelude. (?) 721
738 La Notte, **165**, 2 for violin and piano. See **696** 722
739 Tristia, from Vallée d'Obermann, **25**, 6 for piano, violin and cello 723

For Piano Solo

740 Rondo; Fantasia. 1824. (Lost) 724
741 3 Sonatas. 1825. (Lost) 725
742 Étude in C major. (?) 726
743 Technical Studies, Vol. 3 (?) 726*a*
744 Prélude omnitonique. (?) 727
745 Sospiri (companion piece to **58**) 728
746 Ecce panis angelorum. (?) ? pub. John Church 729
747 In Memoriam. (?) ? pub. John Church 730
748 Valse elégiaque. (?) 731
749 4me Valse oubliée. See **83**. Pub. Presser 732
750 Ländler in G major. See **103**. Pub. Curwen 733
751 Ländler in D major. (?) Unpublished 734
752 Air cosaque. (?) 735
753 Kerepesi csárdás. (? not by L.) 736
754 Trois morceaux en style de danse ancien hongrois. Pub. 1850; not by L. 737

755 Spanish Folk-Tunes. (?) 738
756 Overture, Coriolan (Beethoven. Prob. lost) 739
757 Overture, Egmont (Beethoven). (?) 740
758 Overture, Le carnaval Romain (Berlioz). (?) 741
759 Duettino (Donizetti). (?) 742
760 Soldiers' chorus from Gounod's Faust. (Prob. lost) 743
761 Paraphrase on the fourth act of Kullak's Dom Sebastian. (?) 744
762 Funeral March (?) 745
763 Andante maestoso. (?) 746
764 Poco Adagio from the Gran Mass. (?) 747
765 Overture, The Magic Flute (Mozart). (?) 748
766 Radovsky. Preussischer Armeemarsch No. 120. Pf. score 749
767 Introduction et Variations sur une Marche du Siège de Corinth (Rossini), 1830 (?) 750
768 Nonetto e Mose (Rossini), Fantaisie. (?) 751
769 Gelb rollt (Rubinstein). (?) 752
770 Alfonso und Estrella (Schubert), Act. 1. Pf. score. 1850–51. (Prob. lost) 753
771 2a Mazurka di P. A. Tirindelli, variata da F. L. (Prob. not by L.) 754

For Piano, Four Hands
772 Sonata. 1825. Lost 755
773 Mosonyis Grabgeleit. (?) 756

For Two Pianos
774 Le triomphe funèbre du Tasse. (?) 757

For Organ
775 Symphonic poem. The Organ, after Herder. (?) 758
776 Consolation No. 4 in D flat, **38** (? not arr. by L.) 759
777 Cantico del Sol, **176**. Cf. **650** 760
778 Chopin's Funeral March for organ, cello and piano. (?) 761

Songs with Piano
779 Air de Chateaubriand. (?) 762
780 Strophes de Herlossohn. (?) 763
781 Kränze pour chant. (?) 764
782 Glöckchen (Müller). ? companion piece to **320** 765
783 L'aube naît (Hugo). 1842. Lost 765*a*
784 Der Papsthymnus, **175**, 8, for S or T and pf. (? not arr. by L.) 766

Other Vocal Works
785 Excelsior, **178**, 1, for voice and organ. (? not arr. by L.) 767

Recitations with pf.
786 Der ewige Jude (Schubart). (?) 768
787 Un faux pas (from **642**)!

2. Planned
Operas
1842 Le Corsaire
1845 Stage version of La Divina Commedia, text by Autran
1846 Two Italian operas
1846–54 Opera on Faust
1847 Richard en Palestine (Scott)
1848 Spartacus

1856–58	Hungarian opera, János or Jánko
1858–59	Jeanne d'Arc

Chorus

1845	Les Laboureurs, Les Matelots, Les Soldats (Lamennais), companion pieces to **253**
1849	Oratorio after Byron's Heaven and Earth; text by Wagner
1856	Two Masses
1860–61	Liturgie catholique, Liturgie romaine
1862	Manfred
1869	St. Etienne, roi d'Hongrie, or Fire and Water
1874	Longfellow's Golden Legend as a recitation (cf. **178**)
	Theodor Körner's Fiedler der hl. Cäcilia
	Sketches for Psalms 14 and 15, a plainsong Magnificat, Les Djinns, and a Miserere

Orchestra

1853	Music to The Tempest
1861	The History of the World in Sound and Picture (after a series of pictures by Kaulbach): The Tower of Babel, Nimrod, Jerusalem, The Glory of Greece
1865	Continuation to Hungaria, **156**
1871	Two works of Chopin for pf. and orch., incl. Fantasy Op. 49
1885	Ungarische Bildnisse **72** for orch.

Pianoforte

1850	Schubert's C major Symphony
1860	Polonaise martiale
1863	Transcription of Beethoven's Quartets
1877	New ed. of Mendelssohn's Songs Without Words
1880	Bach's Chaconne
1883	Piano score of Rousseau's Devin du Village
1886	Fantasia on Mackenzie's The Troubadour. Sketch for Somogyi Csárdás

3. Works by Other Composers, Edited by Liszt

Bach, Kompositionen für Orgel. Revidiert und mit Beiträgen versehen von F. L. (includes **645** and **646**).
Chromatic Fantasy
Three Preludes and Fugues in C sharp minor
(In *Anthologie Classique*, Schlesinger, Berlin)

Beethoven. Three piano concertos (opp. 37, 58, 73) edited and arranged for 2 pianos, with cadenzas, 1879.
Works for piano, 2 and 4 hands, ed. 1857
Duos for piano with violin or cello, horn, flute or viola
Trios for piano with violin (or clarinet) and cello
Mass in C. Mass in D
Piano quartets, ed. 1861
Trios for string and wind instruments
Menuet, revu par F. Liszt

Chopin. Études, pub. 1877.

Clementi. Preludes et Exercises, corrigés et marqués au metronome par le jeune Liszt, suivis de douze de ses Études. Cf. **1**. Pub. 1825.

Field. 18 Nocturnes, redigés et accompagnés d'une preface, 1859.

Gottschalg. Repertorium für Orgel, Harmonium oder Pedal-Flügel. Bearbeitet unter Revision und mit Beiträgen von F.L. Cf. **138, 645–49, 652, 653**.

Handel. Fugue in E minor.

Hummel. Septet, Op. 74, for piano, flute, oboe, horn, viola, cello and bass. Also as quintet for piano, violin, viola, cello and bass.
Mädchenlieder. Unter Mitwirkung von Hoffmann von Fallersleben und Franz Liszt herausgegeben von A. Bräunlich und W. Gottschalg. Pub. 1851.
Schubert. Selected sonatas and solo piano pieces (2 and 4 hands). Ed. 1868–80.
Scarlatti. Cat's Fugue.
Viole. Gartenlaube. 100 études for pf.
Weber. Selected sonatas and solo piano pieces. Ed. 1868, 1870
Paraphrase on the Invitation to the Dance, 1843
6 pages of variants to the Konzertstück
Zámoyska, Ludmilla. Songs. Unpublished.

4. Literary Works.

Gesammelte Schriften. Ed. Lina Ramann. Pub. 1880–83
Vol. I. F. Chopin (1852)
Vol. II, 1. Essays from the *Revue et Gazette Musicale*:
On future Church music (1834)
On the position of artists (1835)
On popular editions of important works (1836)
On Meyerbeer's Les Huguenots (1837)
Thalberg's Grande Fantaisie, op. 22, and Caprices, opp. 15 and 19 (1837)
To M. Fétis (1837)
R. Schumann's piano compositions, opp. 5, 11, 14 (1837)
Paganini; a Necrology (1840)
(This volume does not include the article on Alkan's Trois Morceaux dans le genre pathétique, op. 15 (1837).)
Vol. II, 2. Essays of a Bachelor of Music (1835–40). 1–3. To George Sand. 4. To Adolphe Pictet. 5. To Louis de Ronchand. 6. By Lake Como (to Louis de Ronchand). 7. La Scala (to M. Schlesinger). 8. To Heinrich Heine. 9. To Lambert Massart. 10. On the position of music in Italy (to M. Schlesinger). 11. St. Cecilia (to M. d'Ortigue). 12. To Hector Berlioz.
Vol. III, 1.
Gluck's Orpheus (1854). Beethoven's Fidelio (1854). Weber's Euryanthe (1854). On Beethoven's music to Egmont (1854). On Mendelssohn's music to A Midsummer Night's Dream (1854). Scribe and Meyerbeer's Robert le Diable (1854). Schubert's Alfonso und Estrella (1854). Auber's Muette de Portici (1854). Bellini's Montecchi e Capuletti (1854). Boieldieu's Dame Blanche (1854). Donizetti's La Farorita (1854). Pauline Viardot-Garcia (1859). No Entr'acte Music! (1855). Mozart; on the occasion of his centenary festival in Vienna (1856).
Vol. III, 2. Richard Wagner.
Tannhäuser and the Song Contest on the Wartburg (1849). Lohengrin and its first performance at Weimar (1850). The Flying Dutchman (1854). The Rhinegold (1855).
Vol. IV.
Berlioz and his Harold Symphony (1855). Robert Schumann (1855). Clara Schumann (1855). Robert Franz (1855). Sobolewski's Vinvela (1855). John Field and his Nocturnes (1859).
Vol. V.
On the Goethe Foundation (1850). Weimar's September Festival in honour of the centenary of Karl August's birth (1857). Dornröschen; Genast's poem and Raff's music (1855). Marx and his book 'The Music of the Nineteenth Century (1855)'. Criticism of criticism; Ulibishev and Serov (1858). A letter on conducting; a defence (1853).
Vol. VI.
The Gypsies and their Music in Hungary (1859).
Vol. VII (not published) was to contain two more letters of 1837–8 and 1841, the Illustrations to Benvenuto Cellini (1838), and L's forewords to his musical works.

Published separately:

De la fondation Goethe à Weimar, 1851.

Lohengrin et Tannhäuser de R. Wagner, 1851.

F. Chopin, 1852.

Des Bohèmiens et de leur musique en Hongrie, 1859.

Über John Field's Nocturne, 1859.

R. Schumann's Musikalische Haus-und Lebensregeln. French translation by F.L., 1872.

Liszt also took part, together with Marschner, Reissiger and Spohr, in Eduard Bernsdorf's *Neues Universal-Lexicon der Tonkunst* (1856–65). A manual of piano technique, written for the Geneva Conservatoire (1835(?)) is apparently lost.

General Index

Index of Liszt's Works Discussed in this Volume

CHAMBER

SONGS